15 impact on students conc.
17 com & soc (CS)
3 com & soc
    obligated (co)
5 not
5 CS

351
71
357
365
383
429
439

Man-Computer Interaction Research
MACINTER-I

Man-Computer Interaction Research
MACINTER-I

Proceedings of the First Network Seminar of
The International Union of Psychological Science (IUPsyS) on
Man-Computer Interaction Research
Berlin, German Democratic Republic, October 16-19, 1984

Edited by:

F. KLIX and H. WANDKE

Department of Psychology
Humboldt University, Berlin
German Democratic Republic

1986

NORTH-HOLLAND
AMSTERDAM ● NEW YORK ● OXFORD ● TOKYO

ISBN: 0 444 87910 2

Published by:
ELSEVIER SCIENCE PUBLISHERS B.V.
P.O. Box 1991
1000 BZ Amsterdam
The Netherlands

Sole distributors for the U.S.A. and Canada:
ELSEVIER SCIENCE PUBLISHING COMPANY, INC.
52 Vanderbilt Avenue
New York, N.Y. 10017
U.S.A.

Library of Congress Cataloging-in-Publication Data

Network Seminar of the International Union of
    Psychological Science on Man-Computer Interaction
    Research (1st : 1984 : Berlin, Germany)
    Man-computer interaction research MACINTER I

    Bibliography: p.
    Includes index.
    1. Computers--Psychological aspects--Congresses.
2. Man-machine systems--Congresses. I. Klix, Friedhart.
II. Wandke, H. (Hartmut) III. Title. IV. Title:
MACINTER-I.
QA76.9.P75N47 1984   004'.01'9   85-27530
ISBN 0-444-87910-2 (U.S.)

PRINTED IN THE NETHERLANDS

PREFACE

The accelerating introduction of interactive computer devices
in all spheres of life results in important changes in various
areas of public life (e.g. labour, education, communication,
etc.). Humans are affected as individuals, members of a group,
organizations and social systems. They are in touch with computers at work, as customers, as traineees, in consumption, and
in play. Since computer systems consist of both hardware and
software components, they have physical, psychological and
sociological impacts.

Every discipline of human science therefore has to investigate
very special problems in its man-computer interaction research.
On the other hand, there are significant interactions between
the above-mentioned areas and the levels of human life. This
calls for interdisciplinary cooperation.

The subjects of research in every case require a second kind of
interdisciplinary work: cooperation with computer science. Up
to now, this cooperation has mainly consisted in deriving
problems for human sciences from technical development. But it
may make more sense to derive the directions of technical
development from human capabilities, needs and difficulties.
To strengthen both kinds of cooperation - this is the aim of
the MACINTER Network. Although there are a lot of national and
international organizations holding series of conferences on
man-computer interaction (e.g. IFIP, IFAC, and ACM), it seems
to us that the role played by psychology is often ambiguous.
We believe that psychology can contribute to this interdisciplinary field of research in a very specific manner:

One of the essential theses of modern psychology is that human
activity is based on information processing and that human
behaviour can be interpreted as information exchange with the
environment. It is a very fascinating point that the computer
(forming part of the technical environment of man) also processes information, even if on the basis of very different
principles from those that humans rely on. The analysis and
optimization of information exchange in man-computer systems
is therefore a domain of psychology par exellence.

It is intriguing to see how basic and applied research in
psychology meet in this domain.

The general frame of the analysis and optimization process for a special man-computer system can be described as follows:

(1) An analysis must be made as to what kind of problem or class of problems should be solved in an interactive system. In what way is the knowledge that is required for solving a problem represented in human memory? What are the human prerequisites (knowledge, capabilities, cognitive skills etc.) that form the basis of system design?

(2) It must be decided how the human interface of the system can be constructed so that it matches, at least in its main parts, the prior knowledge of the humans involved.

(3) The additional knowledge necessary for interaction with the system and the solution of problems with the help of the system, has to be imparted to the persons who will use the system.

(4) The problems that can be solved with the help of the system usually form part of higher order tasks of human activity, especially in work processes. The embedment of man-computer interaction in job organization provides the essential framework for information exchange in man-computer systems.

(5) The quality of man-computer interaction must be assessed. The point is to evaluate the psychological results - both positive, like well-being and mental health, and negative, like overload, fatigue, and stress.

According to these main psychological approaches the editors devided the papers into several chapters in this publication.

The first contains those papers that deal with general topics which are related to various phases of the analysis and optimization process.

The second is dedicated to knowledge representation and knowledge acquisition i.e. learning processes and training procedures.

Knowledge is here seen as falling into two categories: the knowledge necessary for understanding and solving problems (content knowledge), and the knowledge necessary for interacting with a computer (interaction knowledge). The aspect of storage principles for knowledge in human memory and their application in expert systems is also considered in this chapter.

The third is about psychological questions related to designing the human interface. Papers concerning the visible interface - the physical layout of the screen - and semantic and syntactic aspects of the interface can be found in this chapter.

The fourth is made up of papers evaluating man-computer systems. Evaluation is made by analyzing both short-term consequences, like mental load, fatigue, and stress (often including physiological methods), and long-term consequences like changes in job satisfaction and health.

Finally, the last chapter takes a look at job organization, especially the problem of dividing functions between man and computer.

We hope that this book will encourage discussions not only among psychologists working in man-computer interaction, but also among other scientists, such as software engineers, computer specialists, researchers in artificial intelligence and informatics, and, last but not least, among persons who use interactive computer devices.

We believe that psychology can - among other disciplines - contribute substantially to better use being made of modern information technologies in human life, and that research into man-computer interaction may provide new insights in cognitive psychology. This is why we are looking forward to future research activities being reported in MACINTER II, III ...

Friedhart Klix and Hartmut Wandke

CONTENTS

Preface   v

Acknowledgements   xiii

GENERAL ASPECTS OF MAN-COMPUTER INTERACTION

MACINTER - Aim and Goal (Opening Address)
F. Klix   3

Cognitive Ergonomics: An Approach for the Design of
    User-Oriented Interactive Systems
N.A. Streitz   21

An Approach to Metacommunication in Human-Computer
    Interaction
M.J. Tauber   35

Personality Traits of the Worker within the "Man-Machine"
    System at Automated Production
Ph. Genov   51

Analysis of the Competence of Operators Confronting New
    Technologies: Some Methodological Problems and Some
    Results
M. De Montmollin   59

Methodological Problems of Designing Dialogue-
    Orientated Components in Information Systems
K. Fuchs-Kittowski, K. Koitz, and Ch. Rudeck   65

Smaller Sizes - Changing Roles: New Dimensions of the
    Man-Computer Interactions
P. Gelléri   71

KNOWLEDGE REPRESENTATION AND ACQUISITION

Exploratory Investigations in Acquiring and Using
    Information in Interactive Problem Solving
B. Krause and H. Hagendorf   79

Necessary Contributions of Cognitive Psychology to
    Computer Knowledge Representation and Manipulation
    Systems
H. Helbig   89

Memory Research and Knowledge Engineering
F. Klix   97

Psychological Methods for Assembling Procedures in Text
    Management Systems
J. Hoffmann, M. Ziessler, and R. Seifert   117

Internal Representation of Externally Stored Information
W. Schönpflug   125

Problems in the Design of Information Retrieval Systems:
    User Competence and Information Complexity
W. Battmann   131

Computer Assisted Knowledge Acquisition: Towards a
    Laboratory for Protocol Analysis of User Dialogues
W. Dzida   139

Effectiveness of Training as a Function of the Teached
    Knowledge Structure
R. Schindler and F. Fischer   151

Designing Learning Processes for Work Activities in
    Automated Technologies
B. Matern   161

System Issues in Problem Solving Research
J.M. Scandura   173

Understanding Learning Problems in Computer Aided Tasks
Y. Waern   185

Learning Styles in Conversation - a Practical Application
    of Pask's Learning Theory to Human-Computer
    Interaction
G.C. van der Veer and J.J. Beishuizen   195

INTERFACE DESIGN

Machine Adaption to Psychological Differences Among
    Users in Instructive Information Exchanges with
    Computers
E.Z. Rothkopf   209

On Complexity of Command-Entry in Man-Computer Dialogues
H. Wandke and J. Schulz   221

Intuitive Representations and Interaction Languages: An
    Exploratory Experiment
D.L. Scapin   235

Computer Languages: Everything You Always Wanted to Know,
    But No-One Can Tell You
T.R.G. Green   249

Design of Programming Languages Under Psychological
    Aspects
R. Schmitt, E. Schulz, and E. Frank   261

Problem Oriented Design of Interaction Structures
H. Kiesewetter   273

User Requirements in Natural Language Communication
    with Database Systems
U. Koch   285

The Efficiency of Letter Perception in Function of Color
    Combinations: A Study of Video-Screen Colors
G. d'Ydewalle, J. van Rensbergen, and J. Huys   295

On the Temporal Stability of Signal Detection Processes
F. Nachreiner, K. Baer, and A. Zdobych   301

Coding of Information in Man-Computer Systems Based on
    Cognitive Task Analysis
E. Wetzenstein-Ollenschläger, and U. Scheidereiter   307

Visualization of Process Information in Improving Work
    Orientation
L. Norros, A. Kautto, and J. Ranta   321

Experimental and Theoretical Analysis of Visual Search
    Activities
B. Chalupa   331

Alternative Information Presentation is a Contribution
    to User Centered Dialogue Design
H. Raum   339

EVALUATION OF MAN-COMPUTER INTERACTION

Effects of Computerization on Job Demands and Stress:
    The Correspondence of Subjective and Objective Data
A. Leppänen, R. Kalimo, and P. Huuhtanen   351

Assessment of Mental Load for Different Strategies of
    Man-Computer Dialogue by Means of the Heart Rate
    Power Spectrum
K.W. Zimmer and B. Guguljanova   357

Performance in Cognitive Tasks and Cardiovascular
    Parameters as Indicators of Mental Load
P. Quaas, P. Richter, and F. Schirmer   365

Influences of Mental Load on Reaction Times in
    Man-Computer Dialogues
F.M. Kühn, K.H. Schmidt, K.-Cl. Schoo, and U. Kleinbeck   373

Some Remarks on a Measure of Computer Operator Workload:
    Changes in Pupil Reflex
T. Marek and Cz. Noworol   383

Subjective Load in Introducing Visual Display Units
Th. Wolff, H. Hugler, H.-J. Selle, J. Weimann, and
    E. Schulz   389

JOB ORGANIZATION

Job Organization and Allocation of Functions Between
    Man and Computer: I. Analysis and Assessment
W. Hacker and E. Schönfelder   403

Job Organization and Allocation of Functions Between
    Man and Computer: II. Job Organization
E. Ulich and N. Troy   421

Psychological Principles for Allocation of Functions in
    Man-Robot-System
K.P. Timpe   429

Social Psychological Prerequisites and Consequences of
    New Information Technologies
B. Wilpert and S.A. Ruiz Quintanilla   439

What Should be Computerized? Cognitive Demands of
    Mental Routine Tasks and Mental Load
W. Hacker   445

Name Index   463

Subject Index   469

ACKNOWLEDGEMENTS

The editors gratefully acknowledge the sponsorship of the
International Council of Scientific Unions (ICSU), which gave
the MACINTER Network financial assistance as one of the first
IUPsyS projects after IUPsyS became a member of the ICSU. This
support allowed the organizers of the First MACINTER Seminar
to invite a wide range of researchers from countries all over
the world.

We also wish to thank for the advice and recommenditions given
by Dr. Peter Grootings of the International Social Science
Council (ISSC) when we were preparing the scientific programme.

Special thanks are due to Berlin Humboldt University, which was
helpful in solving organizational problems in the preparation
of the seminar.

The editors wish to extend their gratitude to the contributors
to this volume for supplying their manuscripts promptly and
in accordance with the standards required.

Mrs Grobe, Mrs Breitenfeld and Mrs Ulbrich were kind enough
to type the manuscripts, and Mrs Kessler turned rough sketches
into accurate drawings.

Friedhart Klix and Hartmut Wandke

GENERAL ASPECTS OF
MAN–COMPUTER INTERACTION

Man-Computer Interaction Research
MACINTER-I
F. Klix and H. Wandke (Editors)
© Elsevier Science Publishers B.V. (North-Holland), 1986

MACINTER – AIM AND GOAL
(Opening address)

F. Klix
Sektion Psychologie
Humboldt University
Berlin
GDR

Computers are like nerve cells in modern industrial societies.
Their impact in almost all fields of social life changes human
existence itself. The new role of psychology is to contribute
to the optimization of the interface as a pivot between psychology and technology. The interface problem is explained in its
asymmetric partition of the same features. In two selected
fields - expert systems and the use of computers in the class-
room - psychological tasks are derived which are explicitely
dealt in the contributions of this volume.

SOME INTRODUCTORY REMARKS

It was at Queens Hall in Edinburgh on Thursday, July 29, 1982 (during the
XXth International Congress on Applied Psychology) that a group of some
20 psychologists met to discuss opportunities for a systematic information
exchange on man-computer research from the psychological point of view. It
was agreed at the meeting that mutual information on this young research
field might not only be of benefit to the institutions themselves but would
also serve to concentrate and strengthen the impact of psychological research
on recent trends in modern technological development. This might, in turn,
increase the social value of psychology and enrich existing research opportunities. But it was also stressed that the strengthening of that impact
would also increase the humanitarian role of psychological research.

Computer are like nerve cells in modern industrial societies, irrespective
of whether they are installed in western, socialist or developing countries.
 They interlink different groups of persons or institutions - both govern-
mental or non-governmental - and do not only allow automating mechanical,
but also cognitive performances or presuppositions in mental sections of
human work. They allow collecting and sharing knowledge and experience with
the help of huge data bases. They allow preparing effective decisions in
complex environments. And they finally allow individualizing standardized
goods by means of varieties of modular products. Computers change the
division of labour and extend what are called white-collar jobs and diminish
the role of so-called blue-collar jobs (Fig. 1).

All in all, computers in modern industrial societies do not only change
the productivity of human labour. Their impact in almost all fields of
social life (labour, leisure, science, art, transportation and other
services) changes human existence itself since it produces deep changes
in the sociological architecture of modern industrial societies.

for benefit of mankind & pers. welfare
com should exist.

4

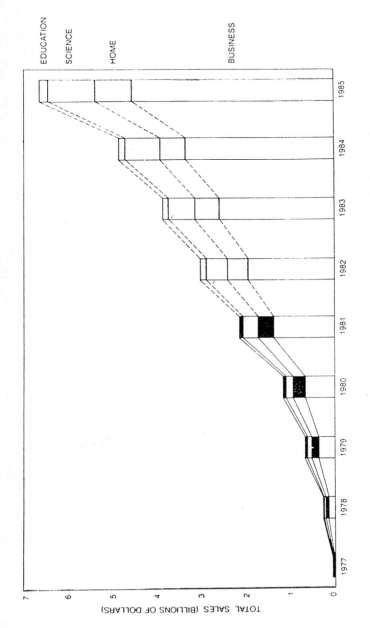

Figure 1: Rough estimate of the increase in the number of microcomputers between 1977 and 1985. It can be assumed that the (predicted) increase between 1984 and 1985 has been underestimated, especially with regard to education and science (from Sci. Amer. Sept. 1982).

← stats

But computers as such accomplish nothing. Their increasing role in our
societies depends on how effective people are in using those powerful
opportunities to the full. And the more effectively this can be done, the
more powerful will be the impact of those cognitive tools on the efficiency
of social organization and the productivity of human labour – with all the
ensuing economic consequences that depend on the social system in which
this technology is applied. It is generally true to say that the extension
and optimization of the opportunities offered by these tools constitute
a great challenge to psychologists. The main aspect related to this
challenge is not how to help develop new and more powerful systems but
how to increase the affection towards these systems and therewith indirectly also the efficiency of the human user. Most engineers and technicians feel that a lot of the decisions that they have to take require
psychological knowledge. This may also be the reason why an increasing
number of psychologists are invited to IFIP or IFAC congresses, conferences of more local computer societies, societies of automatic translation
and societies of Artificial Intelligence. But the selection of the
psychologists invited is usually haphazard. On some occasions the groups
invited are very competent; and on others they are not. And here we come
to the first aim of our project: to define the fields in which psychologists can competently answer (or prepare answers to) questions concerning the optimal design of CRT (cathode ray tubes), the nature of CRT's,
abbreviations in command languages, error-signalizing or error-correcting
devices, principles for making complex programs transparent and trans-
ferable to other users, etc. You all know the main topics of our conference: design of man-computer dialogues; learning of novices in the
dialogue; representation of information on visual display units; adequate
work sets; knowledge representation; mental load, overload and stress due
to computer requirements; job organization and allocation of functions
between man and computer, the mental image of computer functions; and
related topics – all of them indicating that psychologists are competent
in questions concerning the optimization of man-computer interaction;
and this competence is based on actual research results.

SOME ASPECTS OF THE ROLE OF PSYCHOLOGY (AND PSYCHOLOGISTS) IN MAN-
COMPUTER INTERACTION RESEARCH

The title we have chosen excludes areas of psychological research that
influence hardware design, the mechanical lay-out of CRT's or mechanical
properties of interface. It rather draws our attention to the aspect of
communication. What does it mean: communication?

We will agree on this: communication is the exchange of information by
means of encoded messages for which there is a common knowledge (between
at least two systems). The encoded messages rely on a set of symbols (an
alphabet) and rules of concatenation and production that build a language
in the formal sense of the word.

Concentration on the communicational aspect means that the core of the
project will have to be the optimization of interface. Interface in this
sense is the pivot between man and the frontiers of the machine. Optimization depends on two conditions:

(1) on the kind of systems; and (related to that)
(2) on the level of machine capability.

Ad (1):
Concerning the different kinds of systems, we have to distinguish between
action-controlled ones and those which are restricted to information processing capabilities. In the action-controlled ones (to which robots
belong) specific capabilities are necessary: three-dimensional pattern
recognition, identification of scenarios, programming and control of
motion, and continuous feedback of the executed motion (especially the
identification of its bias by accidental environmental influences).
Pattern recognition, identification and change of three-dimensional cues,
distance estimation by disparate mappings, texture density as distance-
cue are well-known kinds of performance by the visual system. Some results
of this research have been used by engineers. More difficult are the
programming and storage of action and action control. Although there is a
large amount of psychological literature on action and goal-dependent
motion patterns, the knowledge gained so far does not seem sufficient
for engineers to use for the storage and control of action-related
behaviour. In our context, all the problems related to this field of
application should be left out of consideration. Instead, I would like
to concentrate on psychological problems of the second aspect, i.e.

Ad (2):
Different levels of machine capability and related psychological problems.
First of all, we should define the range within which to look for the
specific key questions. I would not like to tackle the spectrum going
beyond free programmable minicomputers. The lowest level that I propose
should be included is defined by TI59 or the HP41C, CV, SX series. On
the other hand, at the highest level, we include computers using highly
developed programming languages, like the HP-extended BASIC, PASCAL,
PROLOG, and LISP (see Schmitt in this volume). The IBM A-T PC, HP 150,
200, Apple II, MACINTOSH, right up to the WAX machines may be imaged. Let
us exclude unique systems like CRAY1 or CYBER205 with cycle times of some
nanoseconds. And we will also exclude the socalled non-von-Neumann machines
and parallel processing techniques, although they may make completely new
demands on psychological research.

Within the spectrum so defined, we have well-defined office computers,
personal computers and also computers with an extended memory for large
data bases of the kind used in expert systems. This spectrum is homogeneous inasmuch as it allows selecting and tackling common psychological
problems. Most of the contents of our present network seminar is related
to these common topics: computer dialogues, symbol representation on
visual display units, knowledge representation, mental load and stress,
job organization and allocation of functions between man and computer.

Instead of dealing with these topics in advance, I would rather like to
define some other common, but quite specific problems. They centre round
interface as a pivot between user abilities and hardwired information
processing capabilities. It is a characteristic feature of this topic
that it embraces applied as well as basic research fields of psychology.

INTERFACE AS A PIVOT BETWEEN PSYCHOLOGY AND TECHNOLOGY

Although computers can only work with binary digits, the units at the
interface are usually numbers, characters, sequences of symbols, texts,
lists, or tree structures. In almost all cases, there are several kinds
of hierarchical levels with short cut or substitution rules. (This principle is now also used in the spreadsheet technique.)

One of the special features of the interface problem is its asymmetric
partition of the same topics. Fig. 2 gives an unfold impression of what
is meant by asymmetric partition:

(1) We have two imput-output devices. They both are prewired: one by
    engineers and the other by the biological history of evolution. Both
    frontiers have sensori-motor units which interact, and both may or
    may not be easily compatible with each other. Making them compatible
    is one of the jobs that psychological research has to perform.

    I would like to outline with a few examples: what it means to make
    them compatible.

(2) We have a display on the one side, and receptors on the other. Vision
    and perception governed by laws of their own: contrast, form dis-
    crimination, colour satiation, the size of the figures, etc. are
    usually given an intuitive estimation and are rarely set up by
    experimentally identified parameter data. The point is that there are
    no general data for all cases; they rather depend on the frame or the
    context of the lay-out.

(3) We have operating compartments to which short-term or intermediate
    storage mechanisms belong just as much as procedures and algorithms
    do. Whereas on the computer side the algorithms are well-defined and
    determined throughout (also when they include random numbers or
    probabilities for decision-making), we have, on the other hand,
    procedures whose dependencies are not clear cut on many occasions
    and are not transparent in terms of dependencies. There are proce-
    dures and strategies in human thinking (Simon, 1984; Bruner, 1956;
    Klix, 1984) that involve different kinds of heuristics. What matters
    here is that such kinds of software organization should be developed
    as allow the human operator to make use of such techniques and pro-
    cedures. Different programming languages differ in their feasibility
    in this respect since they restrict genuine modes of human problem-
    solving and thinking to a considerable degree.

(4) There is language comprehension on either side, but it differs very
    much indeed: symbol identification by 0-1 strings, on the one hand,
    and context-dependent sound, word, and phrase identification, on the
    other. There is a formally defined grammar, on the one hand, and a
    (mostly) fuzzy-rule set obeying language competence and comprehension,
    on the other. For this reason a natural language may easily be used
    as a sophisticated programming language. But to make syntactic rules
    comparable and, in consequence, compatible with natural language
    habits in order to make command similar to natural meaning (and
    therefore also resistant to confusion) - all this can be done, and
    the solutions will be of particular benefit to naive users.

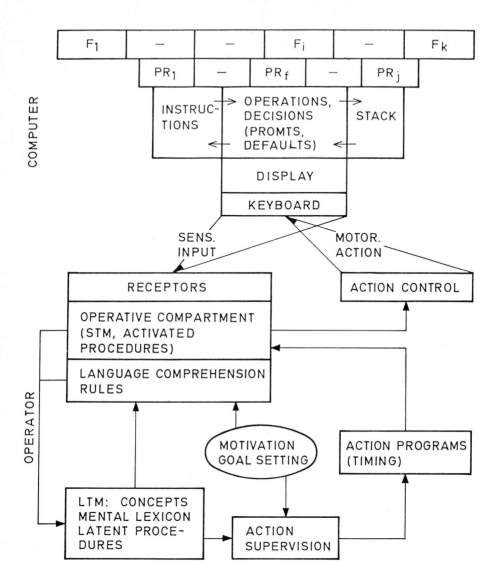

Figure 2: Some functional asymmetries in man–computer activities.
           (For explanation see the article.)

(5) We have two different kinds of long-term memory: one is divided into files and stored programs with specific names, the other is built up by a 'mental lexicon', consisting of phoneme, lexeme, and grapheme concatenations that are associated with sets of conceptual properties. These 'conceptual nodes' and the relations between them create a semantic network. I should not like to consider aspects of phoneme and grapheme representation (which allow reading and writing); instead, I should like to restrict myself to conceptual knowledge representation. The main asymmetry between knowledge representation in man and the computer are related to lexical entries. These entries are, in the computer, restricted to words, word lists and concatenations between words, generally subdivided into files that programs have access to. Restriction to words only instead of words defined by conceptual properties seems to me to be the main barrier today for creating an effective device of language translation. If this asymmetry could be diminished by the principles underlying genuine human concept representation, this could result in a new break through and produce a more effective solution to the translation problem.

(6) The knowledge representation just mentioned is not closed: it can be added to by learning. Learning devices are widely different in the two systems. Man's learning capacity exists a priori: by trial and error, insight learning, higher-order inference rules, or as a result of problem-solving strategies (which include heuristics). In human beings there is an interdependence between learnability and background knowledge, and there is also a kind of non-logical reasoning in the sense that well-defined conjectures are not derivable from the predicate calculus. Computer learning, on the other hand, presupposes the application of learning devices, the specification of thresholds for generalization, specification and inductive inferences (for examples see Michalski (1984)). Though efforts are being made to overcome the restrictions of the predicate calculus, it is at present one of the most promising challenges for psychological research to overcome these classical borderlines. Examples may be the detection of mechanisms of non-monotonous reasoning, the evaluation of thresholds at which to switch from inductive to deductive reasoning, and the application of analogous reasoning whenever an ill-defined problem is given (see Carbonell, 1984, Klix, 1985).

A practical aspect of this point is the drafting of training programs for naive users. The use of a priori knowledge for establishing the efficient performance of a given programming language is a specific job for psychologists. One condition for doing that effectively is the availability of psychological knowledge concerning problem-solving techniques, strategies of information processing and inferential rules. The application of this knowledge for the teaching of programming, especially of dialogue programming, is a first step, which must be followed by further specific research work. Fig. 3 gives an idea of how this task is related to what we have called a problem space (see also Tauber, 1984). Local and global strategies, transformation of local states, the concatenation of states by search strategies, etc. - all these well-known components of problem-solving activities become relevant in the training of naive computer users. Psychologists are at present challenged to help use this functional technique of human intelligence as a constituent part of computer capacities. This field of psychological research is, in particular, linked with

1.) $Z = (E_i, R_i)$

2.) $Z_o = (E_o, R_o)$

3.) $Z_e = (E_e, R_e)$

4.) $\varsigma(z_i, z_e) = f\left[d(z_i, z_e)\right]$

$$= \varsigma(z_i)$$

5.) $\lambda(\varphi_i \quad z_i^j) = g\left[d(z_i, z_e) - d(z_j, z_e)\right]$

Figure 3: Essential properties of a problem space:
(1) an original state Z with a set of properties E_i and
relations R_i between them.
(2) Intermediate states, e.g. Z_o with properties E_o amd
relations R_o. Such sets of states are created during
programming and activated one after another as the program
is carried out. Z_e = goal state with which the programming
task (and/or its fulfilment) ends.
(3) Evaluation function, defined by the distances between
a given state Z_i and the goal (or subgoal). The expenditure
to bridge the gap is a quality expression of the efficiency
of a program, measured by different decision steps.
(4) Evaluation function for the comparison between two
or more states, concerning their distance from the goal.
This function allows identifying the best step for the next
decision.

developments in Artificial Intelligence and makes psychology an active
section of cognitive science.

I have mentioned asymmetries between some specific principles responsible
for higher computer capacities and also some background conditions responsible for human intellectual capacities. To diminish the degree of
these asymmetries does not only make computers more feasible for naive
users (this alone may be reason enough for dealing with this topic), but
also enlarges the given computer capacities in well-defined and significant
dimensions.

At this point I should like to disregard other aspects that underline
the importance of these asymmetries between man and computer one again:
motivation and goal setting behaviour, supervision of cognitive and motor
actions, action plan development, action control, and factors that influence the compatibility between motor action control and the keyboard
layout. Some of these aspects are especially relevant in connection with
higher-level robot development, a topic that cannot to be tackled at this
point.

Changing this general approach I would now like to come to more specific
tasks and briefly explain how they have stimulated recent trends in psychological research. I will select two fields: expert systems, and some aspects
of the use of computers in the classroom.

PSYCHOLOGY AND THE MANIPULATION OF LARGE DATA BASES

The paradigmatic field of expert systems is that of structural data bases,
which provide relevant information e.g. for the taking of difficult diagnostic or prognostic decisions.

The first part that includes psychology refers to automated classification
procedures. As Unger and Wysotzki (1981), Kulka (1972), Krause and
Wysotzki (1984) and others have indicated, it is possible to use human
concept formation strategies for developing automated classification
procedures. K. Goede developed a classification algorithm that is now
realized in a general screening procedure pursued to detect heart
diseases at an early stage (Fig. 4).

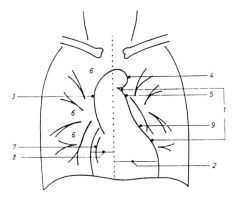

Figure 4: Schematic pattern of heart contours as they appear on a X-ray
          plate. Sets of specific properties allow identifying specific
          kinds of heart disease at a very early stage. The algorithm,
          derived by Goede, Unger, and Wysotzki, is equipped with a
          capacity for learning: after a learning period the system can
          classify the disease with a high degree of precision, provided
          the feedback series of + and - examples is guided by expert
          knowledge. (1) taille curvature, (2) degree of left extension,

(3) stress of the aorta ascendens, (4) aorta button, (5) pulmonary segment, (6) pulmonary nestles, (7) double contour of the
heart shadow, (8) degree of the enlargement to the right, (9)
left heart bend. Specific combinations of these properties are
so-called concepts of heart diseases.

This is one example of many. We know from Lenat (1983), Feigenbaum (1983),
Lederberg (1981), and others that they have pursued classification procedures in order to make a highly complex information input transparent
and feasible. In this first part, psychologists are engaged in preparing
expert knowledge and transferring it to an available section of what is
stored.

The second part with possible essential contributions of psychology is the
internal organisation of the data base. Very different kinds of organisational principles are used to cluster relevant information according
to given similarities.

One of the most crucial problems is the so-called combinatorial explosion.
It is very often impossible to come to a decision as a result of random
search. An example is the MYCIN program, developed by E. H. Shortliffe.
MYCIN can e. g. decide (with a certain degree of probability) whether there
is a bacterial blood infection, and, if there is one, what the nature of
the infection is. About 500 heuristic rules are applied, simple as well
as complex ones. They allow drastically reducing the decision effort
required under the pure resolution method.

Backward checking, questions about class features, similarity appearances
and other information processing principles are implemented in the DENDRAL
system. DENDRAL is able to give a correct structure description on the
basis of a molecular formula with 43 million candidates. Lenats EURISCO
program (1984) uses heuristic rules, e.g. the rule of looking for extreme
cases. The reason for the application of such techniques is their capacity
for reducing the given amount of complexity. But the rules applied are
usually found and defined on an intuitive basis. The human aspect of
solving complex problems is systematically investigated in cognitive
psychology (e.g. Dörner, 1983; Lüer, 1973). It is comparatively well-known
how problem-solving techniques work with subgoal formation, how context-
dependent knowledge specification works, and how conceptual generalizations
are made; and we are relatively familiar with some kinds of non-monotonous
or analogical reasoning.

The selection of optimal search strategies requires a kind of metaknowledge,
which may also be used for self-up-dating procedures. All these procedures
come under what is called knowledge engineering. In my special paper I will
give some examples of how cognitive research in psychology can qualify
the transfer of expert knowledge to an effective representation so that
the knowledge-based programs are more effective than the devices that
are intuitively derived. The background to this particular competence of
psychological research is perfectly easy to see. It is the biological
history of man. The human central nervous system has been confronted with
highly complex situations for more than two million years. It is therefore prewired to keep a huge simultaneously given amount of information
transparent, reduce complex situations down to a decision-relevant degree

and gain access to precisely that kind of information which is necessary and sufficient under the given circumstances. It can be shown that there lies the core of human intelligence.

Learning from man leads to another consequence that I would like to mention in this connection. It is the phenomenon of natural language comprehension. We have to take into consideration that artificial sentence or text comprehension may be very useful for the fulfilment of significant tasks, especially for the rendering of services in cases when the naive user is confronted with immediately available computer facilities.

Up to now, all efforts to allow Artificial Intelligence to comprehend language have basically been linked with a mental lexicon consisting of words, phrases and morphemic rules. The parsing procedures of sentences or texts are well-known. Fig. 5 indicates some crucial aspects in this context (see also Winograd, 1984).

But Winograd wrote only recently that "... there have been no breakthroughs in machine translation" (1984). In my opinion this is mainly due to the neglect of conceptual properties in connection with the translation problem. Almost all so-called semantic net connections in AI have so far been restricted to lexical links. But as I have shown in connection with Fig. 1, there is some evidence that man's semantic memory is built up by property-bound links and not primarily by links between lexical entries.

If this statement is correct, the consequences for the way in which psychological research ought to be able to influence the automation of speech-comprehending, text-comprehending and text-producing mechanisms are hard to overestimate.

THE COMPUTER IN THE CLASSROOM: A NEW CHALLENGE TO PSYCHOLOGISTS

The availability and systematic use of computers in the class-room changes the didactics of teaching and learning more than any other educational mean since the introduction of printed books.

And this has been the case approximately since Comenius's time. At first strong objections were raised to the introduction of books in the class-room: children were expected to have stored their knowledge in their brains. Analogical objections were made to the introduction of computers. We have to admit, however, that there are reasons why we should be careful and cautious with the compulsory use of these tools. UNESCO is aware of this aspect and has made some efforts in this field (under its medium-term research programme).

In view of a new field of this kind, we should stress the competence of psychologists in this field. This gives rise to a real change for fruitful cooperation with computer scientists. I should like to mention a few important points in this connection:

(1) First of all, I would like to say that this topic is a kind of focus in which different areas of psychology met: cognitive psychology, developmental psychology, personality research, and educational psychology. They will all have to give joint answers concerning the

F. Klix

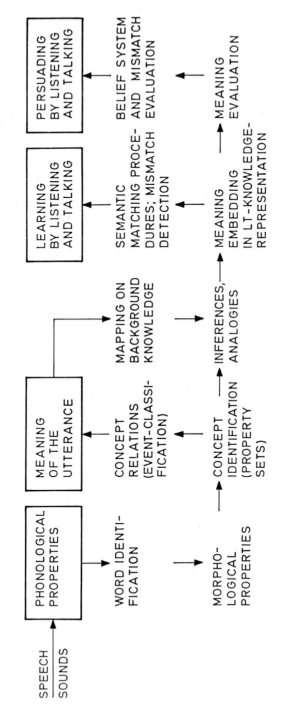

Figure 5: Steps in language comprehension. Top row (framed):
consciously verifiable steps; bottom rows: procedural steps, generally unconscious,
which deepen different levels of language comprehension: meaning recognition, cognitive
learning and persuasion are the main results on the surface.

new role of teachers, new contents of different curricula, the
suitability of different programming languages, and the age-dependent
levels for the use of computers. The availability of alpha-numeric
input-output devices widens their applicability in new fields. Data
bases on historical events and visual information on geographical
facts, literature and grammatical rules will change the wellknown
situation tremendously: instead of being banned from using any information source but their own memory, pupils will now be able to
rely on all the knowledge that exists. What matters is to instruct
pupils on when and how to use that potentially available information.
The teaching of strategies of problem-solving and information search
in a large data base or in an expert system is a central element
of a new kind of didactics.

(2)   Computers in the classroom change the didactics of science teaching.
      It becomes possible to simulate experiments that cannot be carried
      out in the classroom. And they allow visualizing hitherto latent
      properties of laws, e.g. the dynamics of physical laws, inter-
      relations between algebraic and geometrical terms during sophisticated
      training in mathematics, or the demonstrations of the role of co-
      efficients in different kinds of partial differential equations.

(3)   Computers in the classroom are in a very general sense a stimulating
      enrichment of the mental environment of pupils. Their impact on the
      development of mental skills will be the most striking consequence.
      But we will have to wait and see whether there are any more conse-
      quences, some of which may even lead to changes in the personality
      structure itself. The extensive use of computers might in the end
      lead to considerable individualization or perhaps more than that:
      some kind of isolation in mental and social life, in social behaviour
      as well as in developmental psychology. Muylwijk, van der Veer and
      Waern (1983) showed the dimensions of changeability, mentioning four
      categories of learner variables: (1) Extra-intro-version as far as
      personality factors are concerned (highly stable), (2) cognitive
      styles, (3) preferred personal strategies, and (4) personal knowledge
      structure. It is impossible to say now to what extent different
      components may be affected or changed by (or resist to) the influence
      of computer use; but that there will be an impact in various areas
      is shown by two studies: a Dutch study (covering 15 years and carried
      out in Amsterdam /van der Veer, Beishuizen, 1984/) and the Brooklyn
      LOGO project (Watt, 1979, cf. Tauber, 1984). What are the principal
      results?

      Although restricted to some selected topics in teaching, the projects
      show that the mental enrichment of the environment mainly stimulates
      children (of 12 to 14 years) in general exercises, but in particular
      also in practising skills. It is indicated that the multiple-choice
      device is not effective but that series of questions for deepening
      or extending the given information are most welcome and used indi-
      vidually in different ways. This means that the Skinner Technique, as
      it was used for programmed instruction, is not the most appropriate.
      The Dutch study also shows that the interactive display with automatic
      syntax checking and some restricted modules for programming are most
      adequate. Specific styles of programming behaviour have been detected.
      Van der Veer mentions the versatility dimension (after Pask, 1976),
      which is well-known from problem-solving research (roughly spoken: the
      attempt to get an overview vs. focusing on a given detail, see also

van der Veer in this volume). The results lead to two new didactic
problems: how to provide training in strategy development, and how to
introduce coding devices. Pupils have to learn to code information like
a translation. The most promising outcome from the Brooklyn project
was, I believe, the detection of 'hidden talents'. This means that
there are pupils who feel quite stimulated specifically by this kind
of environment. And everybody who worked out one of the large programs
has discovered that there are well-done parts and also some more
stupid modules, but that, all in all, such programs allow tapping an
existing intellectual potential and that there is a large area in
which creative behaviour is required.

(4) All in all, this challenge opens up completely new fields for psycho-
     logy and its interaction with computer scientists:

     - Decisions have to be drafted concerning optimal programming
       languages.

     - The LOGO experience should be evaluated and systematically adapted
       to specific requirements.

     - Teaching the coding of information, in particular to different age
       groups and with consideration given to different intellectual
       abilities, which is a new research field.

     - Ways are taught of coping with problem-solving exercises, evolving
       different kinds of strategies and adapting all this to specific
       individual differences.

     - The systematisation of different levels of difficulty has to be
       taken into consideration. Programming means thinking not in terms
       of isolated problems but in classes of problems. A given simple
       formula does not require (e.g.) to calculate the size of the sur-
       face of a circle but the surface of every circle possible and
       realizable by prompts. What is the best age for such insight?
       According what we know, it is between the age of 12 and 14 years.

     - All the other problems that we have to tackle in this connection
       are also related to the very specific requirement of reducing
       complexity and making a problem formalisable and, in consequence,
       programmable; devising abbreviation rules; deciding what kind of
       error signalisation is most effective, what kinds of error correction
       are most appropriate, and what number of independent commands should
       not be exceeded. Finally, we should be aware that these systems very
       often generate considerable motivation for good performance. Mental
       load and overload has to be recognized. This presents a challenge
       to personality diagnostics.

A BRIEF LOOK AHEAD INTO THE FUTURE

There are now discussions going on about certain computer ghosts: there
are the so-called fifth generation ghost, the optical computer, non-von-
Neumann machines, storage concepts for "meta-giga-bytes", etc. I believe
that the demands made on psychologists by existing machines are high
enough. We are hardly called upon to help develop new kinds of computers;
we had rather help increase the efficiency as well as the welfare of the
so much challenged human user. It is our job to make full use of the
existing opportunities for the benefit of mankind and consider man's
personal welfare. So our task is linked to the negative consequences just
as much as it is to the positive ones. We know that this is not only a
task for psychology to fulfill. (If the network works it will be one of
our next tasks to enlarge the topics within our competence. I was by far
not exhausting: the psychological aspects of computer-aided design and
computer-aided manufacturing (CAD/CAM) raise exciting new prospects for
research into labour psychology. The effective use of graphics, programming graphics and especially the accomplishment of dynamics in graphics
in efficient ways - all these are requirements that point to largely
unresolved psychological problems.

SOME ORGANIZATIONAL ASPECTS: PROPOSALS FOR THE NEXT FEW STEPS

I have outlined some areas in which the introduction of computers are changing social life, irrespective of the kind of social organization in
hand. The examples I have given are such which affect almost all the
fields that may possibly be influenced by these new technological opportunities. The challenges to psychology are overwhelming. They concern
both basic and applied research. The investigation of cognitive processes
and the simulation of cognitive performance link psychological research
to computer sciences and efforts made in other sciences.

We should try to link the different research activities and look for new
applications suitable to help man make use of these new tools for his own
benefit.

REFERENCES:

(1) Bruner, J.S., Goodnow, J.H. and Austin, G.A., A Study of Thinking.
    New York, London 1956.

(2) Carbonell, J.G., Learning by Analogy: Formulating and Generalizing
    Plans from Post Experience. In Michalski, Carbonell and Mitchell,
    1984.

(3) Dörner, D. et al., Lohhausen (vom Umgang mit Unbestimmtheit) Bern
    1983.

(4) Feigenbaum, E.A. and Lederberg, J., Mechanization of Inductive
    Inference in Organic Chemistry. In: Kleinmuntz, B.: Formal Represen-
    tation of Human Judgment. New York, Sydney 1968.

(5) Goede, K. and Klix, F., Lernabhängige Strategien der Merkmalsgewin-
nung und der Klassenbildung beim Menschen. In: Klix, F., Krause, W.
and Sydow, H. (eds.): Kybernetik-Forschung, H. 1, Berlin 1972.

(6) Klix, F. (ed.), Gedächtnis, Wissen, Wissensnutzung. DVW Berlin 1984.

(7) Klix, F., Denken und Gedächtnis. Über Wechselwirkungen kognitiver
Kompartments bei der Erzeugung geistiger Leistungen. Z. Psychol. 3
(1984).

(8) Klix, F., Über die Nachbildung von Denkanforderungen, die Wahrneh-
mungseigenschaften, Gedächtnisstruktur und Entscheidungsoperationen
einschließen. Z. Psychol. 2 (1985).

(9) Krause, W. und Wysotzki, F., Computermodelle und psychologische
Befunde der Wissensrepräsentation. In Klix, F. (Ed.): Gedächtnis,
Wissen, Wissensnutzung. Berlin 1984.

(10) Kukla, F., Untersuchungen zu Eigenschaften und Erwerbsbedingungen
unscharfer Klassen. Forschungsbericht Nr. 131 des Zentralinstituts
für Kybernetik und Informationsprozesse der AdW der DDR, Berlin 1972.

(11) Lenat, D.B., Toward a Theory of Heuristic. In: Groner, R. and M.
and Bischof, N.: Methods of Heuristics. New Jersey, London 1983.

(12) Lenat, D.B., The Role of Heuristics in Learning by Discovery: Three
Case Studies. In: Michalski, R.S. et al. (eds.): Machine Learning.
Berlin, New York, Tokyo 1984.

(13) Lüer, G.: Gesetzmäßige Denkabläufe beim Problemlösen. Weinheim 1973.

(14) Michalski, R.S., A Theory and Methodology of Inductive Learning.
In: Michalski, R.S. et al. (eds.): Machine Learning. Berlin, New York,
Tokyo 1984.

(15) Pask, G., Conversational techniques in the study and practice of
education. Brit. Journal of Educational Psychology 46 (1976).

(16) Simon, H.A., Why Should Machines Learn? In: Michalski, R.S. et al.
(eds.): Machine Learning. Berlin, New York, Tokyo 1984.

(17) Simon, H.A. et al., Rediscovering Chemistry with the BACON System.
In: Michalski, R.S. et al. (eds.): Machine Learning. Berlin,
New York, Tokyo 1984.

(18) Tauber, M.J. et al. (eds.), Readings on Cognitive Ergonomics. Berlin,
Heidelberg, New York, Tokyo 1984.

(19) Unger, S. und Wysotzki, F., Lernfähige Klassifizierungssysteme.
Berlin 1981.

(20) van der Veer, G.C., van Muylwijk, B., van der Wolde, G.J.E.,
Introducing statistical computing - Evolution of the cognitive system
of the navice user. In: Tauber, M.J. et al.: Readings on Cognitive
Ergonomics. Berlin, Heidelberg, New York, Tokyo 1984.

(21) van der Veer, G.C. and Beishuiz, J.J., The computer in the class-room. In: Tauber, M.J. et al.: Readings on Cognitive Ergonomics. Berlin, Heidelberg, New York, Tokyo 1984.

(22) Waern, Y., On the implication of user's prior knowledge of human-computer interaction. In: Tauber, M.J. et al.: Readings on Cognitive Ergonomics. Berlin, Heidelberg, New York, Tokyo 1984.

(23) Winograd, T., Computer software for working with language. Sci. Amer. Vol. 251, No. 3 Sept. 1984.

Man-Computer Interaction Research
MACINTER-I
F. Klix and H. Wandke (Editors)
  Elsevier Science Publishers B.V. (North-Holland), 1986

C O G N I T I V E   E R G O N O M I C S :
An approach for the design of user-oriented interactive systems

Norbert A. Streitz

Institute of Psychology, Technical University Aachen
D - 5100   Aachen
Federal Republic of Germany

As it becomes possible to delegate mental work to
interactive computer systems (ICS), the traditional
scope of human-machine studies needs extending to
include the complex cognitive processes of comprehension, communication, and problem solving. A problem
solving model of human-computer interaction (HCI) is
proposed being based on the distinction between content problem and interaction problem. Subsequently, a
thesis on human-computer cognitive compatibility is
presented and followed by a discussion of the role of
mental models, metaphors, and misconceptions in HCI.

In the past, the use of machines enhanced physical strength and
skills of men with respect to the transformation and transfer
of material and energy. Nowadays, prodigious machines   are
available - exemplified by powerful computers - which are able
to encode, store, organize, process, retrieve, and transfer
information. This development is closely connected to the possibility of delegating parts of mental work to this kind of
machines. Due to the development of highly interactive computer
systems (ICS), humans and computers have to cooperate in an
interactive fashion. As a consequence, this requires a new
specification for the dynamic allocation of tasks between them.

So far, only a limited number of people are exposed to this
kind of working environment. Given the proliferation of personal computers and individual workstations becoming an integral
aspect of our work situation, we proceed to a point where
information technology will be present in all areas of life
throughout our society. This development has to be paralleled
by a change of focus of research in this field. There has to be
a considerable increase in the awareness of the growing shift
in who uses computers: from the computer-trained individual to
the person who has no specific knowledge about computers
(computer novice). Users of office systems, individual work
stations, personal computers, and public information technology
are very different from professional programmers. This opens up
a range of new topics of research especially for psychologists.
Psychological research on human-computer interaction (HCI) is
needed as a science base aiding system engineers and computer
scientists in designing user-oriented ICS. The consideration of
human factors in the design of ICS is important for all areas

of new applications. To name a few prominent examples: text processing, electronic mailing system, computer-aided design and manufacturing (CAD/CAM), expert systems, intelligent computer assisted instruction (ICAI).

Against this background, the objective of this contribution is to propose a framework for the investigation of psychological aspects of HCI. The specific intention of this framework is to establish relationships between some areas of cognitive psychology (e.g. problem solving, knowledge representation) and HCI.

COGNITIVE ERGONOMICS

As computer systems become more sophisticated, the consideration of human cognitive processes are increasingly relevant. Therefore, the traditional scope of human-machine studies needs extension to include the complex cognitive skills of comprehension, communication, and problem solving. The term "software ergonomics" has been introduced in order to distinguish this area of research from "hardware ergonomics" (e.g. the design of keyboards, screens, office equipment). The understanding is that software ergonomics is concerned with the adaptation of software (e.g. command languages, application programs) to the human user, especially to the non data processing specialist. Not limiting this area to computers - although it is most obvious in this context - but extending it to cognitively demanding work situations in general, one might introduce the label "Cognitive Ergonomics". Accordingly, cognitive ergonomics deals especially with the analysis of cognitive aspects and processes of work (e.g. planning and regulation of actions in their relationship to mental representations). As a consequence of this analysis of the conditions of work methods, means, and tools are getting adapted to the cognitive prerequisites a human worker brings to bear in this type of work environment.
SHACKEL (1980) points out that this approach "is concerned with the ergonomics of perceiving, thinking, deciding and remembering, i.e. the relation of these aspects of human performance to the occupation and equipment involved". DZIDA (1980) introduced this label while raising the question which parts of mental work should be delegated to the computer and how much control should remain with the user of an ICS.
The application of cognitive ergonomics to HCI presents a challenging development in research on human factors and is at least as important as the underlying technological development itself.

As a side remark, I like to make a comment on possible research strategies. So far most of the research has been concerned with evaluation of existing systems, e.g., by running case studies or comparing different interfaces. Thus, research topics were mainly determined by existing technology ('Nachlaufforschung') or prospects of the near future. This is a valuable thing to do because feed back has to be provided to the producers of the systems. A second strategy is to be part of a team doing "rapid prototyping" allowing to be very close to new technologies

('Begleitforschung'). In addition, I would strongly argue for
complementing these approaches by trying to progress one step
ahead of existing technology ('Vorlaufforschung') and to develop conceptional models of HCI which provide frameworks for
future interactive systems. The possible role of psychologists
would then be to propose boundary conditions for the design of
new systems which would be based on principles of cognitive
ergonomics.

GLOBAL MODELS OF HUMAN-COMPUTER INTERACTION

The before mentioned point of view requires the application of
theories and models from cognitive psychology in human factors
research. Talking about the design of ICS, two kinds of modelling are of interest. In order to avoid confusion, one should
distinguish between models of the global situation, i.e. the
user-task-computer interaction with its various constituents,
and (cognitive) models of the user him/herself. Whereas cognitive models of the user can be proposed by relying heavily on a
substantial body of research in psychology, models of the
global situation have to consider additional aspects given by
the structure of the ICS. Of course, the central aspect of
modelling the user-task-computer interaction is the modelling
of the user in relation to his/her task. Viewing the user
within the information processing paradigm, currently prevalent
in cognitive psychology, provides a common and consistent terminology for the two partners of the interaction in question.
Global models of HCI should be geared to provide a taxonomy of
interaction modes and be able to specify the level of dependence resp. independence of the interface and the application
under consideration. This requires the integration of user
analysis and task analysis.

In order to approach the novel domain of research on work with
ICS, various theoretical frameworks have been proposed. They
might be distinguished by different metaphors used or different
views of the role of computers.
There is the concept of the computer being a "tool" (e.g.
DZIDA, 1982) similar to and at the same time different from a
traditional tool (e.g. a hammer or - more sophisticated - a
camera). Various additional attributes have been assigned to it
("selfexplanatory" or "symbiotic"). Problems which arise from
the use of this metaphor have been discussed, for example, by
WINGERT (1983).
Another point of view is connected with the notion of man-
machine "communication" (MMC). Accordingly, a computer is supposed to be not only a tool but at the same time a "partner"
in a communication situation. In this role, it has not only an
internal model of itself but it also might be capable of building up a model of the human user as its partner. And it is
intended to make it act in accordance with certain principles
like: "Do what I mean, not what I say". In order to characterize this kind of communication, the notion of formal communication has been introduced (KUPKA, MAAS, & OBERQUELLE; 1981)
and discussed in contrast to natural communication .

A third aspect of HCI is emphasized by the concept of the computer being a "medium". This stems from the point of view that the user does not communicate with the computer but rather with the programmer or the software designer. The computer (including software) then provides a medium for the exchange of information.

Of course, criticism of these positions are dependent on or might be resolved by the definitions of communication used. Our opinion is that the terms communication and dialogue imply already a certain model of HCI and should only be used for that specific connotation. Therefore, we prefer – at this level of analysis – the not so loaded term "interaction".

A PROBLEM-SOLVING MODEL OF HUMAN-COMPUTER INTERACTION

Analysing a variety of work situations, one can state the following observation. A user comes to the computer with a goal in mind and an outline of the individual tasks necessary to achieve it. We propose to describe the relevant factors of such a situation as components of problem solving.

This is in accordance with a definition given by ANDERSON(1980) considering problem solving as "any goal-directed sequence of cognitive operations". Problem solving involves finding a sequence of operations, or operators, that tramsforms the initial state into a final state in which the goal is satis-fied. In order to distinguish problems from (routine) tasks it is necessary that the transformations are not immediately available. Instead, search and inference processes are required to a substantial extent (KLIX, 1971). Therefore, problems are characterized by the existence of a barrier between initial and goal state and can be classified by the type of barrier (DÖRNER, 1976).

In the context of HCI, the user's objective is to solve a problem in a given content domain. (An engineer who has to construct a certain piece of equipment provides a typical example.) We call this aspect of the work situation the content problem. In addition, we assume the user to be knowledgable about the content domain. He/she might have specific strategies and routines to work on the content problem at his/her dispo-sal. This relates to ANDERSON's (1980) distinction between creative problem solving that requires the development of new procedures and routine problem solving that uses existing pro-cedures. This availability of routine cognitive skills will be-come important, as we go along.

In order to achieve the goal, the engineer is interested in using certain means which provide optimal support for the job to be done. A CAD-system would be one of this sort for the construction problem. Assuming that the user is not a computer specialist, he will not be interested in learning special computer languages in order to interact with this device. Thus, he is confronted with an additional problem: the interaction problem. It consists in finding ways to convey the content problem to the computer and to efficiently use the system

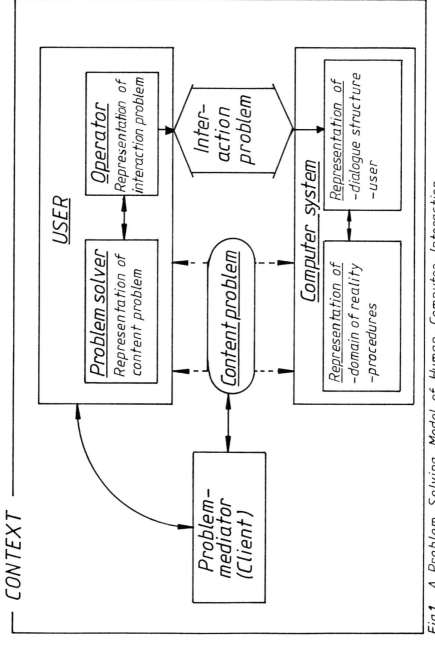

Fig.1 A Problem Solving Model of Human–Computer–Interaction

during the construction process. The interaction problem is superimposed on the content problem (or task) the user has to solve in the first place. Although we distinguish between these two problems at this point, it will be shown later that they are not completely independent of each other.

We give now a more detailed description by making use of Fig.1 which provides a schematic representation of the situation in terms of problem solving.

On the one hand, the user of an ICS is a problem solver. In order to work on the content problem he has to built up a representation of the content problem relying on his prior knowledge of the domain in question. In a number of situations, the content problem has not been posed by himself, but is the result of the demand of a client (or the boss) who functions as a problem mediator. This has the effect that the original content problem will be transformed by the communication process.

On the other hand, he has to act as the operator of an ICS. In order to make use of the system he has to know something about operating the system (e.g. dialogue structure) and how the system represents those aspects of the content domain which are relevant for his current content problem. This includes knowledge about certain procedures or subroutines he can call on when working on the content problem. All this is part of the user's representation of the interaction problem. The type of knowledge necessary to solve the interaction problem could be described as intrumental knowledge - maybe in the sense of the usage of tools. Assuming that the ICS in question does not only consist of a large database but is rather close to what one would call a knowledge-based system, inference and integration procedures should be available. Their implementation and the structure of the knowledge base are mainly determined by the ideas the system designer had about this domain of reality. Possible discrepancies between these representations will be discussed later.

In summary, the accessibility of the computer's knowledge base (data and procedures) depends on the "bottleneck interaction problem". Therefore, it is the extent of the interaction problem which determines the usefulness of an ICS for a user, e.g. a CAD-system for the construction engineer, to a large degree.
Accordingly, two problems define the limits of any interactive knowledge-based systems:

- the quality of the knowledge base of the content domain
  (extent and structure of the data base incl. procedures)
- the "dialogue" capability of the system
  (possibility of user-oriented ("natural") communication

Discussing the usage of this kind of systems, one has to keep in mind that the knowledge must itself be given to the system before it can be used and this may also involve interaction in terms of a dialogue. Therefore, the dialogue structure forms an essential part of any such system. This is especially true for expert systems and ICAI-systems (STREITZ, 1984c). Both types of systems derive their capability and competence from the know-ledge already in the system.

How is this knowledge acquired by the system? Again, it is the interaction problem which is central. Providing ways of trans-fering experts' knowledge to a system might involve an question asking component of the interface. The system itself would then take the role of actively acquiring and updating its knowledge base. This approach would require a cognitive theory of question-asking specifying the conditions of when and how and what type of questions are possible and appropriate at a given moment. There are some ideas towards a theory of question asking behavior of humans (e.g. FLAMMER, 1981; STREITZ, 1984b) which might turn out to be useful for this application.
A similar problem appears in ICAI-systems where one has to distinguish between the learner system and the author system, the latter one being used to produce the course ware. Obvious-ly, these two parts of a system require different ways to minimize the interaction problem.

One way to tackle the problem of minimizing the interaction problem is to provide the ICS with knowledge about the dialogue process itself. This leads to the implementation of a component which is based on an artificial intelligence approach. But most of the systems, so far, are lacking this source of knowledge.

Closely related to the distinction between content problem and interaction problem are those aspects of dialogue design which deal with the implications of task allocation between user and computer. This again has consequences for the global and ad-ministrative organization of work and the cooperation between different workers on related tasks.

HUMAN-COMPUTER COGNITIVE COMPATIBILITY

Since we proposed to consider the work situation as a problem solving situation we will now apply this frame of reference. What do we know about humans' ability to solve problems and about the factors enhancing or degrading human performance? Although cognitive psychologists are still far from being able to give a detailed and comprehensive account, there is quite a body of research on this topic. We do not intend to review the literature at this point, but rather focus on some relevant aspects.

In research on problem solving, we have witnessed a change of emphasis from the study of merely the product of a problem solving activity to the cognitive processes responsible for this product. But only until recently, this shift in interest has neglected the role of memory resp. the role of subjective knowledge representations on which the processes are supposed to operate.

It has been pointed out (STREITZ, 1983a, 1984b) that the initial representation of a given problem domain determines the
course and the products of problem solving to a high degree.
Empirical evidence was demonstrated by inducing different problem representations in different subjects for the same problem
structure . It was possible to predict processes and success of
problem solving by a measure for the degree of adequacy of the
initial representation based on the encoding behavior of the
subjects . In turn, this raised the question of what are the
determinants responsible for the initial problem representation. STREITZ (1984a,b) approached this by proposing an integrated view of text processing and problem solving for which
the concept of understanding is central. Determinants of text
comprehension, as e.g. goals and interests controling encoding
and retrieval strategies in connection with prior knowledge
(STREITZ, 1982), are responsible for the initial problem representation.

Within this framework, we propose a <u>thesis on the conditions of</u>
<u>user-orientation of an ICS</u> in the sense of <u>human-computer</u>
<u>cognitive compatibility</u>.*)
This thesis is based on two assumptions. First, a (physical
symbol) system has to have a representation of the domain
relevant for the information to be processed in order to be
able to process this information. Second, different systems
built up different (subjective) representations of the same
domain dependent on determinants which are effective during the
encoding phase.

> An interactive computer system(ICS) is the more user-
> oriented the less discrepancies do exist between the
> relevant knowledge representations on the user's side
> and on the side of the ICS, respectively. The request
> for cognitive compatibilty refers to the represen-
> tations of the content problem as much as to the
> representations of the interaction problem.

This leads to the following conclusion: The more compatible the
initial representations are with respect to these two problems
- there might even exist isomorphic mappings - the more successful the user will be in using the ICS for achieving his
primary objective, i.e. solving the content problem. The notion
of compatibility used here is different from consistency.
Whereas compatibility refers to relationships between user and
system, consistency refers to relationships within the user or
the system. Of course, consistency of a system is important as
well.

Since these are very general statements, one has to amend and
elaborate on them. One aspect is to specify the domain of
validity. This thesis is meant to apply especially to initial
or casual encounters of a user with an ICS and will hold for
the learning phase of a user. Thus, in this context, learning

---

*)   This represents a reformulation of an earlier proposal of
     the author (STREITZ, 1983b).

to use an ICS consists of solving the interaction problem. Learning or the acquisition of knowledge about the system by the user will be more or less facilitated dependent on the degree of cognitive compatibility.

Due to the limitations of space, we will not be able to give a detailed account of the application of this thesis. Instead, we will limit ourselves to some remarks about mental models (just another term for subjective knowledge representations) in HCI.

THE MENTAL MODEL "ZOO"

Returning to the design of ICS, one can state that the role of the user as an operator of the system (being concerned with solving the interaction problem) requires understanding the design of the system. This, in turn, should lead to the request of designing for understanding. How to proceed ?

As mentioned before, comprehension, problem solving, decision making, and actions are based on subjective representations of the domain of reality under consideration. Recently, the label of an (internal) mental model has become popular again to describe this aspect (e.g. GENTNER & STEVENS, 1983). NORMAN (1983a) applies this concept to the interaction of people with computers and considers four different things:
The target system t, the conceptual model C(t) of that target system, the user's mental model M(t) of the target system, and the scientist's conceptualization C(M(t)) of that mental model.

It is not quite clear from that article who's conceptual model is meant by C(t). We think one should further distinguish between the conceptual model $C_d(t)$ of the designer and the conceptual model $C_p(t)$ of the psychologist. Obviously they represent the target system in different ways. The same argument applies especially to the scientist's conceptual model. Therefore, we also introduce $C_d(M(t))$ and $C_p(M(t))$. One thing we can learn from this is that the $C_d(M(t))$ is probably the main guideline for the designer in designing the system's surface image. And here we find a lot of misconceptions on the side of the designer about M(t). In terms of our proposed thesis, there is very few compatibility. Interdisciplinary research would lead to improvement of the conceptual models by integrating $C_d(M(t))$ and $C_p(M(t))$ for their use in design.

To be complete on different types of models, one also has to mention a model of the user which is given to or built up by the system itself. Therefore, we introduce S(M(t)) as the system's model of the mental model of the user. This kind of model becomes relevant for the design of knowledge-based, adaptive, or intelligent interfaces and in the area of ICAI - systems for intelligent tutoring.

To make things even more elaborate, I like to refer to the problem-solving model and direct attention to its implications for mental models with respect to the distinction between content and interaction problem. What is meant by t ? Is it only the aspect of the target system in terms of the inter- action problem? Our thesis deals with both aspects and I think it is necessary to include the mental models of the content problem as well. We assume thereby again that the represen- tations of the content relevant knowledge differ between the user and the system. The designer's conceptual model $C_d(c)$ of the content domain becomes the systems model of the content domain being different from the user's model M(c). Again, the designer should acquire an adequate conceptual model C(M(c)) and use this in designing ,e.g., the structure of the data base of the system. Because of limited space, we will not deal with this aspect here but did mention it as a consequence of the distinction in the problem-solving model.

In terms of M(t), the question has to be raised what kind of conceptual models of the system should be communicated to the user either by the system's surface itself and/or by manuals, documentation, and on-line help functions. The decision how to convey depends mainly on what concept of learning is preferred. If one thinks about learning as a rather passive storage of concepts in memory an explicit description of a conceptual model of the system is the choice. From the view of a more active process of learning by problem solving, a conceptual model must be derived by the learner through experience which then leads to the mental model M(t).

A quite useful way to investigate and then improve HCI is the analysis of errors users make during interaction. Errors can be categorized into slips and mistakes. Slips have been defined by REASON (1979) as "actions not as planned" or by NORMAN (1981) as "the errors that occur when a person does an action that is not intended". Whereas a mistake is an error when the plan or the intention is already wrong. One can argue, that mistakes might be based on misconceptions a person has about a domain of reality. They are part of people's view of the world and might include their own capabilities, as e.g. the ability to perform a certain task. NORMAN (1983b) proposes that design rules can be derived from analyses of human errors in a systematic way.

MENTAL MODELS AND MISCONCEPTIONS

In this section, we will give some examples on how different conceptual models provided to the user effect their mental models and performance.

1) The notion of saving a file is compared to being like a (virtual) document which can be filed into a file cabinet. Having filed (saved) a document it is still visible on the screen. The user is confused, because in the office world docu- ments which are filed are physically transfered and not only copied. What happened here? Has the command been carried out? What and where is the original, what and where is the copy?
2) Next, we consider a situation where a user is in insert mode of a text processing system. Naive users tend to split the line

before inserting although it is not necessary since the already existing text is continually pushed to the right side. This observation is often quoted in order to demonstrate how the "typewriter" metaphor produces behavior which is not making full use of the system's features. But this argumentation is overlooking the fact that people might also split the line in order to have a better structured view of this passage. Therefore, this kind of behavior is not a valid indicator for the use of an inappropriate metaphor. *)

3) Allen Cypher at UCSD designed a system called "notepad" with which one can – among other things - create notes and put them into (labeled) "bins" and later retrieve them again. You are able to put the same note into different bins. A metaphor from the physical world around us is used in order to communicate an organizational structure. But what happens to the metaphor when we make a correction or an addition on the note N retrieved from, say, bin B_1 ? Using the "bin" metaphor, we would predict that this change effects only the note N in bin B_1. But, if we retrieve the note labeled by N from a bin B_2 we find that it has been changed, too. This is in conflict with the metaphor's prediction. One could say that the metaphor collapses. There are some problems with this metaphor: How can you put the same note into different bins? How and why does the change in bin B_1 effect notes in bin B_2?

Abstracting from the specific examples, one is confronted with the following problem. On the one hand, one would like to provide a metaphor from the familiar world so that the user can draw on prior experience and existing mental models. But this might easily lead to misconceptions about the system's structure and possibilities. On the other hand, one does not want to limit the system's capabilities so that they are compatible with the user's experience of the metaphor's properties in the outside world. There is no easy answer to this problem and no space in this article to discuss it in detail.

CONCLUDING REMARKS

In summary, we would like to argue for further exploration of the problem-solving framework in modeling HCI. The importance of initial problem representations for problem solving leads to more emphasis on the investigation of how people acquire and built up mental models of systems and content domains. The role of (text) comprehension as the encoding component of problem solving implies the request of "design for comprehension".

One has to be careful in choosing metaphors and try to avoid or minimize the conflict between the advantage of drawing on familiar concepts and limiting the system's capability.

As a final remark, I would like to add that I consider it a fascinating situation to be part of the development of the tools we will have to use in our work environment in the near future.

*) Thanks are due to Allen Cypher (University of California, San Diego) for demonstrating the notepad system and to Gerhard Dirlich for pointing out the mentioned problem.

REFERENCES

(1) Anderson, J.R., Cognitive Psychology and its Implications (Freeman, San Francisco, 1980).

(2) Dörner, D., Problemlösen als Informationsverarbeitung (Kohlhammer, Stuttgart, 1976).

(3) Dzida, W., Kognitive Ergonomie für Bildschirmarbeitsplätze, (Humane Produktion/Humane Arbeitsplätze 10 (1980) 18-19.

(4) Dzida, W., Dialogfähige Werkzeuge und arbeitsgerechte Dialogformen, in H. Schauer & M. Tauber (eds.), Informatik und Psychologie. Wien, Oldenburg 1982.

(5) Flammer, A., Towards a theory of question asking, Psychological Research 43 (1981) 407-420.

(6) Gentner, D. & Stevens, A. (Eds.), Mental Models (Erlbaum, Hillsdale, N.J. 1983).

(7) Klix, F., Information und Verhalten (VEB Deutscher Verlag der Wissenschaften, Berlin 1971).

(8) Kupka, I., Mass, S. & Oberquelle, H., Kommunikation - ein Grundbegriff für die Informatik, Mitteilung Nr. 91 des Fachbereichs Informatik, Universität Hamburg (1981).

(9) Norman, D.A.,Categorization of action slip, Psychological Review 88 (1981) 1-15.

(10) Norman, D.A., Some observations on mental models, in D. Gentner & A. Stevens (eds.), Mental Models (Erlbaum, Hillsdale, N.J. 1983a).

(11) Norman, D.A., Design rules based on analyses of human error, Communications of the ACM 26 (1983b) 254-258.

(12) Reason, J., Actions not as planned: The price of automatization, in G. Underwood & R. Stevens (eds.), Aspects of Consciousness. Vol. 1 (Academic Press, London, 1979).

(13) Shackel, B., Dialogue and language - can computer ergonomics help? Ergonomics 23 (1980) 857-880.

(14) Streitz, N., The role of problem orientations and goals in text comprehension and recall, in A. Flammer & W. Kintsch (eds.), Discourse Processing. Advances in Psychology, Vol.8 (North-Holland, Amsterdam, 1982).

(15) Streitz, N., The importance of knowledge representations in problem solving: An example of text comprehension and problem solving, in G. Lüer (ed.), Bericht über den 33. Kongreß der Deutschen Gesellschaft für Psychologie in Mainz 1982. (Hogrefe, Göttingen, 1983a).

(16) Streitz, N., Die Mensch-Maschine-Schnittstelle unter dem Blickwinkel der Kommunikation. Positionspapier zur 3. Arbeitstagung "Mensch-Maschine-Kommunikation" in Bad Honnef (1983b) (organized by the GMD, St. Augustin).

(17) Streitz, N., An integrated view of text processing and problem solving, Paper represented at the 23. International Congress of Psychology, Acapulco, Mexico (1984a).

(18) Streitz, N., Subjektive Wissensrepräsentationen als Determinanten kognitiver Prozesse, Unpublished manuskript, Aachen (1984b).

(19) Streitz, N., Kognitionspsychologische Aspekte der Gestaltung von Dialogstrukturen bei interaktiven Systemen, Paper presented at the symposium "Lernen im Dialog mit dem Computer" (1984c).

(20) Wingert, B., Werkzeugerfahrungen und Qualifikationsveränderungen beim CAD, Office Management, Sonderheft "Mensch-Maschine-Kommunikation" (April 1983) 22-25.

Man-Computer Interaction Research
MACINTER-I
F. Klix and H. Wandke (Editors)
© Elsevier Science Publishers B.V. (North-Holland), 1986

AN APPROACH TO METACOMMUNICATION IN HUMAN-COMPUTER INTERACTION

Michael J. Tauber

IBM Germany, Science-Center
Heidelberg
FRG

ABSTRACT

In many dialogsystems the computer is used as a tool.
For solving tasks of an underlying task space the work
of the user is to delegate task solving to the computer. For this work he needs knowledge about the virtual machine defined by its functionality.
The design process has to start with the specification
of the knowledge which the user must have for his delegating work. The specification of the knowledge is the
conceptual model of the interface. Providing the user
with the conceptual model by means of metacommunication
as communication about the virtual machine is discussed
in the paper.

INTRODUCTION

Research in Human-Computer-Interaction (HCI) is an issue of interdisciplinary work. Designing interfaces in HCI can be regarded as a modelling
process which is mostly influenced by methods of computer science and
psychology (Rohr & Tauber, 1984). Whereas computer science regards the
interface as a virtual machine, psychology emphasizes modelling with
respect to the cognitive structure of the user. Taken together, this
requires designing the interface as a virtual machine which is understandable for the user. Therefore, the user's knowledge of a system
(conceptual model) has to be determined and specified for the design
process from the beginning. The advantage of such an explicitly specified
conceptual model of the interface is twofold (Moran, 1981; Norman, 1983).
- it serves as a representation of the virtual machine
- it serves as a mental model of the system which the user has to acquire.
The conceptual model should be made transparent for the user and be present
in any context. In the case of incomplete user knowledge communication not
only with, but about the virtual machine is neccessary. This kind of
communication is furthermore called metacommunication.

There are two basic but different approaches to apply methods of the
cognitive science to human-computer interaction. Within the first the user
is regarded as an understander which must be helped in understanding the
system and in communicating with the system. Defining an understandable
interface based on a conceptual model, teaching the user the model, and
interpreting all communication steps by means of the model, all belong
to this first approach, which also is the background of the present

paper. The second approach aims at making the system intelligent and adaptive to the user. Since this approach is beyond the aim of the present paper, the reader is referred to the work of Rich (Rich, 1983) on the concept of stereotypes and Gunzenhäuser (Gunzenhäuser, 1984) on the concept of an user agent. However, both approaches can not be seen independently. Many results and models achieved by the first approach can contribute to the second approach and vice versa.

Many different problems can be tackled by means of using a computer in a dialog situation. The predominant are

(a) solving tasks: whereby the interface provides access to specific objects and functions working on this objects, both represented in the system; users delegate these tasks by communicating with the system

(b) information retrieval: whereby the interface provides access to an information systems; the aim of the communication process is to get detailed information from the system (Traunmüller, 1984).

(c) controlling complex processes: whereby mainly the system controlls the process and informs the user about the state of the process. At critical points the user is requested to control and change the process (Rasmussen, 1980).

In the following the discussion is restricted on case (a): the computer as a tool for solving tasks.

THE SYSTEM AS A TOOL FOR PERFORMING TASKS

In using a system as a tool for task solving the following aspects are relevant.
- There is a well defined class of (formal) tasks,
- the space of which is defined by a world of objects and a set of system functions working on the object world.
- Each task is described by an initial state, a goal state and a procedure consisting of system functions which produce the goal state as the result of the application of the function.
- Users must be able to delegate tasks of the task space to the system by specifying the proper functions by the help of commands and physical actions.

(1) The system and its task space

Each tool oriented system is build up and used for tasks which must be defined related to the system. The underlying task space is defined
- by the set of tasks which the system can perform
- by the set of objects manipulated by the tasks and represented in the system (object world)
- and by the set of system functions manipulating the represented objects.

A task is defined by an initial description of objects or the object world and by a goal description of objects or the object world. Tasks can be related to each other in a hierarchic task structure which defines tasks as a procedure consisting of subtasks.

Real entities are represented in the system as objects . They can be
related in an object structure defined by relations like consists-of,
named-by and so on.

Finally there are functions defined by parameters (arguments are objects
from the task space), results (defined as objects) and conditions for
failure.

If the system is asked to perform a task from the task space the task has
to be described by means of the object world and system functions (see
fig. 1)

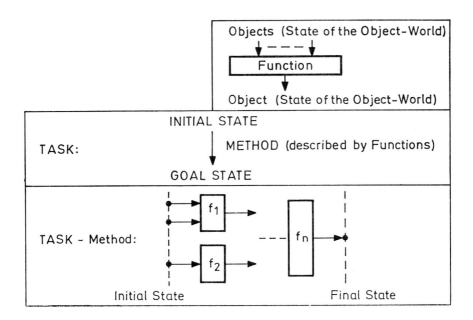

Figure 1:
The functionality of the system: tasks, objects, functions

With respect to the definition of the task space many problems of psychological importance arise. The use of computers can require new definitions
of tasks and their related tools (a text-editor is not a type-writer) and
therefore the existing external task space must be redefined with respect
to the new internal task space required by the computer (Moran, 1983).The
kind of the representation of the objects and the choice of the actual
system functions must be driven by models of human cognition. As discussed
by Rohr & Tauber (Rohr & Tauber, 1984) reduction of complexity of the task
space is of great importance for the user. These questions we will not
discuss in the following. We assume that the choice of an actual task space
is already based on sufficient knowledge of the cognitive structure of the
user.

(2) The functional paradigm

Central for understanding tool oriented systems is the functional
paradigm which describes using the system as
- manipulating objects by applying functions to it,
- composing functions in application by the application
  of other functions,
- constructing functions in some cases by means of old ones.

In this paradigm the functions can be regarded as black boxes, whereby the
inside is not of interest for task solving. Only the effect of the function
is of interest.

The idea to represent manipulation of objects by the application of
functions to the object world, to solve complex tasks by composition of
such functions, and to extend the set of functions constructing new functions by procedures defined by old functions is well known in the field of
dialog languages (Kupka, 1983). Moran, defining his semantic level of the
C(ommand) L(anguage) G(rammar) (Moran, 1981), showed that the functional
paradigm is essential for all tool oriented systems. With respect to the
functional paradigm differences between different dialog systems (form
strong dedicated systems to dialog languages) are not essential. The systems only differ in their degree of universality of the object world, the
degree of universality of the applicable functions, and the degree of
possibility to extend the set of functions (see fig. 2).

	DIALOG LANGUAGES	DEDICATED SYSTEMS
OBJECTS:	general (Lists, ...)	special (Word, ..)
TASKS:	all algorithmic solvable tasks can be performed	can be enumerated explicitly (insert, ..)
EXTENSIONS:	without restrictions possible	not possible
FUNCTIONS:	very elementary (FIRST, APPEND, ..)	domain-specific (MOVE, ..)

Figure 2:
Range of tool-oriented dialog systems

USING THE SYSTEM -DELEGATION OF TASKS

Considering the "ideal" user who knows the task space, "using the system"
can be regarded as a delegation of a task to the system which performs
the task by means of its functions. The procedure of these system functions is defined by the underlying task space. The competent user must
know the procedure. However, he has not to know the solution which is to
construct by the system on the object world. For the work of delegation
user are requested to know the task space in general, the single functions by its effect and to work driven by the functional paradigm.

It is often discussed whether using a system is a problem solving activity
or not. On the system's side this never will be the case, because systems
perform deterministically the delegated tasks specified by the user. On
the user's side it depends on the overall task which the user has in

mind. Using the system means to decompose complex tasks in subtasks of which come can be performed by the system, other might be performed by the user. If the overall task is a problem in the sense of the definition of Dörner (Dörner, 1976) - a problem is described as a task influenced by some barriers, considering either the operations or the goal state - then the overall activity is a problem solving process. However, the subtasks delegated to the systems are not problems in this sense, because the function and its effect is known. In the case of an unexperienced user who tackles tasks by means of the system by trial and error, "using the system" can be regarded as a problem solving process activity. However, the only problem is to learn the system.

For delegating tasks to a system, it must provide commands for describing the procedure of functions, descriptors to specify the considered objects and specifications as user actions on physical devices must be possible. The whole conceptual world of the user's knowledge needed for the del- egation of tasks is illustrated in figure 3.

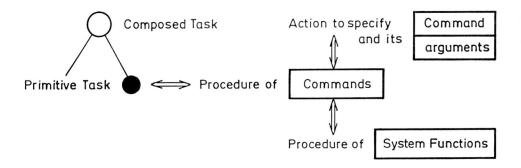

Figure 3:
Delegation of tasks to the system

THE SYSTEM SEEN AS VIRTUAL MACHINE

To perform the tasks of the underlying task space the system must be defined towards the task space. All aspects of the machine which are necessary to perform the tasks must be specified and only these aspects. The only machine of interest is the virtual machine described by terms for task performing. This machine must be understandable for the user. The actual implementation must be defined on lower levels. For the definition of the virtual machine we need a representational framework. This framework serves to determine

- the functionality of the system
- the kind of access to this functionality (language)
- the action of the user and the reactions of the system.

Following these aspects the virtual machine is defined at three levels with respect to the internal task space as proposed by the CLG (Moran, 1981).

The first level is the SEMANTIC LEVEL. It contains the system's
representation of the objects and the system's operations applicable on
the object world. Operations are characterised by parameters (objects)
and by their effect, i. e. the kind of the result. The system operations
are the representations of functions considered in the task space. In
addition to the system operations there are also user operations (cognitive
operations performed by the user) applicable to the object world.

The main components of the semantic level are demonstrated in terms of
the CLG by the following example. This example is part of a complete
specification of a special text-editor which serves as an experimental
tool for psychological experiments at the IBM Science Center Heidelberg.

```
TEXT-EDITOR = (A VIRTUAL-SYSTEM
              OBJECTS = (SET: ED-TEXT-FILE    ED-TEXT-DIRECTORY
                              ED-TEXT-NAME    ED-TEXT   ED-WORD
                              ED-STRING   ED-POSITION   ED-LINE
                              ED-CHARACTER)

          OPERATIONS  = (SET: GET SHOW REMOVE DELETE
                              PRINT SEND SAVE FORMAT
                              DELETE-S  INSERT-S  MOVE-S  INSERT-L))

ED-STRING   = (A LIST

                MEMBER = (AN   ED-CHARACTER))

ED-LINE     = (A LIST
                MEMBER = (AN   ED-WORD))
                    .
                    .
                    .
```

The CLG uses a frame-like notation for modelling the conceptual world of
the virtual machine. The description of operations is shown in the next
definitions.

```
SHOW        = (A SYSTEM-OPERATION
                OBJECT = (A   PARAMETER
                              VALUE = (AN  ED -  TEXT - NAME))

                RESULT = (AN   ED - TEXT)

                ( Der mit ED-TEXT-NAME bezeichnete Text wird am
                Schirm gezeigt   )

INSERT-S    = (A SYSTEM-OPERATION
                OBJECT 1  = (A   PARAMETER
                                 VALUE = (AN  ED - TEXT))

                WHERE     = (A   PARAMETER
                                 VALUE = (AN  ED - POSITION))

                OBJECT 2  = (A   PARAMETER
                                 VALUE = (AN  ED - STRING))

                RESULT    = (AN  ED - TEXT)

                ( Fügt ED-STRING vor ED-POSITION ein   ))
```

The SYNTACTIC LEVEL determines how the functionality of the system can
be evoked. Access to the system operations is given by the means of
commands, access to the objects by the means of descriptors. Commands
can be grouped together in contexts (realised in states, windows, ..).
Each context has its specific state variables as objects which will be
kept by the system between the application of commands.

Commands trigger procedures of system operations if the argument are
determined by means of the descriptors. This is the syntactic aspect of
the input side to the operations.

There is also the need to specify the syntactic aspects of the output of
the operations. Usually the output is presented visually on the screen.
Therefore the structure of the screen, for example the meaning of
different parts of the screen belongs also to the syntactic level. All
these elements of the syntactic level are illustrated in our example
extended now.

```
TEXT-EDITOR-SYNTAX  =  (A  SYNTAX-SPECIFICATION
                           CONTEXTS = (SET: DO-WITH-DOCUMENT-CONTEXT
                                            EDIT-CONTEXT))

EDIT-CONTEXT        =  (A  COMMAND-CONTEXT
                           NAME  =  "SCHREIBE"
                           STATE-VARIABLES = (SET: CURRENT-TEXT)
                           COMMANDS = (SET: INSERT-LINE  INSERT-STRING
                                            DELETE-STRING  REPLACE-STRING

                           ENTRY-COMMANDS = (SET: EDIT-DOCUMENT)

                           DISPLAY-AREAS  = (SET: COMMAND- AREA
                                                  STATE-AREA TEXT-AREA
                                                  MESSAGE-AREA INPUT-AREA))

CURRENT-TEXT        =  (A  STATE-VARIABLE
                           CONTEXT  =  (SET: EDIT-CONTEXT)
                           VALUE    =  (AN  ED-TEXT)
                           NAME     =  "AKTUELLER TEXT")

SPECIFIED-STRING    =  (A  DESCRIPTOR
                           NAME   = "Eingegebene Zeichenkette"
                           FORM   = (A  STRING)
                           VALUE  = (AN  ED-STRING)
                           DOES (CASE: (IF  (  Wenn String länger als
                                               50 Zeichen    )

                                        THEN (   Zeile wird überschrieben   ))

                                       (RETURN (   als  ED-STRING
                                                 die aktuelle Form    ))))

INSERT-STRING       = (AN  EDIT-COMMAND
                           NAME = "FUEGEIN"
                           OBJECT 1 (AN  ARGUMENT
                                         FORM = (A  SPECIFIED - POINT))
```

```
OBJECT 2 =  (AN  ARGUMENT
                      FORM = (A  SPECIFIED-STRING))
       DOES (SEQ:  (INSERT-S  (THE CURRENT-TEXT)
                              (THE SPECIFIED-POINT)
                              (THE SPECIFIED-STRING))
                   (FORMAT (THE CURRENT-TEXT))
                   (SHOW    (THE CURRENT-TEXT))))
```

The interaction level entails the detailed description of the physical
user actions on the physical devices for specifying commands and arguments
to the system. The physical responses of the system belongs also to this
level. In terms of the interaction level the observable sequences of user
actions and system's reactions are described.

The aim of the CLG-technique is to specify the virtuality of the system
on different points of view, whereby the interaction level in the only
observable part of the machine but the two other levels are also
necessary for using and understanding the machine. In the level approach
of defining the virtual machine each task of the task space is described
on each level by terms of this level.

HUMAN-COMPUTER INTERACTION AS AN COMMUNICATION PROCESS

The relations between a delegating user and a virtual machine based on a
dialog about a task space outlined above, are more and more considered
as a communication process in general. In informatics a general model of
communication is proposed by Oberquelle et al. (Oberquelle, Kupka &
Maass, 1983). They give the following definition of communication
(Figure 4):

1. Communication serves to co-ordinate (real and symbolic) actions of
   several agents.

2. Communication is determined by the objectives of all participants
   (intentions).

3. Communication depends on comparable premises for understanding
   (knowledge and conventions).

4. Communication can refer to the communication process itself and to
   its preconditions (metacommunication)

5. Communication is always coupled with expectations concerning the
   partner (partner model).

6. In communication there is a trend towards economical behavior.

This model emphazises the symmetric view of both partners with respect
to the single components relevant for communication. In this paper the
view of communication is restricted in some aspects (Figure 5):

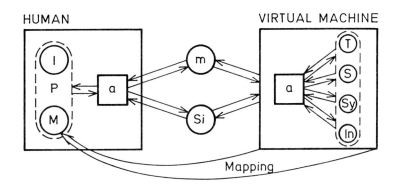

Figure 5:
Restricted model of communication with the system for task
solving

I : Intentions   T : Task-space

M : Model about the   S : Semantic-Level
     virtual machine   Sy : Syntactic-Level

P : Plan   In : Interaction-Level

a : Activity   Mapping: Mental Representation

m : Messages   of the virtual machine

s_i : Situation

CHARACTERISING THE USER

A central role for using the system plays the component "partner model".
At first the question arises what the partner model means. Recently the
term mental model becomes very popular (Gentner & Stevens, 1983; Norman,
1983). The partner model has a similiar meaning as the mental model. What
means the partner model for tool oriented systems? It is the knowledge of
the user about the specified virtual machine. Therefore the partner model
is the mental representation of the virtual machine (see fig. 5).

Understanding by the user (in his process of delegating tasks) is
described in terms of the representation. One aspect of understanding
is the match between the specified virtual machine on the one side and
the actual mental representation on the other side. The degree of the
match can be considered as the degree of the competence to use the system.
Mismatch between the specified virtual machine (furthermore called the
conceptual model) and the actual mental representation can be caused by
wrong concepts on the user side or by incomplete mental representations
seen from the level based definition of the virtual machine. One could
imagine that the representation of one level of the machine is missing.
Another aspect of understanding is to run the representation mentaly and
thereby to change states in the representation in the sense of mapping a
process onto the system. This kind of understanding is the ability to

predict or to explain system's behavior by means of the representation. Both is important for the activity to specify tasks to the system, for inter-preting the results and for analysing and remedying errors, all done by the user.

Using the system can be performed concept-driven - more conscious - or skilled - and more unconscious (Rasmussen, 1980). The skilled user is not focused in this paper. A prestage for the skilled user is always the conscious concept-driven way of using. In the case of concept-driven use users build up and execute plans consciously. The plans are based on both, the partner model, and the actual intentions.

So long as the partner model is not sufficient, the mental model is changing. Sources for changing the mental model are the communication process and the metacommunication. Changing the mental model in the communication process can be explained by a simple feed-back model sketched as follows.

(1) Intentions and partner model leads to a plan.
(2) The plan is executed by user actions.
(3) The user's actions determine system responses.
(4) Evaluating the system responses has an effect to the mental model. Not expected responses lead to the need to change the partner model. (see fig. 6)

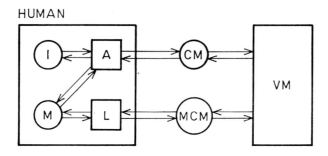

HUMAN

Figure 6:
Changing the partner model

I	: Intentions	Vm : Virtual machine
m	: Mental representation	CM : Communication message
L	: Learning activity	MCM: Metacommunication message
A	: Delegating activity (task solving)	

The need to change the mental model causes metacommunication which can take place in different ways.

- The user is speaking to himself about his partner model and makes some inferences from the system responses affecting his mental model

(METACOMMUNICATION BY SPEAKING TO ONESELF)

- The change of the mental model is influenced by the presentation of the system to the user. In the presentation some aspects of the conceptual model can be directly perceived by the surface of the machine. The use of icons, metaphors, names and so on makes several aspects of the conceptual model more directly perceptible.
  By the interpretation of the perceived presentation of the machine metacommunication takes place implicitly.
  (IMPLICIT METACOMMUNICATION WITH THE SYSTEM)

- There are facilities to communicate about the conceptual model or parts of it explicitly. There must be a communication instance able to "metacommunicate". The instance can be a person or a medium or the system itself.
  (EXPLICIT METACOMMUNICATION)

Characterising the user and his knowledge in this rough way has some important impacts for designing the system in both directions, designing the interface and designing the metacommunication process.

THE INTERFACE - WHAT MEANS IT AND WHAT IS TO DESIGN?

By beginning with the description of the world of tasks a top down modelling process is started which for the design should be oriented on a chain of several representations describing aspects of human-computer interaction (Jagodzinski, 1983). In this chain of representations the system is regarded as a representation of the task world. The system itself can be described by layers of virtual machines above the real machine. Each virtual machine has its typical notation and can be seen as the realisation of special aspects of the machine. The machine on the top is the interface. The lower machines are parts of the implementation. But what is the interface? There are several ideas quite different to each other. Designers define the interface in a more technical sense as a set of commands for accessing the functions of the machine and as a collection of techniques to specify the messages to the system and to structure the perceptible output of the system to the user. All other aspects of the virtual machine are often called the implementation.

But only knowing the perceptible part of the system is not sufficient for using. For example for using a texteditor it is necessary to know that the system is remembering the actual text between the commands, or for programming in a functional language the user must know whether the allocation of a value to a variable is only local to the function or whether it is causing a side effect. In most systems the actual assignment of the value to the name is not visible in the real interface in the sense out-lined. Also, to know only the names of the commands visible in menu is not sufficient. At least the user must know what happens by the application of the command.

The more general way to define the term "interface" is a psychological approach. Stating the interface as a set of mutual suppositions, leads to the conception to define the interface in terms of the user's knowledge. The user knowledge (its partner model) is a representation of the virtual machine, the interface is seen as a possible representation of the virtual machine. The question is to define the interface as a representation of the

machine taking into consideration the cognitive structure of the user.
First of all designing the interface means conceptually modelling the
user's knowledge needed for a competent use of the machine. The kind of
human performance and cognitive activities has to be take into account.
Both engineers and psychologists are requested to participate in the
design process. The following figure demonstrates the different kinds of
representations of the task space considered in human-computer interaction.

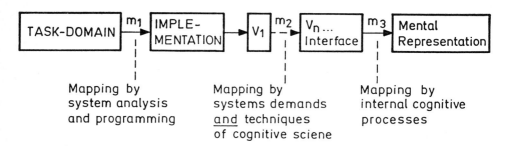

Figure 7:
Representations in Human-Computer Interaction

Evaluating the conceptual model means to consider the model of the user's
knowledge under cognitive aspects. The reduction of complexity of the
system worked on by the user is one important point. The conceptual model
has to be designed toward this reduction (Rohr & Tauber, 1984). Partial
aspects of this elementary cognitive strategy are perceived as consistency
(Payne & Green, 1984).

Up to now the representational framework of the CLG is the best method
for describing the conceptual interface as a model of the desired user's
knowledge. The CLG is developed under psychological considerations.

The impact of the cognitive knowledge-based approach to human-computer
interfaces is to distinguish two parts of the interface

- the CONCEPTUAL INTERFACE, and
- the PERCEPTUAL INTERFACE as a realisation based on the conceptual
  interface.

The perceptual interface should reveal the conceptual interface so far
as possible. The implicit metacommunication already mentioned takes place
by means of the perceptual interface. Many aspects of perceptual interfaces
- supporting the development of knowledge in the direction of a conceptual
model - are discussed by Jagodzinski (Jagodzinski, 1983) and Rohr (Rohr,
1985).

Additionaly to the two design steps already outlined

- definition of the conceptual model
- designing the perceptual interface

the designer has to design

- the acquisition of knowledge about
  the conceptual interface by the user.

He has to decide about manuals and their form, training courses and their
contents and methods, and about the possibility of metacommunication with
the system. Only the third aspect is discussed furthermore.

METACOMMUNICATION WITH THE SYSTEM -
CONVERSATION ABOUT THE CONCEPTUAL MODEL

As mentioned above metacommunication is defined as communication about an
explicit defined virtual machine. Metacommunication starting with a
communication process by delegation of tasks can have different causes.

- The user is not able to build up any plans.
- The plans of the user are incomplete.
- The system's responses do not contribute to the actual task solving
  process.
- The system is not able to interpret the task specified by the user's
  actions.

At which points of the communication process metacommunication should be
possible? Following the causes sketched above for starting with metacommunication - started by the system or by the user - metacommunication
should be possible everytime during the communication process. That means

- before starting with the delegation of any task
- instead of any action of delegation.

In the first case metacommunication is provided for supporting the
cognitive process of building a plan, in the second metacommunication is
an excursion out from the communication process and back to it
(Darlington & Dzida, 1983).

Metacommunication has always to refer to the conceptual model of the
virtual machine. The model has to be used explicitly in the dialog
process.

Metacommunication can refer

- to the conceptual model in general
- to single aspects of the conceptual model
  like levels, single elements of a level, or
  relations between the levels,
- or to discuss wrong user specifications in terms
  of the conceptual model (error handling).

Finally, metacommunication has to be designed under didactic aspects
(Tauber, 1983).

METACOMMUNICATION AND INDIVIDUAL DIFFERENCES

The aim of metacommunication is not only to support the process of
building up knowledge about the system. Metacommunication can also
contribute to the fact that users are different in the development of
their knowledge, and in the kind of their acquired knowledge about the
system (Muylwijk, Tauber, Veer & Waern, 1984). An experimental approach
to metacommunication and individual differences is reported by Tauber
(Tauber, 1985).

Acknowledgements

Thanks are due to Grabriele Rohr (IBM Science Center, Heidelberg) for
intensive discussions about modelling in HCI and to the co-members of
the COST-11bis Working-Group "Human Factors in OSI" Gerrit C. van der
Veer, Bert von Muylwijk and Yvonne Waern for many discussions about
metacommunication and individual differences.

REFERENCES

(1) Darlington, J., Dzida, W. and Herda, S., The role of excursions in
    interactive systems, Int. J. of Man-Machine Studies 18 (1983) 101-112.

(2) Dörner, D., Problemlösen als Informationsverarbeitung (Kohlhammer,
    Stuttgart, 1976).

(3) Gentner, D. & Stevens, A. (eds.): Mental Models (Erlbaum, Hillsdale,
    N. J., 1983).

(4) Gunzenhäuser, R., Lernen als Dimension der Mensch-Maschine-Kommunika-
    tion, in: H. Schauer and M. J. Tauber (eds.), Psychologie der Compu-
    terbenutzung (Oldenbourg, Wien-München, 1984).

(5) Jagodzinski, A. P., A theoretical basis for the representation of
    on-line computer systems to naive users, Int. J. of Man-Machine
    Studies 18 (1983 215-252.

(6) Kupka, I., Paradigmen des Programmierens, in: H. Schauer and M. J.
    Tauber (eds.), Psychologie des Programmierens (Oldenbourg, Wien-
    München, 1983).

(7) Moran, T. P., The Command Language grammar: a representation for the
    user interface of interactive computer systems, Int. J. of Man-
    Machine Studies 15 (1981) 3-50.

(8) Moran, T. P. Getting into a system: External-Internal task mapping
    analysis, CHI' 83 Proceedings, SIGCHI, ACM. 1983.

(9) Muylwijk, van B., Tauber, M. J., Veer, G. C. van der and Waern, Y.,
    On the interaction between systems, task and user charcteristics,
    COST 11 internal paper (will be published), 1984.

(10) Norman, D. A., Some observations on mental models, in: D. Gentner
    and A. Stevens (eds.), Mental Models (Erlbaum, Hillsdale, N. J., 1983).

(11) Oberquelle, H., Kupka, I. and Maas, S., A view of Human-Machine Communication and Co-operation,Int. J. of Man-Machine Studies 19 (1983) 309-333.

(12) Payne, S. J. & Green, T.R.G., The users perception of the inter-action language - a two level model, CHI' 83 Proceedings, SIGCHI, ACM. 1983.

(13) Rasmussen, J., The human as a system component, in: Smith, H. and Green, T. R.G. (eds.), Human-Computer Interaction (Academic Press, London, 1980).

(14) Rich, E., Users are individuals: Individualizing user models, Int. J. of Man-Machine Studies 18 (1983) 199-214.

(15) Rohr, G., Understanding visual symbols, Proceedings of the IEEE Workshop on Visual Languages, Hiroshima Dec. 6-8, 1984 - IEEE Computer Society, Silver Spring, 1985 (in press).

(16) Rohr, G. and Tauber, M. J., Representational frameworks and models for human-computer interfaces, in: G. C. van der Veer, M. J. Tauber, T. R. G. Green and P. Gorny (eds.), Readings on Cognitive Ergonomics-Mind and Computers, LNCS Bd. 178 (Springer, Berlin, Heidelberg, New York, Tokyo, 1984).

(17) Tauber, M. J., Rechnerverwendung für das autonome Lernen, Notizen zu interaktiven Systemen 11 (1983).

(18) Tauber, M. J., Entwicklung mentaler Modelle und kognitive Stile in der Mensch-Rechner-Kommunikation, in: Bericht über den 34. Kongreß der DGZP 1984 (Hogrefe, Göttingen, 1985)

(19) Traunmüller, R., Information Systems Design Methodologies and their compliance with cognitive ergonomy, in: G. C. van der Veer, M. J. Tauber, T. R. G. Green and P. Gorny (eds.), Readings on cognitive Ergonomics - Mind and Computers, LNCS Vd. 178 (Springer, Berlin Heidelberg New York Tokyo, 1983).

Man-Computer Interaction Research
MACINTER-I
F. Klix and H. Wandke (Editors)
© Elsevier Science Publishers B.V. (North-Holland), 1986

PERSONALITY TRAITS OF THE WORKER WITHIN THE "MAN-MACHINE"
SYSTEM AT AUTOMATED PRODUCTION

Philip Genov

Department of Psychology
Academy of Social Sciences and Social Management
Sofia
Bulgaria

An inquiry into workers (operators and tunners) of a
workshop with supple system of automated production
(SSAP) and into engineers of a semi-conductor plant is
carried out. It is based on the hypothesis that some
essential changes of work-related functions of the
worker come about under conditions of automated production. Structures of specific work-related qualities of
worker's and engineer's personality are established and
discussed.

INTRODUCTION

An important part among the variety of psychological problems of increasing
"Man-Machine" system's efficiency in modern automated production pertain to
social psychology. They concern worker personality in connection with the
system, the group, the psychic barriers against full automation of the production processes, the social-psychological mechanisms of increasing the
efficiency of the system, etc. In the present paper only the features of the
work-related trait structures of worker's personality connected with the
"Man-Machine" system under conditions of full automation of the process of
production are considered.

Some requirements of psychic processes (attention, reaction speed, perception, thinking, memory, etc.) applying to workers, especially to operators
under conditions of automated system for management of the production, are
described in literature (B. Lomov, V. Venda, Yu. Zabrodin, etc.). They are,
surely, of a great importance for the psychological preparation of the
workers. Nevertheless, together with these individual psychological requirements, a decisive significance in such cases have some specific alterations
in the personality traits of the worker. They concern not only his technological functions, but his other work-related functions, too. Thus, the development of specific work-related personality qualities which characterize him
as worker of a new type is determined. Changes also come about in some other
of the basic personality functions of the worker: the reproductive, the communicative and the self-regulative ones. The aim of the present paper was to
investigate the structure of the personality qualities developing in workers-
operators and engineers in connection with the successful performance of
their work under conditions of automated management of the production.

METHODS

For the above purpose, an inquiry was carried out into workers (operators and tunners in equal parts) in a workshop with supple system of automated production (SSAP) and into all the engineers of a semi-conductor plant. The subjects investigated were asked to give their opinion of experts about their work-related functions and the qualities necessary for successful performance in their profession. In other questions they were also asked to specify the operator's qualities necessary for timely perception, identification, processing and responding to the information input during performance in a "Man-Machine" system relationship, as well as for good communication with the machine.

ANALYSIS OF THE RESULTS

(1) Functions of the workers (operators and tunners) in a SSAP workshop

The data obtained show that the prevailing function of the workers engaged in a SSAP is the attending to the machines (operating) - pointed out by 71,6 % of the subjects (for 64,5 % it was the main function, and for 7,1 % - a secondary one). 45,2 % reported that they perform a control function upon the course of the technological process, while 38,1 % prevent break-down situations. Other 30,7 % point out among their functions the correction of deviating parameters situated beyond the technological limits. Performance of other functions is indicated as follows: complex functions - 21,4 %, observation of quantitative parameters and break-down settle - 21,3 %, repair - 19 %, etc.
The functions numbered characterize the worker of new type (operator and tunner) as observing, controlling, correcting serving and repairing the machines.

No	Function	Pointed out by % of the subjects		
		Total	as main	as secondary
1.	Attending to the machines	71,6 %	64,5	7,1
2.	Control upon the course of the technological process	45,2	28,6	16,6
3.	Break-down preventing	38,1	26,2	11,9
4.	Correction of deviating parameters	30,7	21,2	9,5
5.	Complex functions	21,4	14,3	7,1
6.	Observation of quantitative parameters	21,4	7,1	14,3
7.	Break-down settle	21,3	2,3	19,0
8.	Repair	19,0	–	19,0
9.	Others	19,1	14,3	4,8

Table 1
Functions of the subjects working in SSAP workshop

(2) Main personality qualities of SSAP workers necessary for performance of
their work-related functions

The qualities freely indicated by the subjects were systematized into 6
groups named main qualities, each embracing a number of specific qualities
necessary for good performance of work-related functions (Table 2).

No	Main quality	Relative part in %
1.	Competency	23,7
2.	Discipline	23,0
3.	Diligence, persistence and assiduousness	21,1
4.	Studiousness and ability of getting into new technique	12,7
5.	Handiness and exactness	10,2
6.	Adherence to principles, exigence and kindness to colleagues	9,3

Table 2
Main personality qualities of the SSAP worker necessary for
good performance of his work-related functions (relative part in %)

The qualities connected with Competency ranked first obtaining 23,7 %, followed by Discipline - 23,0 %, and Diligence-Persistence-Assiduousness 21,1%.
Also important, although represented with smaller percentages are the other
groups: Studiousness-Ability of getting into new technique - 12,7 %, Handiness-Exactness in the work 10,2 %, and Adherence to principles - Exigence-
Kindness to colleagues - 9,3 %. The above main qualities could be further
unified in still more generalized groups. If, for example, Studiousness-
Ability of getting into new technique, and Handiness-Exactness in the work
are referred to Competency, they attain 46,4 %. About one half of the qualities pointed out by the subjects are connected with the need of high occupational competency of the SSAP workers.

The other half concerns specific social personality traits of the worker
- consciousness, discipline, sense of responsibility represented all with
44,1 %. The social responsibility of the individual worker increases at automated production, as well as the social results of his activity. His Consciousness, Discipline and sense of responsibility should, therefore, be
further developed. The quality group of the interpersonal relations between
workers is very important, too, although being a small one - 9,3 %.

The above data show that together with the occupational training a specific
social preparation should be envisaged for the workers.

(3) Qualities of engineers necessary for their good performance under automated production conditions

The results obtained in the investigation show that the structure of the
work-related qualities of engineers differs from the corresponding structure
of operators and tunners (Table 3). The greatest is the relative part of the

qualities reflecting high sense of responsibility - 24,7 %, followed by
Competency - 21,3 %, Discipline - 20,4 %, Studiousness - 11,8 %, Adherence
to principles - Exigence-Kindness to colleagues - 5,6 %, General knowledge
- 5,2 %, and Organizational knowledge - 2,9 %.

While for operators and tunners handiness and exactness in the work are required, for engineers initiative and creativity are necessary, as well as
general and occupational knowledge.

No	Qualities	Relative part in %
1.	Sense of responsibility	24,7
2.	Competency	21,3
3.	Discipline	20,4
4.	Studiousness	11,8
5.	Initiative, Creativity	8,1
6.	Adherence to principles, Exigence, Kindness to colleagues	5,6
7.	General knowledge	5,2
8.	Organizational knowledge	2,9

Table 3
Relative part of the main work-related qualities of engineers and
technicians of an enterprise with automated production (in %)

If for the subjects directly participating in "Man-Machine" system competency is mostly needed, for engineers the Sense of responsibility is of
greatest importance. Their designer's and modelling work is to a great extent determining the quality of the work of the machines and of the personnel operating them. That's why at planning the specialist training for the
"Man-Machine" system the functions of these two kinds of personnel should
be taken into account, as well as the structure of their respective qualities.

(4) Qualities of the operator necessary for perception, processing and
    responding to information input

Personality structure of the individual persons complex and multifarious.
At performance of various social functions different substructures are activated. This point of view was supported by the results of the investigation on the qualities of the operator for timely perception and processing
of the information input as well as for his successful communication with
the machine (see Tables 4 and 5).

For the successful activity of both operator and tunner very important is
the timely perception of the relevant information, as well as its quick
processing and responding. Such is the opinion of the subjects investigated
(43,0 %). This ability of the operator is based both on his technical-tech-
nological preparation (24,9 %), and on his other qualities: power of observation (13,0 %), self-possession (9,0 %), operative thinking (9,0 %),

and production experience (6,0 %).

No	Qualities	Relative part in %
1.	Quick wits and ability for quick reaction	43,0
2.	Appropriate technical and technological qualification	24,0
3.	Power of observation	13,0
4.	Self-possession	9,0
5.	Operative thinking	7,0
6.	Production experience	6,0

Table 4
Relative part of the operator's qualities for timely perception,
differentiation, processing, and reaction to the information input (in %)

No	Quality	Relative part in %
1.	Appropriate technical and technological preparation	23,9
2.	Permanent improvement of the qualification	29,6
3.	Diligence	14,1
4.	Power of concentration	9,9
5.	Technological discipline	9,9
6.	Self-denial in the work	8,5
7.	Quick-wits	4,8

Table 5
Relative part of the worker's qualities necessary for
the process of communication with the machine

The data in the tables show that the performance of some specific functions
of the operator is based on specific qualities.

(5) Qualities of the worker determining the effective communication with the
machine

We examine the interrelation and the interaction within the system "Man-
Machine" as a communication process. It is different from the ordinary view
where the machine is considered as an instrument in the hands and the mind
of man. Some kind of specifically objectificated human intellect is contained in the machine by which it enters not only into physical, but also
into intellectual interaction and mutual influence with the operator. Both
direct and feedback information is circulating between them, which practi-

cally is developing as a dialogue. Subjects in this dialogue are, undoubtedly, not only man, but the machine also. The last may appear as a partner of
the dialogue only in presence of the competent and active partnership of
man. He must understand the "language of the machine", the language of technological process. Without that there would be no efficient dialogue. Therefore, in the communicative "Man-Machine" - "Machine-Man" relationship the
role of the worker is determinative and he must possess definite qualities
to perform it successfully.

Every worker participating in the above system should have appropriate technical and technological knowledge (according to 23,9 % of all opinions). He
must be acquainted with the parameters of the technological process, to detect the deviations from the norms, to reveal their causes and to be in a
position to undertake measures and to ensure additional help for their removal. That means he must perfectly know his "partner" in the "Man-Machine"
system, to understand its "language" and how to respond to it. The partners
in this system are in a continuous development. New problems arise inces-
santly in the course of the production, such as renewal of the output, rationalization of some operations or of parts of the machine, improved organization of the process of production, etc.

In essence, this is an enrichment of both the machine and the technological
or/and organizational intellect contained in it. In its turn, this requires
corresponding enrichment of the occupational intellect of the worker by a
continuous rise of his qualification. This aspect of the performance qualities underlined as the most important one by 29,6 % of the subjects investigated. After it follow Diligence (14,1 %), Concentration in work
(9,9 %), self-denial in work, and quick-wits (4,1 %). Worthy of note are
the requirements to the worker for continuous concentration upon the behaviour and operation of the machine, as well as upon the results of each
stage of the production process. The observance of the technological discipline is very important. Deviations from it often lead to break-down or
to deterioration of the quality of the output. In such cases the dialogue
is not equivalent and becomes a way for the worker to imose his subjective
will which is against the interests of the machine and of the enterprise.

CONCLUSION

(1) The investigation showed that under SSAP conditions the functions of the
worker essentially change. His work is not directly productive any more - he
is attending to the machines. The functions of observation, control, correction, and repair come to the fore. They determine a specific personality
structure of the new type of worker - operator and tunner.

(2) Together with the general structure of the personality traits of the
worker in the "Man-Machine" system, new specific structures of qualities
for good occupational performance are necessary and they develop in connection with the different functions and subfunctions.

(3) Worker's personality traits necessary for his successful occupational
performance differ from the corresponding qualities of the engineer and
technician staff.

(4) A specific kind of communication is present in the "Man-Machine" system.
For the favourable development of this communicative process the worker

must possess the respective qualities.

(5) For a good training of the worker in the "Man-Machine" system the preparation of his functions and subfunctions is necessary, and on this basis
- the development of the respective qualities for performance. They are the
starting position for working out programmes and plans of an efficient
training of the different types of workers and specialists in modern production.

Man-Computer Interaction Research
MACINTER-I
F. Klix and H. Wandke (Editors)
© Elsevier Science Publishers B.V. (North-Holland), 1986

ANALYSIS OF THE COMPETENCE OF OPERATORS CONFRONTING NEW TECHNOLOGIES:
SOME METHODOLOGICAL PROBLEMS AND SOME RESULTS[1]

Maurice de Montmollin

Laboratoire Communication et Travail
Université Paris-Nord
Paris
France

Analysing the activities of operators confronting new
technologies results in two main approaches, which can
be characterized roughly as the American and the European ones. The first is mainly oriented on taxonomies,
physical aspects of work, and laboratory studies. The
second is mainly oriented on processes, mental aspects
of work, and field studies. Ergonomics for new technologies is particularly challenged by this methodological dilemma. The concept of competence is an attempt
to meet both the need for some generalization and the
requirements of some realistic explanation of mental
activities. The competence here could be defined as the
specific articulation of knowledge, modes of reasoning,
and strategies, corresponding to some specific task, or
family of tasks. The examples given are related to the
necessary limitation of knowledge, the influence of experience, the nature of the 'natural logics', the impact
of communications in the team, etc.

SOME METHODOLOGICAL PROBLEMS

Analysing the activities of operators confronting new technologies results
in two main approaches, which can be characterized roughly as the American
and the European ones[2]. The first is mainly oriented on Taxonomies, Physical and psychophysiological aspects of work, and Laboratory studies. The
second is mainly oriented on Processes, Mental aspects of work, and Field
studies. Let us now examine these three interrelated contrasts.

Taxonomy or process

The main difference concerns the approach to the nature of work. The American approach consists, largely, in describing tasks and activities by plac-
ing them in taxonomies (e.g. types of informations and types of human errors), classing them into general categories which permit some immediate
generalizations.

In European approach, in contrast, attempts to describe the activity of the
operators as a process taking place within a specific situation. Thus it
gives (for example in process control tasks) primary importance to reasoning, to procedures for problem solving, particularly when these procedures
are insufficient or faulty. This explains the importance given, in this
area, to the verbalisations of the operators, and this is why the European

approach gives great attention to the process of 'learning' a task (taking
its inspiration in part from the methods of developmental psychology). To
understand why an operator behaves as he does, it is important to know how
he learned the behaviour. European ergonomics, in summary, is less concerned with classifying the operator's behaviour than with explaining it. To
quote some examples with which we are familiar, neither the four American
studies for process control reported at the International Conference in
Occupational Ergonomics (Toronto, May 1984), nor those cited in the conference review on 'Human Factors in the Nuclear Industry', contain any observation concerning the diagnosis of incidents by real operators. It seems
as if ergonomics must limit itself solely to the area of information presentation.

Other characteristic examples of this opposition between 'Taxonomies and
Processes' can be found in the many studies of the work of people using
computer terminals. The American approach is almost entirely concerned with
study of the 'interface'. It attempts to identify the characteristics of
those terminals which are best adapted in general to the characteristics of
operators in general. Within such a perspective, it is impossible to take
into account the semantic and cognitive aspects of the information which
appears on the screen, its 'meaning', because such things are too diversi-
fied and specific. There are precisely these cognitive aspects which are
being studied as one of the most active strands of European ergonomics,
which tries to understand how the introduction of computers (in offices and
control rooms in particular) affects not only the presentation of information but also its treatment which is always complex.

This contrast also explains the importance given by the Americans to the
concept of 'mental load', a notion which everyone tries to measure, apparently in vain. It appears more useful to Europeans to understand how
operators think, rather than to know the hypothetical 'cost' of their
thinking.

The development of taxonomies leads to the elaboration of 'standards' which
are concerned with average imaginary workers. These standards are therefore
applicable to a great variety of working situations, and this is an advantage. Europeans, with the notable exception of German ergonomist, distrust
standards, as prompting to some bureaucratic work analysis.

Physical versus mental aspects of work

The heavy predominance given by the Americans to physical (anatomical, physiological, or psychophysiological) aspects of work contrasts clearly to the
tendency in Europe, where studies of cognitive and mental aspects are perhaps in the majority. This American orientation completely dominated the
conference at Toronto: less than 1 % of the communications were concerned
with cognitive or mental aspects of work. The study of VDTs provides a
typical example. American studies are essentially concerned with the 'workplace': physical dimensions, lighting, etc. However, in our experience the
main difficulties which operators meet in these types of tasks are concerned with work content, i.e. with its meaning. It is not a question of deny-
ing the importance of physical aspects, even in tasks which are considered
to be purely 'intellectual'. But one must not diminish the importance of
what appears today to be the most conspicuous aspect of the adaptation of
workers to their work (in particular in the case of technological transfer
in developing countries).

Laboratory or shop-floor

This opposition follows directly from the preceding ones. When, in Europe, we want to understand how the workers behave during their work we are naturally led to observe them at work. We are sometimes constrained to studying simulations (in the nuclear industry for example), but use simulations which do not try to isolate variables from a complex situation but to recreate this situation with as much realism as possible. Laboratory experimentation is considered as an impoverished reduction, used in rare circumstances to test a regularity in the observed behaviour.

In contrast, it seems that American ergonomics gives higher status to laboratory experiments. This is linked with the way in which work is broken down into general categories. The experimental studies which choose students as subjects are numerous: apparently one is not interested in particular groups of workers but in the most general aspects of human adults. The search for 'laws' with great power of generalization has always been linked to experimental laboratory research. That is the classic scientific approach. According to this, one might say that American ergonomics forms a science while European ergonomics does not. European ergonomics is grounded on work analysis (that is: analysis of the actual process of work) which is more technological than scientific.

THE COMPETENCE OF OPERATORS. SOME EXAMPLES

Let us now see some example findings of such technological analysis in the case of operators confronting new technologies. The following examples result from work analysis in process control (oil refinery, nuclear plant, cementery, plant fertilizer, float-glass) and in sequential processes (automatized machines for cigarettes, soap, pills, and robots for assembling TV sets).

The concept of competence is an attempt to meet both the need for some generalization and the requirement of some realistic explanation of mental activities. In this acceptation, competence is a narrower structure than skill. It could be defined as the specific articulation of knowledge, modes of reasoning, and strategies corresponding to some specific tasks or a family of tasks. Every competence is learned, stabilized, and can be transmitted. Competence has both cognitive and social aspects.

Knowledge

Sometimes, the knowledge of the operators is just erroneous; it is then easily rectified. But more often the knowledge is 'semi-erroneous': it is limited to some aspects of funtioning. This knowledge is adapted to the majority of the problems the operators (at different levels) have to solve, but do not work for some of them, generally the less frequent. These limitations (or simplifications) of knowledge cannot be avoided. You cannot replace all the operators by sophisticated engineers. But you can check the actual knowledge of the operators (by a protocol analysis of their activities in real work situations and a consecutive questionning), and, if necessary, improve it by some adapted training, which has to start from the initial representations used by the operators.

One of the main findings, in this domain, is the mismatch of knowledge regarding the functioning of installations and the knowledge regarding the use of those installations. On the other hand difficulties often arise which are due to temporal delays (concept of hysteresis, for instance).

When it is possible to follow the genesis and evolution of the body of knowledge, in a sort of 'longitudinal work analysis', the results are sometimes surprising. For instance, you can observe a 'closure of knowledge': during the first stages, experience improves knowledge, but later it could have a negative influence, impeding the operator to become conscious of his limits. That is partially due also to some social factors: the lower one's position is in the technical hierarchy, the less he has the possibility to confess his ignorance. Heuristics are officially the privilege of the engineers and the ordinary worker is too often (and erroneously) supposed to be 'routinized'.

Modes of reasoning

The 'natural logic' (so the logicians of Neuchatel would say), as we can observe it by the verbalizations of operators, particularly when they have to give some explanations concerning their work, is far from the normative logics they are supposed to use. And that is also a necessity. The normative logics - for instance in algorithmic form - are too costly (particularly time consuming) when you are confronted with an incident (when, for instance, an alarm is flashing and ringing). You have to use some short-cuts. But this can also result in some false conclusion. As for the knowledge, ergonomists have to optimize (and not maximize) the efficiency of modes of reasoning.

For instance, the very frequent use of <u>analogies</u> is dangerous, but convenient. Here also we can observe the ambiguous role of the operator's experience: it can provoke the mere aggregation of symptoms rather than the explanation by some specific diagnosis.

Strategies

How does the operator construct his 'problem space' (as Newell and Simon said)? What sort of meta-cognition is required, not to solve the problems, but to 'organize' them? Adapted knowledge and reliable modes of reasoning are not sufficient for the real operator in real situation. He must also 'manage' his knowledge and his logical tools.

That is a new challenge for cognitive ergonomics. We do not have much data about this aspect of the operator's competence. Presumably one of the reasons is the impossibility to gather them outside of the field itself, in real time, by some time-consuming observations and recording. But we cannot escape this work, if we want to understand how one type of competence differ from another, what is really the temporal stress, why suddenly operators happen to change their objectives, what is planning and anticipation, or why an operator's behaviour is different when working alone or in a team.

Concerning this last topic which is yet practically a <u>terra incognita</u> in ergonomics the first studies point out the importance of the communications (mainly verbal interactions) between the members of the team. That is a good opportunity for the ergonomists to complete their own competence by some contribution from social psychology and from linguistics.

FOOTNOTES

[1] The first part of this paper was discussed with Lisanne Bainbridge (University College, London). For the second part we are largely indebted to the field research of post graduates students: Maud Boel, Pierre Fichet-Clairfontaine, Nadine Herry, and Antoine Lestien.

[2] This is a simplification of European ergonomics. This is the main approach in France, Belgium and Great Britain, and has a noticeable influence in other countries. It is also a simplification of American ergonomics: we could may be distinguish between "Ergonomics" and "Human Factors".

Man-Computer Interaction Research
MACINTER-I
F. Klix and H. Wandke (Editors)
© Elsevier Science Publishers B.V. (North-Holland), 1986

METHODOLOGICAL PROBLEMS OF DESIGNING DIALOGUE—ORIENTATED COMPONENTS
IN INFORMATION SYSTEMS

K. Fuchs-Kittowski, K. Koitz, Ch. Rudeck
Humboldt-University
Berlin
GDR

Dialogue systems are increasingly becoming an effective
mean to fulfil tasks and functions of work processes.
A purposeful design of the dialogue work within the
work processes demands to set priorities of designing
in accordance with this differentiated character.
A methodological approach was developed in which these
priorities for the design can be derived from an analysis of demands in the work with the dialogue system.

Informatics and organisation theory provide an essential theoretical reference framework for the design of information systems. A system theoretical
approach to the design of systems highlights the fact that the hitherto
predominant analytical method in the development of information systems does
not take into account the organizational and social problems involved.
Needed is a social system design, a synthetic approach. Dialogue systems
are increasingly becoming an effective mean to fulfil tasks and functions
of work processes.

These systems immediately influence the work contents of the users. For an
positive development of the users' working content it is necessary to
grasp the relationships between

- the dialogue work as the utilisation of physical and psychological functions in the solution of the data processing task and

- the primary working activities.

These relationships are extremely differentiated and varied. A purposeful
shaping of the dialogue work therefore demands to set up priorities of
designing in accordance with this differentiated character.

A methodological approach was developed to allow the derivation of priorities for systems shaping from an analysis of work demands in dialogue work.

The date processing task which is solved with the help of the dialogue
system within the primary work task forms the methodological reference
magnitude.

1. Demands of work

In the literature the work are called as "... the demands of work on the
working capacity ..." (1). Within the dialogue work the work demands
comprise:

a) demands on qualification in data processing,
b) demands on the organism.

When assessing the demands of work, the approach of work classification was adopted (2).

Differences in the work demands primarily consist in:

- the extent of the necessary qualifications in data processing,
- the amount and structure of the demands on the organism,
- the proportion of demands in the total activities.

According to our findings the causes of differentiated demands of works consist in:

a) different data processing task classes,
b) different functional relationships between dialogue work and the primary working activity,
c) different personal preconditions.

A concentration takes place on the complexes a) and b).

2. Demands of work dependent on different data processing task classes and implications for designing the dialogue work

The task of data processing has an extremely different character (this goes from a simple data acquisition task to a sophisticated programme development).

Hence, the data processing task sets forth different priorities in the demands. To grasp these priorities of demands a classification of the tasks in data processing was developed. The basis of these classification is provided

a) by the investigation the function of dialogue work in the primary work,
b) by analyzing the dialogue work as an activity with regard to its cognitive demands.

As to a):
By the investigation of the function of dialogue work in the primary work it is possible to determine the character of the date processing task. If the dialogue work helps to execute a solution, then the data processing task has the character of an execution task, when it supports the finding of a solution it has the character of an development task.

In the sense of informatics, execution tasks corresponce to the utilisation of programmes. They comprise the utilisation, the later application and the combination of known processes, methods and solutions. That means, the user works in the framework of a fixed solution pattern.

In the sense of informatics, development tasks constitute the development of programmes. Both types of tasks can refer to rigidly defined or to variable spheres of application.

Independent of their specific features in terms of content, most data processing tasks may be attributed to these two classes.

Dependent on the nature and extend of possibilities for intervening with the course of the dialogue, the user has a varying influence on the course of the task solution. These possibilities for intervention constitute points of decisions. Apart from the character of the data processing task they essentially determine the structure of demands.

From the character of the data processing task and from the possibilities for intervening the course of solution, it is possible to make at first statements on the necessary demands on qualifications.

As to b):
The definition of the character of the data processing task is insufficient to the derivation of differentiated work demands. A classification of the tasks must take into account the specific features of dialogue work with regard to its cognitive demands on the users. The determination of these demands was made dependent on the basis of prerequisites under which the user produces an input information within one step of the dialogue.

There were distinguished 3 basic forms of possible user activities (UA):

UA 1: the input information is an unambiguous, direct allocation of information items to one input demand of the computer system without any
alternatives

UA 2: the decision on the next input information is made on the basis of a
comparison of variants; the variants are offered by the computer
system as alternatives for decisions

UA 3: the decision on the next input information takes place as the result
of a problem solving process (according to Raum, 1980, in an internal information integration).

Within a dialogue, the UA can exist in a pure form or in combination. The level of intellectual demands is determined by the fact, in what share the individual UA occur in the course of the dialogue. The level is lowest, the higher the share of UA 1, and rise with the share of UA 3.

If an interrelation between the character of the data processing task and the possible forms of the UA is established, then certain data processing task classes occur.

Within the framework of our investigation, 4 task classes were considered. The formation of classes can be extended.

UA within a dialogue	Character of the data processing task	
	Execution task	Development task
1	Task class 1	–
2	Task class 2	–
1,2,3	Task class 3	Task class 4

Table A

Possible task classes of data processing

In the task classes various priorities exist in demands. From these priorities result class-specific primary aims for the shaping of dialogue work.
These are directed at the designing the external objective working conditions.

TC	Priority demands	Primary aims in the fashioning of the working conditions
1	Information allocation - extensice perception operations - manual demands	to support - information perception, - information coordination, - information allocation, to reduce manual demands
2	Decision on variants	to support - the visual and content-oriented perception of the variants presented
3	Integration of information - Grasping the information represented on a display - Generating the required information	to support - the visual and content-oriented perception of information - the generating of information
4	Integration of information on the basis of high intellectual demands	to support - the cognitive processes - the content-oriented grasping of information

Table B

Demand priorities in various task classes

3. Demands of work dependent on various functional relationships between
   dialogue work and primary work activity and implications for designing
   the dialogue work

The manifestation and intensity of the physical and psychic activities in
the classes are different and dependent on the degree and duration of the
demands. Within one class, they exist as group differences. They can be
determined by an investigation of functional relationships between dialogue
work and primary work activities.

Functional relationships occur under quantitative and qualitative aspects.
The qualitative aspect describes the manifestation of the content-oriented
relationships between the data processing task and the primary work task,
the quantitative aspect, the temporal utilization of the dialogue system in
relation to the entire daily working time. It covers the user frequency (UF),
the utilisation duration (UD) and the utilisation intensity (UI).

As a result of the analysis of functional relationships it can be stated, whether the area of a work task (as an essential factor for shaping a content conducive to personal development in work) is relevant for the design work in data processing. According to our view, the shaping of the content of a work task of the users is only effective at a high frequency of utilisation in combination with high forms of utilisation duration. As a compelling necessity this shaping is proved in execution task with low intellectual demands (TC 1 and TC 2). Then this shaping must be pursued with the aim of extending the scope in the activity.

At an only low UF, it is not significant to shape a work task, in order to influence the content of work of the users. It is influenced here primarily via the shaping of the objective execution conditions.

From the functional relationships, it is possible to derive the following statements on the shaping of dialogue work:

1. From the analysis of the qualitative aspects there follow some special demands on the organization of work,

2. The user frequency is closely related with the formation of knowledge and experience in dealing with the dialogue system. They increase with the user frequency. Here it is necessary to distinguish between task classes with high and only low intellectual demands. In task classes with high intellectual demands, the formation of knowledge and of experience has a positive effect on dialogue work. The user is increasingly better enabled to use the potential of the system. In task classes with only low intellectual demands this can sometimes entail a devaluation of the work activity, especially if the dialogue work has led to a narrowing down of the content of the work task. Here the necessity of an explicit shaping of the work task becomes imperative.

   With a low user frequency only, as a rule, special knowledge and abilities in handling the dialogue system are not manifested. Investigations show that in these cases the user is only rarely ready to acquire this knowledge. An assistance to the user by the system at all stages of work on the task is to be guaranteed.

3. The utilization duration and utilization intensity provide statements on the amount and intensity of the utilization. At the same time, high forms of utilisation duration have a staringing effect in physical and psychic terms. The degree of influence is compared with a growing utilization intensity. They lead to physical and/or mental fatigue. The evidence or reduction of wrong psychic strains calls for a purposeful change of utilization. At the same time, attention must be paid to the problems of a favourable ergonomics shaping of the working environment. A high psychic strain is not compellingly linked with a longer utilization duration. High and very high forms of utilization intensity (working under time pressure, compulsion to act or to respond, insufficient qualifications, course of the dialogue and so on), even at a lower utilization duration lead to negative effects of strain. This applies especially to task classes with high intellectual demands.

For task classes with low intellectual demands, in the literature manifestations of monotony are pointed out with a high utilization duration. An aggravating influence is brought about here by very specialized tasks (low number of different steps of dialogue, high repetition frequency of brief dialogue courses and so on). This points out to the fact that the work has become a matter of routine. The utilization intensity must be influenced here primarily via a purposeful task structuring. This structuring can be conceived in 2 directions:

- content-oriented extension or enrichment of the data processing task itself by

  . summarizing several specialized partial works on one job (the number of various dialogue steps is increased, the dialogue courses are extended),

  . provision of possibilities for decisions in the dialogue work, by admitting several solution variants and by allowing interventions by the users,

  . integration of exacting operator functions into the primary work processes;

- purposeful structuring of tasks between activities at the display and other activities in the primary work processes.

4. Results of practical investigations

To provide empirical evidence for the outlined methodological approach, extensive investigations were carried out in the Medicine Department of Humboldt-University. In this investigations the working hypotheses have been confirmed as a tendency.

REFERENCES

(1) Lexikon der Wirtschaft, Band Arbeit (Verlag Die Wirtschaft, Berlin, 1970) p. 49.

(2) Arbeitsklassifizierung, Einführung in die Grundmethodik, Teil A und B (Verlag Die Wirtschaft, Berlin, 1980).

(3) Raum, H., Gestaltung der Arbeit an Bildschirmen - Erkenntnisstand und offene Probleme, Sozialistische Arbeitswissenschaft 24 (1980) 4, p. 285-293.

Man-Computer Interaction Research
MACINTER-I
F. Klix and H. Wandke (Editors)
© Elsevier Science Publishers B.V. (North-Holland), 1986

SMALLER SIZES - CHANGING ROLES: NEW DIMENSIONS OF
THE MAN-COMPUTER INTERACTIONS

Peter Gelléri

Department of Psychology
Kossuth Lajos University of Sciences
Debrecen
Hungary

Due to the ever changing nature of the micro
computer product on the one hand there are a lot of
problems - regarding its purpose and its ergonomics
- and on the other hand it is difficult to solve
within the scope of time. We try to give help in how
to overcome this by way of a new approach and we
point out where it is advisable to intervene, and what
kind of researches are needful for this action.

INTRODUCTION

It could be an interesting task for historians to compare the so-called
"computer phenomenon" of our days with others when new scientific results
shocked both the economic and everyday life. It may well be true, that this
earthquake is stronger than any others were. However, one might establish
the really important feature of our case, that it is rather an almost permanent series of earth-shaqes.

One of the most important direction of these strong waves is the dramatic
change in the sizes of computers.
There is a considerable amount of literature dealing with the existing and
possible effects of the personal, home, professional and hobby-computers
(there is some disturbance with the usage of these categories) which have
entered into the everyday life. Fantastic new hardware ideas (e.g. different
types joysticks, the mouse) and software solutions (e.g. windowing, menu
driven program selection) have born to make the micros more popular.

Some years ago the portable breafcase computers have entered into our lives.
It is already not surprising that just recently arrive the first members of
a new family, the pocket computers. And there is no reason not to take seriously these new developments or to suppose that after these no more important steps would be taken.

It is really not an easy task to get a total picture regarding this area,
where every new week brings a lot of novelties. However, without a serious
investigation I would like to summarize my observations from a specific
point of view. This view point is determined by my interest on the possible
roles of psychologists in this area among the existing circumstances.

THE CONNECTIONS BETWEEN THE SIZES OF COMPUTERS AND THE FIELD OF THEIR USAGE

(Please, note: speaking about computers I mean here the result of an addition, what the hardware, firmware and software capacities can produce together.)

	Desktop	Breafcase	Pocket
		computers	
General purpose	+	+	
Science	+	+	+
Business-management	+	+	+
Household	+		
Amusement	+		+
Education	+		
Personal (e.g. diary)			+

While a user can find a nice selection of micros on the market which will suit almost any special purpose, the breafcase and pocket computers (say, the hyper micros) have more specific roles. Furthermore, some pocket computers have found for themselves a relative new area of usage, having special personal type functions.

It is obvious that the connection between the size of these machines and the necessary level of the users' knowledge is relatively close but not general.

We must add to this picture that among the normal micros there are computers only for one purpose (e.g. for video games) and multi-purpose devices as well. The pocket computers have more a specialized role.

THE NEW (OR PARTLY NEW) DIMENSIONS OF THE MAN-COMPUTER INTERACTIONS IN THE WORLD OF MICROS AND HYPERMICROS

There are two main types of dimensions.

The ergonomic type (in a narrow sense of this expression) aspects of the evaluation deals mainly with the quality of the controlling possibilities on the computers. In this context the final questions are that at which level
- easy-to-produce,
- easy-to-use,
- effective-to-use the devices.

The other type of dimensions try to describe the role which is fulfilled in the life of the user by the machine. As you will realize this aspect is not the same then the "fields of usage". Among others the following <u>role dimensions</u> have to take consideration:

- the quantity of the time spent "together" (with the computer),
- the structure of the time spent together,
- the level of specialization for different users (not only for the tasks),
- the level of independence of the conditions (when the users would like to use the machine),
- the level of "intimacy" (how personal is the role of the computer in the user's life),
- the level of indispensability (can the user live without the machine?).

Of course - in principle - one can describe with these types of variables characteristical differences between groups of users, between periods of a learning process or between computers.

SOME TYPICAL PROBLEMS OF THE EXISTING MICROS AND HYPER-MICROS

Here there is no room to touch the well-known fundamental question; whether this process is "for better or for worse". Nevertheless, the extremely quick rush of the new products to the market evidently coexists with special "growing troubles".

From our point of view the main symptoms are the following:

- There are some products on the market which represent in their elements high technology, but, on the other hand, if they are integrated devices then they do not represent a good concept regarding their everyday usage.
- More often there are quite serious ergonomic problems with the products; mainly at their first series.

To analyze the aftermaths of the mentioned troubles in our life will be an unavoidable task. However, the opposite direction of this chain of reactions is more interesting for us.

SOME POSSIBLE CAUSES OF THESE GROWING TROUBLES

As the origin of a lot of problems it might be important to emphasize, the well-known fact, that the quick tempo of developments are forced by the new technological findings. In other words: the champion to create and launch new products is determined first of all by those findings and only subordinately by the demands of the existing or potential users. Of course, this is not the speciality only of the industry of micros. Nevertheless, in the case of the micros and hyper-micros this powerful push of technologies comes across through specific conditions.

There seems to be a strong interaction between three main factors:

- The results of the developments often reflect the engineers' very limited and sometimes false knowledge about the man; about his needs, interests, intellectual capacities, handling abilities, desires.
- The larger part of the users is relatively uncritical in some aspects.

Most of them are simply amazed by the novelties and do not intend to examine the usefulness, effectiveness of the machines for their purpose.

- Comparing to other goods one can judge that the computer market has some
anarchic, or, say, jungle-type features. Let me point out only one in this
rush the new products are often tested on the market - before their development had finished in the labs. There is a popular ideology that just
this is the role of the market and the better product will be the winner,
but I am sorry to say, that it is not right even in the case of a normal
market.

CONCLUSIONS

After the briefly summarized observations let me try to evaluate our position. What could the psychologist do in this rush of new developments if he
would like to do more than to deal with only the consequences of these developments? Our delay is significant, but this is not the point. The program of this conference reflects how the scientists and experts focused
their attention to the new questions and built up new methods to answer
those. The point is that how we could to jump up on a fast, running train,
because this is just the same condition for the use of our knowledge in time.
Another question is that who will be our partner?

First of all we have to make clear for ourselves our approach. This includes a double task.
Probably it would be a mistake to suppose that we have already deliberate
and realistic ideas about the preferable values in the case presented. To
fix for ourselves, a hierarchy of values due to be relevant not only today
but tomorrow as well, this is not an easy situation.

The other part of the same task is to build up a general frame for the investigations. This frame has to comply with the special requirement to include the mentioned time dimension. There were some dimensions proposed
here earlier which might be relevant variables of that frame.

Another question is that where could we step into the process discussed
earlier and through who is it possible to influence it.

In other cases we have accustomed to work together with the engineers, this
is one of the basic idea of ergonomics. It is - in theory - partly the same
story; to help them in the really adequate realization of a product. The un-
usual feature in the case of micros and hyper-micros comes in an earlier
phase, to help the engineers to find a good object for a possible product,
that is to look for promisful aims for the developments together with them.
To refer the name of some microcomputer firms which have been able to a-
chieve so high acceptance and success in the market just because of their
excellent ergonomic ideas, might be a good password for us to enter into
this business.

The other possible place where we could step in the process are around the
customers. There have to be some ways to teach them to better articulate
their own demands and to build up a more critical attitude toward the existing products. It would be a great advantage if their interests could in-
stitutionalize in any form, for instance in the well-known form of a business federation of the users. Of course the micro- and hyper-micro computer
market has not only these two participants, the engineer (including in his

role the programmer too) and the customer (or user). To explore this jungle will be a fine work for sociologists and economists.

Anyway, the chief condition for jumping up on the running train is to be able to predict the next developments. For this work we have three types of references.

The first type are the forecasts about the new findings and technologies. What will these things be able to produce and at what prices?

The second type of reference could be the result of a dedicate investigation to explore the engineers value- and belief-system in the mentioned relation.

The third type will be again the result of a series of investigations on different groups of the existing and potential users.

These researches hopefully will not avoid the following points:

- Among professional and other groups how general and strong is - and will be - the fear of backwardness in achievements and in social acceptability in the case of neglecting the computers?

- These devices are evidently prestige-holders. Which relations are and could be the most sensitive from this point of view?

- The permanent flow of the novelties on the market of micros and hyper-micros makes dizzy the naive users indeed. What is the nature of this dizziness and what are its effects in the short and the long run?

- The computers are highly mythicized by the most wide groups of people. What does this myth consist of, what is its structure?

Altogether, these questions and tasks mean a real challenge for us. Anyway, these might be the necessary requirements to get a role of significance in this exciting process and use it for the advantage of science and the people.

KNOWLEDGE REPRESENTATION
AND ACQUISITION

Man-Computer Interaction Research
MACINTER-I
F. Klix and H. Wandke (Editors)
© Elsevier Science Publishers B.V. (North-Holland), 1986

EXPLORATORY INVESTIGATIONS IN ACQUIRING AND USING INFORMATION IN INTER-
ACTIVE PROBLEM SOLVING

B. Krause and H. Hagendorf

Department of Psychology
Humboldt University
Berlin
GDR

The importance of knowledge on problem solving for the
design of properly functioning man-computer-systems
has often been stated. Some results from the literature on problem solving are discussed with respect
to the design of interactive systems. Results of a
study carried out by the authors on question asking
are presented. The dependence of selectivity of
question asking on the problem situation and on individual cognitive capabilities has been proved.
Consequences for further studies are discussed.

INTRODUCTION

In connection with the design of knowledge-based interactive systems new
tasks originate for cognitive psychology. According to Hollnagel and Woods
(1983) knowledge on cognitive processes under conditions of restricted possibilities for interacting with such systems is the prerequisite for
achieving improved cognitive coupling (Dzida, 1983, Schindler, 1983).

The importance of knowledge on problem solving for the design of user-
friendly software has often been stated, but up to now consequences for
psychological research are rarely derived. Various authors have complained
about this (Hammond et. al., 1981, Fischer, 1983, Rasmussen, 1981, Sackman,
1981, Tikhomirov, 1983).

We remember only one example demonstrating the importance of knowledge on
problem solving for the design of properly functioning man-computer systems.
In the field of medicine the well-known expert system MYCIN has been developed. Clancey (1981) designed an instructional system on the basis of MYCIN.
He emphasized that there is a need for knowledge on training of strategies
of problem solving. As a consequence we have the task to develop an empirical and theoretical basis for man-computer problem solving (e. g. Streitz,
in this volume). The aim of such research is to give support for the acquisition, representation and use of knowledge for man-computer interaction.

Achieving this goal is possible on the basis of two approaches interrelated
with each other:

(1) Results gained in research on problem solving in the last decades have
    to be checked for their relevance in developing a basis for interactive

problem solving (e. g. Klix, in this volume).

(2) To answer specific questions in connection with interactive problem
solving we have to carry out special studies in new relevant problem
fields such as in programming or searching information in unknown
fields.

PROBLEM SOLVING RESEARCH AND USER-FRIENDLINESS

It is the concern of this subsection to illustrate the first point.
Important results gained in analyzing human problem solving concern
strategies, evaluation of information, the influence of motivational and
emotional factors in controlling complex dynamic systems, and knowledge
structures as a basis of problem solving skills in particular subject
matter domains (Anderson, 1981, Dörner, 1982, Klix, 1971, Krause and
Krause, 1980, Lüer, 1982, Simon, 1979, Sydow, 1980).

The general structure of a problem solving process is accepted. This can
be used to consider new problems such as man-computer interaction (e. g.
Streitz, in this volume).

In the framework of the problem space overall strategies like means-end
analysis, planning and subgoaling have been investigated and formalized
(Laird and Newell, 1983). In connection with a corresponding knowledge
base they can be used in designing system functions giving advice to
users.

Changes in strategies as well as transitions between performance levels
according to Rasmussen (1981) have been identified by various authors. This
knowledge could be a basis for deriving recommendations for the design of
adaptive knowledge-based interactive systems. But we should also mention
that Hollnagel (1981) complained on a lack of knowledge concerning factors
for selecting and transforming strategies.

The role of the abstraction level of a knowledge base has been investigated in research on memory (Klix, in this volume).
In conneciton with search of information and inferential processes this
question is of importance for realizing self-explaining systems as well
as for designing systems in the field of CAI.

For many years we have known the importance of information searching
processes in problem solving behaviour. Knowledge on strategies for information search is the basis for user-friendly delivery of information
by the computer as well as for navigating through a knowledge base. This
problem is connected to the work of Schönpflug (1982) on storage and use
of external information. In the following we will concentrate on one aspect
of this question, too.

QUESTION ASKING IN INTERACTIVE PROBLEM SOLVING

In considering information search we have to keep in mind that using information by a person working on a problem is equivalent to changing its
problem representation by integrating a new element, at least. In the past
questions of active information search in problem solving have been at-

tacked by various authors. Krause et al (1977) established a decision rule for selecting a goal-oriented solution strategy or a strategy of information search. Streitz (1982) reported on correlations between the adequacy of the initial problem representation and question asking whereas Hesse (1982) found a dependence of question asking on the semantic embedding of the problem.

We started with some first studies (Schumacher,1984) on question asking in interactive problem solving, too .Active information search that means asking questions is considered as a result of cognitive processes and is an indicator of productivity and goal formation in problem solving (Tikhomirov, 1983). According to the framework developed by Flammer (1980) these processes start with the establishment of a shortage of information and end with the decision to ask a question. Question asking can give us information on the regulation of knowledge-based problem solving behaviour.

The following questions are in the focus of our research:

(1) If question asking is determined by the relationship between the knowledge accessible in memory and the perceived cognitive require-ments, then strategies of question asking have to be based on char-acteristics of the structure of the problem. That means the questions asked should be in relation to goalrelevant information in the Problem situation which is not actually represented in mind.

(2) It is well known that problem solvers differ in their ability to evaluate the adequacy of their goal-relevant knowledge base as well as in the efficiency of acquiring such knowledge within solution attempts. That is why we expect differences between problem solvers in the selectivity of question asking.

For our first experiment we used a complex version of the travelling salesman problem (Oerter et al., 1977). The subject is in the role of a person planning the routes of various cars for bringing containers from a depot L to various locations A, B ..., F. A map is given which contains these locations and the depot as well as the roads connecting locations (depot included). The distances between locations are also given. Beside this map the person has at his disposal three cars with different hold, fuel consumption and mean speed:

Example: By using car 1 you can transport 5 containers. The speed is characterized by 4 min/km and fuel consumption for this car is 12 l per 100 km.

The task of the subject is to bring a certain number of containers from depot L to each location A, B, ..., F within a given time limit:

Example: You have to bring 2 containers till 9,30 pm to location B.

Another restriction concerns the ammount of fuel that the person has at his disposal:

Example: You have at your disposal no more than 20 l fuel.
Now the subject has to plan what cars should bring containers along which routes to the various locations. In planning the subject has to take into consideration possible disturbances in traffic. Similiar to experiments

carried out by Kornilova et al. (1978) our subjects were allowed to ask
questions.

Answers were given by the experimenter on the basis of data from a computer
(simulated man-computer interaction). In table 1 the types of questions
which could be asked by subjects are presented. We differentiate between
general and concrete questions as well as between time-related and fuel-

	general questions	concrete questions
Time-related questions	What time is it?	How long does it take to go by car N on road X?
Fuel-related questions	What amount of fuel has been consumed already?	What amount of fuel is used up by car N on street X?

Table 1:
Types of questions which could be asked by subjects

related questions. The last two categories of questions are related to
the types of problems in the experiment:

Time problem 1/m: The restrictions in the task are formulated in such a
way that there is only one possibility to fulfill the restrictions given as time limits. It is easy to fulfill the restrictions for fuel consumption because there are several
possibilities for fulfilling these restrictions. For solving
this type of problem time-related questions are the most informative ones.

Fuel problem n/1: There is only one possibility to fulfill the restrictions
for fuel consumption and several possibilities to fulfill time-
related restrictions. For solving this type of problem fuel-
related questions are the most informative ones.

A third type of problems will be not considered here because it was used
only in a control condition.
21 subjects had to solve a series of three problems. All three problems
were of one of the types mentioned. Subjects had no more than 30 minutes
for solving one problem. Within this time limit various trials for solving
the problem were allowed.

In a first step the number of informative questions asked has been analyzed.
We awaited more time-related questions in solving time problems and more
fuel-related questions in solving fuel problems. In table 2 the ratio of
time-related to fuel-related questions is given for each problem in a
serie.

Position in the serie	1st	2nd	3rd
Time problems	4.4	8.5	22.6
Fuel problems	1.9	2.1	1.4

Table 2:
Ratio of time-related questions to fuel-related questions in dependence on the type of the problem and the
position of the problem in the serie

From this table we can see:

(1) Question asking depends on the position of the problem in the serie.
For time problems there is an increase from 4.4 to 22.6 in the ratio
of questions, whereas for fuel problems there is a decrease from 1.9
to 1.4. If we look more thoroughly on the data (Schumacher, 1984) we
see that the frequency of time-related questions increases and the
frequency of fuel-related questions decreases over positions of time
problems (TG = 4.6, p .o5). For fuel problems the frequency of fuel-
related questions is constant over positions (TG = .o, p .1). This
is an indicator of the dependence of the selectivity of question asking
on learning over the three problems in a serie.

(2) The frequency of time-related and fuel-related questions depends on the
type of the problem, too. Subjects prefer the more informative questions. The ratio of time-related to fuel-related questions is 11.8 in
the mean for time problems and a mere of 1.8 for fuel problems. So we
have to register a dependence of selectivity of question asking on the
problem type, that means subjects prefer more informative questions.

In a second step we analyzed the frequency of general and concrete questions. The result is presented as ratio of concrete to general questions
in table 3.

	Time-related questions	fuel-related questions
Time problems	2.2	.6
Fuel problems	2.2	2.4

Table 3:
Ratio of concrete to general questions in dependence
on the type of the problem and the type of the question

What we can see for informative questions (time-related questions for time
problems, fuel-related questions for fuel problems) is that subjects prefer
concrete questions. With regard to fuel-related questions for time problems
and time-related questions for fuel problems there is a clear difference in
the ratio of concrete to general questions. This once more demonstrates the
selectivity in question asking.

To sum up, subjects adapt their strategy of question asking to the type
of the problem. That means, on the basis of implicitly given information
subjects change their behaviour. This change becomes more clearly in the
course of solving several distinct problems of the same type.
Now we shift to our second problem. As a first step in analyzing individual
differences we have carried out a classification of subjects on the basis
of their efficiency in problem solving. Subjects were classified as good
problem solvers if they were able to solve each of the three problems in the
second trial at most. Subjects in the group of bad problem solvers were able
to solve a problem on the third trial at the earliest or failed to solve at
least one problem. From the data we see the following:

(1) Good problem solvers ask more questions than bad problem solvers. On
    an average the first group asks about 5.1 questions whereas bad problem
    solvers ask about 2.6 questions.

| | Time problems | | | Fuel problems | | |
Position	1st	2nd	3rd	1st	2nd	3rd
Good problem solvers	3.1	6.2	8.2	1.7	1.5	.9
Bad problem solvers	5.6	28.4	50	2.5	1.9	2.7

Table 4:
Ratio of time-related to fuel-related questions in dependence
on the position of the problem in the serie, on the problem type
and on the level of problem solving performance

(2) On the basis of the ratios given in table 4 we can generalize one result
    of our first findings: question asking depends on the type of the prob-
    lem as well as on the experience with problems of each type. But there
    are some additional effects. In solving time problems either group
    prefers asking time related questions and reduces the frequency of
    fuel-related questions. Differences between the groups exist in solving
    fuel problems. Whereas good problem solvers take into account more the
    informative fuel-related questions (ratio decreases) the bad problem
    solvers do not show such a selectivity in question asking. It might be
    that there is a preference for working with the time dimension. Bas
    problem solvers seem to have difficulties to shift from time aspects
    to the other dimension, to fuel consumption.

CONCLUSION

In this exploratory investigation on question asking in problem solving
uder conditions of a simulated man-computer dialogue it has been proved
that active information search indicated by question asking depends on the
problem situation as well as on individual cognitive abilities for solving
problems.

The influence of the type of the problem and of the state of learning or
experience expressed by the position of the problem in the sequence on
question asking as well as the relationship between question asking and the
quality of the solution process is the empirical basis for coming to such a
conclusion.

Although in general subjects take into consideration features of the problem situation in planning their question asking strategy the good problem solvers much better adapt to only implicitely given knowledge on the problem type than the bad ones. The knowledge necessary for recognizing the type of the problem has to be derived from the restrictions given in the instruction of the problem and on the basis of problem solving exercises in reality or internally.

One conclusion we can draw on the basis of our results is that access to knowledge or to data has to be flexible. We have to take into consideration the high variability inthe organization of cognitive processes if we look at the man-computer interface.

In evaluating our results we have to keep in mind the exploratory character of the investigation. A lot of questions concerning information search are not answered. Two directions for doing research aimed at explaining the individual differences can be characterized: (1) We have to raise the question what factors beside lack of information determine when and on the basis of what information subjects ask questions. Approaches based on a theory of motivation might be successful in answering this question (Lehwald, 1983). (2) We need a deeper understanding of the cognitive basis of question asking and of the effect the information in the answer has on the internal representation of the problem. This is one of our approaches to come to models of knowledge-based problem solving in interactive systems.

REFERENCES

(1) Anderson, J. R., Cognitive Skills and Their Acquisition (Erlbaum, Hillsdale, 1981)

(2) Clancey, W. J., The epistemology of a rule-based expert system - a framework for explanations, J. Artif. Intelligence 20(1983) 215 - 251

(3) Dörner, D., Denken, Problemlösen, Intelligenz, in: Lüer, G. (ed.), Bericht über den 33. Kongreß der DGfP (Hofgrefe, Göttingen, 1982)

(4) Dzida, W., Das IFIP-Modell für Benutzerschnittstellen, Office Management 31 (1983) 6 - 8

(5) Fischer, G., Navigationswerkzeuge in wissensbasierten Systemen, Office Management 31 (1983) 49 - 52

(6) Flammer, A., Toward a theory of question asking, Psychol. Res. 43 (1981) 407 - 420

(7) Hammond, N., Barnard, P., Clark, I., Morton, J. and Long, J., Structure and content in interactive dialogue, Paper presented at the 88th Convention of the APA (Montreal, 1980).

(8) Hesse, F. W., Effekte des semantischen Kontextes auf die Bearbeitung komplexer Probleme, Z. f. exp. angew. Psychol. 29 (1982) 62 - 91

(9) Hollnagel, E., What we do not know about man-machine systems, Int. J. Man-Machine Studies 18 (1983) 135 - 143

(10) Hollnagel, E. and Woods, D. D., Cognitive systems engineering:
     New wine in new bottles. Int. J. Man-Machine Studies 18 (1983)
     583 - 600

(11) Klix, F., MACINTER - aim and goal, (in this volume).

(12) Klix, F., On memory research and knowledge engineering, (in this
     volume).

(13) Klix, F., Information und Verhalten (DVW, Berlin, 1971)

(14) Kornilova, T. V. and Belawine, I. G., Tselobrazovanye pri reshenyi
     zadatsh s pomoshyu "sovyetov" EVM, Vest. Mosk. Universiteta 3/1978
     52 - 61

(15) Krause, B. and Krause, W., Human problem solving, in: Klix, F. and
     Krause, B. (eds), Psychological Research. Humboldt-Universität Berlin
     1960 - 1980 (DVW, Berlin, 1980)

(16) Krause, W. and Lohmann, H., Entscheidungsstrukturen als Grundlage für
     Strategiewechsel zwischen Ziel- und Informationssuche im menschli-
     chen Problemlösen, Z. f. Psychol. 185 (1977) 86 - 127

(17) Laird, J. E. and Newell, A., An universal weak method: summary of
     results, in: Proceedings of IJCAI (Kaufmann, Los Altos, 1983)

(18) Lehwald, G., Handlungsorientierte Motivationsdiagnostik - Probleme
     und Ergebnisse, in: Vorwerg, M. (ed.), Zur Persönlichkeitsforschung 5
     (DVW, Berlin, 1982)

(19) Lüer, G., Problem solving, in: Griffin, D. R. (ed), Animal Mind -
     Human Mind (de Gruyter, Berlin, 1982)

(20) Rasmussen, J., Skills, rules, and knowledge. Signals, signs, and
     symbols, and other distinctions in human performance models, IEEE
     Trans. Systems, Man, and Cybernetics 13 (1983) 257 - 266

(21) Sackman, H., Outlook for man-computer symbiosis, in: Shackel, B. (ed),
     Man-Computer Interaction: Human Factors Aspect of Computer and People
     (Sijthoff & Noordhoff, Alphen van der Rijn, 1981)

(22) Schindler, R., Rechnergestützte Bildschirmarbeitsplätze - Entwick-
     lungstendenzen, Gestaltungsprobleme und Stand der Forschung, Z. f.
     Psychol., Suppl. 5 (1983) 7 - 23

(23) Schönpflug, W., Neue Versuche über externe Speicherung, in: Lüer, G.
     (ed), Bericht über den 33. Kongreß der DGfP (Hogrefe, Göttingen,1983)

(24) Schumacher, A., Experimentelle Untersuchungen zum Abruf und zur
     Nutzung externer Informationen, Diploma Thesis, Humboldt University,
     Berlin (July, 1984)

(25) Simon, H. A., Information processing models of cognition, Ann. Rev.
     Psychol. 30 (1979) 363 - 396

(26) Streitz, N. A., The importance of knowledge representation in problem solving: An example of text comprehension and problem solving, in: Lüer, G. (ed), Bericht über den 33. Kongreß der DGfP (Hofgrefe, Göttingen, 1983)

(27) Streitz, N. A., Cognitive ergonomics. An approach to the design of user-oriented interactive systems,(in this volume)

(28) Sydow, H., Mathematical modelling of representation and generation of structures in thought processes, in: Klix, F. and Krause, B. (eds), Psychological Research. Humboldt Universität Berlin 1960 - 1980 (DVW, Berlin, 1980)

(29) Tikhamirov, O. K., Psychologyi Myshlenyi (MGU, Moscow, 1983)

Man-Computer Interaction Research
MACINTER-I
F. Klix and H. Wandke (Editors)
© Elsevier Science Publishers B.V. (North-Holland), 1986

NECESSARY CONTRIBUTIONS OF COGNITIVE PSYCHOLOGY TO COMPUTER KNOWLEDGE
REPRESENTATION AND MANIPULATION SYSTEMS

Hermann Helbig
VEB Robotron-Projekt
Dresden
GDR

The main concern of this paper is the formulation and discussion of some general problems, which are relevant to
the interrelationship between cognitive psychology and
knowledge engineering. We shall focus our interest on six
topics: knowledge representation frameworks, memory types,
partitioning of memory, the existence of a central processing unit, language and knowledge, reasoning and knowledge.

INTRODUCTION

When we developed the question-answering-system FAS-80 (Helbig et al., 1983)
we spent a great deal of effort on the construction of the knowledge representation framework. Of course, there are a lot of investigations in the
field of semantics of natural language expressions but many of them remained
isolated and had not been integrated into a whole system. We believe that
the representational framework as a whole as well as the semantic primitives, the elementary relations and the axiomatic apparatus should have an
universal character. They should be epistemologically founded and they
should meet the practical requirements of a linguistic processor as well as
the needs of the inference mechanisms and the other parts of an integrated
natural language understanding system. Establishing the means for knowledge
representation in FAS-80 we took into consideration the connection between
elementary concepts of the representation framework and grammatical categories and also between these concepts and question classification. We
endeavored to create an epistemological founded universal set of relations,
functions and sorts of entities which are also supported by logical considerations finding their expression in the axioms connected with the elementary concepts. But, inspite of this quite general approach, we always
felt that there should also be a back-up from cognitive psychology for such
knowledge representation systems. One aim of this paper consists in the
stimulation of the cooperation between cognitive psychology and computer
knowledge engineering.

KNOWLEDGE REPRESENTATION FRAMEWORKS

A basic question relevant to the construction of a knowledge base is the
following: "What kind of representational schema is apt to model the human
memory organization?" In Artificial Intelligence (AI) there are several well
developed devices among which we can chose: semantic networks, frames, procedural mechanisms, production rule systems etc. Because the different
models are widely equivalent with regard to the simulation of intelligent
behaviour, we agree with Anderson (1976) in the assumption that this question cannot be decided upon psychological reasons. It is until now mainly
a matter of convenience, methodology and efficiency which model has to be
chosen. In our work we prefer an extended semantic network as a basic paradigm for representing the static knowledge of a natural language understanding system (Helbig, 1983), while procedures are used to represent the
functional meaning of word classes in the linguistic part (Helbig, 1984) and
implications (written in a production rule style) are used to express the
inferential knowledge (Boettger, 1984). Frames, in our opinion are especially well suited to represent more complex semantic structures starting from
simple action concepts (using case frames) up to descriptions of whole standard situations or sequences of actions (the familiar "scenarios" or
"scripts" in AI). Another situation is to be found with regard to the need
for psychological foundations of the elementary concepts of a knowledge
base. In FAS-80 we used a hierarchy of sorts (see Figure 1) on which a set
of about 100 relations and functions had been defined which allow us to
construct the whole knowledge base (Helbig, 1983).

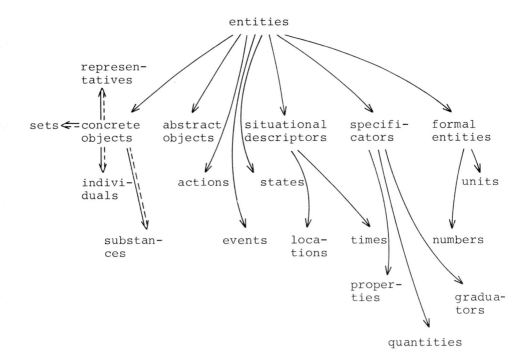

Figure 1

As to the sorts which in the proper sense are classes of concepts representing the entities written in a somewhat simplified way at the nodes of the tree from Figure 1, the question arises what cognitive criteria can be found to classify the entities we have to deal with. To begin with, there are the basic concepts of concrete objects ("a willow", "my house" etc.) which have a perceptual base and certainly an imagery representation in our brain. They are the columns, so to speak, on which the whole building rests. But, what about the mental representation of "justice", "religion" etc.? Where are the cognitive borderlines between concepts representing objects and others representing relations. Let us regard just the sequence "house"-"capital (town)" - "father" - "cousin" - "relative" to illustrate the fuzzy borderlines between objects and relations. Even if "cousin", for instance, has some relational meaning in it, this concept is in no way a fundamental or universal relation (as those mentioned below) to built a knowledge base. Logicians tend to express in their formalisms entirely different entities as the concepts "flower" or "red" in a somewhat superficial way by the same means, namely as predicates (for instance, in a expression like $\exists$ x (FLOWER (x) $\wedge$ RED (x)). Such representations obscure the significant cognitive differences between the sorts "objects" and "properties" (cf. Figure 1). Concrete objects have a shape which is not the case with properties. There is also an unsymmetry in the possibility of attaching the one to the other, objects have properties but not vice versa. The world of concepts representing concrete objects is organized in hierarchies built up by relations as SUB (subordination), PARS (part-whole relation) and so on, while the sort of properties has its own organizing principles, for instance the "polarity principle". Last not least among others the question remains, how the place of abstracta among concreta, properties, states and actions can be determined from the point of cognitive psychology.

MEMORY TYPES

There is a general consensus about the differences between inherited "knowledge" and aqquired knowledge and also on the fact that the former is stored via genetic code on a molecular base what is not the case with the latter. There seems to be also a consensus about other different types of memory as for instance long-term memory (LTM), short-term memory (STM) and ultra-short-term memory (cf. Klix, 1980).

Nevertheless there remains the problem, if the classification of memories and other (more procedural) devices in such models of the function of the brain have a purely logical or functionel character or if there are separate physical areas (memories) in our brain maybe coupled with different neurophysiological mechanisms corresponding to the components of such models.

There are other extreme conceptions stating that "there do not exist any units which would be called memories" in our brain (Kohonen, 1984). If there are no different units with different working mechanisms, why does the STM show another temporal or forgetting behaviour than the LTM. There are researchers in cognitive psychology (see Anderson, 1973, p. 182) who even state that the LTM in contrary to the STM doesn't forget anything in the sense that the stored items are entirely lost; only the access to these items is disturbed. An interesting question from the point of linguistics concerns the transfer of information from the STM to the LTM and how this transfer corresponds to the phenomenon of topicalization in a

sentence. In a phrase like "All lions eat antilopes" the word "lion" belongs
to the topic and "antilope" belongs to the focus of the sentence. In AI-
systems dealing with natural language understanding it is reasonable to
store this information with the concept of "lion" and not with the concept
of "antilope". Is the transfer from STM to LTM during language comprehension with a human being carried out in the same way? How is this process
interrelated with our validation mechanisms and our motivational base?
What concerns the neurophysiological base of our mental processes? I can't
agree with people who state that such data give the same insight into mental processes as the knowledge of electric circuitry of a computer gives
an understanding of the working of an AI-program. While I can image the
representation of a concept in the brain in the form of an activation
pattern (or a "feature map"; Kohonen, 1984) and the representation of links
between concepts being realized by neuronal fibers between neuron sets,
I would be very interested if there is a parallel to the labelling of links
in semantic networks in the physical realization (or is there so such
correspondence at all?).

PARTITIONING OF MEMORY

Besides different memory types of which we can assume that they have a
different physical base we have also to distinguish between partitions of
an otherwise homogeneously organized memory as the LTM. Miller and Johnson-
Laird (1976) distinguish five such partitions: semantic memory, episodic
memory, person memory, geographic memory, action memory. Apart from the
ill-chosen term "semantic memory" (it suggests that there is something like
a "syntactic memory", too) we believe that this is not a convenient partitioning for a knowledge base in an AI-system. With FAS-80 we devided the
non-procedural knowledge in the first stage into three parts which allow us
to look on an entity (modeling a mental concept on the computer) from three
sides, similar to a perspectivical look on three different sides of a cube
(see Figure 2).

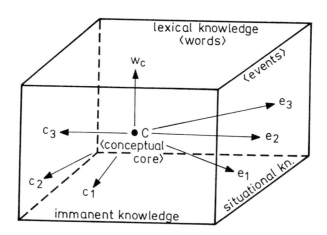

Figure 2

The immanent knowledge contains for each concept c all relations to other concepts c$_i$ characterizing the inherent properties of that concept c which are independent of the situational embedding. This knowledge part is a static one. Typical relations constituting this part are: SUB subordination, PARS part-whole relation, DATTR defining attribute, PROP property etc. (compare also the "intra-concept relations" with Klix, 1980). The situational knowledge bears a dynamic character. It represents events, states, changes in which objects are involved. Typical relations for this part are the temporal relations (TEMP, ANTE etc.), relations describing causes (CAUS) or circumstances (CIRC), the deep case relations (AGT, OBJ, INSTR and so on). These relations correlate with the "inter-concept relations" of Klix (1980). The third part of knowledge often neglected from psychological quarters is the lexical knowledge comprising the morphosyntactic properties of single words which govern the use of the words in the system of language. This must not be mixed up with the knowledge of the grammatic rules of a language which should be represented in a procedural way. On the second stage within the knowledge representation framework used in FAS-80 we distinguish still other layers corresponding to dichotomies which span further dimensions of the knowledge space. To this complex belong the discrimination between individual concepts and generic concepts, between "reals" (mapping real objects or facts) and "pseudos" (mapping objects, which are only thought of, or beliefs). While the usefulness of such conceptions has been proved in AI systems the question still remains to be answered how all this is realized in our brain.

THE CENTRAL PROCESSING UNIT PROBLEM

Nobody will dispute the fact that there are highly parallel processes going on in the brain (let us only hint at playing organ as an example). But, is there also a central processing unit (CPU) controlling these processes and working essentially in a sequential way? There are researchers negating this question (Kohonen, 1984, p. 39). If they are right, why then we are not able to think several thoughts at one time or how could we explain to phenomena of selfawareness and will. Our thesis is that there must be a CPU in our brain, otherwise we would be not able to resolve competing demands from several parts of our organism or our brain (detailed arguments can be found in Becker (1975, p. 91). We claim that processes which are automatized to a high degree can be carried out in parallel, while processes calling our attention are supervised by a CPU which works sequentially. It is not possible to share our attention among several activities at the same time. Persons who are seemingly able to focus their attention simultaneously on more then one activity (as it is said from Napoleon I) achieve a pseudo-parallelity of their CPU by a time-slicing mechanism.

Time-sharing or time-slicing are broadly used in computing technique to share the activity of the computer CPU among several competing tasks.

This technique has found only few attention in integrated knowledge manipulation systems, though it has been discussed in literature (Bobrow, 1975, p. 139). With regard to the modelling of parallel mental processes there should be also a close investigation of modern data flow architecture of non-v. Neumann-computers.

LANGUAGE AND KNOWLEDGE

Anderson and Bower (1973, p. 154) state that our memory basically leans on perceptual descriptions which is a very plausible hypothesis. In linguistically oriented approaches to knowledge representation this has been almost entirely neglected. One of the first problems to be solved is the "labelling problem", i.e. how perceptual patterns or their encodings in the brain (the feature maps with Kohonen, 1984) are connected with words. Only the combination of such patterns with words makes the basic concepts. There is a lot of questions related to this problem. What is the cause for the well known phenomena of polysemy and homonymy? Why show the most frequently used words the highest degree of polysemy (though this is an obstacle for an unique communication)?

Anderson and Bower (loc. cit.) also report on experiments which clearly prove the difficulty human beings have to learn the rules of a language with nonsense terminal words having no referential meaning and how the situation is drastically changed, when these terminal words are connected with optical patterns.

On the other hand, we are obviously able (especially in abstract fields) almost only to think in verbal categories. Notwithstanding this fact, it is not quite clear to which degree even in this abstract fields we make use of an imagery support (for instance of the mental pictures of formulas or curves in theoretical physics). In computer pattern recognition (optical as well as acoustical recognition) we meet an entirely different situation. Most of the systems almost exclusively make use of physical pattern descriptions and their evaluation. There are comparatively few approaches which try to bridge the gap between physical patterns and their conceptual descriptions. A real breakthrough in both fields (in natural language understanding as well as in pattern recognition) will be achieved when we are able to combine perceptual patterns with natural language concepts. Language is not only the form by means of which knowledge is communicated, knowledge is also extensively used during language understanding. In FAS-80, in the phase of understanding of natural language information (in the "teaching phase"), there are accesses to the knowledge base during disambiguation of words and sentences, during resolution of references and during embedding of the semantic structures in a greater context (to mention only the most important effects). Of course, the knowledge base is also the only source for understanding and answering the questions.

REASONING AND KNOWLEDGE

The methods investigated best with regard to reasoning in AI are strictly deductive inference processes. The first theorem provers based on this methods were purely syntactically oriented and showed a rather rigid behavior. Even if only a tiny bit of information did not match the premiss of an implication, a whole chain of inferences being quite in order otherwise would have failed, which is not the case with human reasoning.

There were many attempts to introduce semantic features into the syntactic oriented search, to use heuristics etc. One attempt in this direction had been the "focussing method" in question-answering by the author (Helbig, 1977) which tried to establish a fusion of deductive methods with semantic network representations and heuristic search controlled by valuation functions.

Other authors introduced terms as "fuzzyness" and "nonmonotonic reasoning" into logics (cf. Zadeh, 1979 and McDermott, 1980 respectively). A further problem is connected with the role of conditionals, causes and counter-factuals in reasoning and with their relationship to logical implications. This is very important not only from the logical point of view but also for linguistically oriented knowledge representation systems (see Helbig, 1983, chapt. 9). Johnson-Laird (1983) claims that there is a special kind of "mental logics" and he evolves in this connection a set of schemata for the logic of syllogisms.

One kind of reasoning, which I would like to call "pictural reasoning" is almost entirely neglected in AI (maybe because of the tremendous storage requirements). If somebody is asked: "What colour does your sister's car have?" he doesn't in general find this particular fact being stored in his memory (because he accidentally has been told about that). He also doesn't deduce this fact in the logical sense. He is rather activating a "mental picture" of this car and he is simply "looking" for the colour. How can such a type of reasoning be formalized in an effective way and how can it be connected with the other kinds of reasoning? The common denominator of all reasoning processes is the "pattern matching", that means the comparison of goals, questions, conditions etc. with parts of knowledge structures. What is lacking until now, is an integrated model of reasoning which mirrors all aspects of mental reasoning and also takes into account the typical features of the organization of the knowledge base.

FINAL REMARKS

I am aware that this contribution offers more questions than proposals for solution and the questions presented here are not the only one which are pertinent to the relationship between cognitive psychology and knowledge engineering. One of the most fundamental questions still open to be answered in this context is that for a definition of the concept "knowledge" and how it is interwoven with our skills, abilities and innate properties.

REFERENCES

(1) Anderson, J.R., Language, Memory and Thought,(Lawrence Erlbaum Ass., Hillsdale, New Jersey, 1976).

(2) Anderson, J.R., Bower, G.H., Human Associative Memory (V.H. Winston & Sons, Washington D.C., 1973).

(3) Becker, J.D., Reflections on the Formal Description of Behaviour, in: 4, p. 83.

(4) Bobrow, D.G., Collins Representation and Understanding (Academic Press, N.Y., 1975).

(5) Bobrow, D.G., Norman D.A., Some Principles of Memory Schemata, in: 4, p. 131.

(6) Boettger, H., Inferential Information Retrieval over an Extended Seman-
     tic Network, Computers and Artificial Intelligence, Bratislava 3 (1984)
     2, p. 115.

(7) Helbig, H. et al., FAS-80, ein natürlichsprachiges Auskunftssystem, WIB
     Nr. 18, VEB Robotron ZFT, Dresden (1983).

(8) Helbig, H., Semantische Repräsentation von Wissen in einem Frage-Antwort-
     System, Thesis B, Academy of Science of GDR, Berlin (1983).

(9) Helbig, H., Natural Language Access to the Data Base of the AIDOS/VS
     Information Retrieval System, in: 16, p. 171.

(10) Helbig, H., A New Method for Deductive Answer-Finding in a Question-
     Answering-System, Proc. IFIP Conference 1977 (North-Holland Publ.
     Camp., Amsterdam, 1977).

(11) Johnson-Laird, Ph.N., Mental Models (Harvard Univ. Press, Cambridge
     Mass., 1983).

(12) Klix, F., On Structure and Function of Semantic Memory, in: Klix, F. and
     Hoffmann, J. (eds.), Cognition and Memory (VEB Deutscher Verlag der
     Wissenschaften, Berlin, 1980).

(13) Kohonen, T., Self-organizing Feature Maps and Abstractions, in: 16,
     p. 39.

(14) McDermott, D., Doyle, J., Nonmonotonic Logic I, Artificial Intelligence
     Vol. 13, No. 1/2 (1980).

(15) Miller, G.A., Johnson-Laird, Ph.N., Language and Perception (Cambridge
     Univ. Press, Cambridge, 1976).

(16) Plander, I. (ed.), Artificial Intelligence and Information-Control
     Systems of Robots. (North-Holland Publ. Comp., Amsterdam, 1984).

(17) Zadeh, L., A Theory of Approximative Reasoning, in: Machine Intelligence
     IX (Chichester, Ellis Horwood, 1979).

Man-Computer Interaction Research
MACINTER-I
F. Klix and H. Wandke (Editors)
© Elsevier Science Publishers B.V. (North-Holland), 1986

MEMORY RESEARCH AND KNOWLEDGE ENGINEERING

F. Klix
Sektion Psychologie
Humboldt University
Berlin
GDR

It can be claimed that cognitive psychology is able to
contribute to solving urgent problems in the construction
and use of large data bases. In the first part of the
article psychological experiments are described revealing
principles of knowledge representation in human memory.
The experiments were conducted in order to prove the
discrimination of property-related concepts and event-
related concepts in human memory. The subjects had to
recognize different relations between concepts of both
classes. The recognition times support the assumptions
regarding the storage mechanisms in human memory. In the
second part of the article modules of a computer system
simulating human decision steps and search procedures
are discussed. The results of the simulation runs
correspond to the results of the psychological experiments. In the third part a specific human cognitive
process - the analogical reasoning - is simulated by
a separate module which is able to produce analogies.
Conclusions are drawn regarding the application of the
decribed and simulated memory structures and procedured
in artificial intelligence and software engineering.

KNOWLEDGE REPRESENTATION IN HUMAN MEMORY

At present, there is an obvious convergence of different streams
in recent scientific development. Hardware engineers, software
designers, AI researchers and cognitive psychologists are all
becoming increasingly aware of the fact that knowledge representation is the key for understanding intellectual performance,
irrespective of whether it is natural or artificial. Problem-
solving research in psychology has shown that the knowledge-
representation determines the availability of additional information, the efficiency of inferences and, as a result, also
the derivation of new knowledge.

To the same degree to which the need for large data bases arises
(and this is the case in several areas that enjoy high public
appreciation), the need arises for efficient storage principles.
These are e.g. principles that provide access to the relevant
information at the right moment, and this in view of a tremendous amount of potentially available information. It is well-
known that a solution to this requirement is to be found in
operational principles of the human central nervous system.
These principles are the object of memory research in cognitive

psychology. For that reason we have chosen the representation
of concepts in human memory as our research field. Due to the
methodical feasibility we have started with the investigation
of the detection of relations between concepts. It can be
shown that there are qualitatively different kinds of connections between concepts in memory. We can verify that by self
observation as well as by experiments, carried out to verify
falsiable hypotheses.

As to self observation, fig. 1 shows word pairs which do not
only represent different concepts but also different kinds of
relations.

Property-related concepts			Event-related concepts		
	Type	Level			
yew - tree eagle - bird	sub/sup.	1	customer - buy retailer - sell		Actor 1 Actor 1
yew - plant eagle - animal	sub/sup.	2	teach - pupil cut - bread		Actor 2 Object
lime - birch pigeon - sparrow		1	read - story cut - knife shoot - rifle		Object Instrument Instrument
lime - rose pigeon - carp	coordinate concepts	2	teach - school angle - river		Location Location
oak - trout eagle - mushroom		3	treat - cure calf - roast		Finality Finality

Fig. 1: Different kinds of semantic relation between word pairs;
        left: due to comparisons between properties. (The
        hierarchical level indicates the (mean) step difference
        up to the indicated concept with common properties.
        The smaller the common set the smaller the similarity
        of the classified objects.)
        right: Event-related concepts; they are linked by
        different kinds of semantic relations which indicate
        different roles of the respective concept in the clas-
        sified event. (Actor 1 is in general the grammatical
        subject in a given sentence, actor 2 the grammatical
        object.)

We become aware of the fact that there are quite different relations between concepts. This is already intuitively recognizable with the following procedure: We check whether there are similarities between the paired concepts or not. On closer examination of the left part we can say: yes there are similarities, and we can also detect that they are of different order: We have sub-superordinated concept relations and vice versa; and they differ further on with regard to the hierarchical levels which separate the two concepts from each other (1 vs. 2, right figures); and we have also coordinated concept relations. Having a look at this group we can see that their differences in the similarity degree depend on the distances to that hierarchical (or abstraction-level) on which the first common super-ordinated concept is to be found.

The concept pairs on the right represent meaningful relations, too, but there is obviously no similarity between the concepts. The very question of whether there is similarity seems strange. Quite different conditions for their interrelatedness seem important.

Either of the two concepts is part of an event. But within such an event they play different roles: They denominate actors which represent a situational characteristic activity, there are object- and instrument relations, local indicators and finality connections. It is well known from artificial intelligence research (see Schank, 1975) that these 'case-relations' (Fillmore, 1968) may be used for processing or describing texts or stories. We are indicating with these examples that relations of this kind are parts of classified event representation in human memory.

Fig. 2 shows how we can imagine this kind of memory organisation. The abstraction level is identical for all concepts. From this point of view it may be identified as an horizontal extension of a molecular like concept descriptors of event, there are also quantitavive differences of their roles (expressed by the kind of relation). They are determined by their so called semantic valency. Fig. 3 illustrates how the different relations include different degrees of complexity.

We can now turn to an experimentally verifiable hypothesis. The basis for such a derivation is an assumption on how concept representation in memory may be realized. Fig. 4 shows how we specify the representation of a simple object concept like 'dog', 'horse', 'tree' etc. We have a word-marker (on the left) and a closed set of different kinds of properties that represent subsets of properties or single features (like 'brow', or 'bark'). We have secondly properties (right side) which branch to other concepts, some to one, others simultaneously to two or more different concepts. These branches reflect the different degree of valency. This representation allows using a checking procedure to immediately find the most general (at the top of the string) or the most specific (at the bottom of the list) kinds of properties. Some chunk (or subsets) of properties are attached to lexical entries (words), and some are not.

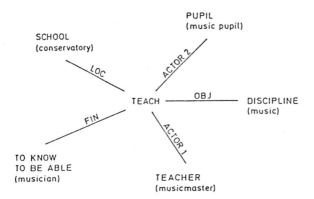

Fig. 2: The concept TEACH as semantic core of a classified
event. The core induces specific relations to other
concepts. Like a molecule with concepts as atoms
describes such a configuration a well-defined class of
events. It is settled in a specific hierarchical level
of abstractness.

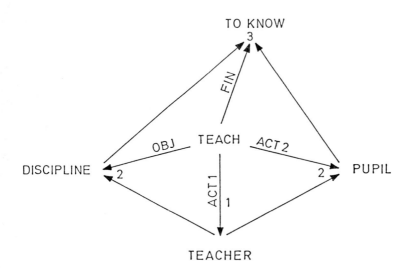

Fig.3: Different valencies of different semantic relations. The
arrows indicate the respective complexity (i.e. valency)
of a relation. (The number of branches determine the
meaning-dependency of the linked concepts.)

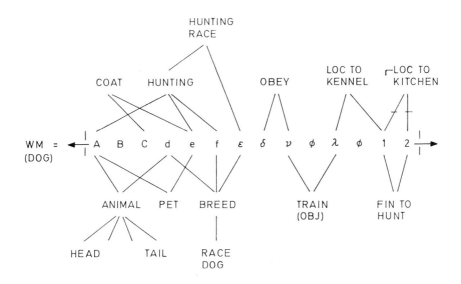

Fig.4: Hypothetical map of the encoded representation of a
primary conceptual unit in long-term memory of man.
A...2: Extensible (denotative) property description
of the concept 'DOG'. Substrings of properties are
indicated only by their word marker. Some substrings
split the denotative set, others branch to other
concepts and set up parts of event representations.

Now we transfer this assumed representation in a hypothesis on
what should happen when subjects have to compare concepts pairs
like those on the left side of fig.1.[1]

Such a concept relation leads to different kinds of consequences. They are outlined with fig.5.[2]

The word pair (NAME1, NAME2) are presented and the respective
property strings are activated. It is checked whether there
are common properties at all. Afterwards the specific comparison procedure begins: (1) Are there specific properties in M1
(Ex mi ?), and, if yes, is there a substring in M1 (TM) which
is identical with M2? If yes, then M1 is sub-ordinated to M2.
If M1 is superordinated to M2 then the procedure (1) fails.
This demands exhaustive search and is a more time consuming
procedure. After the (-)-decision, due to exhaustive search,
the checking procedure is inversed. It is (2) proved whether
there is a substring in M2 which belongs to M1; then M1 is
superordinated. It is transparent now that the super-sub-
concept relation needs more time than the other direction.

F. Klix

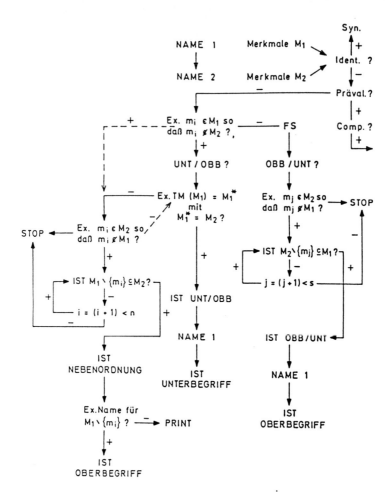

Fig. 5: Decision schema which allows to decide whether a property
determined concept relation is given (left side of
fig. 1) or not. This schema is also realized as part
recognition of a recognition-program: M_1, M_2 - property
sets like the one in fig.3. Ex $m_i \in M_1$ so that $m_i \notin M_2$
looks for specific properties in M_1. $M_1^* = TM(M_1)$ means
a substring in M_1 which is identical with the whole
concept M_2. $M_1 \setminus \{m_i\} \subseteq M_2$ means a set difference of
specific properties which is stepwise enlarged by in-
creasing i until a threshold is realized. (The procedure
is relevant in both cases: for detecting coordination
(=Nebenordnung) as well as for detecting superordination
(= OBERBEGRIFF) of a concept or subordination (= UNTER-
BEGRIFF). It is assumed that software implementation of
such kinds of procedures may ve advantageous for software engineers.

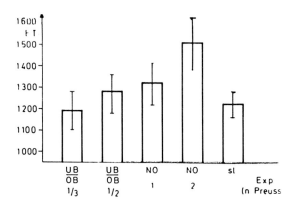

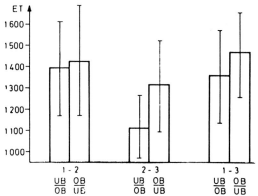

Fig.6: Data which fit consequences of the decision schema
(Fig. 5): sub-superordinated relations (UB) are less
time consuming than the detection of a super-sub-
ordination (OB) of a concept (which lasts longer).
It is also indicated that the detection of coordination
between concepts is still more expensive and (further
more) that it depends on the distance of the first
common superordinated concept (NO1 vs. NO2). These
time differences indicate that there are specific
mechanisms which produce these kinds of relation
detection (data after Preuss, 1983), ET: recognition
time in ms.

The same assumption leads to the consequence that the recognition of a coordinated concept relation is the most time
consuming checking procedure: It has (1) to be decided,
whether M1 has specific properties with respect to M2; (2)
whether M2 has the same specific with regard to M1 and (3)
whether they have common properties. The more they have in
common the easier they are identifiable as coordinated. This

leads to the consequence that the more distant the concepts are
the more expensive is the recognition of this kind of concept-
relation. Fig. 6 gives some of our main results concerning
these predictions.[3] These data are a strong support of our
assumption. But much more detailed results and a more sophisticated argumentation are published in other reports (see Klix,
1983, 1984, 1985).

The possible predictions on recognition times with regard to
the pairs of the right half of fig. 1 are quite different. If
the relations in this second group are actually determined
by finding out whether they are parts of specific event classes
then the recognition time should depend on the semantic
complexity of a given relation (i.e. its valency). Another
possibility concerning this kind of relations is that the
concepts may belong to different events that may be part of
a sequence of events (like: 'accident-hospital-cure' or
'lecture-listen-profession'). In such cases it has to be
established whether there is a possible concatenation between
different events in terms of space and time. Search procedures
are assumed to run along eventrelated concept concatenations
(Klix, 1983, 1984, 1985). The time needed for a pair to be
recognized as meaningful depends on the amount of bridging
steps.

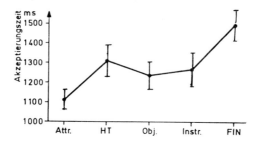

Fig.7: The detection time of event-related concepts depends
       on the valency (see fig.3). Attr: Attribut or single
       property (like DOG and BITE); Actor, Obj and Fin as
       defined in fig.1).

Figure 7 indicates (after Preuß, 1985) that there is a significant dependency of the recognition time on the valency of the
semantic relation.
With regard to the reality of search processes in bridging
distant concepts via branches there is a first result from
Luchmann (1983) which indicates the dependency of the recognition time on the distance between the concepts. This distance
is not determined by common properties but by the more or less

long range which the events have between their occurences
in space and time. In this sense the distance between lecture
and auditory is smaller than the distance between lecture and
examen or profession. Luchmann (1983) verified in a first
experiment that the recognition time depends on that kind of
distances. But there was also an odd result: Due to design-
reasons of the experiment there were also concept pairs without any meaningful connections between them (as 'senseless
pairs' evaluated by the subjects). But in case there is no
meaningful connection this is faster recognizable than the
existence of a more distant relation. This result is not
explainable by search process alone. There must be other recognition mechanisms which are so far unknown. This is mentioned in this connection because it reveals that there are
functional principles in unconscious cognitive strategies of
man which allow to reduce the search expenditure in view of
exclusive decisions in large data bases.

The purpose of this first part of my paper was to give an idea
of how we look for organizational principles in human memory
activity and what the interaction may be like between knowledge
representation, activation and retrieval processes (see also
Schindler and Fischer, this volume). The purpose of it all is
to make these principles as detailed as possible and formalize
them as models which, in turn, may serve as modules for intelligent software engineering.

The crucial point for making such kinds of results useful for
software engineering is to formalize those mechanisms which
are identified as recognition principles in the mental activity of man, and formalisation means an explanation in an
algorithm-like procedure. Our own approach is to define these
principles as modules which are the crucial decision steps in
recognizing a specific concept relation. Continuing our basic
hypothesis that there are two quite different principles of
such recognition processes (namely (1) relation detection by
comparison procedures and (2) relation detection by search
and event-concatenation) we divide our moduls in two different
groups.

SOLID STATES OF KNOWLEDGE REPRESENTATION AND PROCEDURAL MODULES
OF INFORMATION RETRIEVAL AND KNOWLEDGE GENERATION

We will have to tackle the following problems:

- How can we formalize the concept representation in human
  memory (from a structural point of view); and

- How are relations between them identifiable or derivable,
  and how do they guide search strategies in memory?

As to concept storage, we face two possibilities, namely

(1) to define meaning by words in a lexicon-like manner; or
(2) to attach properties to words as an alternative to meaning
    definition.

This double representation is not trivial, since almost all that has so far been done in AI or artificial language comprehension research is based on verbal definition, and the words are classified by grammatical properties. It was my aim to outline an alternative and show what kind of consequences this will have for software engineering. Together with fig. 1 we have discussed how a concept representation in human memory can be imagined. Considering the storage principle one may guess that such a double representation of word marker and property string demand unnecessarily large storage capacity. This objection holds only for very few concepts.

The general rule is: the larger the entries the more efficient is this principle for search and especially for flexible checking procedures. But search procedures or different kinds of kinship detections between concepts are the most practical relevant kinds of knowledge use. One way to demonstrate the benefit of this crucial point is to simulate this kind of concept representation and relation recognition. The point is also theoretically relevant because such kinds of relation detections produce dynamic semantic network structures within latently organized memory entries.

I begin with the property-dependant identification of concept relations. We have to reproduce all kinds of relations on the left side of fig. 1. For that reason we have splitted up the general schema of fig. 5 into crucial decision units, called modules. Fig. 8 shows the structural description of these units.

At first (A) we have the definition of a full concept representation, just as it is given with fig. 4 but rather in a more clear-cut manner. Beyond A there are also concept representations but they are restricted to the decision relevant parts of the respective second concept. (The other parts are assumed to be inhibited).

At first (A'.i1) there is the property description of a second concept as it is relevant for a subordination of A vs. A'(i.1). W,X are the properties. This is a decision-sufficient condition. A'.i2 is subordinated with regard to A since the concept properties of A are completely within A'.

The identification of coordinated concepts (A vs. A'i3) is due to the wellknown three main decision steps: (1) Are there specific properties in A' (not included in Ai (2); (2) are there in the same sense specific ones in A (not belonging to A'i.3) and (3) are there common properties between the two entries? If all three proofs give positive results then the two concepts are coordinated in the defined sense. The result of these procedures are demonstrated as computer outprints in the appendix.

The relevant aspect of this (and other possible demonstrations) are (1) that the modules are derived from experiments with intelligent human subjects, (2) that the time relations subjects need for their recognition is of the same rank order reflected by the modules and (3) that the simulation of the recognition procedure is due to property comparisons and not

Descriptions of the modules

A. 1st concept:

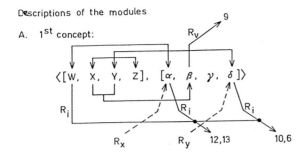

A'. i1: ⟨[W, X], [......]⟩   is superordinated

A'. i2: ⟨[W, X, Y, Z, U, V], [......]⟩   is subordinated

A'. i3: ⟨[W, X, A, B], [......]⟩   is coordinated

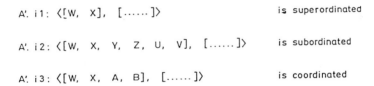

A'. z1: ⟨[N ....], [.... ν ....]⟩   is directly event-related

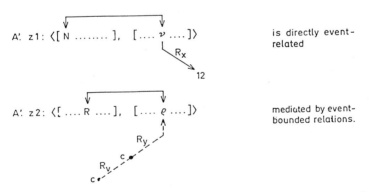

A'. z2: ⟨[.... R ....], [.... ϱ ....]⟩ mediated by event-bounded relations.

Fig.8: Modules of relation detection. Top: The schema of fig. 4 in a more decisive version: denotative properties (W...Z), branchings (, ...,) to other concepts, and inputs (R_x, R_y) from outside. Below: the second concept reduced up to those parts which are relevant for the decision (1 subordination, 2 superordination and coordination). The modules z_1 and z_2 realize the detection of branchings; z_1 by priming (R_x), z_2 by search, for instance in pursuing just one relation R_i (see fig.9)

dependent on concept branches or word markers in memory. Words
are relevant at the beginning and at the end of the procedure.
The advantages of this (3) principle is that it is possible
to compare any given concept with any other one (irrespective
of their embeddings) and to decide which of these kinds of
relations exists between them or whether there is none.
Another consequence of this kind of storage is the inherent
possibility of changing the abstraction level of a given concept. The procedure is meant to inhibit specific properties
and find out whether remaining sub-groups branch out to a
word. In this case, the word refers to a super-ordinated concept (see examples in the appendix). The astonishing thing
of this result is that it was a consequence of the storage
principle that we did not think of while drafting the programme.
Nevertheless, this consequence accords with a well-known performance of our mental activity. And there are more examples
of this kind.

I would now like to turn to event-related concept configurations. Fig. 9 gives an additional example of how we can imagine
the realization. The interesting point there is not activation
spread and the detection of the relation, since they are explicitly stored. The crucial point is rather the direction dependence of the search process. We use the example of the event-
concept BUY and GIVE. They are defined as shown in fig. 10.
We therewith detect the first generalizable rule:

Whenever there is a concept C_x which is a member of two different event representation E_m and E_n. and if there is one
relation R_i which binds this concepts within these different
events then a joint event $E = E_m \cdot E_n$ is deducible. (In our
example we have BUY (for posessing an article) and GIVE (for
receiving a present). In both events MONEY is linked by an
instrument relation. This makes the deduction of a conjoint
event possible.

Another example of devising a meaningful search strategy is
this: let us say a set of n event-related concept pairs belongs
to n different events each. Whenever one of these events
embraces a concept which is again the core concept of an event,
an united sequence of events is producible. Bridged between
these event concepts produce meaningful relations between all
linkable concepts. Fig. 8 describes the idea of the module in
a schematized manner, and in the appendix there are several
examples of computer outputs that demonstrate the feasibility
of our assumptions. It is not possible here to compare these
outputs with results we obtained in carrying out the related
psychological experiments. Instead, I would like to indicate
a consequence that leads to the central point of my paper.
This consequence has something to do with challenges coming
from AI research and also with the need for intelligent software development. In the September 1984 issue of the Scientific
American there is an article by one of the world's most outstanding AI researchers,Douglas B. Lenat. Lenat writes on pp
157-158: "Designing more proficient learning programs depends
in part on finding ways to tap a source of power at the heart
of human intelligence: the ability to understand and reason

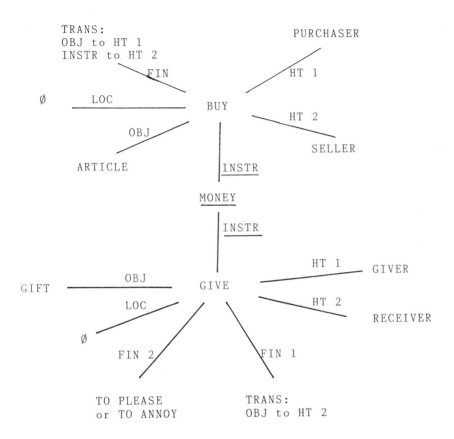

Fig.9: Concatenation of two (conceptually) represented events
       by pursuing an identical relation (INSTRUMENT which
       links MONEY). This is a sufficient condition for pro-
       ducing a compound event.

by analogy ... This source of power is only beginning to be
exploited by intelligent software, but it will doubtless be
the focus of future research. The poor performance of computer
programs in finding and using analogies may be attributable
more to the narrowness of their knowledge than to the inability
of programmers to come up with suitable algorithms."

Lenat is right, I believe, except for the last statement. I will
now show you that it is possible, from the point of view
explained, not only to understand but even to produce analogies.
And analogies are a prototype of human intellectual performance
(see also van der Meer, 1978).

A

1. $E_i \in E$; $R_i \in C_j \times C_R$

2. $C_K \underset{\text{def.}}{=}$ semant. Kern : $C_K \longrightarrow E_i$

3 a.   Wenn $\left[(R_i \in E_m) \wedge (R_i \in E_n) \wedge (R_i \longrightarrow C_x) \right] \Longrightarrow$

$$\exists\, E\emptyset :\ E_m \cup E_n$$

3 b.   Wenn $\left[(R_i \in E_j) \wedge (R_i \longrightarrow C_K) \wedge (C_K \longrightarrow E_K) \right] \Longrightarrow$

$$\exists\, E\emptyset :\ E_j \longrightarrow E_k$$

Fig.10: Formalized conditions on possibilities for concatena-
ting different events. E_i: events, C_j: concepts,
R_i: relations between concepts, C_K: semantic core.
3a describes what is demonstrated with Fig.9. 3b is a
generalized rule for concatenations of semantic cores.
The condition is that one of the concepts in an event
representation is itself a semantic core (like OFFENCE
and CONFESS).

A MODULE FOR ANALOGICAL REASONING

A crucial point that Lenat refers to is the amount that there
is of human memory. From our point of view, this is a wrong
thing to do. The really crucial point is rather to understand
the organization of human memory.

If we arrange concepts around their most common properties, we
will obtain groups of similarities: animate objects, areas
of human interest like labour, leisure, food and art. Other
groups embrace landscape properties (original or artificial)
or goals of activity. This arrangement links very general properties. If we take a look at such an arrangement we can
detect as a result that these families of concepts possess
common properties that link characteristic semantic relations,
which, in turn, determine their specific role within an event
representation. It is the actor relation for organisms (agent
or patient), the object or instrument relation in areas of
human interest, the locational relation for landscape properties, and the purpose relation in the case of human goals or
reasons for activities.

So, organization is at least twofold: it is arranged around
common properties or similarities and at the same time linked
by specific roles in events.

Fig. 11 gives an example of the assumed architecture. (Though
this assumption is speculative it reveals some consequences

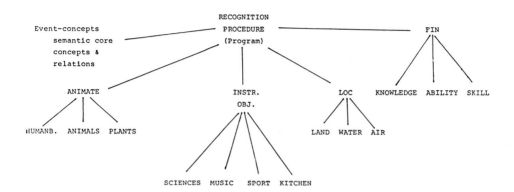

Fig.11: Supposed architecture of the solid structured parts of
human long-term memory. The sensory input (together
with instruction (or motivation)) activates separetely
stored events (left) or the respective kind of concepts.
They are grouped around their main common properties and
divided by subgroups of different sub-classes indicated
by substrings of property concatenations. The main substrings allow to link the most common property with one
of the most prominent semantic relations: ANIMATE with
ACTOR, BUILDINGS, WATERS etc., with LOCATION and MOTIVES
with FINALITY (INSTR. and OBJECT) are self-explaining.

which allow to reproduce performances which are wellknown phenomena of our mental activity, e.g. characteristic sequences in
associative chunking: similarities change vs. antonyms, super-
concept findings vs. characteristic activities, locations vs.
finalities etc.).

Now the final step: what is an analogy? At first, and in a more
general sense, it may be seen as some kind of mapping of a
known knowledge structure into another one which is somehow
related to the original and in the same sense also different.
The question arises what are the constraints by which a comparison becomes the specifity of an analogy? To reveal such
constraints it is necessary to look behind the shimmering sur-
faces of semanticity and to make transparent what we can call

the deep structure of an analogy. I am not convinced that we
can reduce all possible kinds of analogies to the following
explained deep structure. But what I am able to show is that
there exists a lot of analogy examples between natural concepts
which are governed by the following rule: Two structures A and
A' are given and between them there is a set of relations (at
least one, see fig. 12). Then we have a second pair of structures B-B'.

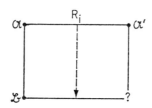

Fig.12: Schema of an analogy-detection. A concept pair A-A' is
        given, a relation between them is found, and the task
        is to identify for a given third concept B the analo-
        gical fourth concept B'. The condition is that the B-B'
        relation is the same as the A-A' relation.

There may also exist some relations between them. And whenever
there are same relations between A-A' and B-B' then the analogy
condition fits whatever the structures are. And to create an
analogy means to find out a non given structure B' which is
with regard to B in the same relation as A' with regard to A.

Turning now to the realization of analogy creation two steps
are required.

(1) identifying the relation between A and A'; and

(2) applying this relation to the third concept B and trying
    to find out which fourth concept meets the condition. Such
    a concept provides a solution to the analogy problem.

The computer-simulated analogy-production works within a program
in 4 main steps (fig. 13):

The first step is the identification of the property strings
of the first concept pair. (They are keyed in by words.) The
result is that there are two words activated and two property
strings are attached to them.

The second step is the identification of the relation between
the two concepts: Of an immediate event-tie is activated then
it has preference (like teacher - teaching or lecture -
audience).
Otherwise it is checked whether there are common properties.
If yes, then the kind of a property-determined relation is
proved. This is essentially performed by the modules of

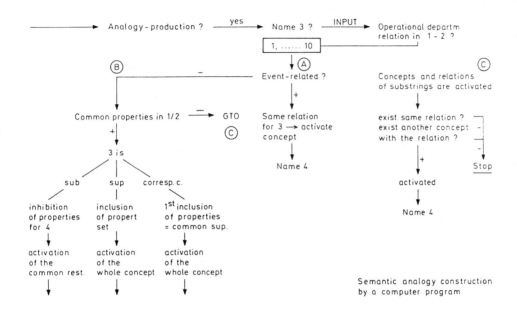

Fig. 13 : Outline of a computer program that identifies concepts
which fulfill the analogy-condition as described with
Fig. 12. It is supposed that the relation between
A-A' is already identified (due to the modules of
Fig. 8). The third concept (B) is keyed in as name 3
and the respective set of attached properties is
activated. Then there are three subprograms: A proves
the event relation, B the property-dependent kind of
relation, and C is a search program. B uses the modules of Fig. 8 1-3 and C the modules 4-5 (see also
Fig. 10). 'Using the modules' means that the detection
procedure is inversed! The checking procedure is used
for constructing properties which fit the analogy
condition (e.g. if A vs A' is subordinated then B' must
have the most general property with B in common and
there must (further on) be a substring in B which is
completely identical with B!).

Appendix: Examples of computer outprints of the
analogy-construction programme. It should be recognized
that the same concept A leads to quite different
concepts with regard to B in dependence on A', e.g.
on the kind of relation between A and A', respectively.

fig. 8A'z2 . This checking part is indicated as 'search procedures in memory'.

The third step begins with keying in the third name. Restricted
by the internal organization of memory (fig. 10) the attached
property set is activated.

The crucial fourth step starts with fetching the identified
relations between A - A'. This relation allows to identify the
responsible module. Just this module is now used as an operator:
The recognition procedure is inverted and applied to the property string of concept 3. In this way the module produces a
'property-image' which satisfied the analogy condition. This
image directs the search procedure until a identical string[4]
is found in the indicated file. This property set fits the check
condition and if it is attached with a word marker then this
word is semantically analog to B as A' is it to A. Alltogether
we have three different cases of analogy production:

Case A: Were the concepts A - A' event-related? If so, activate
        this relation and try to find out whether there is a
        concept in the event to which B belongs, with an input
        of that relation. This is a solution.

Case B: If the concepts A - A' are not event-related but have
        common properties, apply the particular module to
        concept B and look for a word attached to the constructed
        set of properties. This concept (and its attached word
        mark) is a solution.

Case C: The concepts A - A' are parts of different, but linkable
        events. The modules applied ask for whether there are
        branches of the R_x kind going to sub-strings in some
        other concept (i.e. the solution or (if not), whether
        there is an input branching of the R_x type. If so,
        search for a concept which responds to R_x as an output
        branch. This is a solution of the analogy problem.

I would like to sum up the basic idea.

Though outlined very briefly, our main effort is directed at
revealing organizational and operational principles of human
memory. Doing this in as great a detail as possible, we obtain
functional principles, called modules, which allow realizing
effective modes of information storage and retrieval. In the
same way, we are in a position to implement performances which
are similar to what we call intellectual performances. The
intention is that this kind of similarity makes the capability
of computers more transparent and familiar especially to naive
users since their own mental activity works in a related way.
I believe therefore that results of this kind also belong to
these approaches, which are dedicated to the optimization of
man-computer interaction (see also Wandke, this vol.).

But the most challenging task lies still ahead: how are we to
apply the principles of cognitive learning?
Cognitive learning is corrections of memory contents without
immediate reinforcement. Analogy detection is one kind of

cognitive learning. Further examples are generalization of rules, transfer of knowledge from one orientation area to another, non monotonous reasoning, derivation of deduction rules and derivation of metaknowledge.

To combine the two: intellectual modules and cognitive learning capabilities are software features of the future. We are still at the very beginning (Michalski, 1984). But I believe that cognitive psychology will be assigned a specific role in this field of modern scientific development in man-computer inter-action.

I am full aware that I have left open some essential questions. It was my aim in this first report on our approach to indicate that there are primarily psychological approaches suited to qualify the one or the other endeavors in software engineering. And what I have described here with every-day life concepts can immediately be transferred to areas of specific knowledge bases.

FOOTNOTES

[1] S's are sitting before a screen. 500 ms after a fixation point is vanished the word pair is presented. As fast (and exactly) as possible S's have to decide (and to press a buttom after that) and finally to denominate the detected relation. The time is measured, failure are separately evaluated.

[2] This schema is in the same time a decision sequence which allows to simulate this kind of concept identification and relation recognition.

[3] The identification of a now-identy is more expensive than the identification of identity, suppose there are single units.

[4] This is a strong condition. We can weaken it by defining a similarity threshold. Then a semantically more complicated analogy production takes place.

REFERENCES

(1) Fillmore, C.J., The case for case, in: Bach, E. and Harms, R.T. (eds.), Universals in linguistic theory (New York, 1968).

(2) Klix, F., Begabungsforschung - ein neuer Weg in der kogni- tiven Intelligenzdiagnostik? Z. Psychol. 191 (1983) 360-387.

(3) Klix, F., Über Erkennungsprozesse im menschlichen Gedächt- nis, Z. Psychol. 192 (1984) 18-46.

(4) Klix, F., Denken und Gedächtnis - Über Wechselwirkungen kognitiver Kompartments bei der Erzeugung geistiger Lei- stungen, Z. Psychol. 192 (1984) 213-244.

(5) Lenat, D.B., Computer software for intelligent systems, Sci. Amer. 251 (1984).

(6) Luchmann, D., Differenzierung von Prozessen und Strukturen des menschlichen Langzeitgedächtnisses mit ereigniskorre- lierten Hirnpotentialen (ERPs), Diplomarbeit, Sektion Psychologie, Humboldt-Universität (1983).

(7) van der Meer, E., Analogical reasoning - an approach to cognitive microprocesses as well as to intelligence per- formance, Z. Psychol. 186 (1978) 39-47.

(8) Michalski, R.S., A theory and methodology of inductive learning, in: Michalski, R.S. et al. (eds.), Machine learning (Berlin, New York, Tokyo, 1984).

(9) Preuss, M., Experimente über Relationserkennungen im menschlichen Langzeitgedächtnis. Dissertation, Sektion Psychologie, Humboldt-Universität (1985).

(10) Puffe, H., Eine weiterführende Untersuchung zur Unter- scheidbarkeit semantischer Relationen im menschlichen Lang- zeitgedächtnis, Diplomarbeit, Sektion Psychologie, Humboldt- Universität (1979).

(10) Schank, R.C., Conceptual Information Processing (New York, 1975).

(11) Schindler, R. and Fischer, F., Effectiveness of training as a function of the structure of instructed knowledge, in: Klix, F. (ed.), MACINTER I (North-Holland, Amsterdam, 1985).

(13) Wandke, H. and Schulz, J., On complexity of command-entry, in: Klix, F. (ed.), MACINTER I (North-Holland, Amsterdam, 1985).

Man-Computer Interaction Research
MACINTER-I
F. Klix and H. Wandke (Editors)
© Elsevier Science Publishers B.V. (North-Holland), 1986

PSYCHOLOGICAL METHODS FOR ASSEMBLING PROCEDURES
IN TEXT MANAGEMENT SYSTEMS

Joachim Hoffmann, Michael Ziessler and Rosemarie Seifert

Department of Psychology
Central Institute of Cybernetics and Information Processes
Academy of Sciences
Berlin
GDR

Text assembling systems are used to rationalize the
formulation of texts. To be most effectively a text
assembling system has to meet the requirements of its
special field of application. That means each user has
to set up a list of appropriate text units and to formulate special rules for the text assembling procedure.
To solve this problem several steps are proposed which
proved good in their application to different practical
problems.

INTRODUCTION

Modern electronic writing-systems are thought to rationalize clerical work.
A main part of this work consists in formulating and editing of texts. Frequently these texts are not identically but consist of a limited number of
constant single statements. That is,there is a number of texts differing
only in the selection and combination of constant statements out of a total
number of statements. For the formulation of such texts assembling procedures are an effective way of rationalization: The constant single statements are stored in a systematic order as text units. Thereby one has a
text-preserve, which can be used to assemble a text for each case of application.

There are some psychological problems determining the cognitive demands in
the use of text assembling systems by man. These problems concern the construction of the text assembling system, the manner of calling up the text
units, the manner of text editing and others. To ensure a faultless use of
the text assembling systems their properties should be in correspondence to
the properties of human information processing. Doubtless these are very
important problems of a more general nature. But the main problem of our
paper will be another one. To be most effectively the text assembling system
has to meet the requirements of the special field of application. That means
each user has to develop his own special text assembling system. The main
problems in achieving this goal which cannot be solved in general consists
in setting up the list of appropriate text units and in the formulation of
special rules for the text assembling procedure.

In the industrial management there is a need of a suitable inventory. It is
our intention to propose some methods for the building up of special text
assembling systems. It should be noted that these will be heuristic methods.
However, these methods proved good in their application to two practical

problems of different kind: the draft of texts offering industrial equipments, and the formulation of reply letters in an agency. Here we want to present some of our experiences.

In general we propose the following basic steps for the building up of text assembling systems:
(1) the setting up of the list of appropriate text units
(2) the derivation of rules for text assembling
(3) the arrangement of a text manual or a dialogue system.
Mainly the first two steps will be discussed in detail now.

METHODS FOR SETTING UP THE LIST OF TEXT UNITS

In the first place a text is determined by the content, which should be expressed (Kintsch (1974), Anderson and Bower (1973)). The special lingual formulation is only of subordinate importance. That means in the derivation of the text units our point of departure should be the depth structure of the texts rather than the surface structure. The derived text units have to cover all contents of all different texts in the field, they should allow any necessary combination, and their number should be rather small to minimize the expenditure of search in text assembling.

To meet these requirements the first step which is proposed here consists in the derivation of the smallest constant statements necessary to express the contents of the different texts.
Two approaches are possible: The analysis of a sample of available texts or the analysis of the work of the competent officials acting upon the problem the text will be about. This second approach uses the fact that the statements in a text are the result of decisions of a competent official. If the competent official in his work comes to a decision the corresponding statements of the text are determined at the same time. That is, if we identify all the decision points and their possible consequences in the algorithm of the competent official's work we also get the constant statements necessary to express the contents of the different texts. For the analysis of the competent official's work the psychology offers several appropriate methods. The results may not only be used to derive the constant statements but also for a rationalization of the work itself at the same time.

But let us come back to the first approach, the analysis of a sample of texts, in detail. The basic idea of this approach consists in the identification of constant single statements within a multitude of texts already existing. The prerequisite is the availability of a representative sample of all different texts in the field. To ensure that no contents will be lost the texts should be analysed in a systematic manner. Suitable methods to do this were developed in psychology in the context of text processing research. In analogy to Kintsch (1974) we propose a propositional representation of the contents of the texts. Figure 1 gives an example.
If this method is applied to all texts without any gap the result will be the amount of the smallest constant statements, represented as propositions. The smallest constant statements are sufficient to compose all the different texts completely. In principle it would be possible to formulate the smallest constant statements as sentences and to use them as text units for a text assembling procedure. But, it is easy to imagine that such a proceeding would result in an immense amount of text units even for texts of middle complexity. Later, in the synthesis of texts, we would be confronted with a

EXAMPLE: "We acknowledge the mail of your request and can
inform you that we will realize the installation
of the telephone connection as desired."

PROPOSITIONAL REPRESENTATION

(1)   (acknowledge, we, mail of request)

(2)   (realize, we, telephone connection)

(3)   (inform, we, 2)

Figure 1
Example for the propositional representation of a sentence

large expenditure of search for the appropriate text units. Therefore as a
next step the smallest constant statements should be systematically ordered
and reduced by composing more complex statements. In doing this we can start
from the fact that the constant statements identified in the first step cannot appear in any arbitrary order in the texts.

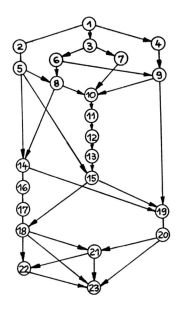

Figure 2
Network of smallest constant statements
(example from Hoffmann and Schmuck (1983))

Following the logical connections in the field only some combinations are
possible and other combinations are not. To find the possible connections
between the smallest constant statements the construction of a network of
the statements has proved to be a suitable method. Figure 2 shows an

example. The nodes of the network are the smallest constant statements. The connections between the nodes represent the possible combinations of the statements in any text out of the sample analysed before. The direction of a connection marks the order of occurence of the connected statements. In addition to this it is recommended to value the connections between the smallest constant statements by the proportion of their occurence in the analysed texts.

Now a systematic reduction of the network will also result in a reduction of the amount of single statements. For the reduction of the network we propose the following general rules:

(1) Sometimes the network falls into several parts which are not connected with each other. Such parts are as a rule in correspondence to the subdivision of the field into several subjects. It is recommended to handle each part separately (cf. Fabeck (1974)).

(2) Often the network shows connections of smallest statements which may appear only in a fixed form. Such constantly connected smallest statements can be composed to more complex statements. An example is given in Figure 3.

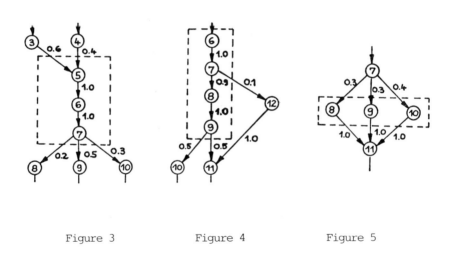

Figure 3   Figure 4   Figure 5

Figure 3, 4, 5
Possibilities to summarize smallest statements. The dotted line marks the statements which may be summarized. The connections between the statements are valued by the proportion of their occurence in the anylsed texts.

(3) It is also possible to compose more complex statements if the smallest statements not always but at least frequently appear in a fixed combination in the tests (see Fig. 4). So for the majority of texts, which have to be synthesized later, one complex statement is available. For the few differing cases corrections are necessary. You should notice at this point that the more smallest statements are summarized the lower is the expenditure of search in the text assembling procedure. But at the same time the expenditure

for corrections in the differing cases is increased. That is, for each field of application you should look for an optimum between the expenditure of search and of corrections.

(4) Occasionally also statements which are alternatively needed with nearly the same frequency can be composed to a complex statement. This makes sense if these statements differ only in one detail, for instance a model name or an other special fact. In the complex statement the detail should be replaced by a variable which has to be completed later in correspondence to the special case of application. This is illustrated by Figure 5.

The reduction of the network results in the minimum amount of constant statements which can be used to produce the variety of the contents of the texts necessary in the field by an appropriate selection and combination of the statements. These statements are the basis for the lingual formulation of the corresponding text units.
After we have presented the steps necessary for the derivation of the contents of the text units, we come now to the second basic problem: the organization of the text assembling procedure.

THE ORGANIZATION OF THE TEXT ASSEMBLING PROCEDURE

A text is produced by the selection of appropriate text units and their combination in the right order for the given case of application. The expenditure of search for the necessary text units and their combinations is decisively determined by the manner of the arrangement of the text units. Two principles should be taken into consideration to arrange the text units: The first one results from the logical connections in the field, the second one takes the structure of texts into account. The first principle ensures the selection of factually correct text units and the second one their combination to formally correct and understandable texts. The structure of text units in correspondence to the logical connections in the field is based on the subdivision of the field in several subjects (cf. Fabeck (1974)). That is, each subject forms a separate category of text units. If the amount of text units within a category is very large yet, a further subdivision which is based on the algorithm of the competent official's work is possible. The algorithm shows the decision points which determine the content of the texts. Those text units selected at the same decision point form a new common category and may be distinguished from other text units of the same subject category. Thus independent of the method used to derive the text units at least at this point an analysis of the competent official's work is unavoidably. To arrange the text units in accordance to text properties the structure of the texts which shall be produced must be analysed. For that we can use again findings of text processing research (e.g. Rumelhart (1975), Thorndyke (1977)). This research has shown that texts may be hierarchically subdivided into functional parts. For instance a commer-cial letter often consists of the salutation, the reference, the information, and the regards.

The information may be subdivided further into the basic statement, an argumentation, and additional information. Choosing an appropriate level of the hierarchy one gets a clearly arranged set of functional categories which can be used to structure the text units.

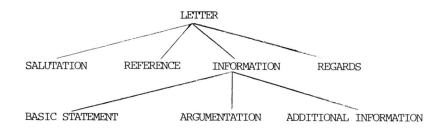

Figure 6
Structure of a commercial letter

As a next step both structure principles have to be combined. That means, we
have two dimensions to structure the text units (see Fig. 7). This results
in the formation of small categories of text units which are represented by
the cells of the matrix in Figure 7. In the most cases only some of the
cells are occupied by text units. This is marked here by the crosses. These
categories summarize text units which are alternatives of the same decision
in acting upon the problem and which have the same function in the text. It
is recommended to ensure that this final categories of text units summarize
not more than 8 text units which have to be processed in text assembling.

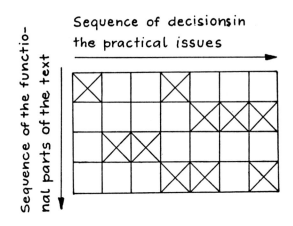

Figure 7
Formation of text unit categories by the combination of two
structure principles. The crosses mark cells which are as an
example occupied by text units and represent text unit categories.

Following this step the creation of a rule system determining the order of
processing of the text unit categories is required. For that it is necessary
to combine two decision processes with each other. At the one hand you have
to decide the practical issues for the selection of the text units and at
the other hand you have to determine the sequential order of the selected

text units in the final draft of the text. According as which side is given the priority two distinct opportunities are given to realize the text assembling system. The first opportunity follows in the first place the text structure. The text unit categories of the special subject have to be processed in dependence on their sequential order in the text. That is, beginning with the first row the matrix presented above has to be processed row by row. Out of each category the alternative determined by the decision in the practical issue has to be selected. As a result of this procedure the final text is available. Since the sequential order of the decisions in the practical issues is not in each case identically to the sequential order of the corresponding text units in the final text, those text assembling systems require the conclusion of the decision process before the text assembling may begin.

The second opportunity for the creation of the text assembling system unites the competent official's work and the text assembling, what should presumably result in a great effect of rationalization. For that, the text unit categories are arranged according to the logical connections in the field. The competent official acts upon the problem, comes to the necessary decisions, and at the same time he selects the text units for writing the text. That means the matrix in Figure 7 is processed column by column. Finally the selected text units have to be ordered in accordance to the decided text structure.

Corresponding to the text assembling system created before, the text unit categories may be arranged in a text manual now. Presumably the text assembling procedures will be especially effectively if the text units are stored in an electronic writing-system and the selection of the appropriate text units takes place in the form of a dialogue between man and computer. In the combination of the competent official's work and the text production the computer may not only be used to offer the text units for selection but also to support the decision process in the practical issues.

REFERENCES

(1) Anderson, R. and Bower, G.H., Human associative memory (Winston, Washington, D.C., 1973).

(2) Fabeck, J., Textanalyse - Textprogrammierung (Wiesbaden, 1974).

(3) Hoffmann, J. and Schmuck, P., Psychologische Probleme der Textbausteinverarbeitung, Z. Psychol. Suppl. 5 (1983) 42 - 55.

(4) Kintsch, W., The representation of meaning in memory (Wiley, New York, 1974).

(5) Rumelhart, D.E., Notes on a schema of stories, in: Bobrow, D. and Collins, A. (eds.), Representation and understanding: Studies in cognitive science (New York, 1975).

(6) Thorndyke, P.W., Cognitive structure in comprehension and memory of narrative discourse, Cognit. Psychol. 9 (1977) 77 - 110.

Man-Computer Interaction Research
MACINTER-I
F. Klix and H. Wandke (Editors)
© Elsevier Science Publishers B.V. (North-Holland), 1986

INTERNAL REPRESENTATION OF EXTERNALLY STORED INFORMATION

Wolfgang Schönpflug

Institut für Psychologie
Freie Universität Berlin
Berlin (West)

Technical devices such as magnetic tapes and disks extend the capacity for information storage. However,
retrieval from external information stores must generally be initiated by the user. For this purpose, the user
acquires knowledge on features of storage devices and
their contents. Acquisition of source knowledge constitutes a complex task as could be demonstrated in an
experiment.

INTRODUCTION

The external storage of information has been a potent principle in the development of human memory (Hunter (1979), Leontjew (1971)). Since the in-
vention of typography external storage devices have surpassed human memory
as far as capacity, stability and speed of encoding is concerned. Especially with electronic devices, information storage has become fast and safe,
and large amounts of information can be preserved with little effort. However, for the time being, there is a substantial difference between internal and external storage mechanisms. Retrieval from internal memory is mostly an automatic process, and follows nicely the changing needs for information and varying human intentions. Retrieval from an external information
store is not automatic, and if that retrieval is to meet the user's information needs and intentions, the user has to make mental and motor efforts in
order to initiate and to control it. For this purpose, he must know the
content, the location, and the functional characteristics of the external
information store used. Thus, the user has to build up an internal representation of the information stored externally, the storage device used,
and the relations between information and device (Muthig & Schönpflug
(1981)).

PROBLEM

A special term is proposed for the internal representation of structural
and functional features of external information storage: Source knowledge.
Source knowledge is that part of the mental model of an achievement situation which enables the user to participate in his interaction with a technical device that preserves information. This information will be useful if
source knowledge can be matched with information needs and intentions which
are also represented internally. The concept of source knowledge is to be
contrasted with another concept: Focal knowledge. Focal knowledge refers to
the information which is identified and retrieved by means of source knowl-

edge. Thus, source knowledge is instrumental for focal knowledge, whereas
focal knowledge is the target of operations based on source knowledge. In
an action theoretic perspective: Focal knowledge serves a final goal,
whereas source knowledge serves intermediate goals.

In man-computer interaction, typical categories of source knowledge are file
names, drive names, user numbers, and formats. Of course, one has to admit,
that source knowledge also can be represented externally. This is done, for
instance, in file directories. However, three limits still remain: First,
not all set-ups provide the user with an extended representation of the information stored. Second, a minimal portion of the internal source knowledge is indispensable for the initiation of active search and retrieval.
And third, users often try to go beyond this minimal portion, since better
source knowledge increases the speed and efficiency with which the external
information stores are managed.

METHOD

Obviously, the use of external storage devices poses a number of problems
for psychology, and, therefore, a series of experiments was conducted to
investigate these problems. The purpose of the present paper is to report
the last experiment in this series. This study compares memory for sources
with memory for focal information. The experiment was run by means of a
DEC 11/40 computer. Subjects were seated in front of a DEC VT 100 screen,
and had a standard keyboard at their disposal. By striking certain keys,
the subjects could display a succession of texts. They were asked to prepare
for a reproduction of these texts following the presentation of the series.
For preparation, the subjects had two options: One option was to memorize
the texts themselves - as is done in conventional experiments on text learning; the other option was to use the computer as an external storage device.
In order to use the computer, however, the subjects had to memorize a reference for each text; if the reference was entered during the testing
period, the corresponding text reappeared on the display and served as an
aid for reproduction.

Actually, the computer analogy was not emphasized while the subjects were
introduced to the experiment; it was rather constructed as a library analogy. In the beginning, the subjects received the following instructions:

> "This year is 1984. Imagine that you retreat to a desert island, with-
> out newspapers, radio, television and other means of communication to
> the civilized world. You stay there for twelve years. When you return
> home, you try to catch up. You talk to friends and neighbours, and you
> read books. Later on, you will be asked about the events that have
> happened. To answer these questions, you can either memorize the events
> themselves or you memorize the persons or the books from which you
> learned what has happened; if you remember the persons or the books,
> you may consult them during the reproduction period. This situation is
> simulated on a computer."

The focal knowledge in this experimental setup refers to the texts which
had to be reproduced. There were 27 texts about fictitious events occurring
between 1984 and 1996 in nine different interest areas, including sports,
architecture, economics and politics. Source knowledge could be acquired
from the indication of the names of authors, of book titles, and of editors
associated with the texts. This is an example:

> "Im Jahre 1992 wurde die neue Schnellbahntrasse Hamburg - Frankfurt -
> München in Betrieb genommen. Der neu entwickelte Express erreicht eine

Spitzengeschwindigkeit von 360 km/Std. und legt die rund 850 km lange
Fahrt von Hamburg nach München in vier Stunden zurück. Eine ähnliche
Verbindung besteht zwischen Köln und Paris; für die knapp 500 km zwi-
schen den beiden Städten benötigt der Express 2,5 Stunden.

Source: Rose Peterson: Im Eilzug durch die Lande. Mannheim: Bilabel."

The experiment tests the tradeoff between memorizing focal knowledge and
memorizing source knowledge. Since individuals make estimates of learning
difficulty, a straightforward prediction is that, in selecting between the
text or the source, they will select whatever is easier to memorize. Thus,
provisions had to be made for varying the difficulties of memorizing the
texts and memorizing the sources. Both difficulty of texts and difficulty
of sources were varied on three levels. Text difficulty was varied by the
number of words and information units contained within the text. Source
difficulty was varied by the number of concepts which had to be entered for
retrieval, just an author or a title, an author plus title, or an author
plus title plus editor.
However, the straightforward prediction that subjects compare difficulty of
texts and difficulty of sources and choose the easier one of a text-source
pair refers to subjective estimates of difficulty rather than to objective
characteristics. Therefore, subjective ratings of difficulty were assessed.
Five-point scales of text difficulty and of source difficulty were presented
on the display, and the subjects gave their judgments by pressing corresponding keys. Individual intentions were also assessed. In a dialogue following
each presentation of a text-source pair, the subjects had to indicate whether they planned to memorize (1) the text and only the text, (2) the source
and only the source, (3) both text and source, or (4) neither text nor
source. This report is focussed on these subjective ratings.

RESULTS

Table 1 shows the proportions of preferences for learning the text and only
the text within a 5 x 5 matrix formed by the ratings of text difficulty and
of source difficulty. Proportions of preferences for learning the source
and only the source are presented in Table 2, also within the 5 x 5 matrix.
Single cell comparisons were made between corresponding values in the rows
of Table 1 and the columns of Table 2. Eighteen out of 25 comparisons were
in favour of text learning which is a statistically significant finding as
evaluated from the binomial distribution (p = .02).
In contrast to straightforward expectations, the notion of a choice between
text and source learning is debatable. In a considerable proportion of instances, subjects make no decision, but rather try to memorize both text
and source, as shown in Table 3. In the cases represented in Table 3, again
a bias in favour of text learning is observed. That is, there are more difficult texts learned in combination with sources than difficult sources
learned in combination with texts. Corresponding values in the rows and in
the columns of Table 3 were compared; with the scores in the diagnonal
excluded, ten comparisons could be made. Eight of these comparisons revealed
more text and source learning with relatively higher text difficulty
(p = .06). The preference for texts becomes still more conspicuous if the
text-only cases from Table 1 and the text-and-source cases from Table 3
are summed to form a measure of overall learning intention.

Rated difficulty of source	Rated difficulty of text				
	1	2	3	4	5
1	41	10	27	0	0
2	59	32	5	0	5
3	78	72	31	12	0
4	95	91	85	41	11
5	100	100	50	90	11

Table 1
Proportions of preferences for memorizing the text and only the text (decimal points omitted).

Rated difficulty of source	Rated difficulty of text				
	1	2	3	4	5
1	3	60	37	80	90
2	0	11	57	79	78
3	0	3	21	45	79
4	0	0	2	22	37
5	0	0	0	0	36

Table 2
Proportions of preferences for memorizing the source and only the source (decimal points omitted).

Rated difficulty of source	Rated difficulty of text				
	1	2	3	4	5
1	57	30	40	20	10
2	39	57	37	18	13
3	22	26	26	32	15
4	5	9	13	17	13
5	0	0	50	0	0

Table 3
Proportions of preferences for memorizing both
text and source (decimal points omitted).

DISCUSSION

These data give evidence for an asymmetrical relation between focal knowledge and source knowledge. The functionality of focal knowledge does not
depend on references from source knowledge. However, source knowledge without reference to focal knowledge is not functional in our test situation.
This means that memory load for source knowledge is systematically higher
than memory load for focal knowledge. Effective use of source knowledge requires both internal representation of external sources, and internal representation of the information to which the sources refer. In comparison,
effective use of focal information does not require the internal representation of information sources. From this point of view, acquisition of
source knowledge appears as a more complex task than acquisition of focal
knowledge. It is not surprising, then, that individuals prefer the less
complex task.
Under these conditions, acquisition of source knowledge about externally
stored information will be determined by several factors. One crucial question is: How economically can external information be represented internally? In terms of cognitive psychology this means: How simple are the macrostructures representing the external information, and how easy is the application of macrooperators producing these macrostructures? Investigations of
this problem are still needed. Another question is: If a macrostructure is
formed, how appropriately is it represented in descriptive terms such as
file names or designation of file types? In the present experiment there
was a specific variation which was relevant for the issue mentioned. Under
one condition, the book titles to be inserted for retrieval were formulated
very generally, for instance, "Crhonicle of the 20th Century"; these general
titles were randomly assigned to the texts. In another experimental condition, book titles were matched specifically to each text, for instance a
title "All about Air Traffic" to go with a text on supersonic planes. Typically, the preferences for sources increased if the titles matched the
texts.
What about actual use of source knowledge? Did subjects expose texts on
their display during the reproduction period? In fact, many of them did. Of

course, retrieval from the external buffer was less frequent than reported preferences for the source. One reason was that the recall of material from the internal memory was satisfactory enough, and subjects felt that they did not need additional exposure to the text. The other reason was forgetting of the source during the reproduction period. The frequency of text exposure was correlated with difficulty ratings. Subjects most likely exposed texts on the screen which were rated as difficult to memorize associated with a source which was rated as easy to remember.

These observations and considerations suggest that external storage of information is a domain of common concern for computer science and psychology. It can be expected that psychological research can considerably contribute to progress in the design and application of future systems for external information storage.

REFERENCES

(1) Hunter, I.M.L., Memory in everyday life, in: Gruneberg, M.M. and Morris, P.E. (eds.), Applied Problems in Memory (Academic Press, London, 1979).

(2) Leontjew, A.N., Probleme der Entwicklung des Psychischen (Volk und Wissen, Berlin, 1971).

(3) Muthig, K.P. and Schönpflug, W., Externe Speicher und rekonstruktives Verhalten, in: Michaelis, W. (ed.), Bericht über den 32. Kongreß der Deutschen Gesellschaft für Psychologie 1980 in Zürich, Volume 1 (Hogrefe, Göttingen, 1981).

Man-Computer Interaction Research
MACINTER-I
F. Klix and H. Wandke (Editors)
© Elsevier Science Publishers B.V. (North-Holland), 1986

PROBLEMS IN THE DESIGN OF INFORMATION RETRIEVAL SYSTEMS:
USER COMPETENCE AND INFORMATION COMPLEXITY

Wolfgang Battmann

Institut für Psychologie
Freie Universität Berlin
Berlin (West)

Users of data base systems have to cope with (1) mental
load related to the dialogue with the system and (2) mental load related to the content of the task. Both forms
of mental load can be reduced by the development of adequate strategies, but a strategy focusing on the reduction of content related load may lead to an increase in
dialogue related load. The tradeoff between both strategies is discussed on the basis of results of
laboratory experiment.

INTRODUCTION

Data base systems have a supportive function in problem solving processes:
they enhance the availability of information; but the processing of information retrieved remains the task of the user. Optimizing the system user interface requires the consideration of two forms of mental load: (1) Load related to the content of task demands and, (2) load related to the complexity of the dialogue. With regard to performance and subjective well-being
both forms of load are highly interdependent: a reduction of dialogue related load will set free capacity to cope with content related load and vice
versa. In recent years system designers have focused on the reduction of
dialogue related load by refinements of data models and the data manipulation languages (Reisner (1977), Shneiderman (1980)). This paper concentrates
on the effects of measures of task design aiming at the reduction of content
related load.

Content related load depends on the design of information in the system. Information can be presented in different forms varying from condensed and
complex to elaborated and transparent. Taking into account that data base
systems should usually support a variety of users each form of presentation
has its advantages: complex and condensed information facilitates decision
making by combining all data relevant to the problem, and proves valuable
for experts able to carry the high content related load. But this approach
puts individuals in a situation of overload, who, due to a lower problem
solving competence, require less complex and elaborated information.

A possible way out of this dilemma is the construction of a multiway information system which offers information relevant to the problem parallelly
in different complex forms. The differentiation of solution paths achieved
by this measure of task design has proved successful in other decision making contexts (e.g. Abernathy and Rosenbloom (1971)), and enables users of
varying competence to work efficiently with the system. Individuals with a

low problem solving competence can attempt to reduce content related load by
the selection of low demanding information adopting a 'content oriented
strategy'. Alternatively, individuals may generate a 'dialogue oriented
strategy' aiming at the enhancement of the efficiency of action by reducing
the extent of the dialogue.

Unfortunately, there is normally no numerical one to one relation between a
condensed and elaborated information, but a self-contained complex or condensed information will have to be dissected into several low complex information. Therefore, individuals using a content oriented strategy must
retrieve and process more information. Thus, the reduction of content related load will lead to an increase in load related to the dialogue. This
load will be reflected in (1) an absolutly higher number of operations and,
due to the extended number of data, which must necessarily be processed,
(2) an augmented retrieval of irrelevant data and search processes. Erroneously exposed data as well as processes of intermittent search prolong
and interrupt the solution of the task. In consequence, relevant information already memorized by the individual is more likely to get lost than in
a short dialogue. Forgetting relevant information should cause two further
indirect effects: (1) relevant information must be retrieved not once but
several times and, (2) experiencing the limits of capacity, the individual
will become insecure about its ability to cope efficiently with the task
and the correctness of the solution found. Similarly, relying on a dialogue
oriented strategy poses a high content oriented load.

A laboratory study was conducted to test the tradeoff between content and
dialogue related load under conditions of a multiway information system.

METHOD

In an office, simulated in our laboratory, subjects were asked to take over
the role of an administrative clerk and had to calculate wages, decide about
promotions and hire new employees. All necessary information (e.g. wage and
tax lists, social security deductions and company guidelines) were stored
in a data base system simulated by a DEC PDP 11/40 computer. Working on a
task was a three step process (Fig. 1): (1) Task analysis. In a text, ap-
pearing on the left side of the screen, the goal of the task was pointed
out to the Ss and some base-information was given. (2) Information processing. Striking appropriate keys on the keyboard, all data necessary to reach
the solution could be requested from the data base and were displayed besides the task text. A directory gave an overview about all available data
from which only a minor part was relevant to the particular problem.
(3) Decision making. Finally, after the request of a special mask, Ss could
enter the result.

In the multiway task, sketched as an example in Fig. 1, Ss were requested
to calculate the monthly wage of an employee. Deductions for taxes, social
security, insurance as well as overtime payments had to be considered. The
relevant data were stored in two ways in the data base system: (1) in form
of separate tables, marked as low complex data (LC) in the figure, and,
(2) in form of one highly complex formula marked HC. Frequent retrieval of
LC-information indicates a content oriented strategy. In contrast, processing the HC-formula indicates the attempt to adopt a dialogue oriented strategy.

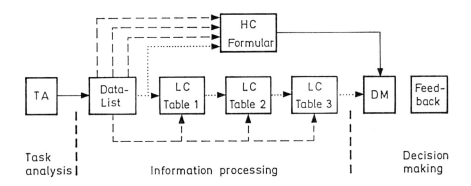

Figure 1
Formal structure of a multiway clerical task

Subjects worked on several types of these clerical tasks for 3 to 5 hours. Seven tasks of each type were presented. Concurrently, every action taken by the subject was recorded by the computer. A total of 86 female and male volunteers participated in the study. The subjects were mostly unemployed clerical workers ranging in age from 18 to 47 years.

RESULTS

The quality of the dialogue in dependence of the dialogue and content related strategy.

The correlations between the number of LC- and HC-data processed over seven trials ($r = -.01$) and their corresponding processing times ($r = -.36$) indicate that both strategies are indeed independent but not used exclusively. It must be considered that these correlations include the period of strategy development in the first trials. An analysis of the last three trials only reveals much stronger correlations especially between the HC and LC processing times ($r = -.60$).

The correlations between dialogue and content oriented strategies and the indicators of dialogue quality as defined above are given in Table 1. As predicted, applying the content oriented strategy is positively correlated with intensified search processes as well as the accidental retrieval of information not relevant to the particular problem. In turn, these parameters are low but positively correlated with the number of wrong solutions ($r = .19$, $r = .27$, $p < .05$). The expectation that retention of relevant information will suffer due to the intensified dialogue is confirmed by the positive correlations found between this strategy and the indicators "relevant informations processed several times (multiple requests)" and "decision attempts".

	content oriented strategy	dialogue oriented strategy
SEARCH TIME	.51	-.23
N REQUESTS DIRECTORY	.43	-.24
N RETRIEVAL ERRORS	.46	.02
N MULTIPLE REQUESTS	.75	.40
N DECISION ATTEMPTS	.26	-.10
N CORRECT SOLUTIONS	-.10	.11

Table 1
Correlations between the strategies and indicators of dialogue quality
(Significance limit r > .18, p .05; N = 86)

The negative correlations between all parameters and the dialogue oriented
strategy indicate that the willingness to carry a high content related load
relieves the individual from the vicious circle of searching new and concurrently forgetting old data. Search processes, erroneous retrievals as
well as the overall time spent on a task are reduced significantly. In
terms of efficiency of action (cf. Eysenck (1979), Schönpflug (1985)) these
data reflect the effort associated with the prefered strategy. This effort
has to be matched with the success achieved (i.e. the number of correct solutions). Considering the tradeoff between content and dialogue related
load within each strategy, none of them can be judged as superior or more
task adequate: the insignificant correlations of both strategies with the
number of correct solutions indicate that the higher dialogue related load
demonstrated for the content oriented strategy compensates the achieved reduction of content related load. Similarly, a high content related load was
traded in for a low dialogue related load when the dialogue oriented strategy was adopted.

Intelligence and strategy generation

The multiway approach was chosen to give especially users of a low problem
solving competence a possibility to reduce content related load by the
choice of the content oriented strategy. Since this strategy did not
prove very successful due to the increased dialogue related load, it is of
interest, (1) whether this strategy was adopted by the subjects despite its
low efficiency and (2) to which extent modifications of the strategy or a
mix of strategies were used to enhance its effectivity. Therefore, it was
tested if problem solving competence determined the choice of strategies.
Since task demands required mainly mathematical skills, an intelligence
test (Amthauer (1971)) was used to assess problem solving competence and to
divide the sample in two groups of 43 subjects each.

Results of an ANOVA analysis confirm the expectation, that subjects with
lower problem solving competence prefered the content oriented strategy:
(1) Low intelligent Ss displayed with a mean of 4.2 retrievals per task LC-

information significantly more often than did high intelligent ones (2.5 retrievals, F = 14,92, Fg = 1,84, p < .001). Displays also lasted for a longer time with low intelligent Ss (73.8 vs. 44.4 sec., F = 15,68, Fg = 1,84, p < .001). (2) Parameters indicate for low intelligent subjects the increased dialogue related load associated with the content oriented strategy. More time was spent on search (25.1 vs. 17.3 secs., F = 5.7, Fg = 1,84, p < .02), and the number of erroneous retrievals is enhanced (15.0 vs. 11.1, F = 14.18, Fg = 1,84, p < .001). But, as in the correlational analysis with regard to the two strategies, there is no difference between high and low intelligent subjects in the number of correct solutions.

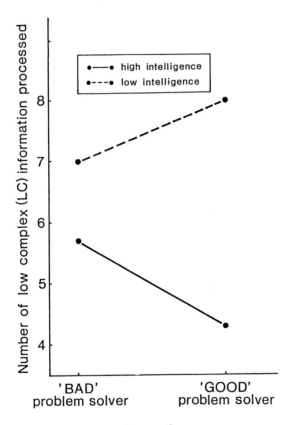

Figure 2
Preference of the content oriented strategy in dependence
of the intelligence and problem solving quality of the subjects

In order to test, whether a modification or mix of strategies could enhance the effectivity, we subdivided the groups of high and low intelligent subjects into two groups of 'bad' and 'good' problem solvers according to their number of correct solutions and analyzed the preference of the content related strategy, indicated by the time spent on LC-information, thereafter (Fig. 2). The significant main effect for intelligence just confirms, that this strategy was prefered by low intelligent subjects. In addition, problem solving quality and problem solving competence interact ordinally

(F = 4.31, Fg = 1,84, p < .05). This interaction indicates that low intelligent 'good' problem solvers relied mostly on the content related strategy
while, in contrast, successful high intelligent subjects avoided LC-information and relied on the dialogue oriented strategy. 'Bad' problem solvers
form a middle group neither fully adopting the content oriented strategy
nor rejecting it in favour of the dialogue oriented strategy. This argumentation is supported by the number of changes between LC and HC data within
the tasks. 'Bad' problem solvers switch more often between these data than
'good' Ss.

The optimization of the content oriented strategy

On the basis of the correlational analysis it was argued that the advantages
of the content oriented strategy are devaluated by the enhanced dialogue
related load associated with this strategy. This argument is contradicted
by the results of good problem solvers with low intelligence who processed
the highest number of LC-information and, in consequence, should suffer
from an intensified dialogue related load reducing the chances to reach a
correct solution. An explanation for this contradiction was found during
the analysis of the temporal distribution of parameters indicating the dialogue related load.

The temporal distribution of time spent on search processes over the trials
for the low intelligent 'good' and 'bad' problem solvers is shown in Figure 3. The significant interaction effect between intelligence and the repeated measures factor indicates, that good problem solvers are engaged in
intensified search during the first tasks only (F = 4.3, Fg = 6,234,
p < .001). Comparable temporal distributions were found for other parameters
indicating dialogue related load: the number of erroneous retrievals and
multiple requests of relevant data show for good problem solvers a peak in
the first trial followed by a drastic reduction. In contrast, dialogue related load is relatively stable over trials for bad problem solvers.

CONCLUSIONS

The notion of the "one best way" to solve a task, which has for a long time
dominated industrial psychology and problem solving research, does not take
into account that one system has to serve a variety of users differing in
competence and experience. An alternative approach has been put forward by
Lewin (1953) who stressed that several "functionally equivalent" courses of
action can be pursued to reach one goal. This approach, which meets the unequivocal demand that the satisfaction of the users should be the ultimate
measure of the success of system design (Hansen (1971), Wasserman (1973)),
was followed in this study using the paradigm of a multiway data base system.
The results of this study point out the benefits and disadvantages of this
approach as well as a more general dilemma of coping with mental load.

As was shown in the correlational analysis, content and dialogue related
load are antagonistic (Tab. 1). By application of a specific strategy individuals trade in one form of mental load for the other. As a result of this
antagonism, the overall load cannot be reduced substantially. Due to this
general dilemma, the multiway system proves disadvantageous for some individuals. If minimizing one form of mental load leads to a maximization of
the other, choice of strategies becomes difficult. The mixed strategy found
for 'bad' problem solvers may express both vain attempts to minimize either

forms of load and resignation facing the dilemma of load reduction.

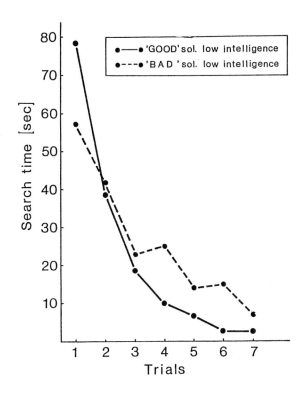

Figure 3
Temporal distribution of search times
for low intelligent 'good' and 'bad' problem solvers

Results showed that abandoning of strategy development was no solution: the mixed strategy was connected to a low problem solving quality independent of the intelligence of the subjects (Fig. 2).

'Good' problem solvers with low intelligence have demonstrated that this dilemma can be avoided if a "metastrategy" taking advantage of the temporal distribution of both forms of load is developed. Using a two step strategy, these subjects reduced the dialogue related load connected to the content oriented strategy (Fig. 3): analyzing the data base intensively, these subjects carry the highest dialogue related load found for all groups in the first trials. On the long run, the improved internal model based on this analysis enabled them to reduce dialogue related load connected to search and erroneous retrievals substantially. Therefore, these subjects experienced the negative tradeoff between dialogue and content related load for a short period only, and achieved a positive tradeoff afterwards. The success of these subjects by within strategy optimization is a direct consequence of the multiway characteristic of the task: the effectivity of action does not depend primarily on the problem solving competence of the individual but on the strategy selected. Since in many cases it will be more easy to teach an adequate strategy than to enhance the problem solving competence, this can be regarded as a major advantage of a multiway system.

REFERENCES

(1) Abernathy, W.J. and Rosenbloom, R.S., Parallel strategies in development projects, Management Science 15 (1969) 486 - 505.

(2) Amthauer, R., Der Intelligenz-Struktur-Test 70 (Hogrefe, Göttingen, 1971).

(3) Eysenck, M.W., Anxiety, learning and memory: a reconceptualisation, J. Res. Pers. 13 (1979) 363 - 385.

(4) Hansen, W.J., User engineering principles for interactive systems, in: Proceedings of the Fall Joint Computers Conference (AFIPS-Press, Montvale, N.J., 1971).

(5) Lewin, K., A dynamic theory of personality (McGraw-Hill, New York, 1953).

(6) Reisner, P., Use of psychological experimentation as an aid to the development of a query language, IEEE Transactions on Software Engineering SE-3, 3 (1977) 218 - 229.

(7) Schönpflug, W., Goald-directed behavior as a source of stress, in: Frese, M. and Sarbini, J. (eds.), Goal-directed behavior (Erlbaum, Hillsdale, 1985).

(8) Shneiderman, B., Software psychology (Winthrop, Cambridge, Mass., 1980).

(9) Wasserman, T., The design of idiot-proof interactive systems, in: Proceedings of the National Computer Conference (AFIPS Press, Montvale, N.J., 1973).

Man-Computer Interaction Research
MACINTER-I
F. Klix and H. Wandke (Editors)
© Elsevier Science Publishers B.V. (North-Holland), 1986

COMPUTER ASSISTED KNOWLEDGE ACQUISITION
TOWARDS A LABORATORY FOR PROTOCOL ANALYSIS OF USER DIALOGUES

Wolfgang Dzida
Institut für Systemtechnik
Gesellschaft für Mathematik und Datenverarbeitung
St. Augustin
FRG

A combination of computer assisted protocol analysis and
critical incidents analysis can be implemented in order
to carry out empirical case studies during sessions of
human computer dialogues. The automated interpretation
of dialogue steps rests on models of human work structure
and work flow. This approach is aimed at a better understanding of users' difficulties in planning and performing
dialogue steps. Empirical and theoretical results serve as
a basis for better adapted interfaces.

INTRODUCTION

Why is it useful to monitor a user's dialogue by means of a special computer
program? Since user's work is actually performed at a interface to a computer
it is convenient to gather empirical data with the help of the computer.
What benefit will accrue from this investigation? There is some empirical
evidence that users of complex software systems do not make use of the
rich functionality being offered nor do they take notice of it (Draper,
1984). Users confine themselves to a small amount of tools. They do not
elaborate an overview of the potential of the system. Therefore, it is up
to the system developer to provide for a presentation of the system to the
users in terms of their models of work, and to find out where there are
mismatches between user's models and the developer's model of the system. At
the end of these investigations the developer will obtain some theoretical
and empirical results that help implementing better adapted human computer
interfaces.

This investigation into user's dialogues with a computer is necessary as it
has been planned to develop a software product called 'dialogue interpreter'.
This program is a tool for knowledge acquisition. It will act as a monitor
that provides a deeper insight into users' interaction with a complex software system. The dialogue interpreter comprises a protocol system and an
inference engine. The protocol system is intended to identify dialogue steps
of a user, and an associated inference engine governs the interpretation
of the dialogue.

As usual in the software development process the planning process of a product, such as the dialogue interpreter, starts with a model of the application case. In terms of this paper the application model is the model of the
users' work flow and work structure. Knowledge acquisition about these domains will be started with the assistance of a rudimentary dialogue inter-

preter, and it is expected that the observation of users' behaviour will give rise to alter the state of knowledge as it is provided by means of this paper. With an increasing amount of knowledge elicited from the users the dialogue interpreter's comprehensional power will be improved. Knowledge acquisition is difficult. It is even almost impossible, if the engineer can not apply a model to map the facts to be gathered.

SOME BASIC PSYCHOLOGICAL ASSUMPTIONS

A well accepted philosophical theorem is that the interpretation of an empirical fact, even its declaration as a fact is explicitely or implicitely theory related. In monotoring a user's dialogue steps one has to distinguish empirical facts (for instance, different types of steps) and the interpretation of these facts. As it has been planned to conduct the collection and interpretation of dialogue steps with the aid of a computer program the underlying theoretical assumptions for these automated processes have to be outlined.

My theoretical assumptions do not refer to a certain theory about human problem solving or work performance. Rather, the list of assumptions should be regarded as a framework. The refinement of this framework, of course, will be guided by theory.

The investigation into human task performance at work stations has led to the inclusion of the 'tool' as an important component that controls the work act. The user's expertise about tools pertaining to his work environment enables him to define properties of the objects that result from his activities. If a work step is performed at a computer terminal it may be called a 'dialogue step', since the application of a software tool is mediated by a sequence of worded inputs and outputs, i.e. an interaction or dialogue.

A basic psychological assumption is that working with an interactive system usually starts after a mental association is found concerning a work activity and a general idea of what sort of tool would be appropriate. In other words, the user's concept of a certain work activity is mentally established if a corresponding concept of a tool is well-known to him. If this assumption holds true, a corrollary can be formulated as follows: Work activities are hierarchically decomposed according to the user's knowledge about the decomposition of operators. Hence, the notion of a tool is inevitably associated with the notion of a work activity. If the planning of an activity comes to an end and the pair of components 'activity/tool' is established a practicability test is involved which anticipates that an expected result is achievable.

Example: By means of a camera one can produce a series of photos which differ merely in respect of 'depth of field' or 'focus'. The user of a camera is capable of achieving these photos intentionally, if and only if he has a mental concept of a 'zone of sharpeness' and how to adjust the focus by means of the light stop or the aperture.

A software tool cannot be perceived by touch as it is with a camera. Software tools are intangible, traditional tools are tangible. A basic psychological assumption may then be derived from this fact: A mental association of an activity with a conventional tool can be more easily achieved than

with a software tool. Consequently, the work psychologist's research
question of highest priority is how to facilitate this mental process with
the aid of a self-explanatory human-computer interface. Our protocol
analysis approach is concentrated upon an acquisition of knowledge that
may give an answer to this research question.

In observing the usability of software tools one feature of them may attract
our attention: Some tools are application specific, but some of them are
generic. For instance, a user wants to insert a digit into a string represented among a text on a display. The user knows about a command "insert"
that provides the specific effect. The same system offers a different
command to the user for the sake of inserting a word into a sentence and
a further command to insert a paragraph into a text. Thus, the user of this
kind of editor has to associate specific activities with specific tools
respectively. However, there may exist another type of editor allowing the
user to carry out all these activities with the assistance of the same
tool, and the user may even "insert" messages, files etc. From this a basic
psychological assumption follows: The user mentally associates activities
with specific tools, however, he deduces specific activities from generic
tools, provided he has captured the concept of a 'generic' operator.

An additional basic assumption has relation with the user's precision in
anticipating the result of an activity. Some properties of the result
appear to be well-defined in advance, whilst some additional properties
happen to be vaguely defined or are even neglected during the planning process. A theoretical assumption that reflects this observation is then
suggested as follows: The user associates an activity with an operator in
a distinct manner as well in a fuzzy way - so far as properties of the
resultant object are concerned. Hence, there will be a twofold association
between an activity and a tool, the first of it treating the primary effect
of an activity, the second one referring to an auxiliary relationship between the result and an operator; in order to distinguish auxiliary properties from primary ones they may be called additional attributes of the
result. Thus, the user's planning process involves a twofold practicability
test, one test being concerned with a precise definition of the main effect
of an activity, another test referring to additional effects and insofar
being indistinct for a while.

Keeping these assumptions in mind, the observation and interpretation of
user dialogues will be planned with the purpose of acquiring knowledge about
the validity of these assumptions.

TWO TYPES OF DIALOGUE STEPS

Basically, a dialogue step is the empirical entity to be observed during the
protocoll analysis of a user's work session at a terminal. A dialogue step
can be literally regarded as a single keystroke or a series of keystrokes
to perform a task (c.f. the "Keystroke-Level Model", Card et al., 1980).
However, the focus of this analysis is close to traditional ergonomic time
and motion studies; this approach does not take into account the work
content of dialogue steps.

A user sitting at a terminal is faced with an interface. One may distinguish
different aspects of the user interface: one instance is the dialogue interface that provides some facilities to handle the positioning or selection

on a screen; another instance is the functional interface that embodies
certain principles of access to a system of application programs (Dzida,
1983). According to this interface model different types of dialogue steps
can be distinguished. Some dialogue steps may change data, and others
merely change the display states. In analyzing these kinds of dialogues by
means of a 'dialogue interpreter' a model of a dialogue step is applied
being concentrated on five different aspects of work content: 1. result
object, 2. activity, 3. initial object, 4. tool, and 5. parameter. (This
model of a dialogue step is referred to elsewhere as "work act model" for
work analysis purposes, Dzida et al., 1984). The total of the five components can also be termed a user's 'task'.

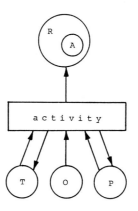

Figure 1

Model of a dialogue step; T = tool, O = object, P = process parameter,
R = result, A = attribute

Example: A secretary uses a typewriter (tool) to print a column of numbers
(= result) on a paper (= object); she sets a tabulator (= parameter) on
a certain position (= value of the parameter), in order to type the digits
more reliable into the column (= attribute of the resultant object).

The model of the dialogue step is semantically based on theoretical
assumptions already been mentioned.

The model is syntactically predicated upon 'means-activity nets' (Oberquelle, 1983). Circles, rectangles and arrows are to be interpreted as
follows:

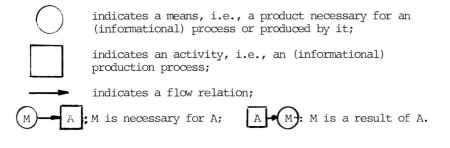

indicates a means, i.e., a product necessary for an
(informational) process or produced by it;

indicates an activity, i.e., an (informational)
production process;

indicates a flow relation;

(M)—[A]: M is necessary for A;   [A]—(M): M is a result of A.

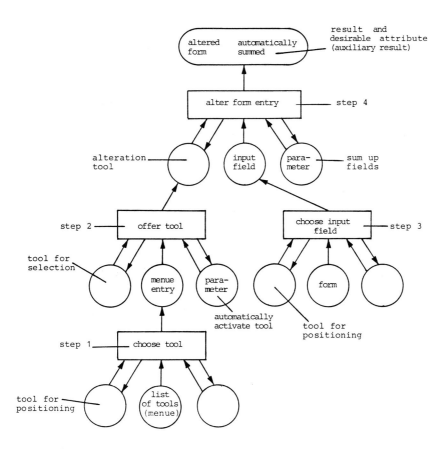

Figure 2

A series of dialogue steps to alter a form entry: 1. Positioning a cursor
in a list of tools, e.g. with the help of a "mouse", 2. Selection of a tool
on the list and automatic activation of the tool corresponding to a default
parameter, 3. Positioning a cursor at the input field to be altered, 4.
Alteration of the form entry and automatic production of altered summation
fields by means of (default) parameters.

Figure 2 illustrates two types of dialogue steps. Steps 1, 2 and 3 change
the display. In terms of this article, these steps are called 'dialogue
step type 1'. These steps are preparatory work acts; they are necessary to
accomplish step 4, i.e., the utilisation of an application program. Step 4
is called 'dialogue step type 2'. It is worth mentioning that both kinds of
dialogue steps can be described by the same model. A bulk of research has
been done to investigate type 1 steps, particularly as regards the advantages of different tools for positioning and selection (Card et al., 1983).
This kind of research mainly deals with the user's manual handling capabilities and how to improve them so that he performs more effectively. The
content of work activities is left out of consideration. The intended
protocoll analysis of user dialogues may be applied on both kinds of dialogue steps. However, our focus is on dialogue steps type 2, because one
objective of our approach is to evolve user's difficulties with application
programs and their heuristic strategies to cope with them.

The model of the dialogue step can be regarded as useful if the 'dialogue
interpreter' is enabled to identify the components of each step in a series
of steps. Recently, it has been shown that an implementation can be
achieved by means of artificial intelligence techniques (Hoffmann et al.,
1983; Dzida et al., 1984).

WORK STRUCTURE AND WORK FLOW

A 'dialogue' may be defined as a sequence of dialogue steps. In traditional
work analysis as in systems analysis much attention has been payed to the
sequential aspect of work, i.e., the work flow. The analysis of work
structure, however, is gaining increasing importance. Both aspects are
relevant to our knowledge acquisition purposes, because it may be of practical and theoretical interest to what extend the user's planning process
is guided by an adequate model of the work structure as well as by a model
of the work flow.

As already outlined the interpretation of an element of dialogue - which
is a dialogue step - depends on an identification of the five structural
components of a dialogue step. The structure of a dialogue step can be taken
as elementary, if an activity is not decomposed moreover. One noteworthy
feature of human work activity is that it is organised at different levels
of abstraction (Volpert, 1982). Hence, the interpretation process of higher
level activities depends on an identification of the corresponding lower
level activities. And vice versa, the interpretation of low devel dialogue
steps can be achieved, if a relation to higher level activities can be
verified.

In interpreting a dialogue step three types of abstraction may be of considerable interest:

1. Some activities belong to a complex of activities, with the complex
   being denoted by a term that indicates an abstraction from more specific
   activities. For instance, in figure 3, the term "process standing order"
   is a higher level activity, summarizing that there exists a composition
   of different specific activities which are attended to the same object,
   namely the standing order of a banking job.

2. Some activities belong to a class of activities which is denotes in terms of the effect being common to a group of resultant objects after a generic tool was applied. For instance, figure 4 illustrates an arrangement of activities which are specific with regard to the object they attend to, but which are governed by the uniform operator "i".

3. Some activities refer to a complex of results. This complex is composed of resulting objects which partially contribute to a complete result. The total of activities is denoted in terms of an abstraction. For instance, in figure 5, the term "renovation" indicates a higher level task that comprises specific tasks on different objects.

The user of an application system is supposed to use a model of the system in terms of the suggested work structures or some structures similar to them. A user's dialogue steps could be interpreted in terms of these structures. If the interpretation fails the models of work structures have to be revised. One may learn from the revision what kind of work structure a user had in mind, how to make the structure of an application system more transparent to the user, and how to overcome a mismatch between subjective and objective work structures.

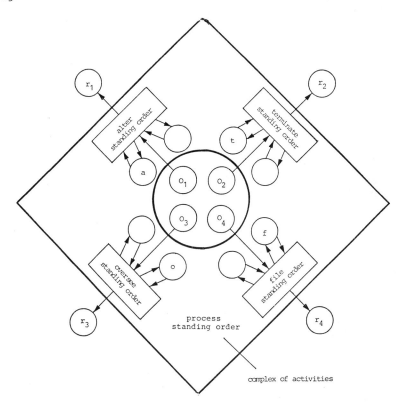

Figure 3
"Process standing order" as a complex of four bank job activities dealing with the same class of objects (o1, o2, o3, o4), and supplying four different results (r1, r2, r3, r4).

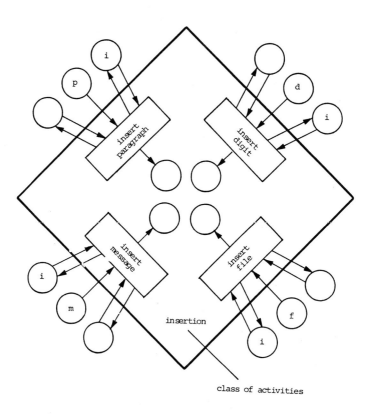

Figure 4

"Insertion" as a class of activities dealing with different kinds of
objects and providing the same characteristic result, due to a generic
tool.

Complementary to the analysis of work structures is work flow analysis.
According to the introductory basic assumptions one may distinguish three
kinds of activities.

1. Preparatory control is an activity aimed at an orientation particularly
   at a system's confirmation that a required object exists or a condition
   has been established. Example: The user checks whether a certain version

of an object still exists.

2. Preparatory activity is aimed at a result that contributes to the accomplishment of a subsequent activity. Example: The user redefines the name of an output device so as to provide for a certain output quality.

3. Execution control is an activity aimed at a check whether a previous dialogue step has supplied the required result object. Example: The user checks whether certain data have been altered.

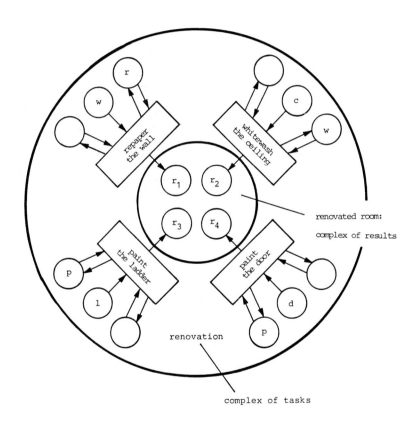

Figure 5

"Renovation" as a complex of tasks dealing with different kinds of objects and contributing to a complex of results (r1, r2, r3, r4).

In our approach, a dialogue step can be interpreted only in the context of a dialogue division, i.e., in relation to successive steps. It is assumed that knowledge of relationships between dialogue steps can be represented in terms of a least the above mentioned three kinds of activities, so that an interpreter is enabled to 'understand' a protocolled dialogue step. Understanding means identifying the structural components of a dialogue step syntactically and interpreting them semantically. The interpreter attempts to identify the structure component of each dialogue step (syntax); with the aid of identified components, an attempt is made to find a meaning for each dialogue step (semantics); this process is governed by rules.

Of course, a large number of rules is used in the semantic interpretation of dialogue steps. The following list provides merely a survey of a few rules that correspond to the above mentioned types of activities:

R1:   IF: a dialogue step is preparatory control
      THEN: a dialogue step can be understood

R2:   IF: a dialogue step is preparatory activity
      THEN: a dialogue step can be understood

R3:   IF: a dialogue step is execution control
      THEN: a dialogue step can be understood

R4:   IF: the user checks a required object
      THEN: checking is a preparatory control

R5:   IF: the user offers a required object
      THEN: the offer is preparatory activity

R6:   IF: the user checks an object
                 AND the object is the result of a previous
                 dialog step
      THEN: checking is execution control

Further rules are application specific. For instance, a rule "R7" may be added concerning an editing task and referring to "R6":

R7:   IF: the user employs the tool for editing
                 AND the object is already present
      THEN: the user checks the object

In addition, rules can be implemented to "understand" dialogue steps with the help of identified work structures, such as "complex of results" or "complex of activities". Example (referring to figure 3):

R: IF: a dialogue step is attended to an object
                 "standing order"
      THEN: a dialogue step pertains to a complex of
                 activities called "process standing order"

A higher order rule may run as follows (also referring to figure 3):

R: IF: a dialogue step pertains to a complex of activities
      THEN: there exists at least another activity attending
                 to the same class of objects

Higher order rules can be regarded as independent; i.e., they are not nee-
ding to apply to a certain application domain. Lower order rules are application specific. This holds for work flow rules as well as for work structure rules. Usually, a representation of a concrete complex of tasks or a
complex of activities has been originated from a deep insight into an
application domain. It makes us probably reluctant to accept that "paint
the ladder" is typically included in a complex of tasks which has been
termed "renovation" (c.f. figure 5). Protocol analysis and subsequent
interpretation of dialogue steps may evolve such a mismatch between structural conceptions of work.

In most cases work flow analysis and work structure analysis complement one
another. One may, for instance, analyze the structure of figure 5 also in
terms of a sequence of activities providing a series of results as follows:
result 2, result 1, result 4, and result 3.

Consequently, protocol analysis of dialogue steps can be supported by two
kinds of knowledge bases, each of them focussing on a certain aspect of
dialogue, either work structure or work flow. A synthesis of both kinds of
interpretations will possibly be necessary resulting in a set of "meta
rules" of human computer interaction. Example:

R: IF: a dialogue step is a preparatory activity
                 AND there exists at least another preparatory activity
                 AND the activities refer to complex of activities
        THEN: there exist degrees of freedom for task performance

CONCLUDING REMARKS

As a matter of fact, empirical case studies suffer from a variety of
methodical deficiencies. Nevertheless, I regard this approach as an
exploration of a field of working behaviour which has got as yet little
transparancy to work psychologists.

It is naive to believe that protocol analysis is capable of interpreting
a series of dialogue steps exhaustively. Since the interpretation just
rests upon models of work, only a section of reality can be comprehended.
Therefore, modelling is not an end in itself. Rather, it is aimed at
special purpose investigations, i.e. the improvement of design decisions
on the basis of empirical case studies. Insofar the protocol system provides a means for user-developer communication. It is intended to accompany
the automated interpretation of dialogue steps by interviews. Thus the
user's planning process can be reconstructed. Critical incidents will be
clarified with the assistance of the user, so as to find out design
deficiencies of the system. Alternative design features of the user interface will be discussed with the user on the basis of the protocolled
dialogue steps.

Knowledge acquisition about user dialogues will also provide a representation of the systems' model in terms of the users' work model. Then, the
user will be allowed to infer from his application specific knowledge to
the peculiarities of the software system. Traditional help systems do
not provide this kind of knowledge. Nevertheless, the more complex an
application system is, the more a user may claim information about
structural features of the available functionality. It is recommended that

the structure of an application system be described so as to make it more
self-explanatory. Our investigations into user dialogues will also contribute to this recommendation.

REFERENCES

(1) Card, S.K., Moran, T.P., and Newell, A., The Psychology of Human-
    Computer Interaction (Lawrence ERlbaum, Hillsdale, 1983).

(2) Card, S.K., Moran, T.P.,and Newell, A., The Keystroke-Level Model for
    user performance time with interactive systems, Communications of the
    ACM 23 (1980) 396 - 410.

(3) Draper, S.W., The nature of expertise in UNIX, Proceedings of
    INTERACT '84, First IFIP Conference on Human-Computer Interaction,
    vol. 2 (1984) 182 - 186.

(4) Dzida, W., Das IFIP-Modell für Benutzerschnittstellen, Office Manage-
    ment, Sonderheft (1983) 6 - 8; may be requested from the author.

(5) Dzida, W., and Valder, W., Application domain modelling by knowledge
    engineering techniques, Proceedings of INTERACT '84, First IFIP
    Conference on Human-Computer Interaction, vol. 2 (1984) 320 - 327.

(6) Dzida, W., Hoffmann, C. und Valder, W., Wissensbasierte Dialogunter-
    stützung, in: Tauber, M.J. und Schauer, H. (eds.), Psychologie der
    Computerbenutzung (R. Oldenbourg, Wien, 1984) im Druck.

(7) Hoffmann, C. und Valder, W., Dialogunterstützung durch Expertensysteme,
    in: Balzert, H. (ed): Software-Ergonomie (Teubner, Stuttgart, 1983).

(8) Oberquelle, H., Nets as a tool in teaching and in terminology work, in:
    Brauer, W. (ed.), Net Theory and Applications (Springer, Berlin, 1980).

(9) Volpert, W., The model of the hierarchical-sequential organization of
    action, in: Hacker, W., Volpert, W. und von Cranach, M. (eds.), Cogni-
    tive and Motivational Aspects of Action (North-Holland, Amsterdam, 1982).

Man-Computer Interaction Research
MACINTER-I
F. Klix and H. Wandke (Editors)
© Elsevier Science Publishers B.V. (North-Holland), 1986

EFFECTIVENESS OF TRAINING AS A FUNCTION OF THE TEACHED KNOWLEDGE STRUCTURE

Raimund Schindler, Frank Fischer

Humboldt-University
Berlin
GDR

To teach the knowledge required for accomplishing word
processing tasks by means of a computer text-editing
system the task-solving knowledge has been arranged into
three types of internal substructures termed operative
units representing different levels of abstraction
(task-oriented operative units, state-oriented operative
units, and state-and-action-oriented operative units). It
can be shown by experimental investigations that the user's
training can be make more effective if the task-solving
knowledge is arranged into generalized operative units.

THE PROBLEM

This paper deals with a particular problem of user's training. We concentrate
on the knowledge the user of a computer system has to aquire to operate the
device successfully. The work described in this paper is based on a particular computer text-editing system.

Similiar to the distinction made by Kieras and Polson (1982) we distinguish
two major components of the user's knowledge: the user's device representation and the user's task-solving representation. The device representation consists of the knowledge which the user has with regard to the structure and the functioning of the device itself. The user's task-solving
representation is the user's knowledge of how to carry out a task using
the device. We shall only discuss the task-solving knowledge in some
detail.

We assume three major components of the user's task-solving knowledge: the
task knowledge, the goal knowledge, and the action unit knowledge. The task
knowledge comprises the tasks which can be accomplished by means of the
device and a related set of concepts and symbols (termed: task features)
which must be known, for example to interpret the notations used to indicate
modifications in a rough draft. The goal knowledge consists of a set of states or modes of the system which the user will have to gain to solve a task
and of a related set of alpha-numeric signs (termed: system state features).
For each state of the device there is a specific combination of alpha-numeric
features displayed on the screen of the system. In order to accomplish a
particular anticipated state of the system the user has to perform a specific
keystroke sequence on the keyboard. We shall call these keystroke sequences
units of actions, and these units of actions are the components of the
action knowledge. Each action unit is defined by a definite sequence of key-

stroking to the keyboard.

Card, Moran and Newell (1980, 1981) have provided evidence for the fact that computer text-editing can be characterized as a routine cognitive skill. Such behavior occurs in task situations where no extrem requirements on performance are made and which people master with training and practice, but where the variability of tasks prevents them from becoming completely routine and requires cognitive involvement. One important feature of routine cognitive skills is that in the course of practice the actions of skilled users in accomplishing the tasks are guided and controlled by a limited set of cognitive substructures which will with certainty lead to success. That means, with practice and training the components of the task-solving knowledge described here are arranged into cognitive substructures in such a way that the different tasks can be performed effectively. These substructures we will call operative units. Operative units, like production rules, have the form of a rule that specifies a cognitive contingency. They are composed of two components. The first is a condition that specifies the circumstances for which the operative unit can be applied and the second is a sequence of actions which steps the user has to take when the operative unit is applied. If the condition is true than the action component of the operative unit is to be executed.

Thus, one of the problems with which the designer of a training programm is faced is how to arrange the components of the task-solving knowledge into such operative units. This problem is difficult because it is the designer's business to ensure both effective learning and effective task accomplishment by the trainee. One prerequisite to effective learning is that the trainee understand the use of what he or she is learning. Thus, it may be necessary to arrange the task-solving knowledge into opperative units in such a way that their condition part represents a particular text editing task. Alternatively it could be argued that the operative units used by experts may be characterized by abstraction from single tasks. That is to say they are based on generalized regularities of the human-computer interaction, that means, on relations between classes of variables and not on relations between single entities. Klix (1971, 1976) and Anderson (1982) have described such processes of generalization in some detail. The problem is that the understanding of such elaborate operative units can be too difficult for novice. To find a good solution for the text-editing system on which this paper is based we have developed three training programmes which have been designed on the basis of three hypothetical types of operative units. In the following we are going to describe their structure.

HYPOTHETICAL TYPES OF OPERATIVE UNITS

The basis for arranging the task-solving knowledge into different operative units is given by the regularities which the designer of the software has utilized. In our investigations we are concerned with only three possible types of operative units.

Generally, the structure of the operative units is formed by slots and by relations between them. We use the "unit notation" proposed by Nilsson (1983) to describe their structure. In this notation the slots are represented by units which have the following general structure:

```
S
f1: S'1
f2: S'2
```

S is a variable symbol or a constant symbol used to represent particular
components of the task-solving knowledge. The symbols f1, f2 stand for
functional expressions (called slotnames) which are used to represent other
knowledge components which are related to this unit. The symbols S'1 and
S'2 are called the slotvalues. The condition part of an operative unit is
marked by ANTE and the action part by CONSE.

The first type of operative unit which we consider shall be named the task-
oriented operative units. This type is based on a classification of tasks
which can be grouped into classes of tasks and into types of tasks. Examples
of different classes of tasks are typing of a text by means of single letters
or of text units stored in the computer. There are different types of tasks
in each class of task, that is, the user has to accomplish different typical
combinations of component tasks. Examples might be making corrections from
a marked-up manuscript in a text file stored in the computer or typing a
new text from a manuscript with well-defined instructions. The produced
text can be printed out in various forms and it can be stored on diskette
etc. The arrangement of the task-solving knowledge into operative units on
the basis of such types of tasks would mean that for each type of task
there is a action programme for solving this task. The general structure of
the task-oriented operative unit can be characterized as follows:

```
    ANTE: AT1        self: (element-of TASK TYPES)
                     taskfeat: TF1

          ST1        self: (element-of SYSTEM STATES)
                     statefeat: SF1

   CONSE: AP1        self: (element-of ACTION PROGRAMMES)
                     sysstate: (element-of-the-set-of (ST2, ST3)
                     action: (element-of-the-set-of (AU1, AU2)
                     statefeat (ST2): SF2
                     statefeat (ST3): SF3
                     key (AU1): K1,K2,K3
                     key (AU2): K4,K5
                     trans (ST1, ST2): AU1
                     trans (ST2, ST3): AU2
```

The condition part of the task-oriented operative unit is denoted by ANTE
anc consists of two units which are related to each other by a conjunction.
The first conjunct (AT1) represents a type of task for which a particular
combination of task features (TF1) is characteristic. The slotname "self"
indicates that the entity described by the unit is an element of a set.
The slotname "taskfeat" represents the features of the type of task while
the symbol TF1 describes the slotvalue. The second conjunct represents a
basic state the computer system is in (ST1). It is characterized by a
specific combination of alpha-numeric features (SF1) displayed on the screen
of the device. If both units of the ANTE are matched by fact units than the
AP1 unit is to be executed. This unit can be regarded as an action programme
to accomplish a given type of task. It consists of a set of system states
(ST2, ST3) and of a set of action units (AU1, AU2). The system states

can be regarded as goals which the user has to achieve. They are represented by functional expressions of the form "statefeat (ST2): SF2". To achieve these goals in a given basic system state the user has to perform particular units of actions which are denoted by the slotname "action". To denote the keystrokes which the user has to perform in executing an action unit we use expressions of the form "key(AU1): K1, K2, K3". The symbols K1,K2,K3 represent the single keys. The sequence of the system states which the user has to achieve is indirectly represented by expressions such as "trans (ST1,ST2):AU1". These indicate that the action unit "AU1" transforms the system state "ST1" into the system state "ST2". All slotnames listed for one unit are related to one another by conjunctions. The number of slots in the action part of the task-oriented operative units depends on the number of states which the user has to attain for accomplishing a particular type of task. In the given example only two states have to be achieved.

In the second type of operative units which we considered in this paper the task-solving knowledge is not arranged in accordance with the types of tasks but rather with the set of transitions between the states or modes of the system which the user has to perform in order to solve a class of task. We call this type of operative units state-oriented operative units. Their structure depends on the number of states which the user has to perform for accomplishing all tasks of a particular class of tasks. If a given system state can be transformed in only two new states then the structure of the state-oriented operative unit can be described as follows:

```
ANTE:    ST1          self: (element-of SYSTEM STATES)
                       statefeat: SF1


CONSE:   T1           self: (element-of SYSTRANS)
                       ausg: ST1
                       folge: (element-of-the-set-of (ST2,ST3)
                       action: (element-of-the-set-of (AU1, AU2))
                       statefeat (ST2): SF2
                       statefeat (ST3): SF3
                       key (AU1): K1,K2,K3
                       key (AU2): K4,K5
                       trans (ST1,ST2): AU1
                       trans (ST1,ST3): AU2
```

The ANTE structure of the state-oriented operative units consists of an element of the set of system states that is relevant to accomplish a class of task (denoted by the constant symbol "ST1" and by the slotname "self"). It is characterized by a specific combination of alpha-numeric features displayed on the screen (represented by the expression "statefeat: SF1"). The CONSE structure represents a transition function that maps the given state into new states. The slotname "folge" denotes the states in which the system can be if elements of the set of action units (denoted by the slotnames "action" and "key (AU1)" and "key(AU2)") are performed by the user of the keyboard. The alpha-numeric features of these new states are represented by functional expressions like "statefeat (ST2): SF2". Expressions like "trans (ST1, ST2): AU1" denote the action unit that transforms the current state (represented by "ausg: ST1) into a possible other state.

The third and last type of operative units which we have developed is based on the state-oriented operative units. It is called state-and-action-oriented operative unit. In this type the action units which the user has to perform for accomplishing the transition functions are classified in accordance with the keys the user has to strike in executing an action unit. The state-and action-oriented operative units are subdivided into two rules (R1,R2):

R 1

ANTE: CF1   self: (element-of CLASSES OF STATEFEATS)
                           feat: F1

CONSE: CAU1, CAU2   self: (subset-of-the-set-of CLASSES OF ACTION
                                  UNITS)
                           poss: F1
                           key' (CAU1):(element-of-the-set-of (CK1,CK2))
                           key' (CAU2):(element-of-the-set-of (CK3,CK2))

Rule R 1 represents the classes of action units possible to be performed by the user in a given class of system states. The ANTE structure of this rule consists of a classified system state (represented by the constant symbol "CF1") which is characterized by a particular combination of features (marked by the function "feat" and by the slotvalue "F1"). The classes of action units as denoted by "CAU1", CAU2" in the CONSE structure are applicable for the user in the given system state (represented by the expression "poss:F1"). Each class of action units is defined by subsets of particular classes of keys. This is represented by expressions of the form "key'(CK1): CK1,CK2".

Rule R 2 has a structure similar to that of the state-oriented operative units. It represents classes of transition functions.

R 2

ANTE: ST1   self: (element-of SYSTEM STATES)
                           statefeat: SF1

         CF1   self: (element-of-the-set-of CLASSES of
                                  STATEFEATS)
                           feat: F1

CONSE: T1'   self: (element-of CLASSES OF SYSTRANS)
                           ausg: ST1
                           folge: (element-of-the-set-of (ST2, ST3))
                           statefeat (ST2): SF2
                           statefeat (ST3): SF3
                           action: (element-of-the-set-of (CAU1,CAU2))
                           key (CK1): K1,K2,K3
                           key (CK2): K4
                           key (CK3): K5, K6, K7
                           trans (ST1, ST2): CAU1
                           trans (ST1, ST3): CAU2

The condition part of the rule R 2 consists of a conjunction of which the first term is a specified state of the system and the second is an element of the classes of features of the system states. The CONSE structure represents possible transitions of this state and the classes of actions to be performed by the user to enter them.

In summarising the three types of operative units which we have described in this paper, here are their main differences:

- Task-oriented operative units relate a particular type of task and a basic state of the system to an action programme which the user will have to execute for accomplishing this task. For different types of tasks, these action programmes are not disjunct, that is, there are slotvalues in different task-orientated units which are identical. Thus, is may be difficult for the trainee to discriminate between the different types of the task-oriented units.

- Both, the state-oriented and the state-and-action-oriented operative units describe only components of action programmes that have to be combined by the trainee in accomplishing a text-editing task. They do not explicitly contain pieces of information concerning the goals the user has to achieve in accomplishing a particular task. Thus, the important question is, wether the trainee can infer this information from the features of the system states.

- The state-and-action-oriented operative units are based on relations between classes of variables and not on relations between single elements. Such generalized relations can simplify the selection of action to be executed for accomplishing a goal. The critical point in this type of operative unit is, that the trainee must be able to understand the processes of abstraction developed by the designer in constructing these operative units.

EXPERIMENTAL PROCEDURES

On the basis of the three types of operative units described above three training programmes have been developed to present the task-solving knowledge needed for accomplishing one particular class of tasks with the aid of the computer text-editing system. Thus, the amount of knowledge to be acquired by the trainees is the same. The only difference is that this knowledge has been subdivided into different types of operative units. The three training programmes have been designed in the same way to make them comparable: All information is presented step by step in a written text which is to be learnt and repeated orally by the trainee until he can reproduce it correctly. Following this, the trainee has to perform exercises using the device in order to practice the components of the operative units he has learnt. For each programme groups of 10 students of psychology who had no previous computer or word-processing experience were instructed in a one-on-one situation, i.e. by individually teaching each novice the text-editing system.

Training has been evaluated by scoring the time of training and by scoring the number of different word-processing tasks in which the subjects has shown their ability to do this immediatly after the training process. Secondly measurements were made of the ability to transfer the acquired task-solving knowledge to another class of tasks. Thirdly, after a period of 14 days the trainees were given the same types of tasks which they had originally done immediately after the training process to test their stability of performance. Of course, the text of these tasks had been changed.

SELECTED RESULTS AND DISCUSSION

Figure 1 shows the duration of training for the three training groups. It can be seen that the training of the task-oriented group (TO-group) has taken the longest time (224 minutes) and that there is no signiticant difference in the duration of training between the state-oriented group (SO-group, 179 minutes) and the state and action-oriented group (SAO-group, 195 minutes).

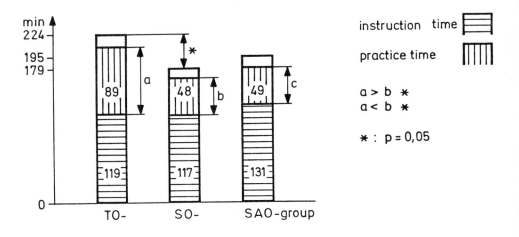

Figure 1
Duration of training
(TO: task-oriented training;
SO: state-oriented training;
SAO:state- and action-oriented training)

Furthermore, there is no significant difference between the three training
groups concerning the time spent in training to instruct the subjects. Thus,
it can be concluded from these results, that the trainees experienced not
less difficulties in acquiring concrete operative units than in learning
generalized operative units. To gain more detailed information on this
question, the subjects had been asked to evaluate the readability of the
three training programmes after training. In this evaluation the model of
Langer et al. (1974) was used. As a result of this it can be shown that
the state and action-oriented training programme had been evaluated by the
subjects as being the best of these. They characterised it as being shorter,
easier to understand and more precise than the other two training programmes.
Of course, it cannot be entirely execluded that there are characteristics in
the methods used for the three training programmes which have affected
these results. We assume however that the structure of the operative units
to be acquired by the trainee has to a large extent influenced the evaluations given by the subjects. It must be tested in further investigations
whether these results can be generalized.

Surprising results have been obtained immediately after training. Since the
task-oriented units can be regarded as action programmes for accomplishing
text-editing tasks using the device the TO-group can be assumed to achieve
the best performance after training. But this is not the case (see Figure 2).

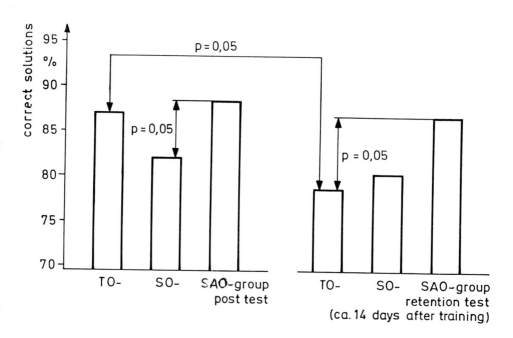

Figure 2

Performance after training

Immediately after training there were no differences between the TO-group and the SAO-group in accomplishing the text-editing tasks. The SO-group achieved the worst results. Figure 2 also shows that about 14 days after training the performance of the TO-group had decreased whereas the performance of the other two groups remained stable. The SAO-group achieves the best results in the retention test. This result supports our assumption that generalized relations existing between classes of variables help the user to make selections necessary to solve the tasks.

The results provide evidence for the fact that the SO-group and the SAO-group can infer the sequence of states of the system which they needed to accomplish the text-editing tasks from the system states. Of course, this result cannot be generalized for all computer systems. It may only be valid for such dialog systems using the menu technique to display the attainable system states. In this paper only a rough description can be given of the results indicating the transferability of the acquired knowledge to another class of tasks. Generally, the subjects of the SAO-group have an advantage over the two other groups in accomplishing the new tasks. But, this result is only valid if the generalized transition functions acquired can also be used to solve the new tasks. There is no evidence for the fact that one of the constructed types of operative units prevents the subjects from acquiring existing regularities in operating the device. The opposite is not true either. To assess this result properly it must be taken into account that there were only a few tasks which the trainees had to perform indepedently. In summarizing these results we may say that, the results obtained give evidence for the fact that user's training can be made more effective if the task-solving knowledge is arranged into operative units in such a way that generalized relations between classes of variables existing in operating the device are taken into account. Seen from this point of view the designer of the system software also creates the basis for effective user's training.

REFERENCES

(1) Anderson, J.R., Acquisition of cognitive skill, Psychological Review 89 (1982) 369-406.

(2) Card, S.K., Moran, T.P. and Newell, A., Computer text editing: An information-processing analysis of a routine cognitive skill. Cognitive Psychology 12 (1980).

(3) Card, S.K., Moran, T.P. and Newell, A., The psychology of human-computer Interaction (Lawrence Erlbaum Associates, Hillsdale, New Jersey, 1983).

(4) Kieras, D. and Polson, P., An approach to the formal analysis of user complexity, Working paper Nr. 2, University of Arizona and University of Colorado (1982).

(5) Klix, F., Information und Verhalten (VEB Deutscher Verlag der Wissenschaften, Berlin, 1971).

(6) Klix, F., Über Grundstrukturen und Funktionsprinzipien kognitiver Prozesse. in: Klix, F. (ed.), Psychologische Beiträge zur Analyse kognitiver Prozesse (VEB Deutscher Verlag der Wissenschaften, Berlin, 1976).

Man-Computer Interaction Research
MACINTER-I
F. Klix and H. Wandke (Editors)
© Elsevier Science Publishers B.V. (North-Holland), 1986

DESIGNING LEARNING PROCESSES FOR WORK ACTIVITIES IN AUTOMATED TECHNOLOGIES

Bärbel Matern

Department of Ergonomics
Technical University of Dresden
Dresden
GDR

Reasons for dealing with the design of learning processes
in automated technologies are seen in changes of human
task in process control. The content of learning processes
depends on the design of technology and the organisational
plan. The developed strategy for the acquisition of activities consists of three parts, namely a teaching strategy
based on the causal-genetic method of Davydov, learning
techniques and learning aids and materials.

REASONS FOR DEALING WITH THE DESIGN OF LEARNING PROCESSES IN AUTOMATED TECHNOLOGIES

The installation of process computers and small control rooms with visual
display units changes human tasks in process control. The increasing level
of automation influences the allocation between man and machine. Control
and stabilization tasks are carried out by computers. This means that
man is only necessary to correct unexpected deviations of parameters and
to change control strategies. So the frequency of activity initiated by
man is dropping. But the complexity and difficulty of the process which
must be controlled do not decrease. That's why the acquisition and maintenance of work-related qualification is a problem. That part of working
time which is devoted to actions amounts to less than half of the total
working time according to our pilot investigations in chemical industry
(see figure 1) and it decreases as the computerization increases. Brasch
(1983) analyzed 56 working shifts and found only 5 situations in which
control actions by man were necessary. These rare demands bring not only
the danger of dequalification of man but also of mental load. Non-sufficient
action competence will always result in uncertainty and in the fear of an
imperfect performance. Mental load is not generated by an objective task
but by anticipate refusal (Hackman 1978). Figure 2 shows the relationship
between saturation and stress and the amount of activity achieved during
the working time.

Learning to perform a new activity requires support and this is an increasing demand in developing software (Dzida 1980, Spinas, Troy and Ulich,
1983, Tauber 1983, Müller 1982, Nullmeier and Rödiger 1983). The intention
of this paper is to describe the aim and the content of learning processes
of operators based on working analysis in several chemical plants. A
conception for its design is generally seen in support of acquiring of
adequate psychological regulation. Support can take place by stimulation

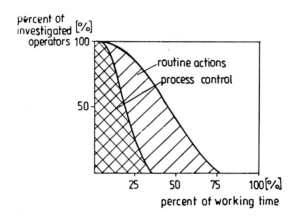

Figure 1

Investigations of the portion of working time of operators in chemical
industry which is filled with activities.

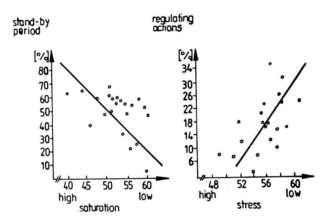

Figure 2

Relations between the amount of active working time and saturation and
stress.

of independent learning, by instruction on signals, rules and strategies and by practice of their use. Experience in design of work-related learning processes will be used in order to derive an appropriate strategy for teaching and learning.

AIM AND CONTENT OF LEARNING PROCESSES IN AUTOMATED INDUSTRY

Man must be able to master network-like dynamic systems with a high complexity which is determined by a large number of partly connected automatic control systems and a large number of sensing devices (1500 to 2500). Disturbances of the process are seldom. They cannot be fully anticipated and they are quite varied. Therefore, man does not possess suitable programmes in his memory but he has to carry out diagnosis and measure-planning in the form of problem solving. Difficulties arise because the amount of information actually available is very often insufficient and must be supplemented by independent research. Differentiated mental representations of the process and the automation equipment are the precondition for information search in memory or with the dialogue equipment.

Many results of research done in the area of industrial psychology show that the efficiency of diagnosis and measures taken depend on the character of mental representations. So operators with high performance are able to think about the process on different abstraction levels and they classify their working situations differently according to specific tasks. Operators with lower performance have only a middle level of abstraction of their mental representations. They are less able to make task-dependent flexible classifications. Acquisition of these mental representations concerning the equipment, the process and its development and the task-depending flexible operating with them is a precondition for independent diagnosis and planning (see figure 3).

The content of the mental representations required is determined by the design of technology and the specific organisational plan of the production process. On principle, the discussion of learning design has to take into consideration that learning of work activities cannot be reduced to the reception of given structures. Effective learning contains cognitive and motivational processes as well and presupposes activities with a motivational potential, with latitude for goal-settings and decisions. The often discussed aim of job design, namely personality promotion, is also important for the design of work-related learning processes because of its effect on learning motivation and generating of learning encouragement (see figure 4).

STRATEGY FOR THE ACQUISITION OF ACTIVITIES

The acquisition of complex activities requires the active analysis of their components and qualities (Leontjew 1979, Dörner 1984). But man has only rarely the possibility for actions because of a high level of automation. Then the simulation of work situations is an appropriate way to create occasions for actions. Free capacity of process computers available can be used for the simulation. Learning design includes several tasks:

1. The development of a teaching strategy
   It is based on simulation models which allow practising the acquisition of complex mental representations, measure-planning, the learning of

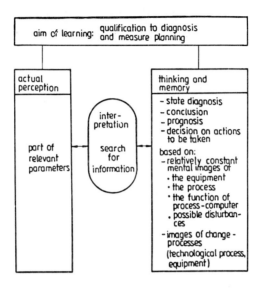

Figure 3

Aim of learning: Providing a man with skills for automated production
processes.

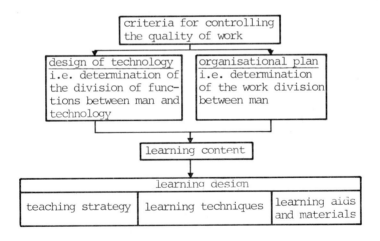

Figure 4
Determination of the learning content and parts of the design of work
task-related learning process.

rules for action generating. The mastering of simulated models is to make possible the transfer to any concrete work situations. The causal-genetic method of the teaching strategy of Dawydow seems to be suitable for this aim.

2. The development of learning techniques
   These can allow the learner to acquire new knowledge, abilities and skills independently. These techniques partly consist of methods for self-analyzing the work situations and the own actions and they ease the transition from a dominante guidance at the beginning of the learning to a supported self-led education.

3. The development of learning aids and materials
   They consist on programmed teaching materials, informative action-related feedback, working activity-related external sources and testing tasks for self-checking. These aids and materials can alternatively be used by the learner.

All three influential factors are suitable to support the general phases of learning processes which are named

- accretion
- structuring and
- tuning

(see Norman 1982). An unequivocal relating of one group of methods to one phase of learning process has been proved impossible. It is their combi-nation that is decisive for designing the learning process. The portion of the components varies during the learning process (see figure 5).

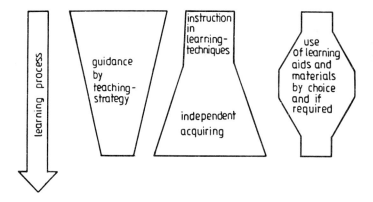

Figure 5

Changing the significance of the components of learning design during the learning process.

The appropriateness of this strategy concerning the acquisition of abilities will be illustrated by means of the results of a pilot study on the design of the working-in activities of a partly automated production process.

EXAMPLE FOR THE APPROPRIATENESS OF THIS STRATEGY

Special aim

The introduction of new technologies usually has a faster pace than the changes in professional training. Consequently there is a gap in the general theoretical knowledge and its selection and structuring for work activities as well as in the development of abilities and skills. This gap caused us to design work activity-related learning. In the trial plant the problem was intensified by small lots contraining frequently changing operations. As a consequence: A great amount of knowledge must be acquired and an insufficient mastering of its technological and activity-related structuring accounts for a lot of mistakes.

Learning aim and learning design

The learning aim was the comprehension of the variant technologies by the learner so that he is able to anticipate and plan the working operations, to be aware of the possible mistakes and to check the results of each processing step. That means the priority of the learning design lies in the support for the action-related structuring of knowledge and the transforming of the knowledge into actions, i. e. in the development of procedural knowledge.

A stone-like design of teaching and learning units was arranged. The parts include:

1. Programmed teaching materials for the technology-related acquirement of knowledge

2. A working procedure-training according to the teaching strategy of Dawydow

3. A system of rules and tasks for the independent knowledge structuring and -checking.

The second part represents the main method for the acquirement of procedural knowledge in our investigation. Figure 6 shows the procedure in a schematic form.

The way to build the initial abstract model starting the learning process was seen in the search for invariants in the technological steps. A rough technological frame which is valid for all productions was the starting point. After this frame has been acquired the further structuring of know-ledge will be supported by the instruction in the organization the activity into actions. Technological variants will be performed by the selection and combination of certain actions. Rules for the selection, the sequence plan-ning and the checking of the results support the acquirement of knowledge.

For practical reasons it was necessary to design the learning units and learning materials in such a way that they could be used as working-in as well as for further education and that their completing was feasable in case of technological alterations.

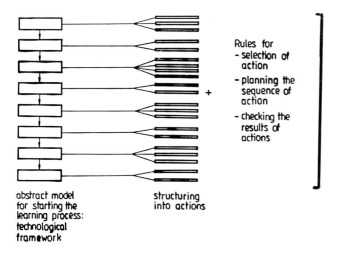

Rules for
- selection of
  action

- planning the
  sequence of
  action

- checking the
  results of
  actions

abstract model
for starting the
learning process:
technological
framework

structuring
into actions

Figure 6

Schematic representation of the teaching strategy for training of work
procedures

METHODS

The appropriateness of the strategy of the learning of activities described
above was tested with apprentices and compared with the traditional working-in. Figure 7 shows the design.

The test-group comprises 9 subjects and the control group 8. The knowledge and the ability of action-related structuring of knowledge and
action planning were checked in the pre- and posttest. The active training
required the application of the learner's knowledge in real working situations. A measurement of the experienced mental load and motivation was
made with the EZ-scale by Nitsch.

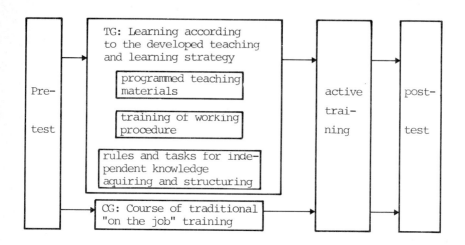

Figure 7

Plan for checking the efficiency of the new design for the learning of work activities.

RESULTS

The developed teaching-learning programme led to a higher amount of action-related knowledge, already visible during a one-week proving time (see figure 8). Differences in the performance between pre- and posttest of the test-group and differences in posttest between test- and control-group are significant. A error recording in test-group 1 during the active training shown 0.55 errors per person. The few errors made are related to incomplete operations and skills but not to logical errors in action-planning. The better performance is not determined by a higher effort. The mental load and motivation of the test group moved in a positive direction (see figure 9).

CONSEQUENCES

The results of this pilot study as well as experiences from the design of learning processes in traditional technologies (Matern, Rühle, Skell 1980, Rühle 1979, Matern 1983, Matern u.a. 1983) confirm our assumption that the combination of teaching units of selected working tasks with learning techniques is a successful way of learning design on principle. Selected working tasks can also be abstract models of the work activity. Learning techniques are aimed at the qualification for independent analyzing of working tasks by the learner so that he learns the own work as a problem analyzer. This procedure can be completed by alternatively usable learning materials and aids. The successful stimulation of learning processes by the causal-genetic method leads to the consequence that by means of process

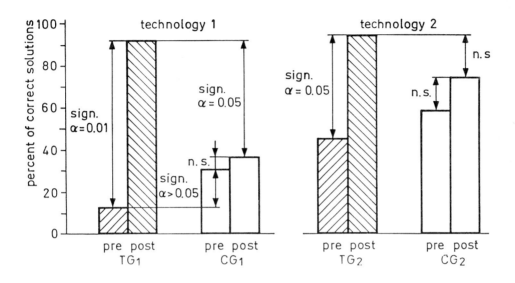

Figure 8

Change in the amount of correct use of work related knowledge in simulated action planning (pre- and post-test) by the developed teaching-learning strategy and the traditional "on the job" training.

invariant supervising-, stabilization-, optimization- and control tasks valid models for starting the learning process can be designed. The guided learning at the beginning and later on only the supported learning can give the preconditions for the independent transfer in order to cope with other not specially trained demands. This is a way to avoid the analyzing effort for the determination of the learning content which is very high at control room activities. Our research is aimed at developing a system of process modules which are suitable as learning units and to test the assumed transfer to analogous demands.

But the transfer of this learning design into industry requires a lot more. A precondition is a changed education of projecting engineers. They should be able to create the conditions for these learning processes, namely

- working contents with permanent learning potences which are determined by the allocation of functions between man and machine

- the granting of the preconditions for learning on simulated simplified process models in hard- and software.

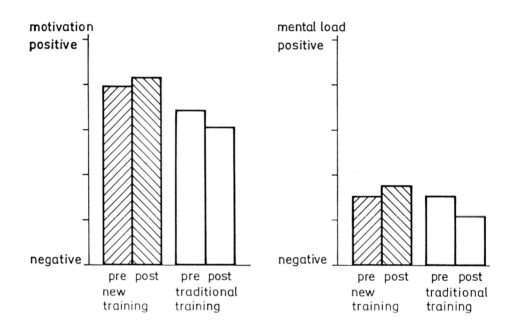

Figure 9

Reported motivation and mental load at the beginning and the end of a one week training.

A consequence would result in giving up the traditional borders between professions in which the operator in a control room has to perform only supervising, stabilization and occasionally process control. An enrichment of these tasks is necessary. Parts of activities which at present belong to other professions should be given to operators, for example

- problem analyzing
- the completing of the software
- the training of new operators.

Changes of the professional structure like these can prevent dequalification caused by limited possibilities for actions.

REFERENCES

(1) Brasch, Chr., Trainingsinhalte für Meßwartenfahrer, Dipl.-Arbeit, TU Dresden (1983).

(2) Dawydow, W.W., Grundlegende Probleme der Entwicklungs- und pädagogischen Psychologie in der gegenwärtigen Etappe des Bildungswesens, Sowjetwissenschaft - Ges.wiss. Beiträge 30 (1977).

(3) Dörner, D., Denken, Problemlösen und Intelligenz. Psychologische Rundschau 35 (1984) 10 - 20.

(4) Dzida, W., Kognitive Ergonomie für Bildschirmarbeitsplätze, Humane Produktion und Humane Arbeit (1980) 18 - 19.

(5) Leontjew, A., Tätigkeit - Bewußtsein - Persönlichkeit (Volk und Welt, Berlin, 1979).

(6) Lompscher, J., Das Aufsteigen vom Abstrakten zum Konkreten als Strategie der Ausbildung der Lerntätigkeit, Päd. Forschung 24 (1983).

(7) Matern, B., Rühle, R., and W. Skell, Training kognitiver Regulationsgrundlagen, Methoden und Ergebnisse, in: W. Hacker und H. Raum (eds.), Optimierung kognitiver Arbeitsanforderungen (Verlag der Wissenschaften, Berlin, 1980).

(8) Matern, B., Lernen in der Arbeit - aber wie?, Techn. Report, Techn. Univ. Dresden (1983).

(9) Matern, B., Thiele, K. und P. Wenzlau, Einarbeitungshilfen für Schaltmonteure - eine psychologisch gestaltete Methode zur Rationalisierung der Einarbeit, Soz. Arbeitswiss. 27 (1983) 227 - 238.

(10) Matern, B., Zur Funktionsteilung zwischen Mensch und Automatisierungseinrichtung, Messen - Steuern - Regeln, 12 (1984).

(11) Müller, G., Entscheidungsunterstützende Endbenutzersysteme (B.G.Teubner, Stuttgart, 1982).

(12) Nitsch, J.R., Die Eigenzustandsskala (EZ-Skala) - ein Verfahren zur hierarchisch-mehrdimensionalen Befindlichkeitsskalierung, in: J.R. Nitsch und I. Udris (eds.), Beanspruchung im Sport (Bad Homburg, 1976).

(13) Norman, D. A., Learning and Memory (Freeman, San Francisco, 1982).

(14) Nullmeier, E. und Rödiger, K.-H., Psychologische Kriterien für die Gestaltung von Dialogschnittstellen, Office Management, Sonderheft Mensch-Maschine-Kommunikation (1983) 32-33.

(15) Rühle, R., Inhalte, Methoden und Effekte der Analyse und Vermittlung operativer Abbilder bei Bedientätigkeiten der Mehrstellenarbeit, Diss. (B) Techn. Univ. Dresden (1979).

(16) Spinas, Ph., Troy, N. und Ulich, E., Leitfaden zur Einführung und Gestaltung von Arbeit mit Bildschirmsystemen (Verl. Industrielle Organisation, Zürich, 1983).

(17) Tauber, M.-J., Benutzen und Lernen, in: Balzert, H. (ed.), Software
     Ergonomie (Teubner, Stuttgart, 1983).

Man-Computer Interaction Research
MACINTER-I
F. Klix and H. Wandke (Editors)
© Elsevier Science Publishers B.V. (North-Holland), 1986

SYSTEM ISSUES IN PROBLEM SOLVING RESEARCH

Joseph M. Scandura

University of Pennsylvania

USA

This article raises the fundemantal issue of whether
various aspects of problem solving should be studied
as isolated phenomena. It is argued that: (a) system
requirements impose constraints on knowledge representation, (b) problem domains may be analyzed systematically and (c) all knowledge, including "extra -
domain" knowledge, is best viewed as relativistic.

INTRODUCTION

The major goal of my introductory remarks is to raise a fundamental issue
in problem solving research - specifically the issue of whether various
aspects of problem solving should be studied as isolated phenomenon - or,
whether problem solving research might better be viewed within an equally
precise, yet broader systems perspective.

The goal of most problem solving research back in the late 1960´s and early
1970´s was to uncover general relationships involving such variables as
aptitude, problem difficulty, meaningfulness, problem solving styles, etc.
By way of contrast, those working in structural learning (e.g., Scandura
1971, 1973, 1977) and various other schools had long come to the conclusion
that any reasonable approach to problem solving research would have to deal
directly with specific knowledge. The various knowledge-specific schools
differ in other respects, of course.

SOME ESSENTIALS OF STRUCTURAL LEARNING THEORIES

As a base for comparison, let me briefly review some essentials of the
Structural Learning Theory (e. g., Scandura, 1971, 1973, 1977) - not only
for the abvious reason that structural learning has been the main focus of
my work - but also because it appears to be unique in its overall concern
for human problem solving as an integrated system.

1. Whereas all cognitive theories recognize a distinction
between domain specific knowledge and control, this distinction in structural learning theories is sharp and fixed. The former refers to knowledge
associated directly or indirectly with given problem domains; the latter,
to such things as a control mechanism governing the use of domain specific
knowledge, processing capacity and speed.

In the case of control, for example, we discovered almost 15 years ago now

that human problem solvers come "wired in" with a goal-switching
mechanism (e. g., Scandura, 1971, 1973, 1974). It need not be taught or
learned because humans behave as if it is already there.

2. A second major problem has been how to deal with individual differences
in problem solving. One alternative has been to employ normative testing
as in most correlational studies. Another, as in computer simulation, has
been to devise theories which directly reflect individual differences.

By way of contrast, structural learning theories make a sharp distinction
between prototypic competence, or idealized knowledge (associated with
given problem domains), and relevant individual knowledge (e. g., Scandura,
1971, 1973, 1977). Prototypic knowledge serves as a standard against which
individual knowledge is measured. Assessed in this manner, individual
knowledge has been shown empirically to provide a highly reliable basis
for predicting problem solving behavior. The behavior of individual problem
solvers on specific problems has been predicted with 80-99 % reliability
depending on the test conditions (e. g., Durnin and Scandura, 1973, Levine,
1966, Scandura, 1967, 1970, 1973, 1977).

3. Given the importance of prototypic knowledge, considerable attention
also has been given to methods for identifying prototypic knowledge.
Originally, task analysis was concerned with behavioral requirements
(e. g., Gagne, 1962). Later, in recognition of major differences between
behavior and the cognitive processes underlying such behavior, the method
of structural analysis evolved over the past 15 years (e. g., Ehrenpreis
and Scandura, 1973, Scandura, 1971 a, 1971 b, Scandura et al., 1974). What
distinguishes structural analysis from other approaches to cognitive task
analysis is the explicit attention given to higher order knowledge or
rules. Higher order rules operate on and/or generate new rules and have
been shown to provide an explicit basis for explaining, predicting and
even controlling problem solving creativity.

COMMONALITIES WITH OTHER MODERN PROBLEM SOLVING THEORIES

Since the late 1960´s and early 1970´s when the Structural Learning
Theory was originally proposed, many aspects of the theory have become
commonplace. Basic ideas have been adopted, implicitly or explicitly, to
some degree in almost all modern problem solving theories.

1. Not only is it generally agreed today that domain specific knowledge
is the most important factor in problem solving behavior, but the term
"rule" itself has been widely adopted, albeit often in modified form.

2. Although details differ, the goal-switching mechanism also is coming
into acceptance. In Artificial Intelligence, for example, it has become
increasingly common to combine both data and goal driven inferencing as
is done in goal-switching.

3. A growing number of investigators (e. g., Seigler, 1976, Holzman et al.,
1976) also have adopted prototypes as a means of assessing individual
capabilities.

4. There is broad consensus on the need for ways to efficiently conduct
knowledge analysis. In education, the process has been quasi-systematized

and goes under the label of task analysis. In artificial intelligence, the term "knowledge engineer" has been coined to refer to cognitive scientists skilled in the analysis of problem domains.

Rather than dwell on similarities, however, or specific variations, I wish to emphasize just a few fundamental issues on which there is little agreement.

TYPE OF REPRESENTATION

Almost everyone agrees on the need for precise representation of knowledge. Nonetheless, many believe that the type of representation, whether declarative, procedural, production system, or whatever, is primarily a matter of taste and preference. Those who deify mathematical formalism, for example, frequently give primary credence to Post-type production systems (productions are often called "rules"). Others prefer relational networks; and still others, sets or procedures.

In one important sense, the above kinds of representations are all alike. Human problem solving behavior can equally well be represented in any of these forms.

Recall, however, that different programming languages are often preferred in different applications. In a similar manner, human problem solving imposes severe constraints on how knowledge might best be represented. For example: (a) The representation chosen certainly should allow for assessing individual knowledge: One would want a representation which provides a convenient basis for representing individual differences as well as prototypic knowledge. (b) Similarly, it should be possible to represent knowledge at arbitrary levels of detail (the desired level of prediction or explanation of problem solving behavior may vary greatly). (c) And it should provide naturally for the acquisition of knowledge. (d) Finally, a useful form of representation should facilitate the process of representation itself. So much the better if knowledge representations underlying given problem domains can be derived systematically.

Neither space nor time allow complete analysis of the various major forms of representation with respect to all relevant criteria. Let me just illustrate by listing some limitations associated with the widely used production systems form of representation.

First, even individuals who have adopted the production system formalism for most of their work use a quite different formalism, based on simple decision trees, in assessing behavior potential (e. g., Seigler, 1976, Klahr, 1978). Decision trees ware just a specific case of structural learning rules.

Second, productions are by definition the basic elements in any production system (used to represent knowledge). To represent the knowledge in more datail requires replacing individual productions with production systems - thus quickly yielding production systems whose elements are production systems whose .... This might be okay if production systems provided a convenient basis for representing individual knowledge - but they do not.

Third, for many years, production systems were used almost exclusively to represent performance during problem solving. Little attention was given

to knowledge acquisition, motivation, or any number of related psychological processes. Indeed, learning was thought to be extremely complex
and difficult to study and for the most part was avoided (e. g., Newell
and Simon, 1972). Even today, learning studies typically involve the
acquisition of individual production rather than production systems per se
(e. g., Waterman, 1974). Since nontrivial problem solving behavior is
explained in terms of production systems, the process of learning viewed
from the production systems perspective must necessarily deal with production systems per se and not just individual productions. Consequently,
explanations of learning have been both less general and far more complex
than they need to be.

Fourth, systematic methods (e. g., Scandura et al., 1974, Scandura, 1982,
1984 a, 1984 b) also see "structural analysis" below) already exist for
identifying the prototypic rules underlying given problem domains. To
date, I am unaware of any conclusive research in this direction with
regard to production systems. This is not to say that it might not be
possible to do so - especially since adapting an existing approach is
almost always easier than creating one in the first place. The basic
question will be how such a method will compare with structural analysis
as regards such things as cohesiveness, parsimony and ease of use.

In structural learning theories, all knowledge is represented in terms of
rules. Like productions, rules have a domain and an operation. They are
unlike productions, however, in two important ways:

(1) Neither rule domains (structures) nor the operations (procedures) need
be atomistic. In general, both are themselves composed of atomic elements -
hierarchically arranged conditions or equivalence classes in the case of
domains, and procedures in the case of operations. (Note: For reasons
beyond the scope of this discussion, rule procedures may not be recursive,
e. g., see Scandura (1981).

It also is worth noting that there is a duality between rule domains and
procedures. The process of rule automatization gradually replaces procedural complexity with structural complexity (e. g., Scandura, 1981).

(2) Rules also include ranges, or structured sets of conditions corresponding to anticipated rule outputs.

From a behavioral point of view, rules correspond as naturally to production systems as they do to individual productions. Production systems,
however, consist of simple lists of productions which both generate
outputs and control which production is tested next. Rule procedures, on
the other hand, reflect the branching structure directly. This enhanced
structure of rule domains and procedures is what provides the natural
basis for assessing and representing individual knowledge. (For further
discussion, see Scandure, 1977).

More important, a long series of studies starting back in the 1960´s has
shown that the rule representation has direct behavioral implications
(e. g., Scandura, 1968, 1969, 1970). If a rule is prototypic of the way
(some) individuals solve given classes of problems, then the rule structure provides a natural way to represent individual knowledge of these
individuals. For example, consider the subtraction procedure in figure 1.

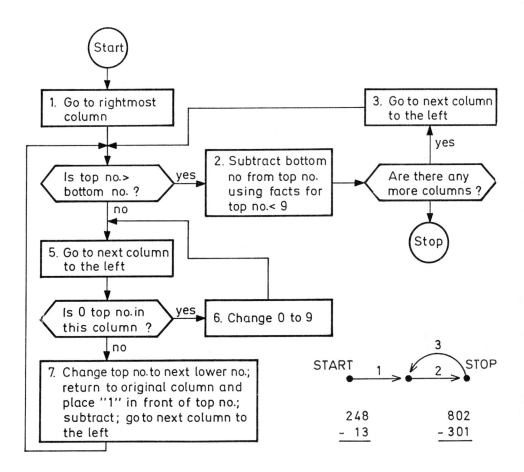

Figure 1
Subtraction Rule (algorithm) and sample subtraction problems

The obvious thought in this regard is that individual knowledge might be represented by including or not including various components of the proto- type. But there is more to it than that. Studies have demonstrated a very direct relationship between individual problem solving behaviour and the representation of individual knowledge. In particular, it is possible to operationally define individual knowledge in terms of highly efficient test procedures which derive directly from the rule representation (e. g., Scandura, 1977). There is, of course, a formal equivalent with respect to production systems but whatever that equivalent is, it certainly is not intuitive. Undoubtedly, the strongest argument in favor of the rule re- presentation (as mentioned earlier) is that rules have been favored even by production system enthusiasts in the case of individual knowledge re- presentation.

Level of representation also is important in problem solving research (e. g., Scandura, 1977). Specifically, prototypes used to asses individual knowledge must be compatible both with (a) the sophistication of the target population and (b) the degree of behavioral detail one wants to account for. Put differently, rules must be represented in sufficient detail that the rule components are behaviorally atomic both with respect to minimal capabilities of problem solvers whose behavior is to be explained or predicted and the precision with which that behavior is to be predicted.

Rules, including domains, procedures and ranges, can naturally be repre- sented at arbitrary levels of refinement by simply replacing atomic com- ponents with more detailed rules. More important, whatever the level of representation, rules naturally lend themselves to individual knowledge assessment.

Allowing arbitrary refinement in the case of production systems would only make matters worse in this regard. Even simple production systems do not appear to lend themselves well to individual knowledge representation. Hierarchies of production systems would be even less natural.

To summarize with respect to knowledge representation: The basic issue is whether general system considerations (e. g., the ability to handle individual differences, learning, etc.) should be primary as in structural learning theories, or whether personal preference should predominate.

ANALYSIS OF PROBLEM DOMAINS

A second major issue (mentioned above) is how to identify the competence associated with given problem domains. It has become clear that the identification of content-specific knowledge requires input from a domain expert. Many also believe that the service of so-called "knowledge engi- neers" is crucial (Kinnucan, 1984). Their job is to help domain experts externalize what they know. In this view, the process of knowledge re- presentation is largely an intuitive process.

In contrast, prototypic knowledge in structural learning theories may be identified via Structural Analysis (e. g., Ehrenpreis and Scandura, 1974, Scandura et al., 1974, Scandura 1977, 1982, 1983, 1984). Structural Analysis is a systematic (largely algorithmic) process which makes it possible for domain experts to represent underlying knowledge without the services of a knowledge engineer. Put differently, Structural Analysis is a systematic and formalized representation of what knowledge engineers do.

The basic issue, of course, is whether Structurel Analysis, or any other method of analysis for that matter will ever be sufficiently robust - whether there are things that will always remain the province of the knowledge engineer.

"EXTRA DOMAIN" KNOWLEDGE AND UNIVERSALS

Let me turn finally to the issue of "extra domain" knowledge - to influences on problem solving behavior that apparently are external to content specific knowledge. Extra domain knowledge may include logical inference, meaning, induction, problem interpretation, problem solving strategies, conceptual foundations, tacit knowledge or whatever.

How to handle this extra domain knowledge? Some as in the case of expert systems take the position that such things as logical inferencing and induction are best conceptualized in terms of system (or human) universals - in that context, they are often labeled "inference engines". In problem solving,more generally speaking, these universals are assumed to work in conjunction with domain specific knowledge. Others have made similiar universal assumptions regarding such things as generalized "learning to learn" (e. g., Mc Keachie, 1984), study skills and descriptions of knowledge versus knowledge itself (e. g., Anderson, 1982).

In the Structural Learning Theory, learning strategies, meaning, and induction, as well as all other higher-order capabilities, are treated just as other rules of knowledge (e. g., Scandura, 1973). That is, they are prototypes against which individual knowledge is measured. The only difference in the case of higher-order rules is that they operate on and/or generate lower-order (content-specific) rules. Obviously, viewing higher-order rules as modifiable prototypes gives more flexibility and precision in behavioral prediction. One does not have to assume, for example, that "A or B" and "not A" will ALWAYS lead one to conclude "B" - or that being able to ride a bicycle NECESSARILY means that the person can describe how to do so. Such universals may provide useful bases for Artificial Intelligence or as prototypes. But, they surely are not universally available to humans in all situations.

In structural learning theories only the "goal-switching" control mechanism, along with processing capacity and speed parameters, are considered universal. This division of universals and specific knowledge, has been shown to provide a very natural and modular basis for explaining problem solving behavior, as well as learning, motivation, meaning, memory, automatization and the like (e. g., Scandura 1971, 1973, 1977, 1981).

To summarize, problem solving behavior may be explained in terms of domain specific knowledge supplemented with universal extra-domain knowledge. Or, such (higher-order) knowledge may be considered of the same genre as other knowledge - as prototypes against which individual knowledge is measured. In the latter case, human problem solving (as well as learning, etc.) is explained in terms of a simple, very basic universal control mechanism together wich lower and higher order rules associated with (i. e., derivable from) the problem domain.

Each of these views has its advantages and disadvantages. Representing extra –domain knowledge in terms of distinctive,universal inference-engines, for example, may appear to simplify the process of building artificial intelligence systems. Such universals as general heuristics, study skills, and the like also may serve a useful purpose in guiding classroom learning and/or instruction where attention to individual variation is not feasible. However, such systems lack the flexibility needed to deal effectively with individual variation (e. g., in inferencing). Moreover, it is far from clear that representing such universals differently from specific knowledge rules is desirable. At the vary least parsimony would seem to suggest otherwise.

There is another facet of the "extra-domain" issue which is not so transparent since it has deeper philosophical roots. Some cognitive psychologists, including some of the contributors to this issue, take the position, explicitly or implicitly, that they are seeking the real truth, that one day we will actually know how people really solve problems. It is just a matter of pinning down the domain specific knowledge and identifying all the extra-domain knowledge insolved.

Alternatively, proponents of this view believe no matter how thoroughly a problem domain is analyzed, that problem solving is always subject to outside, or extra –domain, pertubations which must be identified.

The opposite view is that explanation is relative and not absolute. All knowledge is content (i. e., domain) specific, lower and higher-order knowledge alike. The problem domain itself, provides a sufficient basis for identifying all of the relevant knowledge. Using extra-domain knowledge from other sources is at best a convenience which could be eliminated by more complete analysis. With Structural Analysis, for example, all higher, as well as lower, order rules are identified by direct or indirect reference to the given problem domain. The issue of "extra- (or outside the) domain" knowledge never comes up.

Furthermore,it can be shown that beyond a certain point (e. g., Scandura, 1977), further analysis is futile, whether internal or external. Differential predictions resulting from such (further) analysis can not be distinguished within the given problem solving domain.

Consider, for example, a simple problem domain consisting of column subtraction problems in arithmetic. In this case, a simple column subtraction rule would provide a fully-adequate account of performance on that problem domain. An analysis which was extended to include the meaning of the process, say, or means for deriving the subtraction rule, would add nothing in so far as the original problem domain is concerned.

Of course, if the problem domain were enlarged to include manipulations of concrete objects, involving "take-away" say, then the extra-domain knowledge could be crucial. The important point to remember is that the behaviorally relevant parts of such extra-domain knowledge can be derived from the (enlarged) domain itself. Whatever knowledge cannot be so derived will be behaviorally INDISTINGUISHABLE within the problem domain.

Another important characteristic of the relativistic view is that rule sets associated with proviously analyzed problem domains always provide a useful starting point for analyzing more encompassing domains (e. g.

Scandura, 1977, Chapter 2). Progress is strictly cummulative as might by desired in any science.

I could say more about meaning, meta-cognition and understanding but space does not allow. (For this purpose, I would refer you to Scandura, 1970, 1973, 1977, 1980, 1981). The central point I would make here is that meaning and meta-cognition, for instance, are relative notions. Thus, for example, various kinds of manipulations of concrete objects might be viewed as rules in their own right - or, they might be viewed as meanings for other rules, say a rule for performing column subtraction. Thus, a concrete object rule may actually BE meaning in the sense that it is related to another (in this case more syntactic) rule.

What is important in strucural learning theories is not only whether something is meaningful, but the nature of the relationship between what constitutes the (syntactic) entity and what constitutes the meaning. That raltionship might vary from a simple degenerate higher-order rule, or association, relating the two to a highly general and powerful higher-order rule which operates on any number of meanings and generates their syntactic counterparts. In a similiar vein, meta-cognitive processes refer to higher-order rules representing relationships between rule knowledge and descriptions of that knowledge.

CONCLUSIONS

In conclusion, let me briefly summarize the issues.

(1) Do system requirements - such things as provison for assessing in individual knowledge, learning, level of representation and identifiablility of knowledge - properly impose constraints on the form in which knowledge is represented? I have suggested that they do.

(2) Is the process of knowledge analysis necessarily a human endeavor, or can the process be largely automated as I have proposed? We currently have underway a computer implementation of Structural Analysis which should soon provide a definitive answer to this question.

(3) What is the role of "extra-domain" knowledge? Is knowledge best viewed as relativistic - that is, is all relevant knowledge derivable from given problem domains? Or, is some of the requisite knowledge (i. e., extra-domain knowledge) best viewed as universal, even if tied to particular phenomena such as learning, inference, meaning, understanding, induction, or interpretation (cf. Anderson 1982, compilation).

Finally, let me call your attention to a common thread underlying each of these issues, and others. Should various aspects of problem solving be studied as isolated phenomena, connected largely by human intuition? Or, is it possible, today, to view problem solving, say complex human behavior generally, as a rigorously defined, yet unified theoretical system? My own views on the subject must be clear.

REFERENCES

(1) Anderson, J.R., Acquisition of cognitive skill. Psychological Review. 89 (1982) 369 - 406.

(2) Durnin, J.H. and Scandura, J.M., An algorithmic approach to assessing behavior potential: Comparison with item forms and hierarchical analysis. Journal of Educational Psychology 65 (1973) 262 - 272.

(3) Ehrenpreis, W. and Scandura, J.M., Algorithmic approach to curriculum construction: A field test. Journal of Educational Psychology 66 (1974) 491 - 498.

(4) Gagne, R.M., The acquisition of knowledge. Psychological Review 59 (1962) 355 - 365.

(5) Holzman, T.G., Glaser, R. and Pellegrino, J.W., Process training derived from a computer simulation theory. Memory and Cognition 4 (1976) 349 - 356.

(6) Kinnucan, J., Computers that think like experts. New York: High Technology, 1984, 36 - 37.

(7) Klahr, D., Information processing models of cognitive development, in: J. M. Scandura and C.J. Brainerd (eds.), Structural/Process Models of Complex Human Behavior, Sijthoff & Noordhoff, Alphen aan den Rijn, The Netherland, 1978.

(8) Levine, M., Hypothesis behavior by humans during discrimination learning, Journal of Experimental Psychology 71 (1966) 331 - 338.

(9) Mc Keachie, W., Learning how to learn. Proceedings XXIII International Congress of Psychology, 1984.

(10) Newell, A. and Simon, H.A., Human Problem Solving. Prentice-Hall, Englewood Cliffs, N.J. 1972.

(11) Scandura, J.M., The basic unit in meaningful learning - association or principle? The Proceedings, APA, 1967. (Also in The School Review 75 (1967) 329 - 341.

(12) Scandura, J.M., New directions for theory and research on rule learning: I. A set-function language. Acta Psychologica 28 (1968) 301 - 321.

(13) Scandura, J.M., New directions for theory and research on rule learning: II. Empirical research. Acta Psychologica 29 (1969) 101 - 133.

(14) Scandura, J.M., The role of rules in behavior: Toward on operational definition of what (rule) is learned. Psychological Rewiev 77 (1970) 515 - 533.

(15) Scandura, J.M., Deterministic theorizing in structural learning: Three levels of empiricism. Journal of Structural Learning 3 (1971) 21 - 53.

(16) Scandura, J.M., Structural learning I: Theory and research. Gordon & Breach Science Publishers, London, New York 1973.

(17) Scandura, J.M., The role of higher-order rules in behavior. Journal of Experimental Psychology, 1974.

(18) Scandura, J.M., (with the collaboration of others), Problem solving: A structural/process approach with instructional implications Academic Press, New York, 1977.

(19) Scandura, J.M., Discussion of selected issues relevant to structural learning, in: J.M. Scandura and C.J. Brainerd (eds.), Structural/ process theories of complex human behavior. Sijthoff, Leyden, The Netherlands, 1978.

(20) Scandura, J.M., Theoretical foundations of instruction: A systems alternative to cognitive psychology, Journal of Structural Learning, 6 (1980), 347 - 394.

(21) Scandura, J.M., Problem solving in schools and beyond: Transitions from the naive to the neophyte to the master, Educational Psychologist, 16 (1981) 139 - 150.

(22) Scandura, J.M., Structural (cognitive task) analysis: A Method for Analyzing Content. Part 1: Background and Empirical Research, Journal of Structural Learning 7 (1982) 101 - 114.

(23) Scandura, J.M., Structural analysis. Part II: toward precision, objectivity and systematization, Journal of Structural Learning, 8 (1984) 1 - 28.

(24) Scandura, J.M., Structural analysis. Part III: validity and reliability, Journal of Structural Learning 8 (1984) 173 - 193.

(25) Scandura, J.M., Durning, J.H. and Wulfeck, W.H., Higher-order rule characterization of heuristics for compass and straight-edge constructions in geometry, Artificial Intelligence 5 (1974) 149 - 183.

(26) Seigler, R.S., Three aspects of cognitive development, Cognitive Psychology 8 (1976) 481 - 520.

(27) Waterman, D.A., Adaptive production systems, CIP Working Paper 285, Dept. of Psychology, Carnegie-Mellon Univ. (1974).

Man-Computer Interaction Research
MACINTER-I
F. Klix and H. Wandke (Editors)
© Elsevier Science Publishers B.V. (North-Holland), 1986

UNDERSTANDING LEARNING PROBLEMS IN COMPUTER AIDED TASKS

Yvonne Waern

Department of Psychology
University of Stockholm
Sweden

This paper will analyse three different contributions to
learning problems in computer aided tasks. The first problem concerns the difference between the task as conceived
in the computer system and the task as conceived by a person who is skilled in the task. The second problem concerns
the user's model of the system and the system's model of the
user. These models lie behind the communication between user
and system. I will give some examples from different investigations I have performed on each of these problems.

INTRODUCTION

As the number of people who encounter new computer system is increasing,
the need for computer systems which are easy to learn increases. Also,
as the number of computer systems for different tasks increases, the need
for easy transfer between different computer systems increases as well. To
ease learning and transfer of prior knowledge, we need to consider what
may cause difficulties in the new systems people encounter. The aim of the
present paper is to analyze the situation where people meet new computer
systems. By a careful analysis, I hope that many - if not all - difficulties in learning a new computer system may be predicted, and hereby at
least some of them may be avoided.

Let me start by an overview over the situation, where a person meets a
new computer system to perform a task, and where the task is well-known
to the person. Such situations arise for example when secretaries encounter
word-processing systems, when engineers encounter computer aided design
systems or when business managers encounter decision making systems. This
situation is depicted in Figure 1. Let me explain this figure below.

Firstly, the person who performs the task has a particular conception of
the task. This conception is depicted in the rectangle, called "user's
task model" to the left in the figure. The user's task model may differ
from the model of the task which is used by the system designer. The
reasons for the difference may be several: The computerization may put
certain restrictions on the task (such as for instance that variables
should be estimated numerically rather than intuitively or that only a
certain number of categories is allowed). The computerization may also
imply new possibilities, whereby the task may be more efficiently performed
by being conceived in a different way than when it was performed manually.
There is also the possibility that the task changes through computerization,
without the user noticing this change.

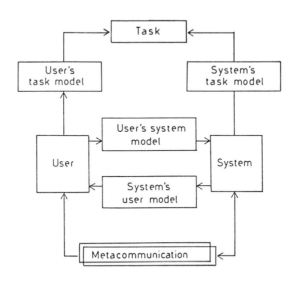

Figure 1

The interaction between user, system and task.

Secondly, the person has to communicate with the system about the task. This communication involves both input from the person to the system and output from the system to the person. In order to be able to communicate with the system, the person needs a model of the system. This model should contain concepts which concern the semantic and syntactical characteristics of the interaction language (whether it be commands or menus) as well as the details of the interactions (such as how many commands may be given in sequence and how long response times to expect from the system). Likewise, the system designer has to have some model of the user in order to be able to make a system communicate with him. This model has to incorporate ideas about for instance how to signal that an action has been performed, and what command words (or menu options) to use.

Finally, the system designer (or the system instructor or system advisor) has to communicate with the system user about the communication between system and user. This may be called metacommunication, and covers all user documentation: manuals, help and error messages. Metacommunication may be carried through outside of the system. Printed manuals and verbal instructions are examples of such external metacommunication. It may also be carried out within the system. On-line help- and error messages are examples of such internal metacommunication. Computer assisted learning is another example, when the learning concerns the system itself.

In the following I will analyze how these three different areas may evoke difficulties for a beginning user, and give some examples of difficulties from each area.

THE TASK MODEL

Whereas the task is concerned, a careful task analysis of the old task as well as of the system's requirements and additional offerings is needed. Much discontent about existing computer systems can be referred to short-comings in this analysis. For instance, Swedish researchers have reported extended dissatisfaction with a computer system for helping health insurance officers to calculate the benefit which different clients are entitled to according to Swedish regulations. Two main sources of dis-satisfaction have appeared. The first is related to the fact that the system only contains certain categories, and that some cases may be very diffi-cult to refer to a particular category. For instance, it was impossible to place in the system the case of a woman, who got sick after having lost her child a week after its birth. The second is related to the fact that the calculations performed by the system are not possible to inspect. This lack of transparency makes the insurance workers feel that they loose touch with their own knowledge, since they cannot practice it any longer (Göranzon, 1982). Of course, it can be said that this system is old (is was installed in the early seventies), and that "user friendliness" was not heeded at that time. It should now be possible to learn by this mis-take and recommend that information systems should correspond both to the prospective users' information needs and allow them to keep or expand their own knowledge about the information covered.

It is however well known that several existing commercial systems, such as word-processing systems or computer aided design systems, have not been developed in actual collaboration with their prospective users. Of course, it may be difficult to get information from a persons who will be involved in using the system. A skilled person cannot always introspect about the tasks to be performed by such systems. Even though some general traits of the task may be consciously understood and possible to communicate, others belong to the area of "automated" habits, and may be difficult both to talk about and to change. Also, the system itself will change the situation, and the coming situation may not be possible to predict either by the system designer or by the prospective user.

I will here give some examples from our laboratory of small but very annoying differences between the conception of the task by a person and a system.

The first task is a subtask of a word-processing task. In order to change a word which has been written in a word-processing system, the user has to move a cursor to the word in question. The particular task to be discussed here concerns a movement of the cursor along the line of text to the right. According to a skilled typist's conception of a type-writer, this task is automatically performed by pressing the space bar. By pressing the space bar on a type-writer, either the paper is moved to the left or the type-head is moved to the right. In both cases, a place to the right of the current place is accessed for typing. In the system studied, the adequate method to move the cursor to the right was to press a key with a right-headed arrow. A press of the space bar resulted in blanks, which were

written on the existing text, thus deleting it. In an investigation performed by Baladi (1983) and analyzed in Waern (in press) three subjects
were studied when learning a particular word processing system. The task
to move the cursor occured as a subtask in several different text correction
tasks. One subject was a skilled typist, the two others were not used to
typing. It was found that the skilled typist primarily had difficulties
with moving the cursor to the right. All other movements of the cursor
(which were as unfamiliar) were performed correctly. After four hour training with the system, the skilled typist still started all attempts to
move the cursor rightwards by pressing the space bar. When the subject
detected that existing letters had been deleted, she recognized her error
and easily found the correct way to perform the cursor movement. However,
next time in a similar situation, she used the space bar again, probably
automatically. The lesson from this observation is that it may take much
more time and effort to inhibit an automated habit than to acquire a new
conscious procedure.
The next example concerns a study of drafting. In this study, the difficulties to perform a simple subtask of drafting, i.e. drawing a straight
horizontal or vertical line was analyzed. The procedures necessary to
perform this task on a drafting board and with the help of a particular
computerized drafting system were compared. It was predicted, that certain
kinds of difficulties would arise, due to the difference in the required
procedures (cf. Waern, reference note). I will here give one example of
an analysis of one ingredient in the task. A crucial difference between
drawing lines on the drafting board and in the computerized system concerned how the endpoints of a line were defined. On the drafting board,
endpoints are defined before drawing the line, by makind dots or utilizing
endpoints of existing lines. In the computerized system, the starting point
was defined by one method, whereas the endpoint was defined by another
method, which created a line at the same time. This conception of the task
is of course rather different from the drafting board conception. In a study of the performance of three persons, who all were skilled computer users,
but did not know the particular system, the following was found. Most difficulties could be predicted from a careful analysis of the task. Twenty
difficulties (out of 65) in drawing lines were due to the mentioned differences in the conception of the task. The largest source of difficulties
(which also was predicted) will be presented below, under the heading of
user-system communication.

To conclude, it may pay much in terms of the possibility to predict learning difficulties to analyze fortcoming users' prior knowledge of the
task that the computer is meant to support. I have presented some further
analyses of the relationships between users' prior task knowledge and
system's task model in Waern (reference note and in press).

USER-SYSTEM COMMUNICATION

This topic has been most extensively studied of all topics in human-computer
interaction. Comparisons have been made between human-human communication
and human-computer communication, to the effect that much seems to be
missing in human-computer communication. Not only is the non-verbal aspect
of communication missing, or most of the natural language possibilities
but also the shared world of experience and common world knowledge which
makes human-human communication most often so efficient and still effort-
less. We must at the moment accept that the language facilities of computer are very restricted. It may even be asked whether the attempts to

design systems with "natural language" capabilities are worthwhile (Fitter, 1979, Shneiderman, 1980).

Given that communication with computers may yet for a long time to come have to be "unnatural", it may be asked, what characteristics of an artificial language that cause difficulties and what characteristics that make such a language easy to learn. There seem to be three principles which are worthwhile to consider: 1. The words of the language should have clearcut and if possible "natural" relations to the "real world" of task related actions (such as delete, type, print, etc.). 2. The words of the language should be easy to discriminate (for novices in LISP, for instance, the difference between "car" and "cdr" just concerns one letter, even though their different functions may be quite clear.). 3. The syntax as well as the semantics of the language should be based upon some consistent rules. It has for instance been found that it is easier for novices to learn a command language that is internally consistent than a command language which is consistent with "natural language" habits (Barnard, Hammond, Morton, Long & Clark, 1981). It has also been shown that if a command language can be described by a consistent rule, it is easier to learn (Green & Payne, 1983).

It may not always be easy for the user to detect which rules are applicable to the computer situation. Let me illustrate this with one example for a case study with a pilot system for CAD (cf. Waern, in press). In this system it was possible to draw straight lines in two different ways: 1. by pointing to two points and ask the system to draw a straight line between these. 2. by pointing to an existing line and ask the system to draw a line parallell (or in a straight angle) to that line (on a certain distance and with a certain length). The first method was always applicable. The second method was applicable only when the user already had drawn a straight line. In the case study performed, it was found that the subject studied attempted in vain to draw a straight line by using the second method. The problem was that he tried to use the visible straight line above the menu as point of departure for this method. However, this line was not existing in the system as a part of the figure. The method was thus not applicable. The inconcistency lay in the fact that the method was applicable in some situations but not in others.

Another kind of problem which resides in human-computer communication concerns the way in which it is possible to express that we are finished with a message or ready to receive another message. In communication between humans a delicate system of eye-movements, voice signals or other nonverbal means are used as "turn-taking" signals. Since such nonverbal signals are not possible in human-computer communication, other turn-taking conventions have to be developed. A common convention to have the user signal when he is ready is to have him press the "return" key. (In systems, where this is sometimes but not always required, problems with inconsistency will occur.) There has been no development of corresponding conventions to have the system signal when it is ready to accept a new command or when it is working with a given command. Therefore, researchers have to some extent been concerned with the effect of systems' response times on users' performance and satisfaction with systems. However, it may well be the case that the response time per se is no problem, as long as the user understands the turn-taking signals.

Let me give an example of difficulties derived from non-existing turn-
taking signals. In this study from our laboratory (also mentioned above,
under the heading of "task model"), three experienced system programmers
had to perform some computer aided drafting task in a pilot system, which
worked with a time-shared computer. In this system, response times could
vary a lot, depending upon the current load on the system. The task was
to be performed by working with a pen on a tablet. This required a particular "working style": pointing with the pen against the tablet in a
close to staight-angular fashion when actually giving commands, and
lightly touching the tablet when moving the cursor around. Even though the
subjects were rather used to the pen- and tablet-input, they often missed
the pen-pointing necessary to get a command through to the system. This
caused them to repeat their commands every time the system hesitated to
perform the action ordered by the command. However, the reason for the
hesitation could be that the system was occupied with something else. In
that case, the system stored both commands and performed the corresponding
actions one after the other. Therefore, double or unwanted lines were
drawn in those cases. These were often not noticed at once by the user,
and caused considerable trouble when they were detected and had to be
erased after other lines had been drawn. It was found that the difficulty
to interpret system delay was the strongest single source of difficulties.
responsible for about 43 % of all difficulties encountered (Waern, reference note).

Here we encounter a problem which may be very difficult to solve: how can
a system ever be able to signal when it has not received a command? A
possible solution is to give the user the possibility to get information
about the status of the system. If the user can see, whether the system
is waiting for input or waiting to be able to carry through an instruction,
some uncertainties regarding the meaning of system delay may be resolved.
This solution requires that the user observes the problem and considers
it worthwhile to prevent it rather than correct eventual mistakes afterwards.

METACOMMUNICATION

Let me finally analyze the problem of metacommunication. This problem
relates to both of the previously covered topics: the model of the task
and the model of the system. The user must be able to get information both
about the task as conceived by the system and about the commands to be
used and feedbacks to be received from the system.

Since computer systems usually are very complex, the main problems concern
selection and presentation of relevant information. Thus we may say that
the problems concern where to get which information when.

Let me start by considering some questions referring to manuals. We may
choose between external manuals, which are always available, or internal
manuals, which are available upon request i.e. on-line manuals. It may be
predicted that ordinary people's book- and journal-reading habits may
make it difficult for them to capitalize on an on-line manual. In a study
from our laboratory it was found that people refrained from looking up
information on-line, whereas they did not hesitate to look up the same
information if it was available on paper (Askwall, in press).

Manuals are the place where information about the functioning of a system may be found as well as information about the actual procedures to handle the system. It can now be asked how this information should best be presented. As to the functioning of the systems, we know that people's models of systems are of great importance for their learning of the system (see above as well as Norman, 1983 and Mayer, 1976). It is therefore important that eventual differences between system's and user's model of the task are pointed out in the manual.

Let me give one example from our laboratory. The example concerns how a person and a computer system conceive a continous text. For an ordinary book or journal reader, a text is continous. If you want to read an article in full you do not care, whether or not it is presented on a single or on several pages. You just turn the page to read the continuation. Now consider the case where you have to proof-read a text. You know for instance that a particular word may have been spelt incorrectly. You scan the text for that word and just continue,when you encounter a new page. In a computer system studied, the system differentiated between "screen" and "rest of the text". It also differentiated between "first word" and "more words". In the manual, these different concepts were not discussed explicitly. Instead, they could be derived from the commands to perform the search task. The commands to be used were presented as follows:

```
s  xxx .  Search for word  xxx  on screen.
n  xxx .  Search for next word  xxx  on screen.
t  xxx .  Search for word  xxx  in rest of the text.
nt xxx .  Search for next word  xxx  in rest of the text.
```

In an investigation reported by Baladi (1983) and analyzed in Waern (in press) it was found that this particular task posed problems for all three subjects studied. The subjects could not see that there was any difference between the four commands, and just used the first one mentioned in the manual. When the word sought for was not to be found on the screen, they got very confused and tried several different solutions. They tried for instance to restrict the search string to three letters. Not until they, with or without the help of the experimenter, attended to the difference between the command descriptions, did they find the correct command (i.e. the third in the list above).

Another problem with communicating models of systems is related to the fact that a computer system seldom can be accounted for by a single model from user's prior knowledge (Norman, 1983). What does it mean to a user that one relevant model is stressed, whereas another relevant model just is mentioned? Some preliminary data from an investigation I am currently performing tells the following, which is valid for a word-processing system: We presented one model which stressed the type-writer as an analogy. Some subjects were then subjects disturbed by the temporary effects of commands (such as overwriting existing text until the return key is pushed). We also presented a "block-building" model, where the effect of deleting was compared to taking away blocks and the effect of insertion was compared to putting in blocks. In this case, some subjects got confused when they hat to search the text forwards or backwards. These people might have broken up the text in small parts (i.e. symbols, corresponding to building blocks), thereby losing the text's characteristic as a linear string. These are but preliminary results, which have to be further confirmed.

The question raised above concern the content of metacommunication. It can also be asked, how the content should be presented. Is it for instance more helpful for a user to get explicit procedural instructions for certain purposes or is it better to just know what effects different commands have? I am currently investigating the effects of these different ways to inform about possible commands and methods on people's learning particular tasks as well as on the transfer of learning to new tasks.

Another important class of metacommunications concerns help and error messages. Let me here discuss only error messages, since the same principles apply to help messages.

We know that people often do not use manuals. Rather they experiment with the system. Therefore, the on-line error messages are crucial for their possibility to learn by their mistakes.

It is important to consider which information that is useful when an error occurs. First, the error must be diagnosed: the user has to know why he did not attain the intended goal. Then the correct way to arrive at the intended goal must be identified. We see that the "intended goal" is central both for diagnosis and remediation. It can be asked, how we can get information about the user's intended goal. It is probably impossible to tell the intended goal solely from the user's low-level actions. To take one of the examples above, a sequence of space bar pressings may signify an intended goal to delete some symbols or an intended goal to move the cursor rightwards. Thus, to understand the intended goal we may have to ask the user. A personal advisor, sitting beneath the user seems to be the ideal solution, although uneconomic and impractical. An on-line error message generating system, which is equipped with ability to question the user seems to be another, less than ideal but may be more practical solution.

We yet know very little about the requirements of a helpful on-line error message generating system, but one fact seems rather clear: it will need a lot of facilities which we hereto only have seen in artificial intelligence systems, i.e. knowledge representation (ro represent intentions as well as current states), search methods (to find possible solutions) and some natural language facilities (to communicate with the user in as natural a way as possible). We do not know either what kinds of error messages users want and need. It is quite probable that different users may want and need different kinds of error messages (cf. van der Veer, van Muylwijk & Waern, 1983).

To conclude, the issue of metacommunication seems to be the one where least research hitherto has been performed. We seem to know very little about the conditions under which external sources of metacommunication (personal as well as impersonal) are more satisfactory than on-line messages. We do not know when on-line metacommunication at all is feasible (considering for instance the difficulty to assess users' intentions). We seem to know even less about the effect of the content of metacommunication: which models should be offered, how should the procedures be presented and how should error messages be voiced? Let us hope that research in the next few years will present at least some answers to some of these questions.

REFERENCES

(1) Askwall, S., Computer supported reading vs. reading text on paper, International Journan for Man-Machine Studies (in press).

(2) Baladi, P., Inlärning av ett ordbehandlingssystem (VIDED). (Learning of a word processing system (VIDED)), B.A. thesis, Department of Psychology, University of Stockholm (1983).

(3) Barnard, P.J., Hammond, N.V., Morton, J. & Long, J., Consistency and compatibility in command languages, International Journal of Man-Machine Studies, 15 (1981) 87-134.

(4) Fitter, M., Towards more 'natural' interactive systems, International Journal of Man-Machine Studies, 11 (1979) 339.

(5) Göranzon, B. et al., Job design and automation in Sweden, Research Report No. 35, Arbetslivscentrum (1982).

(6) Mayer, R.E., Different problem-solving competencies established in learning computer programming with and without meaningful models, Journal of Educational Psychology, 67 (1975) 725-734.

(7) Norman, D.A., Some Ovservations on mental models, in: Gentner, D. & Stevens, A.L. (eds.), Mental models (Lawrence Arlbaum Ass., Hillsdale, N.J. 1983).

(8) Payne, S.J. & Green, T.R.G., The user's perception of the interaction language: A two-level model, Proceedings from the CHI '83 Conference: Human Factors in Computing Systems, The Association for Computing Machinery (1983) 202-206.

(9) Shneiderman, B., A note on human factors issues of natural language interaction with database systems, Information Systems, 4 (1981) 125-129.

(10) van Muylwijk, B., van der Veer, G., Waern, Y., On the implication of user variability in open systems, Behavior and Information Technology (1983) 313-326.

(11) Waern, Y., Learning computerized tasks as related to prior task knowledge, International Journal of Man-Machine Studies (in press).

(12) Waern, Y., To predict difficulties in using a computerized drafting system, Report from the Production System Laboratory, The Royal School of Technology, Stockholm (1984).

FOOTNOTE

The research reported here has been supported by grants from The Swedish Board for Research in the Humanities and Social Sciences and The Swedish Board for Technical Development.

Man-Computer Interaction Research
MACINTER-I
F. Klix and H. Wandke (Editors)
© Elsevier Science Publishers B.V. (North-Holland), 1986

LEARNING STYLES IN CONVERSATION - A PRACTICAL APPLICATION OF
PASK'S LEARNING THEORY TO HUMAN-COMPUTER INTERACTION

Gerrit C. van der Veer, Jos J. Beishuizen
Vrije Universiteit, Amsterdam
Netherlands

Conversation theory as a theory of learning is
applicable to problem solving situations in human-
computer interaction. The learning process will
benefit if the strategies of learning and teaching
match. Learning style may be described with three
factors: inclination to learn, operation learning
and comprehension learning, all showing a significant correlation with the learning time. With
examples we will show the usefulness of Pask's
conversation theory for human-computer learning
situations.

INTRODUCTION

A learning situation is described by Gordon Pask as a conversation between two instances. According to the various publications of his "Conversation Theory" (Pask, 1976a, 1977,1980),
these instances may be located inside the mind of the learner
(the teacher process and the learner process), involved in
developing metaprodecures, that may be employed in structuring
knowledge in a certain domain of problem solving. In alternative
applications of conversation theory, the two partners in conversation are a learner and a tutor. In standard situations
the role of the tutor may be allocated to a computer system.
Examples of dedicated computer systems for the study of learning, called BASTE, INTUITION and THOUGHT STICKER are described
by Pask and Kopstein (1977). In any case the essential characteristics of the partners in communication are their representation of knowledge or "mental organisation". Examples of
domains about which these partners may converse are a taxonomy
of species or the history and political structure at the court
of Henry VIII (see Figure 1).

Aim of the conversation in the learning process in the attainment of understanding, or the ability to reconstruct. This is
reached if the learner has at this disposal an entailment
structure (Pask, 1979) in which each concept may be derived
from other elements, and about which both partners in the conversation agree. This implies that conversation theory as a
theory of learning is applicable only to learning material about
which an entailment structure is reasonable. This includes at
least all kinds of problem solving situations in human-computer

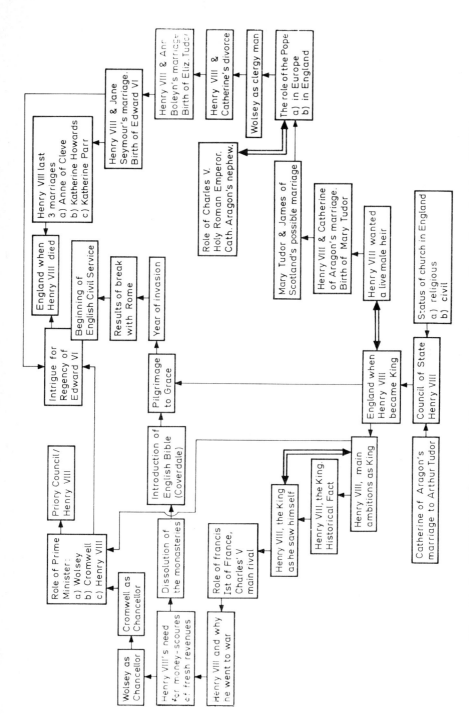

Figure 1: Example of an entailment structure, after Entwistle (1978)

interaction.

In the course of learning the knowledge representation is called an entailment mesh, a knowledge structure under construction, which is shaped via pruning and abduction, processes in which the manipulation of analogies between known substructures and new elements is an important activity. In this behaviour Pask distinguishes between different learning strategies (Pask, 1976b):

- Holism, or attention to global relations and the construction of general hypotheses. Several topics are simultaneously considered and there are several actual goals.

- Serialism, for focusing on direct relations and specific hypotheses. Attention is concentrated on one topic and there is one actual goal.

- Redundant holism, or the creation of new descriptive schemes in combination to a holistic strategy.

These strategies are considered to be individual characteristics that are to a certain extent situation dependent, although they should be considered stable within a single learning domain for relatively short spaces of time.

In more recent publications the strategies are conceived as manifestations of an underlying phenomenon called learning style or competence (Pask, 1980), designating the way in which a learner manipulates the analogies in the learning material, the methods he has at his disposal or prefers. Learners differ in the extent to which these aspects of competence are present:

- Comprehension learning designates a global approach directed at an overview and general relations.

- Operation learning is a local approach concentrated on procedural details and rules.

- If both competence factors are sufficiently available, Pask speaks of versatility: the learner is free to choose the best way of attack, adapted to the situation (see Fig. 2).

If either operation learning or comprehension learning is nearly absent, this is called a pathology:

- Globetrotters are comprehension learners who lack any inclination to operation learning. They misunderstand analogies or they apply them in circumstances in which these are invalid.

- Improvidence designates operation learning without the derivation of general principles. Analogies are not applied when feasible or indispensable.

Figure 2: Competence factors and pathologies

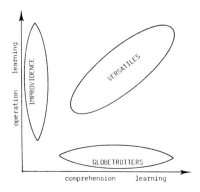

Figure 2: Competence factors and pathologies

In the conversation between learner and teacher, understanding is reached if both agree upon the entailment structure. So during the learning process the developing structure, the entailment mesh, has to be tested to the knowledge structure of the tutor. An efficient learning process should benefit if both structures concur, even in details. The teacher should act with the same kind of competence as his pupil, or the structure of the algorithm in the computer should correspond to the entailment structure the student is developing.

In designing efficient structures for educational situations it is therefor feasible to determine the individual competence of students (and teachers). Pask developed several procedures (Pask and Scott, 1972) to distinguish the different strategies and later on (Pask, 1976c) tests to measure cognitive style aspects.

STRATEGIES OF LEARNING AND TEACHING

Being interested in individual differences in learning behaviour we looked at the feasibility of the distinction serialism-holism. To this end Beishuizen (1984) compared procedures for determining learning strategies in differenz domains. As an example of a non verbal domain a transformation task designed by Pask and Scott (1971) was applied that may be characterised as the development of a motor skill. On patterns of 4 binary visual stimuli discriminating responses had to be learned consisting of the pressing of a corresponding selection of 8 keys. The subjects had to discover the combinations and to learn a quick performance of the appropriate action. They were allowed to start with practicing on any subset of the stimuli. From the order of the subsets chosen, the strategies serialism (selecting subsets as small as possible, combining new subsets one by one with already learned subsets in the way of strings of actions) and holism (combining subsets into chunks in a hierarchical way) could be detected.

As an example of verbal material Beishuizen developed a teach-back procedure, after method used by Pask with fictional material (Pask and Scott, 1972), using a text about night-jars. Students were asked to reproduce the contents after the text was read and removed. From the tape recorded reproduction the Spearman rank correlation was calculated between the order of the single statements reproduced and the order in the original text. A score of 1.00 represents a perfect serialistic reproduction. The scores farthest away from this value were considered to indicate holism. In fact in a experimental situation in which university students participated, the border between the two types of strategies was rather arbitrary drawn at the median value of .92. For 19 students that took part in this investigation there was a small negative relation between the classification in serialists and holists based on the behaviour in the two different domains we mentioned. As the phi coefficient of correlation (-.39) was at the border of significance, it showed at least clearly that there is no positive relation of any importance between these strategies in different domains of learning material.

The strategies as determined in the verbal domain were applied in a computer-assisted learning situation concerning verbal material. Students characterised as serialists or holists in the teach-back task took part in a second session in which they were confronted with a computer directed instruction program about syllogistic reasoning. Part of the students received instruction in a teaching style that could be characterised as serialistic, treating one single operator at a time and thereupon chaining this to the foregoing string of operations. The other group received a holistic program, consisting of a treatment of the single operations followed by an integration of all of them at once. Half of the students were taught in a way corresponding to their personal strategy, the other half was treated with the contrasting method.

Analysis of variance showed there was no overall difference between holists and serialists as to the time needed to solve a number of criterion problems at the end of the learning session, nor was there a difference in this respect between the two teaching strategies. But there was a significant interaction between the two ($F_{1,18} = 7.92$, $p < 0.02$), showing a better learning result if the strategies of lerarning and teaching match (see Fig. 3).

If the goal of the learning process is the mastery of an algorithmic ability in which part operations are sequentially organised, holistic students, preferring a global approach, are best confronted with exercises of the total skill as soon as

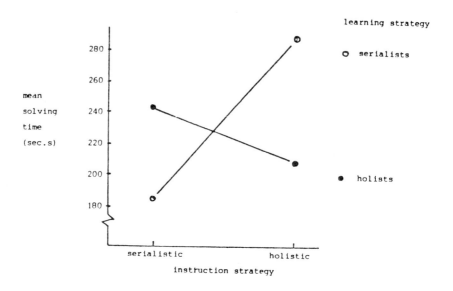

Figure 3: Interaction between teaching strategy and learning
          strategy

possible (after the individual part operations are mastered).
Serialists on the other hand benefit most from a course in
which the skill is constructed step by step from the composing
parts. In any case the learning strategy should be determined
with the help of subject matter that is related to the domain
in which the learning process will take place.

MEASURES OF COMPETENCE

In search for convenient devices to measure competence we trans-
lated and revised the Smuggler test and the Spy Ring History
test (Pask, 1976b, 1976c, 1977), standardising the instructions
and redesigning the procedure. The design of both devices is
identical. Students are confronted with a dossier about an
international gang that changes its structure periodically. The
learner has to study this material with the aim to take part in
a special department of interpol that is to destroy the organisation during the next period. The dossier is composed of
different kinds of information:

- A directed graph of the network for each of 3 previous periods
  in a row (see Fig. 4).

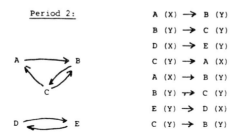

Period 2:

A (X) → B (Y)
B (Y) → C (Y)
D (X) → E (Y)
C (Y) → A (X)
A (X) → B (Y)
B (Y) ⇢ C (Y)
E (Y) → D (X)
C (Y) → B (Y)

Figure 4: Example of a directed graph and a list

- A list representing a possible sequence of transactions for each of these periods.

- Information about the rules of the organisation and the role of the 5 participants (e.g. in the smuggler organisation a member involved in producing heroine needs a batch of morphine before he can produce and send anything to other members).

- Background information about individual members (see Fig. 5).

- Geographical details concerning the 2 of 3 different countries in which the organisation is active.

After study of the dossiers a series of questions is presented to the students about:

- Reproduction of the network, and reconstruction of possible transaction lists. The students are free either to reproduce the original material or to construct new instances according to the role of the members of the organisation and knowledge of the specific situation in the concerning period.

- A prediction of the structure of the network and the transaction list for the next period.

- Facts about the geography of the countries and personal data of the members.

- General rules concerning the organisation and the role of the participants.

- Opinions about the student's own style of structuring the information in order to predict the structure in a future period (meta cognition).

Last name   : Amitaba
First name   : Achmed
Code   : AMI
Date of Birth   : 17-8-1951
Place of Birth   : Maida, Jemen

Source: Ramudian Bulletin, 1976

Amitaba is from Arabian origin, a sportsman, who originally earned his
living as a travelling salesman. He is multilingual. At a party of
the department of trade he met the beautiful daughter of the minister
of agriculture of Ramudia, and he moved to that country. He became a
dealer in farm machinery, specialising in irrigation techniques. He
met Deborah, one of the other members of the circle, in a private gam-
bling house. She was witness to a disastrous loss and paid his debts
out of "sympathy".

Figure 5: Background information about one of the members of
          the network

After 3 factor analytic studies on the original indexes on
data from several homogeneous samples of students of different
ages (13 to 15 years: n = 81; university students: n = 45,
n = 71 for the two parallel tests), we developed scoring
methods for 3 factors or dimensions (Van der Veer and Van de
Wolde, 1983b):

- Factor I: inclination to learn, to put effort in memorising.
  This factor does not indicate a capacity. The student is totally free, the instructions do not necessarily suggest that
  he should memorise, but some students do so spontaneously and
  consistently.

- Factor II: operation learning. Inclination to deduction of
  specific rules and procedural details. This style results in
  the availability of tools to construct procedures when needed,
  and in consistency with regard to related details of the
  knowledge domain.

- Factor III: comprehension learning. Inclination to induction
  of general rules and descriptions, to trace relations between different, even remote, parts of the domain. With this
  style one tends to reconstruct forgotten details on the basis
  of general structure and analogies.

In Pask' original scoring system there is a separate index
called versatility. In our data we could not identify this
style as an independently measurable scale. In case we need
an index for it we will have to combine factors II and III.

COMPETENCE IN HUMAN-COMPUTER INTERACTION

In a group of 63 students (Van der Veer and Van de Wolde, 1982,
1983a) learning a simple computer language, all three competence
factors showed a significant correlation with the time needed
to learn the language, even if we partialed out general intelligence (Raven's Advanced Progressive Matrices):

I	Inclination to learn	-.50
II	Operation learning	-.40
III	Comprehension learning	-.36

The factor Inclination to learn moreover correlated significantly (partial correlations -.36 and -.52) with the time needed to
solve some programming problems after the language was mastered.
In this group factor II and III correlated rather high so we
combined these scores, by simple addition, to a new scale we
call versatile (unlike Pask, who calculated a separate index
for this concept, for which we could not find a statistical
justification). Subjects scoring high on versatility defined
in our way showed a preference for holistic strategies and
moreover turned out to have less difficulties in programming
abstract and hierarchically complex algorithms, than did others
(Van der Veer and Van de Wolde, 1982). This difference disappeared if the problem was no longer abstract but stated in
meaningful terms and familiar semantics, even though the
structure of the problem was identical to the abstract one
(see Fig. 6).

Adding the semantic connotation equalises the possibility of
versatile and non versatile programmers. The flexibility of
choice between operation learning and comprehension learning
in that case is no longer crucial. This may be taken into
account in constructing programming exercises for didactic
purposes.

In another study (Van der Veer, 1983) factor I, inclination to
learn, turned out to have a significant partial correlation
with study results during a several month programming course
(71 students) with the ability to manipulate structural diagrams
(.24) and with programming skills in simple languages like
BASIC (.28), whereas the other competence factors did not show
a systematic relation.

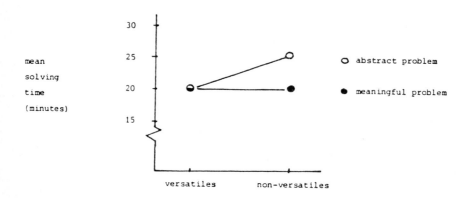

Figure 6: Relation between competence and type of problem
          to be solved

CONCLUSION

Pask's notions about strategies and cognitive styles, developed
from conversation theory turn out to be systematically measurable. The indexes developed are useful in predicting success
at problem solving in man-machine interactions, and are useful
tools in matching or adapting (computer assisted) instruction
style to learning style.

REFERENCES

(1) Beishuizen, J.J., De betekenis van de leerstijl "serialisme-
    holisme" voor een computer-bestuurde leersituatie, in:
    Dirkzwager, A., Fokkema, S.D., van der Veer, G.C. and
    Beishuizen, J.J.(eds.), Lernen met computers in het onderwijs
    (S.V.O., Den Haag, 1984).

(2) Entwistle, N.J., Knowledge of structures and styles of
    learning: a summary of Pask's recent research, British
    Journal of Educational Psychology, 48 (1978) 255-265.

(3) Pask, G., Conversational techniques in the study and
    practice of education, British Journal of Educational Psy-
    chology, 46 (1976a) 12-25.

(4) Pask, G., Styles and strategies of learning, British Journal
    of Educational Psychology, 46 (1976b) 128-148.

(5) Pask, G., Spy Ring History Test Form IV (System Research Ltd., Richmond, 1976c).

(6) Pask, G., Learning styles, educational strategies and representation of knowledge: methods and application (System Research Ltd., Richmond, 1977).

(7) Pask, G., Consciousness, Journal of Cybernetics, 9 (1979), 211-258.

(8) Pask, G., Commentary on Scandura, J.M.: Problem Solving, Academic Press, 1977, Journal of structural learning, 6 (1980) 335-346.

(9) Pask, G. and Kopstein, F.F.J., Teaching machines revisited in the light of conversation theory. Educational Technology (October 1977) 38-41.

(10) Pask, G. and Scott, B.C.E., Learning and teaching strategies in a transformation skill, British Journal of Mathematical Statical Psychology, 24 (1971) 205-229.

(11) Pask, G. and Scott, B.C.E., Learning strategies and individual competence. International Journal of Man-Machine studies, 4 (1972) 217-253.

(12) Van der Veer, G.C., Individual differences in cognitive style and educational background and their effect upon the learning of a programming language, in: Schauer, H. and Tauber,M.J. (eds.), Psychologie des Programmierens (Oldenbourg, Wien, 1983).

(13) Van der Veer, G.C. and Van de Wolde, G.J.E., Psychological aspects of problem solving with the help of a computer language, Computers and Education, 6 (1982) 229-234.

(14) Van der Veer, G.C. and Van de Wolde, G.J.E., Individual differences and aspects of control flow notation, in Green, T.R.G., Payne, S. and Van der Veer, G.C. (eds.), The Psychology of Computer Use, (Adademic Press, London, 1983a).

(15) Van der Veer, G.C. and Van de Wolde, G.J.E., Een Nederlandse bewerking van de smokkelaarstest, in: Lodewijks, J.G.L.C. and Simons, P.R.J. (eds.), Strategien in leren en ontwikkeling (Swets en Zeitlinger, Lisse, 1983).

INTERFACE DESIGN

Man-Computer Interaction Research
MACINTER-I
F. Klix and H. Wandke (Editors)
© Elsevier Science Publishers B.V. (North-Holland), 1986

MACHINE ADAPTION TO PSYCHOLOGICAL DIFFERENCES AMONG USERS IN INSTRUCTIVE
INFORMATION EXCHANGES WITH COMPUTERS

Ernst Z. Rothkopf

AT&T Bell Laboratories

Murray Hill, N. J.
USA

We describe three examples of the application of
empirical procedures and psychological analysis to
adapt computer systems to psychological differences
among users. These involve 1) the relationship between component processes in computerized text-
editing and aptitudes; 2) the use of normative data
on referential language practices in the design of
information retrieval calls; 3) adaption of instruction to learner characteristics.

INTRODUCTION

Our technology and material culture has accommodated physical differences
among humans but it lags in accommodation to psychological differences.
Personal weapons such as swords, battle axes, and golf clubs have been made
to fit weight and size requirements since ancient times. Manufactured goods
such as clothing were long ago systematically adjusted to size differences
among individuals. Fixtures, tools, and machines that are adjusted to physical differences among people have evolved more slowly but substantial
progress has been made. In more recent years, the emerging disciplines
of anthropometry and human engineering have reflected increasing concern
with problems caused by human size differences and have contributed to
solutions for these problems. The main statistical machinery that was used
for adjustment was the arithmetic mean and the range of variation. One of
the pioneer efforts in this area, by example, was by the anthropologist
Hooton of Harvard University. He carefully measured the posterior and other
dimensions of thousands of Americans and used the mean range of these
measurements to design a standard railroad seat. Techniques, similar to his
have since been widely used to design work stations, telephones, control
systems and many other manufactured goods. Even here, however, the dic-
tatorship of the arithmetic mean has persisted. By and large, multimodal
distributions have tended to be neglected. Only recently have we seen
special tools for such distinctive groups as left-handed persons. Even
major population divisions such as women have not been attended to until
lately in the work place. For example, no one manufactured telephone pole
climbing irons for women until very recently. Deliberate systematic adjustment of manufactured artifacts to psychological differences among users
is a much more recent phenomena. Concern with such problems was greatly
stimulated by the widespread use of computers and computer systems. In an
important sense, adjustments of work activities to psychological differences
among people was made possible by growth in computational power.

I want to briefly illustrate several approaches to the accommodation of
psychological differences. I will include accommodation a) to differences
in aptitude and age in designing computer text editors; and b) to differences in referential language in information retrieval systems. The
remainder of the paper will focus on the accommodation to psychological
differences around learners in computer-based instructional systems, the
area that is closest to my own interest. My examples were chosen because
they illustrate different types of problems and different approaches to
their solution, and because they reflect work at AT&T Bell Laboratories.

APTITUDES: IMPLICATIONS FOR TASK DESIGN AND TRAINING

An interesting method for dealing with psychological differences has been
pioneered by Egan and Gomez in our laboratory. They studied difficulties
in learning to use a line-by-line-computer text editor. Their approach was
to a) measure psychological differences among potential users; b) analyze
the work task into psychologically meaningful components; and c) determine
what components were related to measured aptitude. This method parallels
that used by Sternberg (1977) in his componential analysis of test intelligence, but Egan and Gomez applied their technique to a real work task.

Here is what Egan and Gomez (in press) did. First they administered a
battery of psychological tests and an extensive biographical inventory.
They found that two factors predicted success in the experimental computer
lessons. Score on a spatial memory test was positively correlated with
achievement while age was negatively correlated. Neither verbal aptitude
nor reasoning skill nor any of the other measures was reliably linked to
training success.

Egan and Gomez (in press) then performed a cognitive task analysis of text
editing requirements. They decomposed the task into three major components.
These were: 1) finding, 2) counting, and c) generating, as well as several
subcomponents. These are shown in Fig. 1. The analysis was confirmed by
error analysis and by the creation and use of separate tests for these
skills and for combinations of these skills. Correlational analysis
involving aptitude and biographical measures as well as tests of the task
component were then performed. This led to the conclusion that spatial
memory was an important element in finding and generating. Age affected
primarily the generating component. Egan and Gomez (in press) concluded
that individual differences can be accommodated in two ways. First,changes
in task design may offload demands on spatial memory or reduce the impact
of age. For example, a screen-based editor or a context search function in
which the computer does the pattern matching to find the location of a
connection may reduce the spatial memory requirements of editing. Using
simple function keys instead of a complex command language may reduce the
impact of learners' age. Second, special aids during training may encourage
the development of editing practices that are less sensitive to learners'
age and spatial memory.

The study has methodological significance rather than directly practical
implications since there may be other goor reasons for opting for a screen
rather than a line-based editor. Egan and Gomez (in press) concluded:
"Certain domains seem particularly promising for assaying, isolating, and
accommodating individual differences. We think that the approach will be
most useful in those situations where a large number of people from dif-

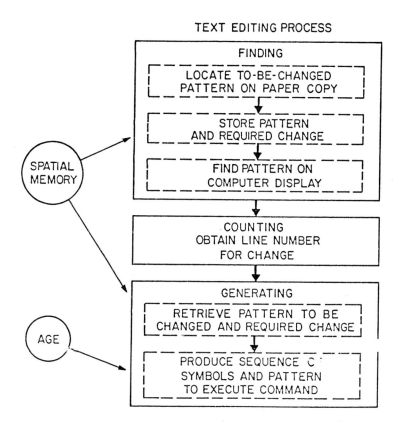

Figure 1
Componential analysis, according to Egan and Gomez (in press),
of text editing with a line-based editor and relationship of
the components to spatial memory and age

ferent backgrounds wish to learn a new complex skill for which there are
good possibilities for accommodating individual differences. Our case study
of computer text editing fits this description precisely. Many other new
skills involving the use of computers or computer-like devices have
characteristics that make them good candidates for this approach. The
number of different people who can accomplish such tasks as troubleshooting,
maintenance, assembly, and decision making also may be increased if the
right kind of changes are made to those tasks.

These studies have demonstrated a set of methods that may free us from the
conventional mentality of selecting the "right" person for a given job. We
have shown that individual differences in learning a complex task can be
sorted out. The components of the task causing some people great difficulty
can be isolated. Task components can be changed to accommondate a greater
range of people. Instead of finding the right person for a given job, we
may be able to focus on developing the right conditions (tool designs,

training, performance aids) to enable a given person to accomplish a
desired objective."

THE DESIGN OF COMPUTER COMMANDS AND STATISTICAL SEMIOTICS

Differences among human beings in referential language are a problem in the
design of computer commands that make use or resemble natural language.
Such commands or calls are commonly used in information retrieval systems
and in certain text editing functions. Furnas, Landauer, Gomez, and Dumais
(1983) pioneered a method for the rational design of command languages,
that is distinguished from earlier efforts by systematic exploitation of
the frequency distribution of relevant traits or dispositions in the
potential user population.

The problem which Furnas et al (1983) investigated was whether there is
sufficient agreement in referential language within a user population to
permit the use of a single common word to retrieve stored information from
a computer. In initial experiments, they found that any randomly chosen
pair of people will use the same word for an object only 10 - 20 percent
of the time. In one study, these researchers asked secretarial students to
name editing operations marked on experimental texts by authors. The three
most popular names for each operation, accounted for only 33 percent of the
total number of responses. The probability that any two people used the
same verb in describing a particular text correction was .08. Clearly,
restriction to a single call term would be troublesome for the general use
of an information retrieval system.

Furnas et al (1983) then explored six major methods for providing cue words
for such an information retrieval system for untutored or infrequent users.
Each of these techniques permitted three mathematical variations. Hence a
total of 18 different methods were tried. Four different situations in which
verbal computer commands might be used were investigated. These were: 1)
editing operations, 2) reference to common objects; 3) a swap and sale
bulletin board, and 4) cooking recipes. The investigators used quantitative
indices of the language experiences and dispositions of typical populations
in these procedures. These were obtained from experiments in which the
frequency with which various words were used to refer to objects or functions were recorded.

The basic data on which Furnas, Landauer, Gomez, and Dumais (1983) based
their analysis, consisted of empirical naming matrices. The objects or
functions to be named formed the rows, and the names given by subjects
formed the columns. The cell entries were the frequencies with which various
names were used to name the various row items.

Success in targetting is shown for the most important three methods for
deriving naming practices from these data are shown in Fig. 2. These
methods were 1) one name per object: weighted random. This is the armchair
procedure, in which computer designers specify reference name and base
their choice on their perception of language habits in the population. This
is probably the most common method by which computer commands are chosen.
The system names are chosen with the assumption that choices are predicted
by the observed relative frequency of word choice in the population; 2)
one name per object: optimized. The word with the greatest observed
frequency of use is chosen as the object or function name; and 3) M

referents for every word: optimized. For every object, all referents were stored, based on the observed usage table. The system responds with the most frequently observed referents for any user input.

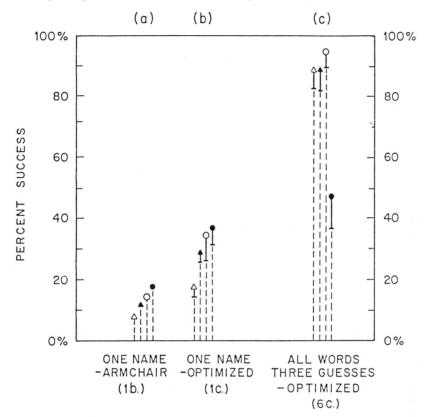

Figure 2
Summary of expected success for three of the most important models presented. (a) "armchair" model; (b) best possible single-name modell (1c); (c) model where the system recognizes all words and returns three guesses (6c).

Figure 2 shows that the third method is most effective, although it appears fairly weak for recipes. The armchair method produced very weak results. It may be noted however, that the designers of system commands are rarely

randomly selected from populations such as those used in this experiment,
i. e. college students, housewives, and cooking experts. The point could
be made, on the other hand, that computer experts, the engineers who usually
choose computer commands, are not necessarily representative of the
population of users. Engineers may actually produce worse results than the
random choices used with the present armchair method.

Furnas and his coworkers conclude that "input/output functions based on
normative naming behavior of users will work much better than systems based
on a single name provided by designers". They comment, "We have ... shown
that a system that made several best guesses, and/or allowed the user to
make several tries, and then returned a menu-like set of guesses to be
chosen among, would substantially improve performance beyond current popular methods. The best approach was to focus on what the user brings to
the interaction, namely a great variety of words, and for each word have
the system make one or more best guesses as to what the user meant". The
analyses provided by Furnas et al (1983) indicate that calling systems can
be substantially improved by going beyond measures of central trends of
user dispositions and making efficient use of remaining information in
frequency distributions of the linguistic disposition of users.

GLOBAL ADAPTIVE INSTRUCTION

Tailoring teaching to the characteristics of learners has long intrigued
educators (e. g. Cronbach and Snow, 1977). The feasibility of such instructional tailoring (often referred to as adaptive instruction) has been
proposed as one important advantage for the educational uses of computers
(Barr and Feigenbaum, 1982). Although there has been a good deal of
optimistic discussion, the psychological bases of adaptive instruction has
not been very thoroughly analyzed. The discussion that follows, focusses
on one special form of adaptive instruction, namely personalization.

Why do we want to adapt teaching to accommodate differences among learners?
It is done with the expectation that by accommodating these differences, by
appropriately matching teaching to students, we can increase chances for
success, speed mastery, reduce exposure to unneeded or unwanted material,
improve transfer of training to jobs and/or more advanced training, make
it more likely that students will complete training, and make learning a
pleasant experience.

Of course, not only can instructional systems adapt themselves to learners,
but the converse is also true. Learners can adapt themselves to instruction.
Good scripted programs make use of this cheerful fact. Adaptive adjunct
procedures, such as questions and other interactive procedures, can be used
to help and encourage learners to adapt themselves to scripted programs.
However, while learners may master the subject matter even under difficult
circumstances, they may find the experience unpleasant and aversive, a very
undesirable outcome.

Teaching can be tailored to students either on 1) global, strategic,
discrete level, or 2) locally tactical, and continuous level. On the global
level, learners are classified and instructional programs or scripted
modules are assigned to each according to their classification. On the
local level, adjustments are continuously made in the teaching sequence on
the basis of analyses that are made of the interactions between computer

and learner. The current discussion is limited to global adjustments to differences among learners, a method of tailored teaching that is aptly described as personalization of instruction.

Before starting, some definitions will help to place personalization in perspective. Stable instructional means[1] can be divided into two categories: 1) scripted and 2) adaptive instructional forms. Personalization comprises elements of both categories.

Instruction is adaptive if it can be directly adjusted to accommodate differences among learners. These may be differences in experience, abilities, interests, or any other factor that plays an important role in instruction. Scripted stable presentations, on the other hand, deliver the same instruction to all. Scripted instruction does not exclude substantial interaction between the learner and the instructional system. But system demands from the learner, and system responses to learner actions follow the same general scenario for all.

Personalization is scripted instruction but not all learners get the same script. Learners are categorized according to one or more relevant characteristics and then assigned to an especially suited script. This is a global approach in the sense that, once learners are categorized, a single switch is thrown to put them on the appropriate instructional track. By contrast, with this global approach, other forms of adaptive instruction involve continual adjustments throughout the course of instruction on the basis of analysis of interactions between computer and learner.

DIFFERENCES AMONG LEARNERS

Pretraining differences among learners that are relevant to personalization include the following five major categories: 1) specific training; achievements directly relevant to the particular instructional subject matter; 2) general experience; 3) aptitudes and abilities; 4) motivation and interests; and 5) expectations about the settings in which targetted subject matter knowledge is to be used.

Specific Training. Students will differ in a) how much they already know about the elements of this domain; and b) in their mastery of enabling knowledges or skills that are necessary for the successful use of the information in the instructional domain.

The advantages of being sensitive to prior mastery of elements of the instructional domain are obvious. A system, responsive to reliable indicators of previous achievement, will not waste students' time by teaching them material that they already know. This homely algorithm is one of the most important practical strengths of adaptive teaching systems.

Learners will differ in how recently they have undergone domain-related training. Relevant test performance is lowered either because of forgetting or because of changes in setting or context. There are important qualitative differences in competence between two learners scoring equally low, if one has never learned and the other learned long ago. Lost competence is often quickly restored and should be handled differently than lack of previous instruction or past instructional failure. This poses interesting, unsolved technical problems because current techniques for discriminating between

competence lost or temporarily misplaced and pristine ignorance are not
well developed.

General experience. The general background of learners is relevant to the
success of specific instruction. Learners differ in their experience with
language, in their differentiation, and mental grouping of events or objects,
as well as in experiences that provide bases for the metaphors, analogies,
and models that can be used to carry new information. General experience
influences the effectiveness of instruction because it determines how well
a particular instructional presentation will work.

For example, unfamiliar vocabulary increases the likelihood that some
instructive event will fail because words are not understood. The likelihood of success of an instructional event is greater if the terms are
familiar generally and if the specific sense in which the term is used is
familiar. This is because: 1) Correct interpretation is more likely; 2)
Interpretation time is faster and demands less processing capacity. Therefore, required integration among terms is more likely to take place; 3)
Because familiar terms require less interpretative capacity, more mental
resources are available for processing and interpreting other terms in the
proximity of familiar language. This is particularly important with exter-
nally-paced material; 4) Familiar terms, particularly figurative and
analogic expressions tie new information to old knowledge. This makes for
stable memory structures.

What holds for vocabulary also holds for other carriers of the instructive
message including phrases, figurative expressions, and pictorial presentations. General experience factors pose similar demands in the development
of adaptive instructional presentations as the adaptive treatment of
aptitudes.

Aptitudes and Abilities. Aptitudes are fairly stable human charcteristics
that influence learning and other performance. Aptitudes that have been
held instructionally relevant include general intelligence, spatial
memory, verbal ability, field dependence, inclination to deal with abstract
representations, and mathematical alibility. The rationale for tailoring
instruction to aptitudes is very similar to that described for general
experiential factors. It is often difficult to neatly distinguish general
experiential factors from aptitudes measured by test.

Adapting instruciton to aptitudes of students is also based partially on
the idea that learners scoring low on a given aptitude actually will do
better with one treatment than another and that the opposite is true for
high aptitude students. This is sometimes called disordinal aptitude x
instructional treatment interaction. The search for such disordinal interactions has stimulated a good deal of exploratory research but few dramatic
instances of disordinal aptitude treatment interactions have been reported
(Cronbach and Snow, 1977).

Another idea that has stimulated interest in tailoring instruction to
aptitudes is the perpetual will-o'-the-wisp that certain instructional
media or sensory modalities are more suitable to persons with particular
aptitudes. According to these views, some learners are more responsive to
visual presentations, for example, while others profit more from aurally
presented instructional material. Experimental evidence in support of this
notion is not strong.

The use of flexible instructional systems such as computers or computer-controlled devices in adapting teaching to aptitudes makes relatively weak demands on the power of such devices. However, computers have been shown to be useful in measuring aptitudes because the number of test items needed for reliable measurement can be minimized by certain algorithms (e.g. Lord, 1977; Urry, 1977).

An aptitude is a fairly stable trait but is, as the term is used, modifiable by certain experiences. It shares many characteristics, as an instructional variable, with the general experience factors that we discussed earlier. In one macrotheory of instruction (Rothkopf, 1981), both aptitude-ability and general experience are postulated to function in the same way. They both influence the likelihood of a successful translation from instructional form to an internal representation sufficient for the instructional goal. Particular aptitudes are associated with the ease with which various types of translations can be handled.

Motivation and Interests

Learners differ in what attracts their attention, in what they find amusing or interesing, and in what they perceive to be their strengths as learners. It therefore seems reasonable to think that advantages may be derived by providing, if possible, instruction that capitalizes on learner interests. This may be done by tailoring optinal aspects of instructional presentations. One possibility is to select instructional examples from fields which the student enjoys or has an interest.

Another somewhat different way of viewing the motivation and interest factor is to think of it as an index of the likelihood that an individual may have had certain specific experiences. People with common motivation and interests are likely to share certain experiences and knowledge. It is possible to weave these experiences into the main instructional fabric through illustrations, metaphors, or other linguistic or graphical devices. Such instructional figures or devices provide familiar representations or schemas into which the main instructional content can be tied. In this way useful mnemonic structures can be created that link the new to the familiar and that will aid learning, retention, and recall. Adaptive instructional systems are expected to succeed here by matching elaborative or illustrative instructional elements to the specific experience and interests of each student or of student groups.

Some experiences, shared by certain groups, although not directly related to the targetted instructional content, can be useful in fashioning instructional treatments that are effective for the particular group in question. For exemple, use of protagonists or narrators who are popular and important to student groups with special interests may be an advantageous instructional maneuver. This is a widely held belief but it is not well established empirically.

Matching content to student interest may prevent tuning out. We can safely assume that certain representations of content will cause erosion of attention and other mathemagenic activities while others will sustain them. Instructional examples from cooking may result in more conscientious study than functionally equivalent examples from chemistry or from leather tanning for affluent, antiscientific kitchen hobbyists.

In summary, adaption of instruction to the motivation and interest of the learner can be expected to have the following two kinds of beneficial effects: 1) Promote mathemagenic activity, i. e. learning-related processing of the instructional matter and prevent physical or mental dropout (see Rothkopf, 1982); 2) Information about learners' motivation and interest can be used to design appropriate materials that are more easily learned and remembered. This is because motivation and interest indicate the nature of experiences shared by certain learners in the past. Embedding new material in material made familiar by earlier experience can readily be integrated with existing memory structures. Such tailored material tends to make fewer processing demands on learners than those outside the domain of interest.

Situations in Which the Subject Matter is to be Used. Examples and exercises are very important instructional elements. Such examples or exercises usually involve highly specific concrete realizations of more general representations of the subject matter. It is usually instructionally advantageous to choose examples or exercises from the situations in which application is contemplated.

For example, an instructional module from a statistics course, aimed at teaching correlational techniques to agricultural students may use agricultural problems or illustrations. Epidemiologists or economists are exposed to the same correlation materials with problems appropriate to their fields. We can expect that such selective assignments would produce better results than if the same problem or illustration set were used for all students regardless of the nature of subsequent application.

The advantage of matching problems and examples to the setting in which they are likely to be applied include the following: 1) problems are likely to be more interesting to the student; 2) problems involving familiar objects and settings provide additional meaning and integrative links for new information; 3) since the instructional problems resemble practical problems to be encountered later, better transfer can be expected to the targetted specific application setting such as job performance; 4) illustrative examples and other instructive events drawn from familiar settings provide extra mnemonic links, perhaps of an incidental nature, and with it useful alternative retrieval paths; and 5) students who may eventually be required to exercise their skills in a variety of settings may be prepared for these eventualities by being exposed to problems drawn from a strategically chosen, central set of concrete instances.

Adapting instructional problems to the student's likely applications is clearly useful in work-oriented teaching. The use of need-specific problems and exercises tends to assure that the problems used in instruction are similar to the problems encoutered on the job or in subsequent narrowly focused advanced instruction. Such similarity makes it more likely that the student remembers appropriate approaches to particular problems and prepares the student for the eventualities of the job.

Rating various possibilities for personalization according to impact and current technical feasibility lead to the following conclusion. Specific previous training is very likely the most powerful and feasible method of personalization, followed by a cluster consisting of motivation and interest, educational goals, and specific application settings. On the bottom are personalization maneuvers based on aptitudes, abilities, and general experience. The last two pretraining factors have very powerful effect on the success of instruction but we do not know very much about how to deal with such differences among our students.

Of the various possibilities for personalization, adaption to previous specific training seems the most feasible and powerful. This is because we have substantial experience with prerequisites and modular instruction and because avoiding unneeded training has substantial, measurable benefits. Personalization by interest, educational goals, and specific application situations also appear promising and well within parctical reach. We can have confidence in this because we know fairly well how these personalization factors can be expected to produce their effects. The most problematical personalization factors are aptitudes, abilities, and general experience because we do not understand very well how to tune instructional materials to these factors. Nor do we have a strong basis for believing that the trouble in shaping appropriate instructional materials for these factors will produce learning effects of commensurate magnitude. Finally, we should also consider the possibility that the mere appearance of attempts at personalization, regardless of its basis, may be sufficient for beneficial instructional results.

Personalization is just one of the ways in which computers can be made to accommodate differences among learners. Space limitation prevents me from discussing in detail the many other interesting possibilities for adaptive instruction.

High expectations prevail about what the computer can do for us in instruction and as a powerful cognitive aid for work and a broad spectrum of other human functions. These expectations are not always based on sound theory and sound experimentation. The excitement in these areas was stimulated largely by the rapid progress in computer technology. The contribution of psychology to effective uses of computers including accomodation to differences among humans, lags behind progress in the computer sciences. We need to play a more active role in defining psychological requirements for the computer technologist and in providing specifications of how these requirements should be met in order to assure efficiency and user satisfaction. Psychologists have developed useful methods for doing so but our current store of psychological knowledge does not meet our needs. We have much work to do.

FOOTNOTES

[1] Stable instructional forms are those that generate equivalent instructive events at each use (Rothkopf, 1976). These forms are either tangible or documentary, or the programs that generate them are tangible and documented.

REFERENCES

Barr, A. and Feigenbaum, E. A. (eds.), The handbook of artificial intelligence, Voll.II. (HeurisTech Press, Stanford, 1982, pp. 223-294).

Cronbach, L. J. and Snow, R. E., Aptitudes and instructional methods (Halsted Press, New York, 1977).

Egan, D. E. and Gomez, L. M., Assaying, isolating and accommodating individual differences in learning a complex skill, in: R. F. Dillon (eds.), Individual differences in cognition, Volume 2. (Academic Press, New York (in press)

Furnas, G. W., Landauer, T. K., Gomez, L. M., and Dumais, S. T., Statistical semantics: Analysis of the potential performance of key-word information systems, Bell System Technical Journal 62 (1983) 1753-1804.

Lord, F. M., A broad-range tailored test of verbal ability, Applied Psychological Measurement 1 (1977) 95-100.

Rothkopf, E. Z., Writing to teach and reading to learn: A perspective on the psychology of written instruction, in: N. L. Gage (eds.), The psychology of teaching methods, The seventy-fifth yearbook of the National Society for the Study of Education (1976, 91-129).

Rothkopf, E. Z., A macroscopic model of instruction and purposive learning: An overview, Instructional Science 10 (1981) 105-122.

Rothkopf, E. Z., Adjunct aids, and the control of mathemagenic activities during purposeful reading, in: W. Otto and S. White (eds.), Reading expository material (Academic Press, New York, 1982, pp.109-138).

Sternberg, R. J., Intelligence, information processing, and analogical reasoning: The componential analysis of human abilities (Hillsdale, N.J.: Erlbaum, 1977).

Urry, V. W., Tailored testing: A successful application of latent trait theory, Journal of Educational Measurement 14 (1977) 181-196

Man-Computer Interaction Research
MACINTER-I
F. Klix and H. Wandke (Editors)
© Elsevier Science Publishers B.V. (North-Holland), 1986

ON COMPLEXITY OF COMMAND-ENTRY IN MAN-COMPUTER DIALOGUES

Hartmut Wandke and Jörg Schulz
Sektion Psychologie der Humboldt-Universität
Berlin
GDR

In an experiment with a command-oriented language for a
special database three different dialogue structures were
tested. Dialogue structures differed in complexity of
commands and complexity of dialogue steps. Computer-
naive subjects prefered in general to enter a chain of
simple commands in complex dialogue steps. Significant
interaction with task difficulty was found. The results
are discussed in relation to the mental load induced by
the use of different dialogue structures.

The designer of dialogue systems has to decide on the layout of several
levels of man-computer interaction (see Moran,1981). One important design
aspect is the dialogue structure, especially the problem how to distribute
the information which should be exchanged in the dialogue on different
steps.

The aim of this investigation was therefore to find out what kind of
dialogue structure should be designed for naive computer users. Because we
conducted our experiment with an user-controlled dialogue styl, based on
a command language, there are following possibilities for structuring the
dialogue as shown in figure 1 by an abstract example. There are three different dialogue structures. The command-entry per dialogue step is organized
in different ways for each structure.

In case A four simple dialogue steps are needed to reach a certain result
which is here symbolized by X, Y, Z.

In each dialogue step only one command is entered by the user and one output is given by the computer.

In case B the same result (X,Y,Z) is reached by one complex dialogue step.
All four commands are entered one after the other and the termination of
command-entry is made not till the last command. Therefore there are no
intermediate results or feedbacks by the computer and the result in shown
immediately.

Please note, that the typing actitity (i.e. the number of key strokes)
remaines unchanged compared with case A.

In case C one dialogue step is needed, too. But instead of those four
commands only one command is to enter.

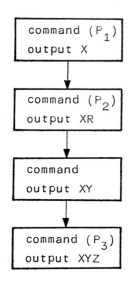

A: Information exchange in four
     simple dialogue steps

command (P_1), command (P_2), command, command (P_3)
output XYZ

B: Information exchange in one complex dialogue step

command (P_1, P_2, P_3)
output XYZ

C: Information exchange in one
   dialogue step with one
   complex command instead of
   a sequence of commands

Fig. 1: Three examples for dialogue structures

Therefore the typing activity is dramatically reduced, while mental load induced by the choice or by the formation of this complex command is assumed to increase considerably.

The problem of this investigation was to find out which of the three dialogue structures is suitable for naive users of computers.
To illustrate this problem it is possible to compare the advantages and disadvantages of the three types of dialogue structure in a hypothetical manner (figure 2).

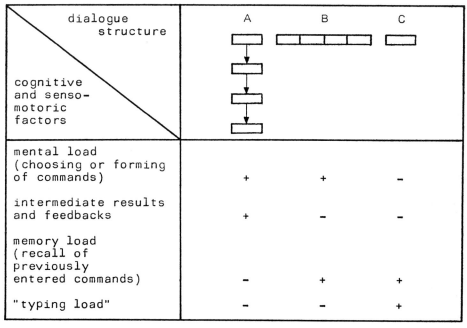

dialogue structure	A	B	C
cognitive and senso-motoric factors			
mental load (choosing or forming of commands)	+	+	-
intermediate results and feedbacks	+	-	-
memory load (recall of previously entered commands)	-	+	+
"typing load"	-	-	+

+ advantage   - disadvantage

Fig. 2: Hypothetical effects on cognitive and sensomotoric factors

Each structure has the same proportion of advantages and disadvantages. A decision about the most suitable dialogue structure is therefore not possible without an experimental analysis. We conducted two experiments: In Exp. I the structure A was compared with B and in Exp. II structure B was compared with C. Because the basic paradigma was the same for both experiments it should be described beforehand.

Figure 3 shows the most essential framework conditions of the paradigma.

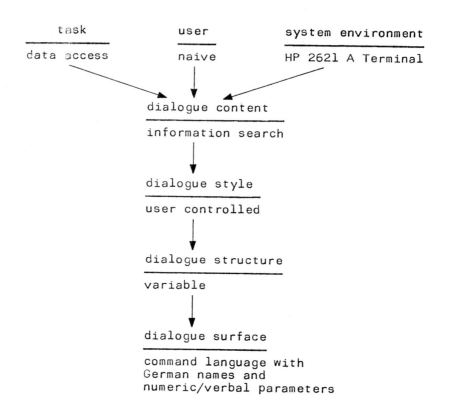

Fig. 3: Frame for the experimental variable "dialogue structure"

We constructed a database which contained 100 simulated commercial orders in a sales division of an industrial plant. The tasks for the subjects were to retrieve information from the database. For instance: How many costumers have ordered more than 200 motors in October 1984 and will be supplied by truck?

There were tasks with one, two, three or more characteristics. In our example task we have four characteristics (date for delivery, this is "October 1984"; number of pieces, this is "more than 200"; product, this is "motor" and means of transportaction, this is "truck"). The subjects could apply following commands (see figure 4).

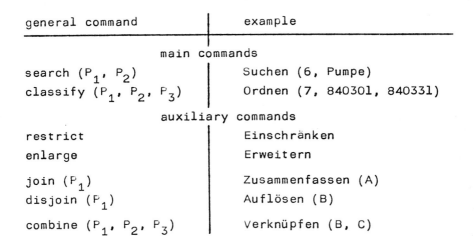

general command	example
main commands	
search (P_1, P_2)	Suchen (6, Pumpe)
classify (P_1, P_2, P_3)	Ordnen (7, 840301, 840331)
auxiliary commands	
restrict	Einschränken
enlarge	Erweitern
join (P_1)	Zusammenfassen (A)
disjoin (P_1)	Auflösen (B)
combine (P_1, P_2, P_3)	Verknüpfen (B, C)

Fig. 4: List of available commands

Command names and partly also parameters were loaned from natural German language to avoid additional learning of abbrevations or numeric codes by the subjects.
By using these commands the subjects could retrieve orders from the data-base. Data access was possible on different and partly alternative ways by using different sequences of commands. Dependent variables were:

- the time the subjects needed for entering the commands
- the overall time for the solution of the given tasks
- errors
- number of requested helps
- scores in a self rating survey (EZ-scale by Nitsch,1976)
- physiological data as parameters of the mental load (see Zimmer et al. in this volume).

Experiment I

In Experiment I two different dialogue structures were compared: The structure A (only one command could be entered per dialogue step) and structure B (several commands could be entered per dialogue step).

Because all commands have to be typed in full length, the "typing load" (number of key strokes) is the same in both structures. At first sight both modes seem to differ only slightly.
But dependent variables show interesting differences between both series. Figure 5 shows the overall solution time for 18 tasks.

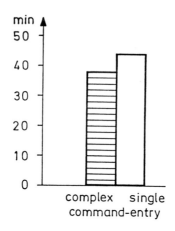

Fig. 5: Solution time for all tasks

The possibility to enter several commands in one step actually results
in a decreased solving time, but the difference is not statistically
significant. (All proofs were made by the t-test for independent samples).

The time for solving a single task (see fig. 6) significantly decreases
when complex command-entry is applied and tasks are relatively difficult.

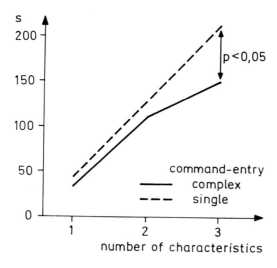

Fig. 6: Solution time per task

Task difficulty is described by the number of chacracteristics which are to meet by the retrieved orders.
Errors show similar relations as solving times do.

Fig. 7 presents the results of the comparison between the two structures.

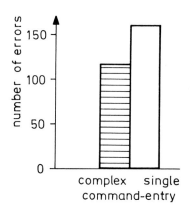

Fig.7: Number ot errors

The difference in Fig. 7 is insignificant. However the consideration of task difficulty (Fig. 8) shows a significant difference with the most difficult tasks.

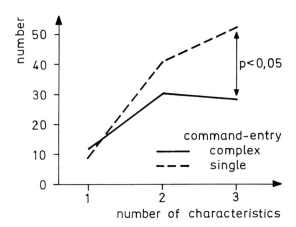

Fig. 8: Number of errors for different tasks

Both series are strongly separated with regard to the number of requested
helps (Fig. 9).

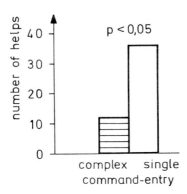

Fig. 9: Number of required helps

The data obtained by the Nitsch-Self-Rating-Scale were interesting, too.
We compared the estimation of factors of mental load and motivation before
and after the experimental sessions. Only those subjects showed changes
in their self-rated motivational and activational state who had the
possibility to enter more than one command per dialogue step, i.e. who
used dialogue structure B. They had a higher degree of self-reliance after
the experimental session as ell as a better temper.

This positive change in motivational factors as well as the relatively
small number of requested helps can be due to a better control of the
experimental situation by the subjects with this dialogue structure.
Control is here understood in the sense of Seligman (1979) and of Spinas
et al. (1981) who used this term in a specific manner for dialogue systems.

Fig. 10 shows the results of a paper and pencil simulation of mental load
using production systems as model. Only one of several possible description
indices, the number of items which are to be recalled from working
memory by solving a task,is shown.

Two different strategies were simulated. With both strategies a dialogue
structure with complex command-entry results in a smaller number of items
in the working memory. On the other hand the strategies themselves cause
different mental load. For detailed information see Zimmer et al. (1985).

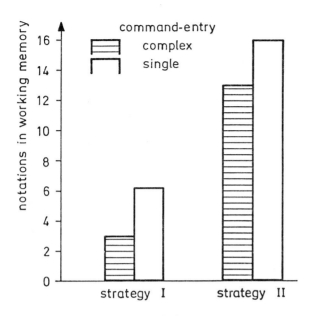

Fig. 10: Simulated mental load

Experiment II

This experiment was designed in following way: The subjects had to choose between the dialogue structures B and C (Fig. 1). In other words, they could choose between

- entering a sequence of several single and simple commands in one dialogue step (this was found to be a good facility in Exp. I) and

- entering of only one but complex command in one dialogue step.

The complex command reduced the "typing load" dramatically but raised mental load. The last is due to a relatively difficult formation rule for the command name. It can be demonstrated by the following example (see Fig. 11).

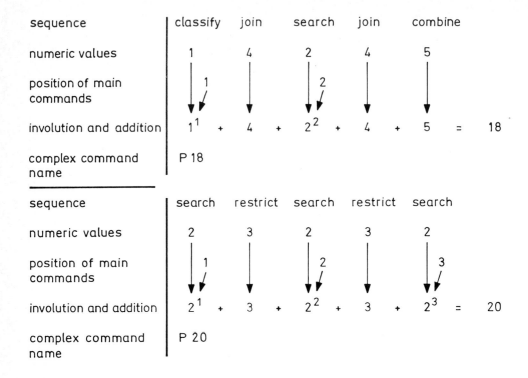

Fig. 11: Formation rule for the complex command names

Instead of a rather boring to type sequence of commands

    classify
    join
    search
    join
    combine

it is sufficient to enter "P 18".

Each command is transformed into a specific numeric value. These values
are

    1 for classify
    2 for search
    3 for restrict
    4 for join and
    5 for combine

The values of the main commands classify and search are involved by the
number of the position the corresponding main command holds in the
sequence of commands without regarding the positions of the auxiliary

commands. In the example presented in Fig. 11 classify holds the first position (its numeric value one is therefore involved by one) and search is the second main command (its numeric value two is therefore involved by two).

After the involution of the numeric values of the main commands by their position numbers all values (including those of the auxiliary commands) are to sum.

A second example in Fig. 11 may make this transformation plain . What was the reason for using this rather sophisticated calculation? This was made mainly, because we were interested in inducing a trade-off between the subjects tendency to minimize key strokes and to minimize mental load of the working memory. Following data were obtained (see Fig. 12).

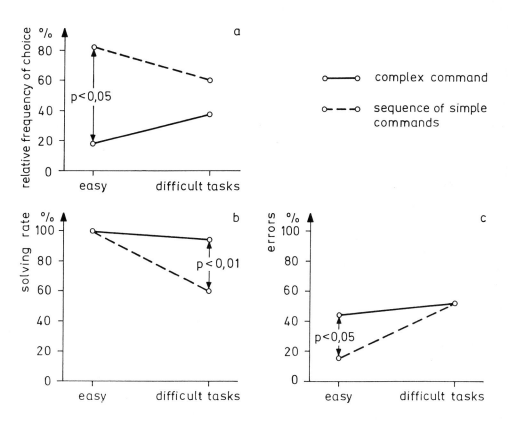

Fig. 12: The choice (a) of complex commands versus sequences of simple commands and performance (b,c) in dependence on easy and difficult tasks

The subjects prefer in general sequences of simple commands in one dialogue
step.

With increasing difficulty of tasks more complex commands were entered
(Fig. 12a).

Subjects solve all easy tasks with both dialog structures. But difficult
tasks are better solved by entering complex commands (Fig. 12b).

When subjects use complex commands they make more errors (12c), but on
the other hand this difference disappears for difficult tasks.

The analysis of the solution time showed no significant difference between
the two dialogue structures. This can be due to the fact that the solution
times contained also time intervalls in which errors were made, detected
and corrected. Correction of errors was easy in the case of complex
commands, because only the letter P and the number have to be retyped,
while in the case of sequences of simple commands a lot of retyping was
to perform, not only retyping but also getting the right state of the
system. The rather high number of breaking offs during the solution process
in the series with sequences of commands can be due to these complicated
conditions for error correction.

From these results the following conclusions can be drawn:

1. Different dialogue structures result in different performance and
   experience in naive users of computers. Cognitive as well as sensomotoric processes are responsible for this effect.

2. The possibility to enter a sequence of single commands in one dialogue
   step results in a significant better performance compared with a
   command-entry with single commands distributed over several dialogue
   steps.

3. This improvement occurs only with difficult tasks.

4. The transformation of sequences of commands into complex commands was
   mainly choosen when sequences were relatively long. Here the shortening
   is very effective.

5. If complex commands were entered more errors were made. But these errors
   were easier to correct. Therefore more tasks could be solved.

REFERENCES

(1) Moran, T.P., The command language grammar: a representation for the
    user interface of interactive computer systems, Int. J. Man-Machine
    Studies (1981) 3-50

(2) Seligman, M., Erlernte Hilflosigkeit (München, Wien, Baltimore 1979)

(3) Spinas, P., Troy, N., Ulich, E., Rohmert, E., Leitfaden zur Einführung
    und Gestaltung von Arbeit mit Bildschirmsystemen (Rüschlikon 1981)

(4) Zimmer, K., Weimann, J., Guguljanova, B., Phasic and tonic heart rate changes related to different strategies of task completition, in: Klix, F., Näätänen, R., Zimmer, K. (eds.), Psychophysiological approaches to human information processing research (North-Holland, Amsterdam, 1985)

Man-Computer Interaction Research
MACINTER-I
F. Klix and H. Wandke (Editors)
Elsevier Science Publishers B.V. (North-Holland), 1986

INTUITIVE REPRESENTATIONS AND INTERACTION
LANGUAGES: AN EXPLORATORY EXPERIMENT

Dominique L. Scapin

INRIA
Rocquencourt
France

This paper identifies a new research direction in the
domain of command language design. Investigating the
intuitive expressions produced by naive subjects giving
commands to a computer and the influence of instructions on the recall performance this study aims at
developing ground for the design of command languages
more flexible for the users. The findings deal with
the caracteristics of the language in terms of vocabulary, sentence construction, preconceived representations of the computer functioning, implicits and lack
of completeness. A few considerations for the design
of computer understanding programs are suggested and
future research steps are identified.

INTRODUCTION

This study constitudes an extension of contemporary research on computer
commands in restricted natural language, aiming to contribute to the design
of command languages more flexible for the user. Command languages are built
from natural language terms because the designers considered that: (a) being
immediately meaningful, (b) such command languages will be easier to use by
the population of naive users. However, if the first statement (a) seems
obvious, the second one (b)does not hold well. As a matter of fact, such
languages represent for the user: a reduction of his/her natural expression.
The user cannot build complete sentences, utilize all the syntactic variations of the language, shortcuts, metaphors, redundancies, etc., he/she
cannot make spelling errors, all these distortions being quite accepted in
the use of natural language; a selection of a few terms (often only one)
among several naming candidates; a standardization of the vocabulary. Being
required to use the same term for the same results seems reasonnable for a
particular system. But at the same time, it is very frequent that similar
functions on different systems or applications are named differently (even
sometimes, the labels are contradictory). Several studies (Barnard et. al.,
1982;Carroll, 1980, 1982; Hammond et al., 1980; Landauer et al., 1982;
Scapin, 1981 a, 1981 b, 1982) have illustrated these users'difficulties in
terms of low recall performance and confusions between terms. Therefore,
command languages have been recommended primarily for more experienced
users. These studies have also demonstrated the high variability of the
naming by the users themselves. Current research has identified some of the
reasons underlying command opacity, important factors affecting the users

performance such as definitions context, redundancy, naturalness, structuring, specificity, sequence order,parameters, etc. However, most work has dealt with the characteristics of existing commands rather than with user created commands and very little has been done concerning the way computer system descriptions influence the users naming and utilization of commands. In order to investigate how ease of use can be enhanced by overcoming some of the difficulties mentioned earlier, the purpose of this study is to gain knowledge about the naming process and to identify the role of the information provided to the users about the computer.

This project has two long range objectives: build a command terms data base and develop grounds for the design of computer interfaces allowing the users to enter their orders with more flexibility. Building a lexical data base, besides it's obvious interest for developing language understanding systems, has an added advantage as a tool for the designer. Such a data base, including cautionary information on possible confusions between terms, data on the generality/specificity of the terms, on their prototypicality, etc., would be a valuable source for the design of commands, an alternative to the sole use of the designer's own judgement and common sense. A first step of that effort (for office automation applications) has been completed (Tasset, 1984), using a systematic dictionary - based lexicographic search previously developed (Bisseret and Scapin, 1980) and experiments itended to explore the relationship between the terms obtained have been conducted. Further data from that research will be jointly used with the data gathered in the present study, for the design of command language understanding programs. Contemplating ways of improving the ease of use of computer applications, some considerations contribute to support the idea of designing some form of command language understanding. It seems unlikely to forecast the availability of natural language computer understanding for office automation in the near future. An approach solely based on linguistic theories and a wholistic approach of language will take a while before triggering the reality of task oriented languages. The characteristics of the language users would utilize when free of communicating with a computer are not known, However, we can hypothesize that they might use some form of extended command language, such as the language used for telex. Besides, experiments (Falzon, 1983; Kelly and Chapanis, 1977, Michaelis et al., 1977) have shown that in some situations, particularly technical work situations, very limited vocabulary and linguistic forms can be sufficient to express most of the orders an individual gives to another one. Therefore, step one of this project is to study the intuitive expressions, produced by subjects involved in a realistic task in order to evaluate the problems that would be raised for the design of command language understanding by computers. In addition, the influence of definitions provided about the computer on the naming and recall processes will be addressed, under the hypothesis that they will reduce the subjects' production variability.

METHODOLOGY

This exploratory study consists of two distinct experiments: Experiment I concentrates on the intuitive expressions created by subjects in a situation where they are required to give orders to a computer. Experiment II is centered on the effect of definitions on the command recall performance. This particular experiment is a derivation of a previous experiment (Scapin, 1981 b), with a different combination of variables and in a different language environment (French). In Experiment I, no command language was provided to the subjects whereas in Experiment II, a command language was

provided. In both experiments, some aspects of two variables related to
the definitions were investigated: procedure and context. The procedure was
or was not provided to the subjects. When it was, the subjects were prompted as to which computer function could be used for each step of the task.
The task requiring the use of the same function twice or more (except for
one function), the definitions were repeated several times. When the procedure was not provided, the subjects had to apply the right function to
the corresponding task step, which means that each definition was stated
only once. The context of the definitions was either operational, functional, or both. The operational definitions were user - oriented, worded
in terms of user objectives and operations. The functional definitions
were computer - oriented, worded in terms of computer functions. Experiment
I consisted of 3 conditions: (A) no information about the computer; information about the computer provided with both operational and functional
contexts: with the procedure (B) or without the procedure (C). Experiment
II consisted of 6 conditions (2 x 3): procedure provided and either
operational (D), functional (E), or both contexts (F); procedure not
provided and either operational (G), functional (H), or both contexts (I).

Procedure and material

For both experiments, the procedure consisted first of reading a task
description. The task was a routine clerical task involving the management of purchase orders and invoices in a garment buying office. The
operations involved in the task were selected so that all of them could
be done with a computer based system featuring electronic mail and data
base retrieval. The task description detailed what a clerk would do with
traditional office tools (forms, folders, paper, pencil, copy machine,
envelopes, etc.), and was organized as a scenario. All subjects in all
conditions read the same task description. Then the subjects were given
or not the various system descriptions and asked to express and explain
the commands they would give to have the computer perform the functions
needed to support the task. The computer definitions included or not a
command language. They followed exactly the task steps (with procedure) or
were only supplied once for each generic function (without procedure). This
also means that, when the command language was supplied, in one case (with
procedure). The command parameters were provided as well, whereas in the
other case (without procedure), the command parameters were not explicitly
provided. The definitions were operational or functional, or both, in which
case both operational and functional definitions were consolidated in one
definition. The task consisted of two sub-tasks involving each five generic
functions (consult an information, create an order or an invoice, send a
message, copy an item, store an item).

In Experiment II, a recall session took place a few days later. The subjects
were not aware that there would be a recall session and were not supplied
with any information about the computer but only with the original task
description.

Subjects

Thirty-four French speaking subjects were run: 16 in Experiment I and 18 in
Experiment II. The subjects were all undergraduate students and clerical
personnel, without any previous knowledge of, nor experience in computers.
All sessions of the experiments were run individually.

Performance Measurements

The language production of the subjects was analyzed with the aim of
describing its variations according to the experimental variables, and most
improtantly with the aim of characterizing the computer representations the
subjects build when they move from a manual environment to a computer based
environment. Therefore the subjects production was analyzed according to
its lexical and syntactical characteristics and according to the occurrence,
complexity and degree of precision of the computer functions expressed. This
was done by taking a programmer's perspective: would it be possible to
program a computer that would perform the functions the subjects suggested,
with the amount of information they provided? For experiment II, the analysis consisted mainly of a comparison of the command language produced
from one session to the other. This paper merely offers a preliminary analysis of the data obtained and should be considered as a pilot study providing directions for further experimentation. The analysis performed in this
experiment are qualitative, based on "clinical" descriptions of the data
rather than quantitative statistics which could not be used with the small
number of subjects run, and the subjects' production variability.

RESULTS, EXPERIMENT I

Vocabulary characteristics

The 16 subjects run in the experiment produced 116 different terms:
36 verbs (including two with two different verbal tenses); 10 substantives;
41 nouns (objects, locations, addresses); 29 miscellaneous terms (articles,
pronouns, conjunctions, etc.)

The total amount of different terms for basically expressing 10 functions
(including similar ones) is quite high (average of 7.25 per subject), but
manageable for a computer data base. However, about half of the vocabulary
produced could not have been predicted by a systematic lexicographic search
(such as in Tasset, 1984). Therefore a computer recognition based solely
on that technique would fail in 50 % of the cases. Of course, other techniques readily available can improve that recognition performance, and
certain terms can be ignored without lossing essential information (e. g.,
articles,pronouns, conjunctions); also interactive clarification dialogue
can be initiated by the computer. However, one of the main reasons why this
vocabularly could not have been predicted is that the subjects imagined
functions or features different from usual office automation functions,
therefore making difficult the choise of key words to start a lexicographic
search. The vocabulary obtained in the experiment confirms the high variability in naming and also suggests the need for qualitative studies of
languages produced in a task environment in order to achieve the potential
benefits of natural language understanding by computers.

Language characteristics

Very few of the expressions obtained can be described as purely natural
(at least written) language, built in the classical fashion: subject -
verb - objects... The 170 expressions produced by the subjects can be
divided into 5 categories:

- only two expressions including a desire were produced (" I would like the retailer's folder"; "I want the manufacturer for this item")

- several expressions (9,4 %) are in a "human communication" mode, personalizing the computer. Among these expressions, half used the casual you (tu) form, in which case they all started with "can you ..." or "do you want to ...", and half used the formal you (vous) form. Among these expressions, about a third included a reflexive pronoun (e. g., "keep me a copy in my file")

- most of the expressions produced are based on the use of the infinitive verbal mode (40,5 %), either correctly (18,2 %) or slightly incorrectly, i. e., with one or more articles missing or variations in the verb-object order (22,3 %)

- another group of expressions consists of title-sentences, i. e. expressions based on a substantive (23,5 %) (e. g. "duplication document in file") or using "... to be ..." (e. g. "copy of the invoice to be filed in the manufacturer's folder") (4,1 %)

- the last group of expressions consisted of the only production of an object name, without any verb or substantive (21,1 %). Most of these expressions were used to obtain, to display a document or information (77 %).

These results show that most of the time the subjects express their orders in a restricted fashion, very much like telex languages or even command languages. In a few cases they use fully natural language sentences. From a computer understanding perspective, this means that in 64 % of the cases, the expressions to be dealth with are much simpler than usual natural language. In addition, putting aside the previous considerations about the vocabulary (50 % predictible), and providing object-based implicit display features, it seems in theory possible to achieve an understanding performance of about 85 % "syntactical" recognition with programs developed for "command-like" expressions. The remaining 15 % could be eliminated by proper instructions (see next experiment) and by initiating clarification dialogues. However, in some cases, the expressions are quite complicated, for instance: "Can you give me the amount of the invoice increased by 10 %?"; "Take into consideration the references of the invoice and join them to the company's file", etc. Looking at the distribution of the expressions in the different categories according to the 3 experimental situations, it appears that none of the subjects in the B condition used expressions in a "human communication" mode and that the group in the C condition used twice has much as the A group did. However, this has an explanation in terms of individual differences. As a matter of fact one subject expressed more than half of these expressions. Another limited difference is that the B group used more title-sentences (36.06 %) than the other groups (23,7 % for A and 22 % for C). For what concerns the object alone category, the A group produced more of these commands (27,1 %) than the B group (21 %) or the C group (14 %). To summarize, very little difference in terms of the formal characteristics of the expressions produced can be attributed to the effect of the experimental conditions.

Characteristics of the intuitive functions

After looking at the vocabulary obtained, at the characteristics of the
expressions produced, it is interesting to examine the different ways the
subjects went from a manual environment to a computer environment, i. e.
what kind of computer functions they imagined to help them perform tasks
that were described in manual terms. First of all, it is noticeable that
very few subjects (3) used manual operations (4 cases) rather than computer
functions (for preparing an invoice, for mailing or for storage). All 3
subjects belong to the group without any information about the system (A).
Four subjects (out of 9) in the B group and 3 subjects (out of 4) in the
C group said they would use a visual consultation to select an information
from a document and therefore did no give any further order to the computer
once they had displayed the particular document, whereas only one subject
(out of 7) did so in the A group. Instead, the 6 other subjects of that
group (and one subject in each other group) used an automatic retrieval
function. This is one example of the sophisticated functions created by
the subjects. The term "sophisticated" is here used to refer to computer
functions that are generally not available on usual software for the office,
and that would require some amount of artificial intelligence. In this experiment, the subjects imagined 9 types of functions that can be divided
into "usual" functions and "sophisticated" functions.[1]

Usual functions	Sophisticated functions
- display of a piece of information or document	
	- automatic retrieval of a manufacturer
- creation of a purchase order, of an invoice	- automatic creation of a purchase order, of an invoice
- copy of a document	
- storage of a document	- automatic recording of all transactions
- sending of a document	- automatic mailing

The five usual functions are quite simple and do not require further
explanation. The 4 sophisticated ones require a few examples of the
subjects production.

- automatic information retrieval, e. g. "automatic search of the
  manufacturer", "Look for the manufacturer of this item", implies a
  retrieval process based on the purchase order message.

- automatic order or invoice production means that the computer is able
  to transfer the right information (e. g. item name, number, price,
  quantity) into the right place (order or invoice). For instance:
  "Call the form, make the order according to the form"; "Can you make
  an order for me."

- automatic storage of all documents and transactions means that in the
  subjects' view, the computer keeps track of everyting without being told
  to do so.(The subjects had more difficulties explaining how the information was retrieved from the computer.)

- automatic mailing means for the subjects either that (as for the
  previous function) the computer knows what, when and where to send, or

that the potential addressees will have direct access to the information without even sending them a message.

- Most of these functions would require sophisticated program modules that would be able to: find the context, i. e. identify in what type of task step the subject is; be context dependent (e. g. if it is an invoice, 10% commission should be added, ..., of it is an order, the manufacturer should be found, ...); recall without notice previously processed information (e. g. price of the item, address of the client, etc.). In addition, most functions would require cross-comparison of data from different sources (messages, manufacturer's files, invoices, etc.) It is noticeable that most of the subjects that imagined such sophisticated functions are subjects from the A group. The average use of sophisticated functions for that group is 2,85 per subject whereas it is only 1,25 for the B group and .80 for the C group. Looking at the individual performances, it appears that: In the A group, 3 subjects used both an automatic retrieval function and an automatic order production function; 1 subject used an automatic retrieval function and considered that the addressee hat automatic access to the information; 1 subject used only an automatic retrieval functions and 1 subject used all sophisticated functions, some of them several times. This particular subject accounts for half the use of the sophisticated functions in that group. Even if this subject is considered as out of the norm, it remains that considering the 6 other subjects (including 2 subjects that performed only half the experiment) the average per subject would then be 1,66 which is still quite higher than the other two groups. Thus, it seems that naive users bring with them a set of preconceptions (and misconceptions) of computer functions that do not always match the systems capabilities. Since providing information about the computer has a limitation effect which reduces their creativity, the choices among possible ways of computer functioning, the use of proper documentation can be a solution to avoid such preconceptions. However, aimed for the occasional user that will not necessarily read the instructions, the design of complex computer functions featuring elaborate artificial intelligence capabilities cannot result from the designer's common sense, but from experimental studies of the naive user intuitive expressions and representations.

Characteristics of the incomplete orders

Another major finding of Experiment I is that the expressions produced by the subjects, if they would be most of the time understood by another individual, would not be understood by a computer. The incomplete orders given by the subjects belong to 3 main categories: The function is not explicitly stated (see previous discussion on the expressions with only the name of the object, e. g. "Manufacturer's folder" for "Display manufacturer's folder"); one of the parameters of the function is missing: action location, addressee, e. g. "keep invoice" for "keep invoice in company's file", "send order" for "send order to client"; or object on which the function operates, e. g. "send to client" for "send order to client"; One of the parameters is missing but can be considered as implicit, or stated by default when the parameter was expressed within the previous order. For instance, "store invoice" for "store invoice in manufacturer's file" when it was preceded by "Open manufacturers's file". Considering all types of missing data together, the results show that the A group is characterized by an average per subject of 9 missing data, whereas this average is 8 for the B group and 7 for the C group. However it is more accurate to use the ratio: number of orders expressed/number of missing

data. Using such as ratio, it appears that the average of the A group
is 1.26, 2.11 for the B group, and 1.97 for the C group. In other words,
the subjects in the A group average about one missing data per command
whereas the two other groups average about one missing data every other
command. Looking at the different types of missing data, the results show
that the subjects from the C group used less implicit functions (23 %) than
the group A (44 %) and B (54 %). The subjects in both A group (37 %) and C
group (33 %) did not express as many parameters as the B group did (16 %).
Both B group (31 %) and C group (37 %) tended to use more implicit parameters than the A group did (19 %). However, the way these differences are
distributed does not allow any conclusion in terms of effect of the experimental variables. As a matter of fact, there are many differences between subjects, within the same group. The graphs obtained for each category of missing data are by far not parallel. Otherwise said, when a
subject does not explicitly express a function, he/she may not supply the
parameters or use them by default, and vice versa.

However, it is possible to distinguish roughly 3 levels of missing data,
all categories compounded, according to the ratio mentioned earlier:
1 (.85, 1.00;) 2 (1.25, 1.71); 3 (1.88, 3.75). Most subjects (6 out of 9)
that were provided with information about the computer (groups B and C)
belong to category 3 whereas one belongs to category 2 and 2 to category 1.
All subjects that were not provided with information about the system
belong either to category 1 (3 out of 7) or 2 (4 out of 7). Thus, the
information provided about the computer, with or without procedures,
appears to have induced the subjects to be more explicit about the functions they imagined. Analyzing further the data, it shows that if the cases
of default information and implicit object for a display function are
removed, then the differences increase (6.28 for group A, 3.6 für group B
and 3.5 for group C). As a matter of fact, both B and C groups are relatively similar in terms of implicits produced, whereas in the group
without information on the computer, the subjects tend to be less explicit
about parameters such as location or addressee, and not a all explicit
about sophisticated functions, even though the measure for these cases is
underestimated since most often, no expression was produced at all. According to the results, there is no strong difference between groups B and C.
This would contradict the hypothesis that not providing the procedure,
i. e. not distinguishing similar objectives for each task step, would
induce the subjects to more consistency in their command language. Looking
at similar task steps, no strong difference occur either. The subjects are
no more consistent in one group than in the other. As a matter of fact, in
most cases, the subjects are similarly inconsistent in lexical terms but
also in terms of implicits and missing parameters.

Discussion

In a situation that requires naive users to express orders to a computer,
it was found that their production has several characteristics: The number
of different terms produced is quite high, but more importantly, many of
them are difficult to predict; the subjects imagined ways of computer
functioning that are quite different from existing computers for the office.
The language produced is not by and large a "natural language" as described
in manuals of written English (or French in this case). Most of the expressions produced are in a "telex style", using mainly verbs in the infinitive tense or title-sentences with substantives. In many cases, only
nouns for objects were used. The experimental conditions influenced very

little the subjects' production in terms of vocabulary and style of expression. However, it seems that instructions about the computer have an
effect on the type of functions created and their completeness. With
instructions, less sophisticated functions were used and the expressions
were more explicit with regards to the functions and their parameters. No
clear distinction was established between the two conditions with instructions. From an artificial intelligence point of view, this study confirms
that further research cannot rely solely on general linguistic theories
about natural language. Research should also be conducted on the production
of "technical" languages involving precise tasks. Some of the topics this
experiment suggests are the need for investigating functions where context
recognition is crucial and ways of taking into account the subjects' tendency to express their orders with implicits, missing information, or information by default.

RESULTS, EXPERIMENT II

General considerations

In the first session, only 2 subjects imagined that one of the computer
features was to be able to automatically create an order from a message
received. Interestingly, the same 2 subjects are the only ones that said
they would manually mail or store an invoice. For all the other 16 subjects, the information about the computer together with the example of
commands curbed their imagination in terms of sophisticated functions. Most
of the commands produced belong to 3 of the categories defined in Experiment
I: (sentences with a verb in the infinitive mode (87 %); title-sentences
with substantives (7 %); name of the object only (2 %). Only one subject
used "human – communication" mode sentences (2 %). In the first session
of this experiment, even more than in experiment I, the very large majority
of the subjects used a "telex" type of language. In session 2 (recall),
none of the subjects used any sophisticated computer function. Again, most
of the commands produced belong to the same 3 categories (sentences with a
verb in the infinitive mode (58 %); title-sentences with substantives
(21 %); name of the object only (14 %). However, 2 subjects used several
"human communication" mode sentences, (7 %), particularly one who expressed all his orders that way (it is the same subject that also expressed
his orders that way in session 1). The difference between session 1 and 2
is basically that in more cases than in session 1, the subjects in session
2 used title-sentences and name of the object only. Some of the sentences,
as for experiment I, if they are understandable by another individual,
might be quite difficult to understand by a computer. Here are some examples: "Message Company file" or "Order message in Company file for
"Store the order message in the Company file" "Send this to the client"
for "Send the invoice to the client".

Comparisons between sessions

In this experiment, the analysis will focus on the comparison of the terms
produced in the first session with the command language provided, and most
importantly between session 1 and session 2. Two separate analysis were
conducted: one on the command verbs and one on the command parameters.

Command verbs

Considering the first session, in general (89,5 %) the subjects tended to
use the verbs supplied in the experiment, with a slight difference according to the existence or not of a procedure. In addition to the cases where
the subjects omitted or changed the verbs supplied, some subjects even
added new verbs to their commands. Considering the second session (recall),
the performance was in general quite poor (38 % of correct recall). However,
the recall performance is not uniform across the 6 different groups. Even
though the size of the groups is quite small, there is some indication that
both type of definitions and existence or not of a procedure have an effect
on the recall performance (see Figure 1).

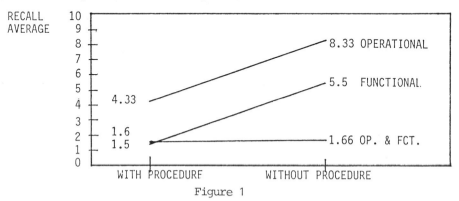

Figure 1

Recall of command verbs

The results indicate that providing the procedure might not be beneficial
for the recall as compared to eliminating the procedure. The verbs supplied, though repeated several times in the case with procedure, were not
recalled better. This holds for both operational and functional definitions
presented separately, but not when both types of definitions are presented
together. The results indicate also that operational definitions produce a
better recall performance than functional definitions (or both). This
result confirms the findings of a previous experiment (Scapin, 1981 b)
for operational definitions without redundancy.

In summary, the results indicate that operational definitions are better,
probably because they relate more to the naive users' task objectives. In
addition when providing both operational and functional definitions,
confusions, might have been created in supplying more verbs as naming
candidates. Also providing definitions for each step of the task does not
seem to be advisable either. In other words, what can be interpreted as
providing too much information can be detrimental to the performance.
Everyone has observed that, computer application manuals that repeat
commands and data fields definitions are often put aside by their users,
because they are too long and cumbersome.

Command parameters

Another interesting aspect of the subjects performance concerns the use of
parameters. Experiment I showed that many parameters are not explicitly
stated. How does providing a command language influences this finding? As

for the command verbs, session 1 was compared to the parameters provided and session 2 (recall) was compared to session 1, except for the case without procedure (i. e. without parameters) where the parameters produced were also compared to the ones supplied in the experiment. The number of parameters presented in the command language was 17 (3 commands needed only one parameter, 7 commands needed 2 parameters). The average per group of production or recall of the parameters was divided into similar parameters, missing parameters, and different parameters. In the first session, when the procedure was provided, the number of parameters stated as in the instructions is very high (95 %) whereas for the group without procedure it is only 30 %. It is interesting to notice that in that latter situation, 56 % of the parameters are missing whereas 14 % parameters are produced with different labels, which means that for this group, in 44 % of the cases, parameters were produced. In other words, in the first session, the instructions not only provided the subjects with labels but with the rule that a command has always (a) parameter(s). Even though not supplied with the parameters (which still existed in the definitions), the subjects without procedure managed to use or create more parameters (44 %) than the subjects in Experiment I (29 %). In the second session, the recall average for the parameters is 54.3 % which is just above average but still better than the recall performance for the command verbs. One of the reasons for this may be that the actual parameters were also stated in the definitions sentences. Looking at the different experimental conditions, the group without procedure and with operational definitions can be distinguished from the other groups (See Figure 2).

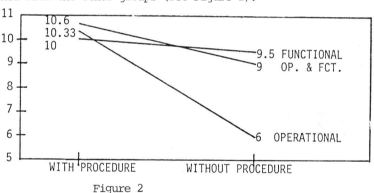

Figure 2

Recall of command parameters

Aside from that group, the subjects did recall almost as well the parameters that were provided to them (with procedure) or the parameters they created (without procedure), with little differences related to the context of the definitions. Also it appears that for the subjects with procedure, the recall performance is lower than the performance in the first session, but that for the subjects without procedure, the recall performance is higher than the performance for the first session. This finding could be considered as additional confirmation of the "generation effect" (Scapin, 1982), , except for the condition without procedure and with operational definitions. Considering the average number of missing parameters, the subject without procedure "discovered" also the rule of adding parameters to command verbs and used consistently that rule during recall. As a matter of fact, in the condition with procedure the subjects tend to omit more parameters during recall than during the first session whereas

it is vice versa for the other group: they added more parameters in the
recall session than in the first session.

Discussion

Experiment II, aiming to explore the role of command definitions on the
production and recall of expressions by naive subjects, supports findings
that confirm certain hypothesis, other research or require further clarification. Instructions about computer functions appear to familiarize
the naive subjects with existing computer functionalities which tends to
limit their representations in terms of sophisticated functions. Providing
a command language appears to provide a language model to which the subjects conform themselves, i. e., produce expressions in a command language
style rather than using human communication modes. However, a certain
number of expressions, even though syntactically simple, would be difficult
to be understood by a computer. The poor results from the recall session
confirm that command languages are quite difficult to manage by naive users.
It seems that operational definitions are beneficial for the recall. Also,
providing more information such as both operational and functional definitions or definitions for each task step is not beneficial. Providing
a command language influences the subjects to produce more parameters
(Experiment II) than when no command language is provided (Experiment I),
even when the parameters were not strictly part of the commands. In
addition to an interpretation in terms of "generation effect", it is
intriguing to observe that many subjects increase their use of parameters
in the recall session. Finally, two findings are somewhat contradicting:
giving the procedure is slightly better for the recall of parameters
whereas it is the opposite for the recall of command verbs.

CONCLUSION

The aim of this exploratory study was to begin identifying the problems
involved in the production and utilization of command expressions by naive
users in order to develop grounds for the design of interfaces more
flexible for the users. The language produced to give orders to a computer
is not, strictly speaking (or writing), natural language but a form of
technical, task oriented command - like language. In terms of vocabulary
but also sentences construction,the language is quite inconsistent between
subjects, within subjects, even for similar sub-tasks. The language produced reveals preconceived representations of the computer functioning and
lack of completeness. These findings suggest that providing interfaces
allowing mispellings, use of synonyms would not be sufficient to take into
account the expressions produced, unless the different concepts are limited
by essence such as for subway station names (Maguire, 1982). Instead, more
elaborate artifical intelligence features, such as context identification,
storage of previous transactions, default object identification, dialogue
clarification modeles, etc., are necessary to cope with such intuitive
languages. Also, the use of proper instructions, particularly expressed in
terms of users' objectives (operational definitions), is beneficial,
particularly in directing the subjects representations of the functions
and leading to more explicit statements, with less missing information.
These findings suggest that more investigations should be done, using
techniques such as the one used here, in order to gain knowledge of the
way users segment their tasks, imagine functions, express them, i. e.
transform their representation from a manual environment to a computer

environment. The next step of this project will be to assess these conclusions be designing software based on the data of this study together with the existing command language data base (Tasset, 1984) and evaluating the rate of computer understanding performance in a real time computer based experiment. In addition, some research questions are worth mentioning such as evolution of the naming in time (after 2 sessions), in other language environments (English, German, etc); how expressions are extended from one application to another that shares common features, general formalization of the operations in the office, etc. In summary, to move on to better interfaces, i. e. to reduce the discrepancy between humans and computers, it is necessary to conduct research on how to make the users better informed, trained (documentation) and how to have the computer understand better the users (artificial intelligence) (see for example (Hayes et al., 1981). For both aspects, it is the increased psychological knowledge of the human user that will enhance the friendliness of computer interfaces.

---

[1] To define these functions, the subjects were asked to explain what the computer would do following their commands, and how.

REFERENCES

(1) Barnard, P., Hammond, N., McLean, A. and Morton, J., Learning and remembering interactive commands, Proceedings of Human Factors in Computer Systems, Gaithersburg (1982)

(2) Bisseret, A. and Scapin, D. L., Ergonomie du service Agora Teletel. II: Etude du language de commande de la messagerie, Technical Report INRIA BUR RO6 du (1980)

(3) Carroll,J. M., Learning, using and designing command paradigms, IBM Research report RC 8141 (1980)

(4) Carroll, J. M. and Thomas, J. C., Metaphor and the cognitive represention of computer systems, IEEE Transactions on Systems, Man and Cybernetics 12 (1982) 107

(5) Falzon, P., Understanding a technical language: a schema-based approach, Research Report INRIA 237 (1983)

(6) Hammond, N. Barnard, P., Clark, I. Morton, J., and Long, J., Structure and content in interactive dialogue, Medical Council Report (1980)

(7) Hayes, P., Ball, E., and Reddy, R., Breaking the Man-Machine communication barrier, Computer March (1981)

(8) Kelly, M. J., and Chapanis A., Limited vocabulary natural language dialogue, International Journal of Man-Machine Studies 9 (1977)

(9) Landauer, T. K., Galotti, K. M., and Hartwell, S. Natural command names and initial learning: a study of text editing terms, Communications of the ACM (1982)

(10) Maguire, M., Computer recognition of texutal keyboard inputs from naive users, Behaviour and Information Technology 1 (1982) 93

(11) Michaelis, P. R., Chapanis, A., Weeks, G. D. and Kelly, M. J., Word usage in interactive dialog with restricted and unrestricted vocabularies, IEEE Transactions on Professional Communication (1977) Pc-20

(12) Scapin, D.L., Evaluation of an electronic mail language, Proceedings of the ACM International Symposium on System Architecture, London (1981 a)

(13) Scapin, D. L, Computer commands in restricted natural language: some aspects of memory and experience, Human Factors 23 (3) (1981 b)

(14) Scapin, D. L., Generation effect, structuring and computer commands, Behaviour and Information Technology 1 (4) (1982)

Man-Computer Interaction Research
MACINTER-I
F. Klix and H. Wandke (Editors)
© Elsevier Science Publishers B.V. (North-Holland), 1986

COMPUTER LANGUAGES:

EVERYTHING YOU ALWAYS WANTED TO KNOW, BUT NO-ONE CAN TELL YOU

TRG GREEN
MRC Applied Psychology Unit
Cambridge, UK

Recently Andrew Arblaster and I started writing a computer language. Now, as a psychologist I've been doing a lot of work on what's wrong with everyone else's computer languages, so I rather hoped that nobody would discover that I was now writing one myself. Unfortunately somebody did. There was a note in a magazine (Pountain, 1984) which was read by someone who had seen my previous work, and I received a letter saying: "Tell me about the theoretical foundations that underlie your new language in the light of your own research." This gave me severe problems. In fact, I had no answer.

Let us start with a statement of faith. One day, I believe, with the cooperation of psychologists, computer scientists, linguists, and others, we shall make our designs future-proof.That is to say, they will not be outdistanced when a new generation of computers is born, because we will have achieved a generalisable understanding of the interrelationships of different aspects of notations. Moreover, one day we shall understand how to avoid 'the Dammit Phenomenon', why people keep on saying "Oh, I've done it wrong ... Oh, I've done it wrong AGAIN!". And a third achievement will be, understanding 'the Language In The Head, the user's representation of the task, the language and the environment.

In this paper I shall consider the first of those three points, and I shall attempt to outline some of the interrelationships that must be understood if we are to achieve our goals. While I do so, I shall assume that programming languages on the one hand, and interactive languages such as text editing languages on the other hand, are closely related. When programming, the results of our actions are not immediately available; when editing text, our actions take effect immediately, but on the other hand the system does not usually preserve a record of what actions we chose - we have no 'program'. So there are clear and important differences between the environments, some of which have been captured for us by Dr. Streitz's paper in which he separates the 'content problem' from the 'interaction problem'. Nevertheless many of the points to be raised about one kind of computer language apply equally to the other, to Pascal as much as Word Star.

Here, first, are some random questions that can be applied to a computer language. How big is it, psychologically? How much 'grammatical work' does it require (and how do we measure that!)? How discriminable are its sentences? How do we formalise the relationship between the external, printed layout and the internal, semantic, structure? Evidently some of these questions are related; they are like economic goods - if you choose to have a great deal of one thing it constrains your other choices. I have tried to express some of the interrelationships in Figure 1, where each segment

can only grow at the expense of the others. Now I shall discuss some of
the interrelationships shown in that figure, trying to show what psychological evidence is available.

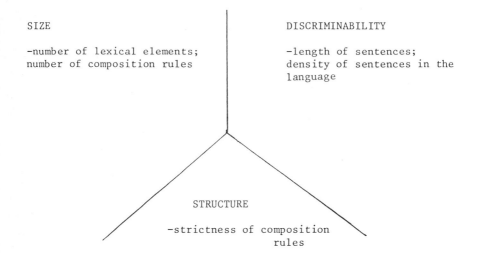

SIZE

-number of lexical elements;
number of composition rules

DISCRIMINABILITY

-length of sentences;
density of sentences in the
language

STRUCTURE

-strictness of composition
rules

Figure 1: Some inter-relationships between aspects of notations.
Size interacts directly with discriminability; discriminability can
also be increased by adding structure rules to reduce the density of
legal sentences; but adding structure rules increases the size. Other
aspects are 'forgivingness' and the 'perceptual parsing' of structure.

DISCRIMINABILITY AND SIZE

The discriminability/size problem is simply stated. In a language with
a small number of elements, it is often hard to distinguish one sentence
from another. Here are some examples:

    s /a\ /.&c/p\ /&c&   (a command for the Unix ED editor)

    ATTACH(OLDPL,$:APPLSRCES.CERNPROGLIB(*MT) ,ST=S19)

                          (from a mainframe Job Control Language)

One can make more than one criticism of such examples, and I shall return
to them below. But at the moment they serve to illustrate obscurity
created by designing a language with a very small vocabulary, so that many
primitives have to be glued together to make a complete command.

Alternatively, one can produce a language that has many different elements,
each of which has a slightly different meaning. Certain versions of Basic
have a multiplicity of slightly different PRINT formats, for instance; or,
as is well-known, the WordStar word processor has a very large number of
commands. Learning all the possibilities, and being certain of precisely
what each one does, can take a long time.

Reasons of space and convenience encourage designers to produce languages
with a small vocabulary, leaving it to the users to cope as best they can
with the resulting problems. Speaking purely as a psychologist one can
hardly criticise designers' decisions, because they have to work within a
complex set of constraints and trade-offs. In fact, I mean no criticism
whatsever of computer scientists, because I feel that it is we psychologists who are not able to supply the answers they need. What constitutes
a 'big' language? What constitutes 'discriminability'?

Although I know very little evidence bearing on this, my group at Sheffield
has reported one relevant study (Morrison et al. 1984). We designed a text
editor which had very few names for commands, each command being relatively
powerful, and we designed a related editor which had more commands but
weaker. In particular, in the first editor there was a command meaning

> move everything between the line containing "A" and the line
>   containing "B" and put it after the line containing "C"

while in the second editor the equivalent commands would be

> Mark the line containing "A" as START
> Mark the line containing "B" as FINISH
> MARK the line containing "C" as TARGET
> Move block

The second method is how WordStar works: more instructions, more things
to learn, each command less powerful. Which is the 'correct' design? Our
evidence suggests that in our situation people would prefer the second
design, at least up to the first four or five hours of use. The paper by
Drs. Wandke and Schulz presents evidence leading to the same conclusion:
they found that subjects preferred to use a sequence of simple commands
rather than one complex command, unless command sequences were extremely
long.

But the picture is not that simple! Suppose we look at the standard flow
chart and at an alternative (Figure 2). The standard flow chart is a very
'small' language, with only few types of box; as a result, one cannot
readily decide whether a particular decision box should be interpreted as
part of a conditional structure (Figure 2a) or part of a loop structure
(Figure 2b). When the diagram gets large (Figure 2c) the problem may be
acute. In the alternative notation there is a separate 'name' for conditionals and for loops, and this problem is eased. What are the pros and
cons here? Clearly, the conventional flow chart notation produces structures that are less discriminable than those of the alternative; at the
same time, flow charts have a simple, uniform structure, which is
frequently regarded as a virtue. (The arguments are developed in more
detail in Green, 1982 .)

To be brutal, as psychologists we have been very slow to provide a study
of the trade-off between language size and discriminability, we are not
even able to take the first step of stating how 'big' a given language is.
As result, we witness the regrettable situation of first-rate computer
scientists bickering about cognitive psychology: Hoare (1981)insists that
the language Ada is too big, both technically, for implementors (which
as psychologists is not our concern), and cognitively, for users (which
definitely is our concern); and Ichbiah (1984, p. 993), Ada's principal

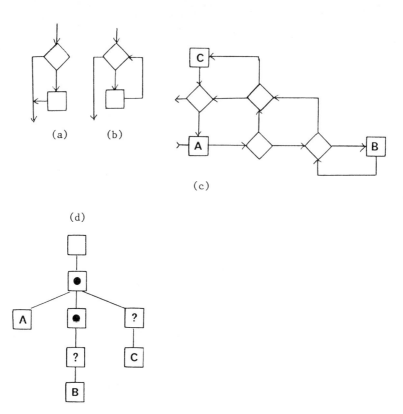

Figure 2: The flowchart language has only two 'words'. Although it is
easy to discriminate between a small conditional (a) and a small loop (b),
it rapidly gets difficult for larger flowcharts (c). An alternative, the
'structure diagram', introduces more 'words': = loop, ? = conditional.
This gives better discriminability (d).

creator, replies that
    "The human mind has an incredible ability to understand structures.
    Provided it understands the major lines of a structure, it will
    make inferences and immediately see the consequences. When you
    judge something, the complexity is not in the details but in
    whether or not it is easy to infer details from major struc-
    tural lines. From this point of view I consider Ada to be very
    simple."

It is most welcome to hear computer scientists arguing cognitive psychology; but it is sad to observe that they do so with no acknow-
ledgement that empirical studies might answer their questions. The
shocking thing is that cognitive psychologists should be able to tell
them whether Ada is 'big' or 'small', and we can't.

STRUCTURE AND FORGIVINGNESS

Although it is not immediately obvious, some linguistic structures are
more forgiving than others. The WordStar-like text editor mentioned above
would allow such 'sentences' as
        Mark the line containing "A" as START ... thinks: no, that's wrong...
        Mark the line containing "X" as START
and so on. Right up to the point where the final command is issued, the
three different marks- Start, Finish, and Target - can be relocated.

The same might be said of Basic and other goto-based languages, and also
of flowchart notations: because they allow the user unconstrained freedom,
they are more forgiving. They accept a larger number of program structures,
and any one program can frequently be modified by a very simple change or
addition. In contrast, more highly structured languages based on nested
hierarchies, as advocated by the school of structured programmers, are less
'forgiving'. That is to say, for a given number of program decision boxes,
one can build a far greater number of different structures if there is no
constraint than one can build under the constraint that the structures be
hierarchically composed.

Forgivingness, as I am using it (idiosyncratically), means that you don't
have to get it right first time; you can patch your work up, by replacing
pointers in your text or by sticking a goto into your code. A forgiving
language allows hacking. In contrast, Pascal encourages the programmer
to work everything out in advance and to get the program right first time.
This is seen as a virtue by structured programmers - and, in many situations,
it is.

Notice how this fact is related to discriminability. A central requirement
for a programmer is to discriminate the given program form other programs
that it might be. It is well-known that performance suffers when materials
are indiscriminable, and it is also well-known that discriminability can
be increased not only by making different objects more different, but also
by reducing the overall number of objects. Thus hierarchically-structured
programs are likely to be more discriminably different.

It has been shown by the Sheffield group and others that small conditional
structures based on gotos are more difficult for novices to write and for
professionals to comprehend (Sime et al., 1977; Green, 1977; van der Veer
and van de Wolde, 1983). But it has also been shown by several workers that
casting an algorithm into a strictly hierarchical, unforgiving structure
is extremely difficult under some circumstances, even for trainee computer
scientists (Hoc, 1983; Siddiqi, 1984; Soloway, 1983), Perhaps most telling
of all, the great mass of amateur and domestic programmers have voted
decisively with their feet. Although Pascal is available for many small
computers, and although it runs faster than Basic and is more secure, they
prefer to use Basic. There are, of course, many reasons given for their
choise, such as preferring the environment of an interpreted language
because it reduces the test-edit cycle time; but one of their major
reasons, if we can judge from their letters in popular computer magazines,
is that they find the syntax and structure of Pascal too demanding.

(A possible compromise solution comes with languages like C, which impose
some degree of structure but less than that of Pascal. It will be interesting to see how it fares. For what it's worth, the language I am
designing has much the same degree of structure as C.)

Here, therefore, we have a second trade-off relationship. This one has
been slightly better studied by psychologists. It is still, a present the
subject of emotional and dogmatic pronouncements from various sides,
proclaiming the virtues of structure or of its absence, the advantages of
Pascal and of Basic. Naturally, as psychologists our job is not to take
sides, but to clarify the cognitive aspects. Central to them are the study
of planning, since unforgiving languages demand forward planning, and the
study of program comprehension, since unconstrained languages are hard to
comprehend.

PERCEPTUAL CLARITY

The next topic in 'Green's tripod' is also related to discriminability:
the relationship between the perceptual display and either the linguistic
structure or its semantic content. This is an area that has received some
degree of attention from psychologists, studying how typographical structure
can improve the comprehensibility of technical prose by mapping the internal
structure of the document onto its layout (Hartley, 1977). Thus the perceptual cues - where the lines of type start and finish, how much white
space precedes them, etc. - can be used to tell the reader where the
junctions are between topics, how important particular parts are, etc.,
an art carried to a high degree of skill by newspaper subeditors. Sloboda
(1981) has shown that skilled pianists find sight-reading easier when the
music is printed with slight spaces between musical phrases, to help them
see the shape. Programmers have long advocated various forms of 'pretty-
printing', where the code is laid out with indentation, and Green and
Payne (1982) extended this idea to concurrent processes (using knitting
as a simple and familiar example where the 'program', or pattern, was
customarily presented with few perceptual cues). Fitter and Green (1979)
present further examples.

Once again I shall argue that the interrelationships need more attention.
But first I shall briefly describe a recent study from the Sheffield group.
The aim of this study was to demonstrate the perceptual cues to linguistic
structure are exceedingly important. How should one make the demonstration?
One method is to take an extremely complicated task and show that it could
be made much easier. This would be a good method in some ways, having good
face validity for instance, but a rather less good in other ways since
everyone outside psychology would say "Well, obviously, what else would
you expect?" We therefore chose the other route, and looked at a task
that was so simple that it would be quite unexpected that perceptual
cues should improve performance.

We designed a simple text-editor in which commands were line-based
instructions, such as

   4pAq

which meant "Find the 4th 'p'and insert After it a 'q'". In this version,
all the command letters were in capitals, but the remaining letters, like
the material to be edited, were in lower-case. Then we compared that to a
second version in which the commands were in lower-case:

   4paq

The results, reported by Payne et al. (1984), showed very clearly that our
users made far more mistakes with the second version.

How can we extend that finding? One simple way is to look back at the very
first example in this paper. There are several problems with that example,
but suppose we laid it out like this:

  change

        a\/.&c

  into

        p\/q\&c&

Already it has become clearer. But it still has problems, because it
contains several symbols which have special effects — and one of them,
"\", means simply 'the following symbol does NOT have a special effect
this time"! What would happen if we put some kind of special marking on top
of all special symbols? For example, those symbols could be in inverse
video. This strains the resources of book production, but even on paper we
could draw a little box round special symbols:

  change

        a/ ⬚ &c

  into

        p/&c ⬚

Thus, <u>even without knowing what the symbols in boxes mean,</u> we have
increased the clarity of the representation, and we have done so simply
by using perceptual cues to separate command fields from argument strings,
and special symbols from ordinary ones. One way to measure the improvement
in performance might be to examine the time taken to copy the command. Dr.
Kühn and his colleagues have described to us the severe difficulties of
typing long strings of random symbols; from my personal
experience, examples (1) to (4) of this paper are likely to rise similar
problems, but the 'improved' version of example (1) which we have just
created ought, if the argument is correct, to be less problematical.

Let us extend this line to the representation of programs. Earlier in this
conference Dr. Schmitt presented evidence about the usefulness of indentation in structured languages, and I would like to mention some comparable
findings obtained by David Gilmore, which have not yet been published.
Gilmore compared the comprehensibility of two styles of language, a
functional style and an assignment style, and he subjected each style to
some manipulations, as shown in Figure 3. Very briefly, he found that for
the functional style the tree diagram was easier to comprehend than the
pretty-printed, or indented, version; and that for the assignment style,
the logically-ordered version was easier to comprehend than the scrambled
version. Overall, the functional style was better than the assignment
style. A subsidiary and unexpected result was that subjects made more
written notes when studying assignment style programs. Let me say hastily
that the programs were very small, that the subjects included both practi-
sed programmers and novices, and that he will shortly be replicating and
extending this study. Assuming that the results are stable, what have we
learnt? Or rather, what questions does it raise?

We might, for instance, ask ourselves just why the functional style is
better. True, it is a matter of folklore amongst thoughtful computer
scientists that functional programming is good — and I seriously maintain
that in their approach to programming language design and programming

```
IF(greater(length([a b c]), length([2 3]),
      IF(islist(letterlist(2) ),
          length([1 2 3]),
          length([d f]) ),
      length([a e i 4 3]) ) = ?
```

(a) Functional style, indented

```
                      ... length.. [a b c]
      ... greater |
      |
      |               '.. length.. [2 3]
      |           ... islist.. letterlist.. 2
      |           |
  IF  |.. IF |.. length.. [1 2 3]
      |       |
      |       |.. length.. [d f]
      |
      |.. length.. [a e i 4 3]
```

(b) Functional style, tree diagram

```
length([a e i 4 3])  ->  W
letterlist(2)  -> Y
greater( length([a b c]), length([2 3]) )  ->  X
IF( X, IF( islist(Y), length([1 2 3]), length([d f])), W ) = ?
```

(c) Assignment style, scrambled

```
greater( length([a b c]), length([2 3]) )  -> X
islist( letterlist(2))  -> Y
IF( Y, length([1 2 3]), length([d f]) )  -> Z
IF( X, Z, length([a e i 4 3]) ) = ?
```

(d) Assignment style, logical order

Figure 3: Variations in typographical layout affect comprehensibility.

environments, computer scientists have produced some outstanding applied psychology by purely intuitive means. Nevertheless, it is also a matter of folklore that it is hard to understand long chains of commands, stuck one into the next; and Dr. Schönpflug has earlier presented evidence bearing on precisely that issue, showing that heart-rate rises and performance falls when subjects work with commands three at a time instead of singly.

MATCHING THE INFORMATION DISPLAY TO THE TASK

I turn now to the problem of defining a 'psychologically complex' program.
Specifically, is complexity a single attribute; or would one expect that
a particular program was 'complex' for some purposes but 'simple' for
others?

Gilmore and Green (1984) compared the comprehension and recall of
miniature programs expressed in two different paradigms. One paradigm was
the conventional assignment style, the 'procedural' paradigm. The other
paradigm was the 'declarative' paradigm used by such languages as pure
Prolog, the production-system interpreter OPS-5 (Hayes-Roth et al.1983),
etc. It was our contention that procedural languages expressed more
clearly one type of information, which we called 'sequential', and that
declarative languages expressed more clearly a second type, which we
called 'circumstantial'. (For procedural languages, differences between
questions demanding these two types of information had already been
reported in Green, 1979; an differences between these two and a third
type, input-output information, had been reported by Sheppard et al.,1981).

We predicted, therefore, that when the question type matched the program
type - sequential question plus procedural program, or the reverse -
performance would be better. This would give a match-mismatch effect.
We also produced another version of each program to which <u>cues</u> were
added to aid visibility of the 'wrong' kind of information; to the
procedural one we added cues to circumstantial information, and vice versa.
Our prediction was that the cues would have no effect on the matching
trials, but would improve performance on the mismatch trials.

It would be going too far to state that the results fully confirmed our
predictions. Nevertheless it was certainly clear that we had been at least
partly right.

One way in which computer scientists have been somewhat unsuccessful as
intuitive cognitive psychologists is in their treatment of psychological
complexity. They have tended to write as though a program could be given
a single complexity value, valid for all purposes (see the large literature
on 'software science', for instance). Our results show that particular
notations have structures which highlight particular aspects of the information they contain, and that complexity is a function of the task as
well as the program. Our results also indicate that conditions of mismatch
between task and program structure can be alleviated by various cues.

The future-proof psychologist should be able to answer such questions as:
What information is highlighted by a given notation? Is that information
sufficient for the following tasks? How can other information be made more
apparent? What is the relationship between a high degree of internal
structure in a language, and the visibility of given information ?

CONCLUSIONS

Needless to say, by concentrating on the first of the three points raised
in the Introduction I have been forced to ignore many equally important
questions. Even within the chosen area I have not touched on problems
of syntax manipulation and its relationship to forward planning, the

importance of user's prior experience, the natural categories of programming (if any), the effects of semantic categorisation of actions, the
possibility of formalising the user's macro-analysis of the program or the
task, and many others.

The message I hope to have conveyed is this. Designing a computer language
requires making a large number of decisions, attempting to meet constraints
that are both technical and psychological.In a great many cases, the decisions are compromises between the claims of two virtues which have a trade-
off relationship. As cognitive psychologists we should attempt to clarify
the interrelationships between such factors and to supply information that
can be used by language designers.

An indication of how far we have to go, convincing at least to me, is to
consider how I as a psychologist specialising in this area designed the
language I mentioned in the Introduction. I did it just like anybody else.
By the seat of my pants.

REFERENCES

(1) Fitter, J.J. and Green, T.R.G., When do diagrams make good computer
    languages?, Int. Jnl. Man Machine Studies 11(1979)235 - 261

(2) Frase, L., and Schwartz, B.J., Typographical cues that faciliate
    comprehension, Jnl. of Educational Psychology 71 (1979) 197 - 206

(3) Gilmore, D.J. and Green, T.R.G. Comprehension and recall of miniature
    programs, Int. Jnl. Man-Machine Studies 21 (1984) 31 - 48

(4) Green, T.R.G., Conditional program statements and their comprehensi-
    bility to professional programmers, Jnl. of Occupational Psychology
    50 (1977) 93 - 109

(5) Green, T.R.G. Pictures of programs, or how to do things with lines.
    Behaviour and Information Technology 1 (1982) 3 - 36

(6) Green, T.R.G. and Payne, S.J.,The woolly jumper: typographic problems
    of concurrency in information display, Visible Language, 16 (1982)
    391 - 403

(7) Hartley, J., Designing Instructional Text (Kegan Paul, London, 1977)

(8) Hayes-Roth, F., Waterman, D. A. and Lenat, D.B., Building Expert
    Systems (Addison-Wesley, Reading, Mass., (1983)

(9) Hoare, C.A.R., The emperor's old clothes, 1980 Turing Award Lecture,
    Communications of the ACM 24 (1981) 75 - 83

(10) Hoc, J.-M., Analysis of beginners' problem-solving strategies in
     programming, in: Green, T.R.G., payne, S.J. and van der Veer, G.C.,
     The Psychology of Computer Use, (Academic Press, London, 1983)

(11) Ichbiah, J., and Anon., Ada: Past, Present, Future, an interview with
     Jean Ichbiah, Communications of the ACM 27 (1984) 990 - 997

(12) Morrison, D.L., Green, T.R.G., Shaw, A.C. and Payne, S.J., speech-controlled textediting: effects of input modality and of command structure, Int. Jnl. Man-Machine Studies 21 (1984) 49 - 63

(13) Payne, S.J., Sime, M.E. and Green, T.R.G., Perceptual structure cueing in a simple command language, Int. Jnl. Man-Machine Studies 21 (1984) 19 - 29

(14) Pontain, D., Two new artificial intelligence languages: POP and SNAP, BYTE 9 No. 11 (1984, October) 381 - 388

(15)Shepphard, S.B., Kruesi, E., and Curtis, B., The effects of symbology and spatial arrangement on the comprehension of software specification, Proc. 5th Intl. Conf. Software Engineering (1981) 207 - 214; reprinted in: Curtis, B., Human Factors in Software Development (IEEE Computer Society Press, Los Angeles, 1981)

(16) Siddiqi, J.I.A., An investigation into problem decomposition strategies used in program design, unpublished Ph.D. thesis, Dept. of Computer Science, University of Aston in Birmingham, Birmingham, U.K. (1984)

(17) Sime, M.E., Green, T.R.G. and Guest, D.J., Scope marking in computer conditionals - a psychological evaluation, Int. Jnl. Man-Machine Studies 9 (1977) 107 - 118

(18) Sloboda, J., Space in music notation, Visible Language 15 (1981) 86 - 110

(19) Soloway, E., Bonar, J. and Ehrlich, K., Cognitive strategies and Looping constructs: an empirical study, communications of the ACM 26 (1983) 853 - 867

Man-Computer Interaction Research
MACINTER-I
F. Klix and H. Wandke (Editors)
© Elsevier Science Publishers B.V. (North-Holland), 1986

DESIGN OF PROGRAMMING LANGUAGES UNDER PSYCHOLOGICAL ASPECTS

Rudolf Schmitt, Eckard Schulz, Elisabeth Frank

Sektion Psychologie
Humboldt-University
Berlin
GDR

This paper presents a comparison between computer languages
taking into consideration some criteria established by using
of psychological results. Two topics are discussed. These are
transparency of program structures and advantageous choice
of string length for keywords, variables and labels. Finally
it is tried to summarize the tendencies in the development
of software from the point of view of programming language
means.[1]

INTRODUCTION

This paper presents a comparison between the well-known universal computer
languages taking into consideration some criteria established by the using
(generalisation) of psychological results. Two topics are discussed. These
are transparency of program structures and advantageous choice of keywords,
names for variables and labels. This is demonstrated by means of some typical examples.

Programming will become the art which influences the common sense. The set
of laymans or amateurs who are dominated by the designer of languages is
very strongly extending. To support the language design process effectively
it is proposed to take into account the results of such parts of psychology
which are dealing with human perception and memory.

Finally it is tried to summarize the foreseeable tendencies in the development of software from the point of view of programming language means.

CRITERIA FOR THE EVALUATION OF COMPUTER LANGUAGES

Criteria that can be incorporated in the comparison of programming languages
should be components of the global evaluation criterion in terms of minimum
consumation time to analyse, to program and to debug a well defined problem.
Furthermore the global evaluation should contain critical statements concerning the possible sources of making or preventing errors.

It seems to be very useful to restrict the comparison to the evaluation of
few special features despite of the danger of overestimating as well as
depressing. Keeping in mind psychological aspects one is forced to abstract
from different more or less effective possibilities to implement languages

and problems on a computer. Efficient man computer interaction is emphasized
in the course of program design. The following criteria defined by Weinberg
(1971) are regarded and extended:

Compactness

The criterion of compactness is derived from the chunking effect by psychological knowledge about the visual information processing. It is predicted
for compact programs that the difficulty to extract the main topics of
large and small sections of programs is minimized. A good program and
data structure will lead to the chunking effect.

Locality, Linearity, and Closeness

The programs should be built up according to the principles of locality,
linearity and closeness. After presentation of a visual structure the most
general features are derived to compare pictures. The principle of
locality demands that all relevant information for one page should be seen
on this page or screen. In particular the structure of the variables are
important global features. Linearity is derived from the sequential human
memory mechanisms and leads to the consequence that decision statements
should be stored in strongly linear queues. One can go back to the early
times of Gestaltpsychology to find the related experiments which led to
the knowledge of the closeness criterion. Closeness means that programs
can be visually devided in parts with some global features establishing
the frames.

Keywords and Names

Keywords were derived from the English language with some exceptions in
LISP: CAR,CDR for instance. There is the similar tendency in the natural
languages too: Most frequently used words are the shortest ones in general.
Regarding an efficient visual perception the following question arises:
Are there optimal string lengths for keywords or statements? The not
reserved words like names for variables and labels should be incorporated
in this question. First of all the results of our scanning experiments
are explained. Figure 1 shows the horizontal eye movements during the
scanning of a string consisting of 40 alphanumeric characters in randomized
order. The subject had the task to recognize the first figure as fast as
possible and to close the eyes after that.

The quick jumping of the eyes on several letters and the fixation movements
can be seen very impressively. The results of the two subjects for 30
alphanumeric strings are drawn in figure 2.

The frequency distribution of the jumps can be seen in dependence on the
string length that were included in the jumps.

The frequency peak on three letters lead to the conclusion that the visual
system can take three letters at once from a fixation point and a parallel
processing of three letters can be estimated maybe. At least it is not
nessesary to jump within a group of three letters. Therefore it can be
assumed that keywords consisting of three letters are recognized with less
effort and very quickly. Fig. 3 gives a comparison of important universal
computer languages according to relative frequency of reserved keywords
and standard functions in dependence on string length.

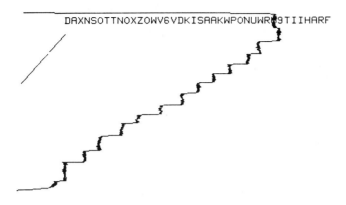

Figure 1: Example for the eye movement during the scanning of one
alphanumeric row. After recognizing the first number the eyes
should be closed. In this example the second number was detected.
The horizontal movements were plotted with equal distances in
the vertical direction.

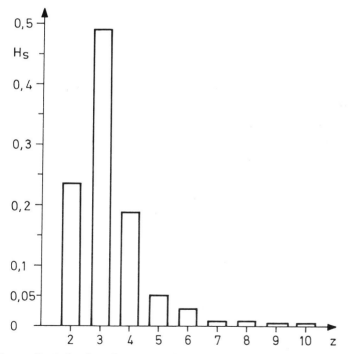

Figure 2: Relative frequency for the occurrence of quick eye movements
H_S in dependence on the number of characters z contained in one jump.

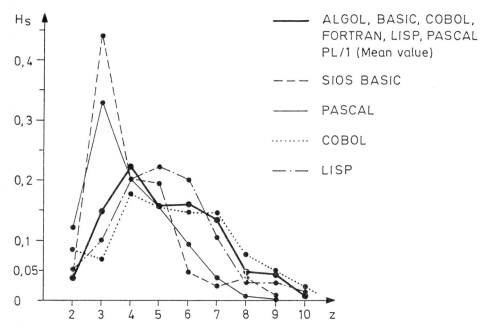

Figure 3: Relative frequency for keywords H_s in dependence on the number of characters used by the computer languages BASIC, ALGOL, COBOL, FORTRAN, LISP, PASCAL and PL/1.

The BASIC dialects show a pronounced peak at three letters. But the language PASCAL offers the same property too. Differing from the top of the mean frequency distribution on all main languages at four letters the relatively old languages LISP and COBOL prefer keywords with a greater number of letters COBOL especially. It seems to be the case that long term experiencies with computer languages are responsible for this tendency being comparible to the use of natural languages. The same conclusion can be drawn for the use of names of variables and labels. Languages allowing names with one or two letters only should be improved in this context.

It seems to be the case that there is an optimal length of keywords, names for standard functions and variables of three letters. The criterion of compactness is satisfied in this context.

Structuring

Each well structured program can be imagined as a pattern. This part of our paper is aimed at supporting such group of programmers which do not think in the actual language, do not have a deep problem knowledge or have to analyse strange or old programs. Which results of psychological research concerning pattern recognition could be used for structuring and producing suitable printouts? What conditions must be fullfilled concerning the compactness that both the main features of great and small compartements of programs can be reproduced with equal difficulties?

Figure 4 presents three typical patterns from a series generated by a Walsh function system. These typical patterns serve as stimulus for our experiments. After recognizing the inherent symmetry the reaction times and the errors were measured. Furthermore the eye movements during stimulus presentation have been recorded on-line by the computer which produced the stimuli too.

Figure 4: Presentation of three patterns ordered according to the inherent symmetry. The difficulty is growing from left to right. The patterns were generated by means of a Walsh system. Reaction times and eye movements were measured.

The following results have been obtained:

First: The increase in the number of identical parts of subpatterns and the increase in the number of different parts of subpatterns are factors leading to longer reaction times to the subjective estimation of a higher degree of difficulties and to more eye movements.

Second: The reproduction of a pattern by a subject and the eye movements are primarily influenced by the number of elements disturbing the inherent symmetry. Disturbances in one pattern lead to more effort in analysing all patterns.

The left pattern in figure 4 consists of two types of picture elements that have a very compact structure furthermore. This can be regarded to be the easiest pattern in comparison with the others. The difficulty to recognize the symmetry is increasing from left to right. Are there tools of programming languages for structuring in such a way that few compact substructures arise with one symmetry property at least?

In the following elements for structuring programs by the languages PASCAL, ALGOL 68 and LISP should be discussed by means of some examples from the mentioned point of view. Fig. 5 presents the statements and general possibilities to create a structured program in different languages.

R. Schmitt et al.

	PASCAL	ALGOL	ALGOL 68	PL/1	FORTRAN	BASIC	EXTENDED BASIC
1. Paranthesis for a compound of statements: BEGIN END DO DOEND	x	x	x	x	–	–	x
2. Complete alternative IF THEN ELSE	x	x	x	x	x	–	x
3. Choices CASE OF ON	x	x	x	–	x	–	x
4. Cycles							
WHILE DO	x	x	x	x	–	–	x
FOR TO NEXT	x	x	x	x	x	x	x
REPEAT UNTIL	x	–	–	–	–	–	x
5. More then one Statement on a line	x	x	x	x	–	–	x
6. Complete block structure	x	x	x	x	–	–	x
7. Definition of new DATA TYPES	x	–	x	–	–	–	–
POINTS	9	7	8	6	3	1	8
PLACE	1	3	2	4	5	6	2

Figure 5: Comparison of universal computer languages according to the
possibilities to create a structured program

The language PASCAL delivers three structures for iterations namely:
1. WHILE   statement,
2. REPEAT   statement,
3. FOR NEXT   statement.

Processing of cycles according to these control structures depends on the
position of the proof before or behind the statements of the iteration.
One point of our discussion is the using of a syntactical frame with BEGIN
and END. These frames should be suitably stressed (comp. figure 6).

The statements in this frame are regarded as a single unit with one entry
and one exit. It is proposed that the frame and the statements should
be arranged in such a way that a horizontally symmetrical impression arise.

```
PROGRAM SP (INPUT, OUTPUT);          PROGRAM SP (INPUT, OUTPUT);

declaration part                     declaration part

BEGIN                                BEGIN
1: X: PSEUDO(X);                     F:='J';
2: WRITELN ('INPUT VALUE');             WHILE F='J' DO
   READ(Y); I:=I+1;                     BEGIN
   IF Y>X THEN WRITE ('VAL.GREAT');        X:=PSEUDO(X);
   IF Y<X THEN WRITE ('VAL.LOW');          WHILE (Y<X) OR (Y>X) DO
   IF Y= X THEN GOTO 3;                    BEGIN
   GOTO 2;                                    WRITELN ('INPUT VALUE');
3: WRITELN ('VALUE RIGHT');                   READ(Y); I:= I + 1;
   WRITELN ('REPETITION ? (Y/N)';             IF Y>X  THEN WRITE('VG');
   READ(F);                                   IF Y<X  THEN WRITE('VL')
  IF F='Y' THEN GOTO 1;                     END;
END.                                       WRITELN('VALUE RIGHT');
                                           WRITELN ('REPETITION?(Y/N)');
                                           READ (F);
                                         END;
                                     END.
```

Figure 6: Comparison of two program parts written in PASCAL

The left part of figure 6 serves for the structure comparison between a PASCAL version without underlining the structure and the structured one right. ALGOL 68 supports repetition by the WHILE and FOR statement only. The frame of the WHILE statement is established by REP and PER (fig. 7). The reserved words REP and PER are especially qualified for delivering an impression of horizontal symmetry because the principle of converting the sequence of symbols.

```
PROGRAM SP;
BEGIN
declaration part
      F: = "J";
      WHILE (F = "J")
      REP
            WHILE (Y<X) OR (Y>X).
            REP
                  WRITE  ("INPUT VALUE");
                  READ (Y); I: = I + 1;
                  IF Y>X THEN WRITE ("VAL. TOO GREAT");
                  IF Y<X THEN WRITE ("VAL. TOO LOW" );
            PER
            WRITE ("VALUE RIGHT");
            WRITE ("REPETITION? (Y/N)");
            READ (F);
      PER
END
```

Figure 7: Program part written in ALGOL 68

ALGOL 68 has several pairs of words for clustering of statements. There
are IF – FI, REP – PER, DO – OD, CASE – ESAC, (–). Figure 8 shows
nested IF THEN ELSE statements leading to horizontal symmetry in case of
suitable engaging.

```
            IF A THEN IF B THEN IF C THEN X ELSE Y FI
            ELSE Z FI ELSE W FI

IF A
   THEN
       IF B
           THEN
               IF C
                   THEN X
                   ELSE Y
               FI
           ELSE Z
       FI
   ELSE W
FI
```

Figure 8: Nested IF THEN ELSE Statements, above in linear sequence
          below with transparent structure (ALGOL 68)

There is a great problem for a programmer who starts to work with the
language LIPS to equalize the parenthesis on both sides. Each convex
clump must have its counterpart.

Figure 9 demonstrates an example of a clear parenthesis structure.

```
( COND ( ( GREATER  Y  X ) ( GO LAB2 ) ) ( ( LESSP Y X )
( GO LAB3 ) ) ( ( T ) ( GO LAB4 ) ) )

( COND
       ( ( GREATER Y X ) ( GO LAB2   ) )
       ( ( LESSP    Y X ) ( GO LAB3   ) )
       ( ( T            ) ( GO LAB4   ) )
; DNOC; )
```

Figure 9: Part of a program from the PASCAL program in LIPS above in one
          sequence; below with transparent structure

Each of a paranthesis which clump a large amount of statements should be emphasised by a comment and a shifting. The comment could be built up by the reverse principle of ALGOL 68. Comments at the end of the frames indicated by END showed to be usefull in the ALGOL like family. The possibilities to structure are poor for all BASIC dialects and FORTRAN too although there are some qualitative differences according to the criterion of compactness. A good BASIC should possess the following possibilities at least:
First: Alphanumeric labels;
Second: Procedures with formal parameter matching;
Third: A full IF THEN ELSE statement;
Fourth: More than one statement after a line number.

In conclusion it should be emphasised that the restriction to little but powerfull control structures with one entry and one exit point leads in connection with shifting and a good arrangement of the statements to global transparency of the program in the sense of pattern recognition. The compact substructures should possess a horizontal symmetry. This fullfill the criteria of compactness and linearity.

Shifting and changing the program lines can be done automatically by pretty print programs and for documentation purposes by a software tool which analyses the structure. The result of an automatic analysis is a so called structogram that fit the mentioned criteria. Structograms can not only be the final point but a good start for automatic programming and editing too.

TENDENCY IN THE DEVELOPMENT OF PROGRAMMING LANGUAGES

GROSS and SCHELLER (1983) mentioned three basic tendencies which are assumed to influence and to dominate the results of soft- and hardware of the fifth computer generation.

First: The development and application of intelligent interface systems is expected. This interface will support the communication with natural language and graphics tools at a very great extent.

Second: Efficient access and processing mechanisms will make it possible to use great data bases (expert systems).

Third: Quick problem solving and interface machines appears with the aim to reach 10^8 till 10^9 logic interferences per second (LIPS).

Which consequences arise for the design and application of universal computer languages? Can the psychological research contribute in the context of interdisciplinary work? The mentioned tendencies emphasize the effective storage and access to complex data and their relations. Each programming language can contribute to these goals more or less. But the intentions for creating the different languages were quite different. Therefore a different efficiency can be stated. FORTRAN is dominant in processing numeric data, LISP in symbolic data, PROLOG serves for logic processing. Problem solving systems written in FORTRAN demand a description of objects and relations between the objects on the basis of numeric features. LISP and PROLOG allow a more flexible and compact description of relations and objects. The last two languages will be prefered as basic languages for the fifth computer generation because of that reasons. PROLOG takes a

favorite position by the Japan computer manufacturer. It can be considered
as the application of predicate logic and it should be suitable for the
design of expert systems. But despite of the favorite position of such
languages which unite logic symbolic and numeric data precessing there are
the obvious tendencies both to extend old languages and to develop quite
new languages with good structuring properties, PASCAL (1971), ADA (1980)
for instance. New computer architectures (DATA FLOW) on the basis of the
well known electronic principles and optical computer in future will
allow a high degree of parallel computation of the statements. There is a
world wide development to establish such kind of languages supporting
parallel computation ALGOL 68, CONCURRENT PASCAL and ADA as languages of
the third and fourth computer generation have explicit parallel working
statements. But the main concept is devoted to a central memory unit till
now. The statements of the type
N: = N + 1
are given up in DATA FLOW machines.

The present dominating of BASIC dialects supporting the dialog programming
is parallized by the trend to automatize the programming. The computer
should be teached to recognize the instructions for automatic programming
in natural language. The way is characterized by languages that allow
us both an efficient problem description (PROLOG) and a proceeding of a
large class of problems.

The border between universal problem oriented languages and a collections
of procedures will be difficult to define. The main reason for that
difficulties is the multilayer structure of language software. That
means one language is realized on the basis of the second: LISP on the
basis of FORTRAN for instance. Time difficulties in proceeding problems
written in the higher level language can be overcome by hardwired processors.

CONCLUSIONS

It is assumed that psychological memory phenomenons can be advantageous
used in future for the design of large data bases and for the development
of new language constructions. The fast and parallel working computer
architectures can only be used effectively if the programmers are
supported by good learning tools and easy understandable languages. The
main fields for parallel working will be the analysing and synthesizing
of pictures. Results of psychophysics and perception in psychology should
be checked concerning their benefit in language design.

In this paper we tried to give two examples how to use psychological
results for the structure and keyword evaluation.

----
[1] The authors would like to thank Dr. Friedrich (ZKI der AdW) and Dr. Kurt
for their helpful discussions.

REFERENCES

(1) Weinberg, G.M., Psychology of Computer Programming,(Van Nostrand, New York, 1971)

(2) Shneiderman, B., Software Psychology, (Winthrop Publishers Cambridge, 1980)

(3) Gross, B. and Scheller, B., Forschungsbericht: Computer der fünften Generation, Z. Phonetik, Sprachwiss. u. Kommunik. Forschung 36 (1983) 6, 755-768

(4) Robinson, J.A., Logic Programming - Past, Present and Future, New Generation Computing 1 (1983) 107-124

(5) Geske, U., PROLOG. B. Grundlagen. Beschreibung. Handbuch, Information des ZKI der AdW der DDR (1983)

(6) Lerner, E.J., Data-flow architecture, IEEE Spectrum 4 (1984) 57-62

(7) Schmitt, R., Rechnersprachen und -dialekte. Auf dem Weg zur strukturierten Programmierung, Wissenschaft und Fortschritt 2 (1984) 36-39

(8) Schmitt, R., Rechner heute und morgen. Von sequentiell zu parallel arbeitenden Rechnerstrukturen, Wissenschaft und Fortschritt 6 (1983) 226-230

Man-Computer Interaction Research
MACINTER-I
F. Klix and H. Wandke (Editors)
© Elsevier Science Publishers B.V. (North-Holland), 1986

PROBLEM ORIENTED DESIGN OF INTERACTION STRUCTURES

H. Kiesewetter

Institute for Informatics and Computing Technique,
Academy of Sciences of the GDR

Berlin
GDR

Interaction structures represent an interface to
interactive problem solving at a problem oriented
level. Exact definitions are given in the form of
INTAK structures; consisting of object contacts
for checking and manipulating characteristics of
objects, process contacts for initializing processes,
and decision contacts for transition between contact
fields, each of which offering a compact decision
situation to the user. The program kernel INTAK
provides unified software means for the design,
generation, utilization and management of INTAK
structures. INTAK structures are in current use at
computers of different type. They open new ways of
mass usage of computers for problem solving.

INTERACTIVE PROBLEM SOLVING

Throughout this paper the term 'interaction' will be used as an
abbreviation for 'man computer interaction' as well as 'user computer
communication'. Questions of interaction have to be considered from rather
different points of view. One guideline for interaction should be the
system oriented one. It is engaged with the questions of hardware configuration and software architecture for interactive systems. Considerable
effort has been made in the last decade for unification and standardization
of hard- and software means for interaction, especially with respect to
graphic output and input (GKS - Version 7.2.) . Having this in mind, ten
Hagen (1980) gave the following interpretation: '... interaction, which
means communicating with a computer program in real time'.

In this paper I follow quite another guideline, which may be called a
problem oriented one. The main question will be: To clarify the role of a
computer as a problem solving machine for its user.

What can a computer (i. e. a programmable digital information processing
unit) do for problem solving in cooperation with its user?

. A computer can thoroughly store information about the problem solving
process.

. A computer can carry out arbitrary algorithmic (i. e. programmable) processes as contributions to the problem solving process.

. A computer can offer output information to the user about the actual state of problem solving.

. A computer can receive input information from the user for further processing.

The user will try to get maximal assistance be the computer in solving his problems. What then else is left to do for the user?

. The user must judge the actual state of problem solving.

. The user must decide, how to proceed further in problem solving, based on his idea of the aimed solution, his knowledge and experience.

There are problems, they will be called algorithmic problems, which can be solved by a computer without the help of man. Three conditions must be fulfilled:

. The problem is uniquely determined by its input and output parameters.

. A program is available, which solves the problem.

. An available program is effective on an available computer; that means it can be implemented and executed according to the required resources and time.

Every non-algorithmic problem will be called a creative problem, that means:

Either   its input or output parameters are not completely determined

or   no program is available, which solves the problem

or   no available program is effective on an available computer.

Creative problems need the work of man for its solution. To give some example: Solving a system of linear equations is an algorithmic problem. Of course this is true under certain suppositions. One condition is,that the number of equations must not exeed a certain limit depending on the performance parameters of the available computer. On the other hand, design of a ship for instance will in every case be a creative problem. One can also imagine, that users prefer creative problem solving in spite of the fact, that algorithmic solutions might be available under certain circumstances.

Interaction delivers means for the solution of creative problems. Interactive problem solving is principally based on the same elementary processes as algorithmic problem solving, but there is one fundamental difference: The user gets information about arbitrary intermediate states and makes decisions, how to proceed further. This implies that the deterministic character of algorithmic processing is lost in interactive processing.

The computer itself is a priori destined for algorithmic processing. As a bare computer it doesn't offer sufficient means for interactive problem solving. Therefore it has to be prepared for its role as a cooperative partner of the user. The potential contributions of the computer must be offered to the user in an understandable and consistent manner. Assistance must be given, how to make decisions. Algorithmic and communicating processes have to be included in a general control scheme. One has to design adequate decision situations and connect it to a creative strategy for problem solving. This alltogether has to be done at a problem oriented level.

INTERACTION STRUCTURES

The central part of preparing computer for interactive problem solving is to design an interaction structure. A verbal prescription of the term 'interaction structure' may be given as follows:

An interaction structure consists of means for defining and connecting potential decision situations, which will be offered by the computer for use in interactive problem solving.

Several techniques have been developed in order to design interaction structures for more or less specialized interactive systems. They use different means of soft- and hardware as well as different control strategies, e. g. menus, command languages, question-answer techniques, alphanumeric and graphic output and input devices, user interface management systems and others. Usually explicit and precise prescription of the underlying interaction structure from the point of view of the user is missing. This however seems to be the essential interface to problem solving.

Now let us precisely define the term 'interaction structure'.
This will be done in the form of a graph, named 'INTAK structure'.
A graph has to be defined by its knots and arcs. The knots of an INTAK structure will be called 'contacts'. They serve as basic elements for making contacts between user and computer. Only three types of contacts have to be defined:

. An object contact identifies a property (attribute) of a class of objects and keeps a value (number, string, characteristic etc.).

. A process contact identifies a process and indicates its state (active or passive).

. A decision contact identifies a contact field, i. e. an ordered set of contacts of arbitrary type, representing a compact decision situation.

Each contact 'co' in a contact field 'dco' defines an arc of the INTAK structure, starting in 'dco' and ending in 'co'.

From a graph-theoretical point of view the set of contact fields represents a follower definition of the underlying graph. Object, process and decision contacts may be arbitrarily arranged in a contact field. Obviously, it isn't meaningful but not forbidden to put a decision contact in its own contact field or to put the same contact twice in a contact field. That means, an INTAK structure can be supposed to be without loops and multiple arcs. Apart from this it may be an arbitrary directed graph.

The contacts of a contact field are numbered. Gaps in enumeration are admitted. The identifier of the contact field and the contact number, both together identify a contact globally in an INTAK structure.

The type of a contact is explicitly indicated to the user in the following way:

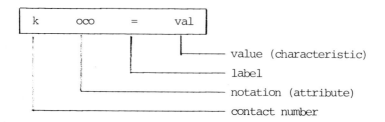

Figure 2.1.
Object contact

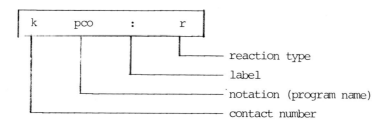

Figure 2.2.
Process contakt

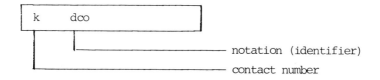

Figure 2.3.
Decision contact

The notation of an object contact has only local meaning in its contact field. Another object contact in another contact field, keeping another value, may have the same notation. For each object contact two values are permanently stored in the INTAK structure: The norm value, defined when generating the structure, and the actual value, generated as result of the last input.

A process in the sense of INTAK is by definition the execution of a program, a so-called contact program, and represents an algorithmic process. The notation of the process contact is identical with the contact program name. It is of global meaning in the INTAK structure. A process contact notation can be repeatedly used in any contact field of the INTAK structure, but it identifies in every occurence the same process. This is in distinction from the application of object contact notations. The reaction type of a process is announced by the symbols 'P', 'A' or 'PA' alternatively. Each process may consist of a prompt reaction (P), an accept reaction (A) or both (PA). The prompt reaction is a once executed, when the user puts the process contact in its active state. The accept reaction is only executed, when the user additionally activates the special process contact 'ACCEPT : P'.

The notation of a decision contact agrees with the identifier of a contact field. Again it is of global meaning in an INTAK structure and may repeatedly be used in any contact field.

The control strategy for processing on INTAK structures is simple and clear:

One contact field is the actual one. It offers a complex decision situation to the user. He can at each state of problem solving activate any contact of the actual contact field.

After activation of an object contact the user can change the actual value, e. g. by means of an alphanumeric keyboard. The new actual value will then be displayed.

Activation of a process contact alters its state. The state 'active' is marked by a label or in another way.

Activation of a decision contact results in the immediate transition to the corresponding contact field.

Three fixed contacts will be put into every contact field. They concern general, problem independent control processes.

1 ACCEPT : P

This is a process contact with prompt reaction. When the user activates contact 1, all accept reactions of all active process contacts are executed. The order of execution agrees with the order of the contact numbers. If one wishes to change the order of execution one has only to change the contact numbers.

2 CFIELD = val

This is an object contact. Its value may be any identifier of a contact field. Contact 2 works together with contact 3. The norm value is the identifier of the restart field (cf. 'RESTAR : P').

3 JUMP : P

This again is a process contact with prompt reaction. It means jump to an arbitrary contact field. The value contact 2 is taken as the identifier of the new actual contact field.

Further problem independent contacts are offered as optional ones.

k NORM : P

This is a process contact with prompt reaction for resetting all actual
values at the object contacts of the actual contact field to its norm
values. This is especially useful, if one wishes to start again with
problem solving in a new attempt, without resetting all actual values
contact by contact.

k RESTEP : P

The result of activating this contact is, that the identifier of that
contact field, which has been the last actual one just before, is
displayed as the new actual value at contact 2.

k RESTAR : P

When this process contact is activated, the identifier of that contact
field, which allows a meaningful restart of the problem solving process,
is displayed as the new actual value at contact 2. The restart fields have
to be assigned, when generating the INTAK structure.

Now INTAK structures have been precisely defined. They represent an
interface to interactive problem solving at a problem oriented level.
Users of INTAK structures may be 'naive experts', that means people with
little knowledge in computer techniques but excellent knowledge in their
own field. This will be important for opening of new ways of mass usage
of computers for problem solving. It should be added, that INTAK structures can as well be designed for the exclusive use by computer science
experts. A computer equipped with an INTAK structure works as an INTAK
machine, i. e. an interactive problem solving machine.

Problem oriented design of interaction structures can be compared with
problem oriented programming of algorithms.

interaction structure	:	algorithm
design	:	programming
INTAK structure	:	problem oriented program
creative problem	:	algorithmic problem

INTAK structures can advantageously be used to develop new forms of
interactive problem solving, not strongly marked or not present in
nowaday systems.

. The user can immediately start his next INTAK session with the last
  actual values, keeping the last activities of the preceding session.

. Norm values can be reassigned (RENORM), for instance when starting a
  new problem solving phase under changed conditions.

. INTAK structures represent a creative problem solving potential.

. INTAK structures are independently designed, generated, used and managed in form of INTAK files.

. INTAK files can be offered for collective as well as for individual use.

. Individual INTAK files, to be applied for special purposes, can be extracted from permanent INTAK files.

. INTAK files can be transfered between computers by means of special data transfer techniques.

PROGRAM KERNEL INTAK

The program kernel INTAK has been developed as a unified basic soft-ware for the solution of the task:

'Design and control of interaction'.

It consists of functions for the design, generation, utilization and management of INTAK structures. It uses the basic functions of the structural kernel ALGRA (Kiesewetter, 1979), since INTAK structures can be treated as special structural objects in the sense of ALGRA.

Generating of an INTAK structure is carried out be means of the following four elements:

. Directive for the generation of contact fields

    !IDENT := cfi1 $\#$ n 1, cfi2 $\#$ n2 , ...

An IDENT-directive serves for declaration of identifiers (cfi1, cfi2, ...) and field lengths (n1, n2, ...) of contact fields.

. Directive for the generation of an object contact

    @ cfi $\#$ k := oco = val

. Directive for the generation of a process contact

    @ cfi $\#$ k := pco : r

. Directive for the generation of a decision contact

    @ cfi $\#$ k := dco

By one of the last three directives the k-th contact of contact field 'cfi' can be made an object, process or decision contact respectively. Executing of those directives results in generation of INTAK structures in form of INTAK files. They contain already the whole information, necessary to be stored for object and decision contacts. Process contacts must yet be provided with contact programs. Special software means give assistance for its implementation. The input and output parameters of contact programs can arbitrarily be connected with actual values at any object contact. This is already all to know about implementation on INTAK structures.

Man works with INTAK structures at two different levels:

. As its user at the level of a naive expert.

. As its implementator with some knowledge in problem oriented programming

The design of an INTAK structure should preferably be originated, checked and improved by the user, while its generation will in general be carried out by the implementator.

Control of interaction is automatically performed by the INTAK control program. Neither user nor implementator must care for it. The INTAK control program works on the INTAK structure. A fixed control cycle is processed for each type of contact, initializing and executing all necessary reactions and subprocesses. All questions of connection with available user computer interfaces are also treated by the INTAK control program. As a minimum installation it is sufficient to have means for:

. The display of the actual contact field.

. The activation of a contact.

. The alphanumeric input.

This can already be offered by cheap configurations.

As a simple example let us consider part of an INTAK structure for the generation of contours:

INTAK

1 ACCEPT : P	2 CFIELD = LINE	3 JUMP : P
4 NORM : P	5 RFIELD = CIRCLE	

LINE

1 ACCEPT : P	2 CFIELD = CONT	3 JUMP : P
4 NORM : P		6 NAME = CONT1
7 LPP	8 OPA	9 LABC
1Ø LPLA	11 LLD	12 LPC
13 LCC	14 LCA	15 LPN

LLD

1 ACCEPT : P	2 CFIELD = LINE	3 JUMP : P
4 NORM : P		6 LINE
7 LLD : P	8 PICT : A	
1Ø L(1) = Ø.	11 L1(1) = Ø.	12 D = 1
13 L(2) = 1.	14 L1(2) = Ø.	
16 L(3) = 1.	17 L1(3) = 1.	
19 L(4) = 1.	2Ø L1(4) = Ø.	

The contact field INTAK is a problem independent root field for the jump into any special INTAK structure. The object contact '5 RFIELD = CIRCLE' keeps and displays the RESTEP field, i. e. the last actual contact field.

The contact field LINE allows to decide, which form of generation of a line will be chosen. For instance, LLD means generation of a line L parallel to a given line L1 with distance D. A line is defined by two non-coincident points. The actual identifier for the generated contour is stored and displayed at the object contact '6 NAME = CONT1'. Transition to the contact field LLD is achieved by activating the decision contact '11 LLD'.

The parameters determining L, L1 and D are kept at object contacts in the contact field LLD. Two processes are present:

'7 LLD : P'

This is for geometric construction. The parameters of L are calculated according to the actual values of L1 and D and displayed as the new actual values at the contacts 10, 13, 16 and 19.

'8 PICT : A'

This is a process contact with accept reaction for the display of the actual picture.

Figure 3.1 shows the essential part of the INTAK structure of another example, named INTMOL (Backhaus et al., 1984). The representation is restricted to the identifiers of contact fields and serves only as a rough survey.

INTMOL has been designed for interactive development and graphic output of molecule and crystal structures. It has been implemented a graphic desk computers. It consists of about 600 contacts and 45 contact fields. It allows different graphic output in form of line models (LIN) or ball models.

Figure 3.1 shows how complex problem solving situations can be well structured by means of INTAK. The contact fields

LININ	input
LINMOD	modelling
LINOUT	output
LINTRA	transformation

represent the main phases of normal traversing through the problem. They give valuable guidance for the user in keeping survey over 600 decision possibilities and to get a good understanding of what can be done next and how can it be done.

282   *H. Kiesewetter*

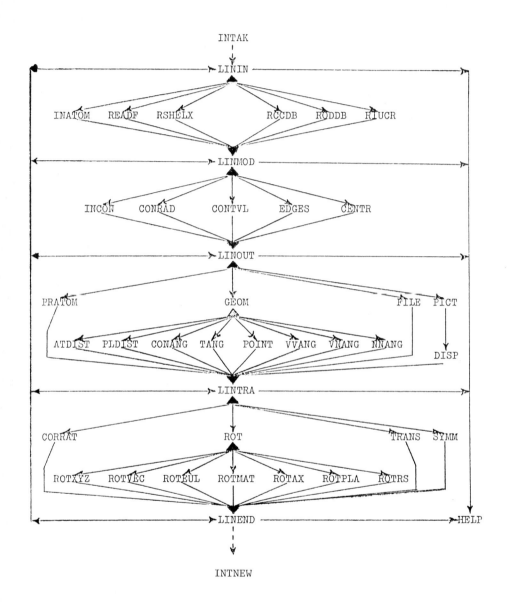

Figure 3.1
Part of INTAK Structure INTMOL

REFERENCES

(1) Backhaus, K.-O.; Grell, H.; Schrauber, H., Storing of Data of OD
(Order-·Disorder) Substances, XIII. Congress and General Assembly of
the IUCr. Hamburg, 9. - 18. 8. 1984

(2) GKS-Version 7.2 (ISO DIS 7942)

(3) Kiesewetter, H., Some Problems of Modelling Graphics Software for
Application in CAD/CAM Systems, EURO-IFIP 1979, London, 509 - 514

(4) ten Hagen, P. J. W., Communicating Graphics, Infotech state of the
Art Report, Computer Graphics, vol. 2 (1980)

Man-Computer Interaction Research
MACINTER-I
F. Klix and H. Wandke (Editors)
© Elsevier Science Publishers B.V. (North-Holland), 1986

USER REQUIREMENTS IN NATURAL LANGUAGE COMMUNICATION WITH DATABASE SYSTEMS

Ulrich Koch

Central Institute of Cybernetics and Information Processes
Academy of Sciences of the GDR
Berlin
GDR

Natural language front-end processors for commercial database systems are designed today without practical experience about what the user really wants. Therefore, the design is made on the base of some imagined user types. We distinguish the enduser, the buyer and the scientific consumer as influencing forces for design and implementation. The criteria posed by these user types are sometimes rather different. We select some advanced concepts in natural-language interfaces to discuss the related problems. The DAD NLI-system developed at our institute is taken to supply the stuff for the discussion.

INTRODUCTION

Natural-language interfaces (NLI) have become a common research subject of the language-oriented Artificial Intelligence. In the last years (since 1982) several NLI-systems have been introduced into practice (e.g., Intellect) or have been evaluated in some experiments (Krause, 1982). Besides the diligent and thorough evaluation experiments made by Krause (1982) and Jarke (1983, 1984) and the work by Michaelis et al. (1977) and Zoltan et al. (1982) there are little objective experiences what the user really wants. Therefore, the designers and implementers of NLI systems are forced to look inside themselves to build up an abstract user image as the addressee of the system. However, if the researchers think about users they have not only the typical or wanted enduser in mind but also at least two further types of users. We describe the three user types to be distinguished in the following way:

1. The enduser. This is the user who sits in front of a display and types in his question to the database in his mother tongue. In this class of users there are several subtypes as casual, naive or professional users of a database. In all papers about layouts of NLIs this kind of enduser is presupposed and it is implied that the system is all right if this enduser is satisfied.

2. The buyer of the system. The buyer need not be an enduser.
   For instance, it can be a software house that wants to
   enriche its database management system production with a natural language front-end processor. Of course, such a user
   will not be interested in the facilities of the NLI if you
   are able to proof or to convince him that the customers of
   the enterprise will be happy to have such an NLI and they
   will be satisfied by the system given. But this is currently
   not the common situation. No NLI designer today is able to
   deliver such a proof because he needs firstly a software
   house or somebody else who carries some risk and helps gather
   practical experiences for testing and improving NLI front-
   ends. To minimize this risk, the buyer will establish his
   own criteria which can be widely differ from these ones the
   real enduser will have and probably they will differ from
   the criteria cur third user type has in mind.

3. The scientific consumer. Because NLI design is up to now
   scientific basic research, the investigators are interested
   in publishing their results to have communication with the
   "NLI community". The first papers on this fields has been
   freed from scientific criteria. The imagined enduser gave
   the design criteria likewise. Now the situation has changed.
   Some independent demands arose that are establishing the
   scientific base for developing natural-language interfaces
   such that some work in NLI is done only for scientific
   purity without worrying about whether the enduser needs it
   or not. Nevertheless, the real or fictitious enduser remains
   the main stimulator for progress in NLI work.

To put meat on the bones, we will discuss our troubles with
these user types on the basis of the DAD NLI-system developed
at our institute. In the next section we will give a short
outline of this system, our test database and a sample dialog
with DAD to make you familiar with the average performance that
a user can expect from an NL front-end. In the third section
we will discuss this dialog with respect to the user types
having been introduced.

DAD-SYSTEM, TEST DATABASE AND SAMPLE DIALOG

The DAD NLI-system consists of three main parts. A linguistic
processor, called SYSAN, a translation module for generating a
retrieval expression from the SYSAN output, and an experimental
database management system to be able to demonstrate a full run
from the question to the answer.

The SYSAN language processor comprises lexical analysis, syntactic analysis, and semantic analysis in an inner linguistic
sense. All these components are independent of discourse and
application. The lexical analysis perform inflexional analysis
and a partial word building analysis, if the word form is not
in the lexicon. A dialog module supports the user to define
word forms which cannot be analysed. The human partner in this
dialog is not supposed to be a linguistic expert, she needs
only a good command of the language. A basic lexicon containing

all functional worlds and representatives of open word classes
belongs to the DAD standard equipment.

Translating the SYSAN-output into a logic expression, which is
the origin for translation into several query languages, is
performed by several steps. The distance between our executable
DAD retrieval expression and this logic expression is very small.
A more comprehending description of DAD can be found in Koch
(1983, 1984).

The experimental database

H (production)			T (parts)			V (manager-of)	
H.P	H.T	H.)	T.T	T.N	T.G	V.P	V.V
P6	T1	800	T4	SCHRAUBE	M7	P4	P2
P1	T2	333	T3	NIET	M7	P1	P3
P1	T1	500	T2	MUTTER	M6	P2	P3
P1	T4	200	T1	SCHRAUBE	M6	P3	P5
P2	T1	300				P6	P1
P2	T2	100					
P5	T1	50					
P6	T3	500					

P (employees)				
P.P	P.N	P.B	P.D	P.G
P6	KRAUSE	SCHLOSSER	410610	1300
P5	MEIER	ABTEILUNGSLEITER	610513	1600
P4	PIEFKE	LEHRLING	550712	100
P3	MUELLER	SCHWEISSER	350611	1000
P2	KRAUSE	SCHLOSSER	420510	1300
P1	MUELLER	ANGESTELLTER	400410	1500

P.P, H.P - person identifyer, P.N - family name, P.B. -
occupation, P.D - birthday, P.G - salery
T.T, H.T - part identifyer, T.N - part name, T.G. - part size
V.P - subordinates, V.V - manager
H.Z - quantity of production

You see there are two so-called basic relations P and T which
describe individuals by some features and two link relations
(H and V) which place these individuals into a relationship
to each other whereby the link relation H gets an additional
attribute which quantifies the relationship between producer
and product.

Sample dialog
=============

(NLI)
BITTE EINGEBEN: (1)
WIEVIEL VERDIENEN DIE SCHLOSSER?
;HOW MUCH DO THE LOCKSMITHS EARN?

GEHALT
1300
1300

BITTE EINGEBEN: (2)
WAS PRODUZIEREN SIE?
;WHAT DO THEY PRODUCE?

PRODUKT   NAME
T1   SCHRAUBE
T2   MUTTER
T3   NIET

BITTE EINGEBEN: (3)
UND WIEVIEL?
;AND HOW MANY?

ANZAHL
 400
1300

BITTE EINGEBEN: (4)
WELCHER SCHLOSSER PRODUZIERT WIEVIEL TEILE?
;WHICH LOCKSMITH PRODUCES HOW MANY PARTS?

ANZAHL   PRODUZENT   NAME
 400   P2   KRAUSE
1300   P6   KRAUSE

BITTE EINGEBEN: (5)
WER PRODUZIERT MEHR ALS MEIER?
;WHO PRODUCES MORE THAN MEIER?

VERGLEICH-ZU   NAME   PRODUZENT   NAME
P5   MEIER   P1   MUELLER
P5   MEIER   P2   KRAUSE
P5   MEIER   P6   KRAUSE

;VERGLEICH-ZU (with respect to) indicates which person with
the name mentioned in the question the answer refers to

BITTE EINGEBEN: (6)
WAS PRODUZIEREN DIE MITARBEITER VON MEIER?
;WHAT DO THE COLLABORATORS OF MEIER PRODUCE?

KEINE DATEN GEFUNDEN
;NO DATA FOUND
P3, the collaborator of Meier, does not produce anything

```
BITTE EINGEBEN:                                      (7)
VON MUELLER?
;OF MUELLER?
```

PRODUKT	NAME	VERGLEICH-ZU	NAME
T1	SCHRAUBE	P1	MUELLER
T1	SCHRAUBE	P3	MUELLER
T2	MUTTER	P3	MUELLER
T3	NIET	P1	MUELLER
T4	SCHRAUBE	P3	MUELLER

```
BITTE EINGEBEN:                                      (8)
WIE HEISSEN DIE MITARBEITER VON MUELLER?
;HOW ARE THE COLLABORATORS OF MUELLER CALLED?
```

NAME	VERGLEICH-ZU	NAME
KRAUSE	P1	MUELLER
KRAUSE	P3	MUELLER
MUELLER	P3	MUELLER

```
BITTE EINGEBEN:                                      (9)
GEHALT VON KRAUSE UND MUELLER?
;SALARAY OF KRAUSE AND MUELLER?
```

GEHALT	PERS-NR
1500	P1
1300	P2
1000	P3
1300	P6

```
;not to give the names in this answer is not a matter of
cooperativity but a real programming error, this happens some-
times, really.
```

```
BITTE EINGEBEN:                                      (10)
WER PRODUZIERT WENIGSTENS DIE TEILE, DIE MEIER HERSTELLT?
;WHO PRODUCES AT LEAST THESE PARTS WHICH MEIER PRODUCES?
```

VERGLEICH-ZU	NAME	Produzent	NAME
P5	MEIER	P1	MUELLER
P5	MEIER	P2	KRAUSE
P5	MEIER	P5	MEIER
P5	MEIER	P6	KRAUSE

```
;it is quite impossible to give also the parts in question.
But you have DAD and you can ask for it, e.g. "which parts
does Meier produce?".
```

```
BITTE EINGEBEN:                                      (11)
WER VERDIENT 1000 M?
;WHO EARNS 1000 M?
```

PERS-NR	NAME
P3	MUELLER

```
BITTE EINGEBEN:                                           (12)
UND WER 1300 M?
;AND WHO 1300 M?

PERS-NR          NAME
P2               KRAUSE
P6               KRAUSE
```

DISCUSSION OF SOME USER REQUIREMENTS

Cooperativity

The sample dialog we are giving demonstrates some capabilities
of the DAD NLI-system. Sometimes, the answers seem too little
cooperative, they are rather literal with respect to the
questions. This happens especially if the questions contain
interrogatives, because the interrogatives tell the system what
the user really wants to know, DAD thinks, but forgets that
the user has his trouble with his mother tongue also. DAD
investigates the question a little more thoroughly if there are
no interrogatives and gives the information the user might be
interested in. But DAD is still in developing and we think
that the problems with more or less cooperativity can be overcome in the next future. The answer to question (1) might be:

        There are two locksmithes.
        Each of them earns 1300 M.

If there are more locksmithes with different salaries, the answer might look like:

        There are n locksmithes with the following salaries:
        1300, 800, ...

Of course, these answers contain information which are not
questioned but this makes the conversation more friendly.
Wahlster (1984) calls this kind of respond preparation "over-
answering". One of the most advanced system with respect to
cooperativity is HAM-ANS from Hamburg University. Cooperativity
is more a demand of the fictitious enduser, scarely of the
buyer because the formal language means for questioning data
bases do not even know this notion.

We are dealing with cooperativity on a rather low level: how
to structure the result table that the questioner can simply
detect his intention.

Presupposition

As with cooperativity presupposition problems arise mainly in
connection with natural language communication although they
exist in using formal manipulation languages also, but nobody
cares about. Every question above contains existential presupposition, for instance: (1) takes for granted that every
body earns something and there are locksmithes in the personell
staff. If some of these assumptions fail the system should tell

the user that it is not able to give information because this
or that presupposition can not be fulfilled. I think that this
requirement will be posed again by the enduser and the scientific consumer, less by the buyer because this domain seems to be
beyond the scope of the classical paradigm. Nevertheless, to
facilitate the system in such a way is not a simple task. DAD
cares about it only in some cases where a missing presupposition
test can lead to funny answer which are logically correct but
surprising for the naive user. For instance, for question (10)
we would get every person in the personell table if Meier does
not produce anything, because the implication is true if the
premise ("Meier produces something") is false.

References, ellipses

One main advantage of natural language communication with databases is that it is possible to maintain a dialog memory and
therefore to put questions which refer to former questions or
answers. (2) and (3) are such successor questions where (2)
is referring by the personal pronoun "they" and (3) is elliptical, i.e. it refers by deleted words. This facility is once
more a scientific requirement especially arising from the
linguistic claim of the system and will be quickly realized and
applied by the enduser.

A type of a not referring but elliptical question is (9). This
type is also demanded by the buyers because NLI is often sus-
pected by them that it is only able to handle complete sentences.

Aggregation, comparatives

Aggregation is to be understood as computation of numerical
values which are not explicitly stored in the database. Such
aggregation can be demanded directly or indirectly by the
question. "How-many"-questions often need aggregation for
answering. But also requests which require to compare numerical
values sometimes need aggregation. In each case, it depends on
the state of the database. For example, comparing salaries does
not demand aggregation because there is only one kind of salery
in our test database, but comparing or how-many-questions with
respect to the quantity of production demand aggregation
depending on the restriction given in the question, e.g. all
parts, screws, screws and nuts a.s.o. Typical questions containing aggregation are (4) and (5). Handling aggregations is
a typical requirement of the buyer because he is well familiar
with this problem. It is not so interesting for scientific
consumer, especially computational linguists, and the enduser
is scarely confronted with this problem immediately, because
he is not supposed to be aquainted with the internal database
structure.

Inferences

To have available inferential capacity in database management
systems is a requirement of all three user types. Perhaps, the
naive user is not always aware where inference is needed. By
inferential capacity it is understood that (besides the facts
and links stored in the database which, of course, also give
arise to find new knowledge) there is some implicit information
about the database that can be employed for finding satisfying
answers. The test database above might provoke to the request:

> "Give all managers of Mueller!"

As you can see, the manager relation only contains the immediate
managers of a person. If we consider "the manager of the
manager of ... Mueller" also as a manager of Mueller (transitive
closure) then it must be stored explicitly (exactly: exten-
sionally) because our relational DBMS can not employ intensio-
nal knowledge like the transivity axiom for manager-of. By the
way, the natural "all" quantifier in the question above would
be taken as redundant because the system is designed to supply
every (non-inferential) answer it can find.

Logical completeness

Logical completeness is a typical demand of the scientific
consumer. Neither the enduser is aware of this problem nor,
usually, the buyer. There are no investigations, as I can see,
whether the enduser tends to write natural requests which
employ complicated logical connections. Question (10) above is
an example for that what we have in mind. But you can build
rather strange questions, e.g. "Does nobody produce nothing?",
to demonstrate or test the ability of the system to handle
first order logic adequately.

CONCLUDING REMARKS

The target group of the NLI development is of course the enduser. Up to now there are only little investigations of the
language behaviour of the real enduser. Particularly Krause
(1982) has done much effort on this field but the evaluation
of his evaluation has to be careful because he experimented
only with the USL NLI-system and the user groups were either
very small or in a laboratory situation. He found some interesting results concerning adaptibility of the user, his
ability to accept totally forbidden concepts and his inability
to obey the prohibition of syntactic and semantic variants.
Also restrictions in the vocabulary are accepted.

There are some experiments (Zoltan et al., 1982) which investigated the errors occuring in man-man-dialog on the one
hand and the man-machine-dialog on the other hand. The results
are not surprising but reassuring: generally a much higher
number of errors mispronounciation misspelling, ungrammatical
utterances, etc. was reported for experiments where people had

communicated with people than it was where people communicated with a computer quoted from Zoeppritz (1983).

Because NLI is quite a new technology its introduction into practize has to be carefully prepared. First, a proper data-base has to be selected. Toy databases like the above one are only sufficient in the research phase and not every existing database supplies good stuff to demonstrate the advantages of NLI. Second, more sophisticated experiments in real environments has to be carried out for getting reliable data for design.

REFERENCES

(1) Artificial Intelligence Corporation, INTELLECT Query System Reference Manual (1982)

(2) Jarke, M., Zur Beurteilung natürlichsprachlicher Endbe-nutzerschnittstellen von Datenbanken, in: Schmidt, J.W. (eds.) Sprachen für Datenbanken (Springer 1983)

(3) Jarke, M., Krause, J. and Vassiliou, Y., Studies in the evaluation of a domain-independent natural language query system, report, Center for Research on Information Systems, New York Univ. (April 1984)

(4) Koch, D., DAD-1 - deutschsprachige Abfrage von relationalen Datenbasen, in: NLI - Arbeiten zur natürlichsprachigen Abfrage von Datenbanken, (Zentralinstitut für Kybernetik und Informationsprozesse, Berlin 1983)

(5) Koch, D., Busse, J., Friedrich, H., Geske, U., Heicking, W. and Werner, W., German language access to databases, Mit-teilungen zur automatischen Sprachverarbeitung (Zentral-institut für Sprachwissenschaft, Berlin, 1984)

(6) Krause, J., Mensch-Maschine-Kommunikation in natürlicher Sprache (Niemeyer, Tübingen 1982)

(7) Michaelis, P.R., Chapanis, A., Weeks, G.G. and Kelly, M., Word usage in interactive dialog with restricted and un-restricted vocabularies, IEEE Transactions on Professional Communication, PC-20(4) (1977) 214-221

(8) Wahlster, W., Cooperative response generation based on an explicit user model, AIMSA 84 (Varna 1984)

(9) Zoeppritz, M., Human factors of a "Natural Language" end-user system, in: Blaser, A. and Zoeppritz, M., Enduser systems and their human factors (Springer, Berlin-Heidel-berg-New York-Tokyo, 1983)

(10) Zoltan,E., Weeks,G.D. and Ford,W.R., Natural language com-munication with computers: A comparison of voice and key-board input, in: Johannsen,J.E. and Rijsdorp,J.E. (eds.) Analysis, Design, and Evaluatic of Man-Machine Systems, (Baden-Baden 1982).

Man-Computer Interaction Research
MACINTER-I
F. Klix and H. Wandke (Editors)
© Elsevier Science Publishers B.V. (North-Holland), 1986

THE EFFICIENCY OF LETTER PERCEPTION IN FUNCTION OF COLOR COMBINATIONS:
A STUDY OF VIDEO-SCREEN COLORS

G. d'Ydewalle, J. Van Rensbergen and J. Huys

Laboratory for Experimental Psychology
University of Leuven
Leuven
Belgium

With our microcomputer, the video screens could work
with 16 foreground and 16 background colors. There are
thus 256 possible combinations. In an initial study,
color preference was investigated. In two following
studies, the efficiency of letter perception was studied
in function of the five most chosen color combinations.
However, within these preferences, the color combinations had no differential influence on the visual process, although it did appear that the subjects performed best with the color combination that they had
chosen.

STATEMENT OF THE PROBLEM

The quality of a text displayed on a video screen is gauged in terms of its
usefulness. How easy is it for the user to find and read information? With
our microcomputer (INDATA), the video screens can work with 16 foreground
and 16 background colors, so there are 256 color combinations possible. One
aspect of the text quality could be the color combinations of the background and the characters. Do people prefer particular color combinations?
Are these preferences the same for everyone or are they peculiar to individuals? Are particular color combinations more efficient than others to
work with? Another question asked was whether there was an advantage to
have certain words or symbols appear in another color than that of the sur-
rounding words or symbols. From the literature, this certainly appeared to
be important to introduce structure or to emphasize certain parts. Nevertheless, some color combinations are more misleading than clarifying. Therefore, we concentrated primarily on the problem of good color combinations.

To answer these questions a study was designed in phases. The first phase
consisted of investigating color preference. With these results, two perception experiments were conducted, a signal detection test and a feature
detection test. For the design of these two tests, we used the existing
CONDUIT tests (Laboratory in Cognition and Perception[1]).

SIGNAL DETECTION AND FEATURE DETECTION

A signal detection test is intended to measure the sensitivity to stimuli:
When and how rapidly does a person perceive a particular stimulus? Signal
detection theory holds that a perception threshold as such is not measurable, because the subject always applied a personal response criterion: When

one is confronted with a situation in which one is uncertain whether or not
one has perceived a particular stimulus, one must still decide whether or
not the stimulus is present. This criterion can be conservative, that is,
the stimulus is judged to be present when one is certain, or it can be
flexible, thus allowing more uncertainty. In this test, we investigated
whether the sensitivity to stimuli is different for different color combinations. For it is important to achieve the highest possible sensitivity so
that the perception can proceed in the most efficient way possible. The
higher the sensitivity, the more rapid and the easier one can discern a
particular word, letter, number, or symbol on the screen.

In the test of feature detection, we investigated how the visual search process proceeded, i.e. how the environment is searched in order to locate a
particular object. The feature detection model does not require all aspects
of the object to be identified, but that a pattern be identified on the
basis of its unique characteristics. These are the characteristics that
differentiate the pattern from other patterns. It is important that this
visual search process can be done quickly. The searching for a particular
word, letter, number, or symbol, the determination of errors, and so on are
tasks that must be able to be accomplished rapidly. This is why the question
of whether particular color combinations can help or hinder this process is
important.

METHOD

Three tests were administered in turn. The first test investigated color
preference. The instructions, which were displayed on the screen, were as
follows:

> This test is very simple. We ask you to set the colors of
> this screen so that they form the ideal combination for
> you to be able to read this text easily and over a long
> period of time. To set the colors, use the arrows of the
> keyboard: the verticle arrows change the background color,
> the horizontal arrows change the color of the letters.

There were 13 subjects - students and assistants in psychology - both men
and women. They were asked to select three combinations out of the 256, a
particular color for the background and another for the letters, after which
the text with the instructions in the color chosen appeared against the
chosen background. Because the intensity of the image could be changed, the
adjustment knob was marked. The subjects could then find the intensity that
they considered best per color combinations. On the basis of the results of
this test, the five most chosen color combinations were used in the subsequent two experiments.

Ten subjects participated in the signal detection test. They were all university students, male and female, who were dispatched by the student job
service and were paid for their participation. Their task consisted of in
discerning whether or not a particular letter was present in a set of other
letters. The task was made difficult by the limitation of the time for the
detection and by the random location of the letters on the screen. The test
consisted of 12 sets. Per set, a number of Fs (friends) appeared at random
location on the screen one by one up to 60. This took 30 seconds. In 8 of
the 12 sets, one of the letters was an E (enemy) instead of an F. The task

consisted of discovering the E. In four sets, the E appeared in the last seconds. This is the "weak signal" condition. Each subject performed the task five times, each time with a different color combination. Thus, each subject was confronted with the five color combinations, and ten measurements were performed per combination. The order of the measurements was structured so that each combination occurred twice at a particular position. In the experiment, therefore, two factors were manipulated: the strength or weakness of the signal and the color combination. Four measurements were made:

hits:	a yes-response when the E is present
misses:	a no-response when the E is present
false alarms:	a yes-response when the E is absent
correct rejections:	a no-response when the E is absent

The instructions, displayed on the screen, were as follows:

> You are among a large group of friends who are generally so nice that you are glad to see them. But be careful of enemies, because they will take advantage of you if you are not careful. Your friends will be indicated on the screen by the letter F and your enemies by the letter E. After each set, the computer will ask you if you saw the enemy. If you did, press the letter P (present); if you did not, press the letter A (absent).

After the subjects had performed this task, they were asked to indicate which color combination they preferred.

Ten subjects participated in the feature detection test (Experiment 3). Again they were male and female students dispatched by the student job service and paid for their participation. Their task consisted of locating a letter in a field of other letters that were either very similar to the target letter or very different from it. To locate a letter in a field that is different requires a less thorough analysis of the various characteristics than when the letter and the field are very similar.

On the screen was displayed a matrix of 96 letters in which the target letter could occur in 12 arbitrary places. The field letters were C, O, D, and G (round-letter field) and Y, Z, V, and K (angular-letter field). The target letter was either Q or an X. The subjects had to find it as quickly as possible, after which the matrix again appeared but then with the letter indicated with which the subject was asked to verify his or her response. When the letter was seen at a different place, the N was depressed and this set was repeated later. The test consisted of 48 sets. Each subject performed the test twice, each with another color combination. Thus, each subject was confronted with two of the five color combinations, and four measurements were made per combination. The color combinations were structured so that each appeared twice as the first and twice as the last measurement.

Thus, three factors were manipulated in the experiment, namely the letter to be located, the field, and the color combination. What was measured was the number of milliseconds necessary to find the Q or the X. The instructions displayed on the screen were as follows:

In this experiment, you will see a matrix of letters.
Your task will be to find a particular letter as quickly
as possible. This letter will either be a Q or an X.
Around this letter will be 95 other letters, which will
be either round or angular. In the search, begin in the
upper left-hand corner, in the same way that you read.
Check first which letter you have to look for and then begin as quickly as possible. When you find the letter,
press on the space bar.

RESULTS

From the results of the color choice test (Experiment 1), we discerned three
tendencies. A number of color combinations were selected by several people.
Certain combinations were apparently perceived better by several subjects.
The color combinations that were preferred are the following (the first color is the background, the second the letters; the color combinations listed
together are very similar):

> grey-blue
> black-white; black-light green
> blue-white; blue-light green
> blue-black
> light blue-dark blue

Nevertheless, we note a considerable number of interindividual differences.
The following color combinations were chosen by only one person: black-grass
green, black-pink, black-grey, dark purple-white, light blue-black, red
brown-black, grey-black, orange-black, white-black, red brown-white, red
brown-blue, blue-dark red, dark blue-light green, khaki green-blue. Finally,
we note that certain color combinations were never selected. They were rejected as being unreadable, disturbing, and so on. Thus the number of colors
that were chosen is limited. The choice of intensity was restricted to three
positions, all of which tended towards the darker side.

The five most often chosen color combinations were used for the following
two experiments, namely, grey-blue, black-white, blue-white, blue-black,
and light blue-dark blue.

The analysis of the results of the signal detection test (Experiment 2)
gave some difficulty. Normally, this analysis would rest on a comparison of
the hits and the false alarms. However, the results show that there were no
false alarms, with two exceptions. Therefore: the analysis was made of the
hits as data. An ANOVA was made with two factors, the strength of the signal
and the color combination.

For the strength of the signal, a clear significance was obtained:
$F(1,81) = 49.78$, $p < 0.001$. The subjects obviously performed better in the
strong-signal condition, which was to be expected. But what we wanted to
examine primarily was the effect of the color combination. This factor did
not yield any significant results: $F(4,81) = 1.213$, n.s. Within the range
of the combinations used here, the color apparently had no substantial effect on performance, and the sensitivity for visual stimuli thus did not
differ for different color combinations. Nevertheless, a number of subjective observations were made. Certain colors were found to be easier and

more comfortable to work with than others. The subjects were also asked which of the five color combinations they preferred. When we compared the hits of the preferred color with the hits of the four other colors, a clear effect occurs: $F(1,27) = 15.063$, $p < 0.01$. With the preferred color combinations, the subjects worked significantly better than with the other combinations, which held true for both the strong-signal condition and the weak-signal condition. Thus, one performs best with the color combination that one chooses oneself. This would indicate that it is very important to have the possibility of choosing oneself.

Three analyses were made of the results of the feature detection test (Experiment 3). The data that were used were the number of milliseconds for each combination of letter and field, averaged over the various positions the letter could appear in. In the first analysis, no account was taken of the various color combinations but only with the letter-field combination and the two measurements. The letter-field effect was very significant: $F(3,20) = 44.64$, $p < 0.0001$. The sequence of the measurements had no effect. Than, two separate analyses were conducted, one for the first measurement and one for the second. Two factors were included: the letter-field combination and the color combination. These two analyses again indicate a significant effect of the letter-field combination: $F(3,20) = 37.24$ and 18.90, $p < 0.0001$. One can locate a letter more rapidly in a dissimilar field than in a similar field, and the Q is easier to locate, certainly in a similar field. These results were expected. As regards the color-combination factor, we found no significant results. Appar-ently, a letter is not found any more rapidly with one color combination than with another, at least for the color combinations tested.

CONCLUSIONS

As regards the color preference, it is obvious that a number of color combinations were chosen several times, while a number of others were never chosen. The combinations that were chosen are, perhaps, rather surprising. In four of the five most chosen color combinations blue occurs either as a foreground or a background color. The fifth combination is black with white letters. When people can make their choices completely freely from a large supply and this while they see the combination before them, thus not purely verbally, a pattern occurs that is valid over various individuals. In addition, a number of choices were made that were purely individual, but that still fall within a limited range of colors. We may thus speak of a preference for particular color combinations.

When we conducted two experiments with the most commonly chosen color combinations in order to determine their effect on a number of visual processes, no differential influences were discerned. The different combinations were roughly all equally efficient. This was to be expected in a sense, because we limited ourselves to the most commonly chosen combinations. Apparently, when a number of good and comfortable combinations have been determined subjectively, it makes little difference what combination is actually worked with. We did find in the signal detection test a more specific indication of the importance of being able to work with a color combination that one subjectively indicated to be the most comfortable. No difference in fatigue was reported for the various color combinations used, although the tests may have been too short in duration for fatigue to occur. Both the tests took about 35 minutes per subject. It is to be noted that a large number of fixations and great concentration were required, so the tests did seem to the subjects to be tiring.

We may ask why a number of color combinations were chosen and a number of others not. There is information in the literature that could help us to answer this question.

First and for most, the contrast between the foreground and the background seems to be very important. A low contrast results in a hindrance of the normal reading process because the visual reading field - the area within which visual information can be acquired during a visual pass - is shrunk, and also because the time necessary for the recognition of a symbol is longer. Low contrast can be due to a poor color combination. One can thus only speak of a good combination when this provides good contrast.

Further, it has been shown that a negative contrast, i.e., darker symbols on a light background, yields better performance than a positive contrast. A negative contrast provides for better readability and a higher degree of visual comfort. It is also better for the adaptation of the eye, certainly as one must often compare the screen and a sheet of paper next to it. This observation applies for video screens of high technical quality. Video screens of a somewhat lower degree of technical quality, however, manifest a number of disadvantages with negative contrast, of which flickering is one of the most disturbing. Here it is therefore of primary importance that the subject himself can set the contrast, because the sensitivity to flickering can vary from subject to subject. Some will, therefore, choose a negative contrast, and others a positive. This we observed in the color-choice test. Both positive and negative contrasts occurred among the most chosen color combinations. Indeed, the screen did show a slight degree of flickering with a light background, which was experienced as disturbing by a number of subjects.

In summary, we may say that it is certainly a major advantage for the subjects to be able to choose a color combination themselves. Indeed, the socio-psychological literature indicates that the freedom of choice generates a positive attitude towards the task and leads to better performance. Within a particular range of colors, the color combination that one chooses oneself and that is subjectively experienced as the most comfortable probably offers the best guarantee for efficient work.

FOOTNOTES

[1] Laboratory in cognition and perception (Conduit, 1979).

Man-Computer Interaction Research
MACINTER-I
F. Klix and H. Wandke (Editors)
© Elsevier Science Publishers B.V. (North-Holland), 1986

ON THE TEMPORAL STABILITY OF SIGNAL DETECTION PROCESSES

Friedhelm Nachreiner, Kerstin Baer, Andrzej Zdobych
Universität Oldenburg
AG Arbeits- und Organisationspsychologie
Oldenburg
FRG

An investigation of time on task and time of day
effects in signal detection at two different tasks
and with randomly presented signals indicates no
performance changes during the day, but changes in
the observer's response strategy over time on task.
No interaction between type of task, time on task
and time of day could be found.[1]

PROBLEM

One of the problems in man-computer-interaction, as has been
well recognized in man-machine-interaction, is the reliable
functioning of man in this dyad. Whereas a lot of literature
has accumulated on determining the reliability of mechanic or
electronic components (cf. Apostolakis et al., 1980 (1)) of
such systems, our knowledge about the reliability of man in
these systems appears rather deficient. The performance of
the total system, however, is clearly dependent on the
reliability of both components, not only on that of its machine
subsystem, with the concrete model for the analysis still to
be specified (cf. Apostolakis et al., 1980 (1)). What is lacking
aside from results on reliability of the human component are
methods for determining human reliability in such systems.

So in man-machine-interaction the reliable detection of critical
signals requiring actions from the human operator against a
background of neutral signals that requires no actions seems
to be a major problem in man-computer-interaction. In this case
reliability could preliminarly be defined in terms of accuracy
at which man can discriminate between critical and neutral
signals over time on task, related to the performance at the
beginning of the task. This problem has been approached for
about 40 years under the heading of vigilance research, and a
lot of results have been presented since then (cf. Mackie, 1977
(2)).

One of these results is that performance decrements over time
on task are usually connected to task with high signal frequency, whereas for low signal frequency no such decrements are
found (Parasuraman and Davies, 1977 (3)). Nachreiner et al.
(1976 (4)) advanced the hypothesis that this effect might be

attributable to rest pauses, which the observer might take
between the signals, when they are given at fixed intervals of
more than 3 seconds duration. They proposed that with signals
presented at random intervals no such rest pauses could be
taken without the risk of missing a signal, and performance
thus should decrease even with lower signal frequencies under
this condition. Since system response times in man-computer
interaction are of this unpredictable nature (Boucsein et al.,
1984 (5)), this problem evidently applies here.

Another aspect of temporal dependence in monitoring behavior
results from the fact that with increasing automatization and
computerization most of these jobs are carried out around
the clock in shiftwork. Referring to the evidence of diurnal
rhythms of physiological functions and performance efficiency
in man (cf. Colquhoun, 1982 (6)) the problem arises as to
how stable or reliable detection efficiency in man-computer
interaction can be assumed to be at different times of the
day.

Results on this aspect of temporal stability of signal detection performance are, however, rather inconsistent. This might
be due to variations in tasks, parameters and methods used
and more consistency might be achieved, if results would be
grouped according to the different types of detection tasks
used. Davies and Parasuraman (1982 (7)) propose to differentiate between tasks requiring successive or simultaneous
discrimination, with the former asking for higher demands on
short term memory. Due to these differential demands on
memory processes Davies and Parasuraman assume differential
performance rhythms, because both tasks should find their
optimal activation level at different times of the day. Whereas performance in terms of hit rate and observers' sensitivity
in simultaneous discrimination is supposed to increase from
morning to evening, performance in successive discrimination
is supposed to decrease.

Contrary to this change in sensitivity or discrimination
efficiency (d' in terms of signal detection theory) Craig
(1979 (8)) and Craig et al. (1981 (9)) attribute diurnal
variations in signal detection performance to variations in
response strategy of the observer (ß in terms of SDT), with
no differentiation for the above mentioned types of tasks.
As both parties support their hypotheses with results from
empirical studies, which, of course, are not completely
comparable, this question should be submitted to further empirical investigations.

EXPERIMENTAL PROCEDURE

We made a first step in this direction by conducting an experiment with 18 subjects, performing the two different types of
signal detection tasks with a low signal rate (mean interval
between signals: 6 seconds). 9 male and 9 female students were
carrying out each type of task at 6 different times of the
day (04, 08, 12, 16, 20 and 24 hours) for a period of 30
minutes, respectively. The period of 30 minutes was subdivided
into three 10-minutes periods, each with 25 critical amd 75
neutral signals presented in random order and at random intervals. The signals consisted of three horizontal bars (white
against black background), that were shown for 1 second on a
vidoeterminal in a soundproof room.

RESULTS

For the successive discrimination the critical signal showed
all three bars longer than the bars of the neutral signal.
Under this condition the signal had to be compared to a
memorized standard. For the task with simultaneous discrimination one of these three bars was longer at one of its ends,
in random order. Here the reference standard was simultaneously given by the two unchanged bars. The difficulty of the
tasks was adjusted to a 70 % hit rate for the well-trained
subjects. They responded to the displayed signals by pressing
a key for 'sure' or 'rather sure' signal or no signal on the
keyboard of the terminal. The experiments were conducted with
the aid of a computer, which generated separate signal
sequences for each trial. Signal quality and associated
responses were recorded, so that hit and false alarm rates as
well as the signal detection parameters d' and ß could be
calculated at once. For these parameters analyses of variance
were conducted (using transformations where appropriate),
using a 2 (type of task) X 6 (time of day) X 3 (time on task)
- design with repeated measures on each factor. Series and
sex effect were controlled by factorially higher designs.

The results showed significant main effects for type of task
for d', ß and false alarms. This was due to the fact that
successive discrimination was still more difficult than
simultaneous discrimination, which resulted in a higher number
of false alarms with associated changes in d' and ß for the
former task. No time of day main effect could be demonstrated
for any of the dependent variables. Nor could any interaction
effect between time of day and type of task be found, as would
have been expected, at least for hits and d', following the
hypotheses of Davies and Parasuraman. This means that there
was no difference in performance at both tasks depending on the
different times of testing. Signal detection - at least for
tasks like those used - seems to be stable throughout the
day.

With respect to time on task a significant main effect for ß
was found, demonstrating a change of the observer's response
strategy with time on task. As shown in Figure 1, observers
adopt a stricter criterion, because they tend to react less
frequently with the response 'signal' in the second and third
period of the session.

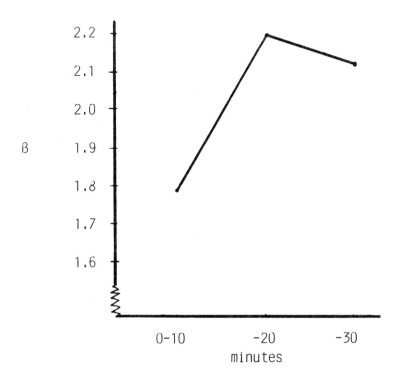

Figure 1: Values of ß for the three 10-minutes periods.

This corresponds quite well to the vigilance decrement usually found in experiments using higher signal frequencies.
Thus, for signal detection at tasks with randomly presented
signals no temporal stability can be expected over time on
task, even at lower signal frequencies.

This instability in performance with time on task is not
modified by time of day (interaction effect not significant),
this implies that there is no interactive temporal dependency.
Thus, it does not seem necessary to assume a differential
change in response strategy at different times of the day.
No other effect approached an acceptable level of significance.

DISCUSSION

So in contrast to Davies and Parasuraman our results reveal
no differential performance rhythms over the day for successive or simultaneous discrimination. This might be due to
the fact that we used a within design, took 6 readings distributed over the complete 24-hour day and presented signals
at random intervals. Instead of using different subjects at
only two times of the day we think, however, that taking
readings round the clock for the same subjects and presenting
signals at random intervals resembles reality quite closely.
On the other hand, time on task will be longer in real life
jobs than in our (or Davies and Parasuraman's) experiments,
and it might have been that subjects in our experiments were
able to compensate time of day effects by investing more
effort. With more extended time on task in the experimental
session circadian variations in performance migh occur, because
compensation by means of investing more effort will no longer
be possible in such substained monitoring.

To test for this hypothesis experiments with more extended
time on task should be conducted, controlling for effort
invested. These are experiments we are planning for the near
future. Analyses of human reliability in man-machine or man-
computer-interaction should take into account that temporal
stability in signal detection could be achieved by increasing
amounts of effort. Thus, from a psychological point of view
the above mentioned conception of reliability in mere terms
of accuracy of performance seems inadequate. This could lead
to belief that the human will still function reliable as a
subsystem when in reality performance is sustained at maximum
effort and a minimal surplus of load will make this system
unrealiable.

FOOTNOTES:

[1] Partially supported by a grant from the Deutsche Forschungs-
gemeinschaft.

REFERENCES

(1) Apolstolakis, G.; Garribba, S.; Volta, G. (Eds.), Synthesis and Analysis Methods for Safety and Reliability Studies (Plenum Press, New York and London, 1980).

(2) Mackie, R. E. (Ed.), Vigilance: Theory, operational performance and physiological correlates (Plenum Press, New York and London, 1977).

(3) Parasuraman, R. and Davies, D.R., Tayonomic analysis of vigilance performance, in: Mackie, R.E. (Ed.), Vigilance: Theory, operational performance and physiological correlates (Plenum Press, New York and London, 1977).

(4) Nachreiner, F.; Obliers, R.; Rutenfranz, J., Zur Frage einer Abhängigkeit der Entdeckungsleistung in Vigilanzversuchen von der Reizereignisrate. Studia Psychologica 18 (1976) 26-40.

(5) Boucsein, W.; Greif, S.; Wittekamp, J., Systemresponsezeiten als Belastungsfaktor bei Bildschirm-Dialogtätigkeiten. Z. Arb. Wiss. 38 (1984) 113-122.

(6) Colquhoun, P., Biological Rhythms and Performance, in: Wilse B. Webb (Ed.): Biological Rhythms, Sleep, and Performance (John Wiley & Sons Ltd., New York, 1982).

(7) Davies, D.R. and Parasuraman, R., The psychology of vigilance (Academic Press, London, 1982).

(8) Craig, A., Discrimination, temperature, and time of day, Human Factors 21 (1979) 69-78.

(9) Craig, A.; Wilkinson, R.T.; Colquhoun, W.P., Diurnal variations in vigilance efficiency, Ergonomics 24 (1981) 641-651.

Man-Computer Interaction Research
MACINTER-I
F. Klix and H. Wandke (Editors)
© Elsevier Science Publishers B.V. (North-Holland), 1986

CODING OF INFORMATION IN MAN-COMPUTER SYSTEMS BASED ON
COGNITIVE TASK ANALYSIS

Elke Wetzenstein-Ollenschläger and Ulrich Scheidereiter

Sektion Psychologie
Humboldt University
Berlin
GDR

In designing man-computer systems one can choose to code
the information presented on the screen by different modes.
Thus, values can be coded as numbers or, graphically, as
heigthts of a column. Factors determining the most
appropriate coding form are investigated. Evidence is
presented that the main factor is the cognitive task.
Situational conditions and individual abilities do not
influence the cognitive performance as strongly. Cognitive
task analysis, bringing together theoretical prediction and
experimental test,is shown to be a successful method for
establishing the optimum coding form.

PSYCHOLOGICAL PROBLEMS IN INFORMATION CODING IN MAN-COMPUTER DIALOGUE

In designing man-computer dialogue systems we have to ask the classical
question of engineering psychology about coding of information presented.
But apart from the earlier experimental determination of the best coding
form for a special type of task (cf. McCormick 1970, Murell 1965, Neumann
and Timpe 1976) we can ask today a few more psychologically interesting
questions, which are essentially a result of the technologically nearly
unlimited possebilities of coding information in man-computer systems. The
universality as to the capacities of information presentation produces for
the first time the conditions for both an adaptive coding fitted to a
given task and a flexible coding defined by the user's own decision. The
adaptive and flexible use of coding forms is an essential supposition to
optimum human information processing as well as an increase in the number
of the degrees of freedom in the activity of the user. At first sight the
implementation of several flexible coding forms thus seems to be a
solution for the hitherto existing problems of coding. In a particular
case of designing however, even when deciding for a flexible coding form
important questions will remain open.

The main problem consists in establishing the psychological criteria by
which to choose from the number of technically feasible alternatives the
ones to be implemented and by which in a particular task situation the
most adequate coding form should be determined.

Psychologically at least the following three factors should be taken into
account when deciding on the most suitable coding form:

- task as inducing cognitive processes,
- individual abilities in the processing of a specific coding form and
  in the use of specific representations,
- situational conditions.

AN APPROACH OF FINDING THE BEST CODING FORM

The aim of this paper is,firstly, to prove that the cognitive task is the
main factor in determining the optimum coding form and, secondly, to
investigate task-adequate coding by means of a cognitive task analysis.

The first assumption is derived from the hypothesis of the task-dependence
of information processing, which has often been confirmed in cognitive
psychology (Hoffmann 1982, Klix 1971, Geißler and Puffe 1983, Hacker 1980).
According to the hypothesis in the cognitive process induced by the task
a task-dependent internal representation is produced. The cognitive
expense for producing this task-specific representation and thus the
efficientcy of the whole process depends on both the task and the coding
form of the information presented.

This leads to the second problem mentioned above of how to determine the
coding form that is highly compatible with the internal representation.
It should be investigated neither just on the basis of a complete
classification of tasks nor by pragmatic testing. Rather, we want to
predict the task-adequate coding form on the basis of processing and
representation models of cognitive psychology and to test these predictions
experimentally. This approach is intended to not only result in statements
concerning the optimum coding but also statements concerning the cognitive
processes and the internal representation to tell us why a coding form
is task-adequate or not (cf. Wetzenstein-Ollenschläger, Scheidereiter and
Geißler 1984).

To resolve these problems the following procedure seems useful:

- On the basis of a description of processes and representations codings
  that are hypothetically considered task-adequate will be selected.

- Process components essential to the task will be tested by an experiment. In the same experiment the efficiency of the cognitive processes
  involved will be determined for various coding forms, and so the task-
  adequacy tested.

- The findings concerning the task-adequate codings will be examined under
  different situational conditions as to how consistent they are. In these
  experiments situational constraints such as real disturbances in the
  man-computer dialogue will be simulated.

- The results obtained will be examined concerning the influence of individually specific abilities in cognitive performance that are achieved
  using a special coding form.

In order to control the effect of the coding form on the task solution, it
is necessary firstly to draft a set of comparable tasks, which fulfil the
following conditions:

- The task are to be solved with at least two different coding forms.

- Particular components of the process have to be provable.

Proving them is possible by the introduction of an additional variable in the reaction time analysis (Sternberg 1969).

- To find out about the internal representation the components have to be differently effective in the individual task.

The selection of the best coding form is based on the general assumption that adequacy of coding is hypothetically definable in terms of the compatibility between the presented information and its internal representation. In some papers on representation using the sentence-picture-comparison paradigm the authors distinguish between an pictorial and a semantic representation (Paivio 1971, 1976, Hoffmann 1982, Klix 1976, 1980). It may well be that in cognitive processes these forms of representation are task-specifically used.

COGNITIVE TASK ANALYSIS

Description of tasks and derivation of predictions

According to general properties required of material and tasks the following conditions for the experiments were defined. On a screen sets of 2 to 7 values were successively presented as external information. The positions of the values in a set were labeled by letters below the number. The values were coded either by numbers or by the height of a column. Therefore the set of values was either a row of numbers or a histogramme (figure 1).

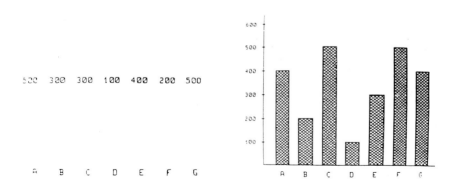

Fig. 1: Set of values coded as a row of numbers (left) or as diagramme of columns (right) used in the experiments .

The tasks simulated the following micro-dialogues between man and computer.

Task 1: Naming of a value in a position pointed out by the experimenter.

Task 2: Simultaneous comparison of two values, each in a different position.

Task 3: Successive comparison of two values from different sets, which are presented successively, the numbers being in the same position.

Task 4: Successive complex comparison of two paires of values from two different sets, presented successively, in which the numbers were in the same pair of positions as pointed out by the experimenter.

It is possible to draw up a stage model from well-known cognitive operations that could implement the cognitive process. Figure 2 shows such models for the naming task and the simultaneous comparison task.

But it is yet an open question whether encoding is a separate stage or whether it is linked to the particular steps of the external search. We are only interested in the stages of search and encoding. Therefore in addition to the external coding, form the size of the set of values was varied. The following characteristics of the internal representations would be required.

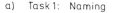

a)   Task 1: Naming

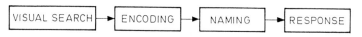

b)   Task 2: Simultaneous Comparison

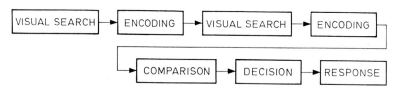

Fig. 2: Tentative models of the cognitive processes for the naming task and the simultaneous comparison task.

- In the naming task the representation has to be a nominal classification of numbers or column heights.

- In the simultaneous comparison task the representation has to be a classification into successive categories, that is a scaling on at least ordinal level, so as to render the comparison possible.

- In the successive comparison tasks several properties of representations are necessary. Firstly, in the retention subtask a representation has to be available that can easily be stored and is resistant to additional simultaneous cognitive processes. It could be a nominal classification as in the naming task. In the comparison subtask both the stored and the presented information must, in addition, have relational properties.

In deriving hypotheses on the task-adequacy of coding forms we start from a comparison of the external coding and the internal representation. A presentation of values by symbols such as numbers does not per se contain information on their quantities. The latter can be obtained only by application of an evaluation rule. For naming and short-term retention quantitative and relational information is not necessary and may indeed hinder the cognitive process, if capacity is limited. On simultaneous presentation a graphic coding in terms of column height may result in a quick comparison, the absolute quantity and the name of number not being necessary. These considerations lead to the predictions on task-adequate coding forms as shown in table 1.

Task	Task-adequate coding form	
	predicted	outcoming
Task 1 Naming	numerical	numerical
Task 2 Simultaneous comparison	graphical	graphical
Task 3 Successive comparison		
a) Retention in memory (1 number)	numerical	numerical
b) Comparison	numerical	numerical
Task 4 Successive complex comparison		
a) Retention in memory (2 numbers)	numerical	not consistent
b) Complex comparison	numerical	numerical

Table 1: Predicted and outcoming task-adequate coding form

The main experiment

Reaction times were always from the beginning of information presentation
on the screen to the S's response. Responses were made in a verbal form.
Mean reaction times were submitted to a regression analysis with the
set size of the presented numbers as the independent variable. The results
are shown in figure 3 and table 2. We regard the coding form with the
shorter mean reaction time as the one adequate to the task.

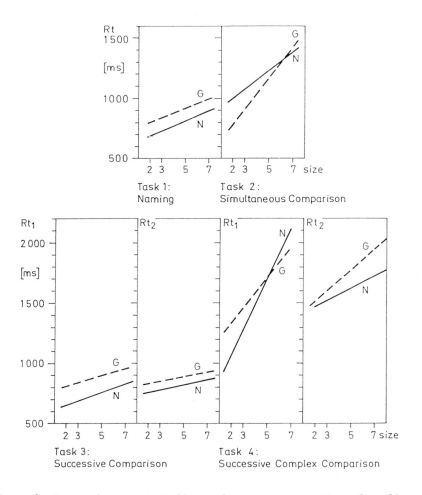

Figure 3: Regression straight lines of mean reaction times for all
tasks and for numerical (N, _____) and graphical
(G, - - - -) coding as function of the size of the
set of numbers presented.

Task 1	Naming	numerical	RT = 42 s + 615
		graphical	RT = 41 s + 763
Task 2	Simultaneous comparison	numerical	RT = 77 s + 851
		graphical	RT =123 s + 551
Task 3a	Retention	numerical	RT = 35 s + 596
		graphical	RT = 30 s + 755
Task 3b	Successive comparison	numerical	RT = 22 s + 715
		graphical	RT = 19 s + 789
Task 4a	Retention	numerical	RT =201 s + 679
		graphical	RT =127 s + 1066
Task 4b	Successive complex comparison	numerical	RT = 50 s + 1376
		graphical	RT = 86 s + 1353

Table 2: Regression functions for all tasks on numerical and
graphical coding form (s - set size)

In 5 of 6 cases the reaction times showed task-adequacy as expected from
the compatibility of coding form and internal representation. It is only
for the retention subtask in the successive complex comparison, that
the results are not so clear. Thus the hypotheses about task-adequacy
are essentially verified.

We can get a more exact interpretation as to localisation of encoding
operations in the stage model by considering the slopes and the inter-
cepts of the regression straight lines. For the naming and the simultaneous comparison task figure 4 presents stage models containing stages
of external self-terminating search and encoding. We find different
structures of the process. In number naming there is a high compatibility.
In column naming the encoding stage needs additional time and external
search is the same. Encoding can be a separate stage as in the simultaneous comparison of numbers or it can occur linked to the individual
search operations. Moreover, figure 4 shows the theoretical reaction
times as a function of set size as predicted by the stage models. They
are completely in correspondence with the data.

Result consistency

The results presented in figure 4 reveal good consistency in that the
adequate coding form proves to be independent of set size. In order to
check if task-adequacy is valid for a large variety of conditions, two
experiments were carried out, simulating situational conditions in man-
computer dialogue. In the first of these experiments disturbances in
presentation were designed to appear. Ss were instructed to identify and
to eliminate them. In the case of non-acceptable presentation Ss has to
ask for the next set of numbers by pressing a key.

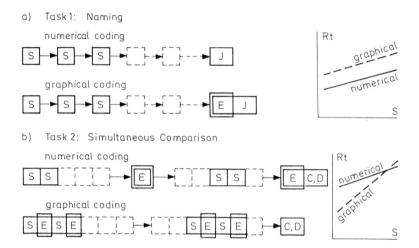

Fig. 4: Different models of the cognitive processes for naming and
simultaneous comparison on numerical and graphical coding
after cognitive task analysis. The double framed stages make
the essential differences between processing the numerically
and the graphicallly coded information. Moreover, the RT-
function of the set size predicted by the models is shown.
(S - Scanning, I - Identification, E - Encoding, D - Decision,
C - Comparison)

In the case of an acceptable presentation Ss had to respond as required
by the task. The results (figure 5) show that in all cases task-adaquacy
of coding forms was consistent, but in general the reaction time is, of
course, longer in the disturbed case.

In the second experiment the variability of system response time was
simulated. In the successive comparison tasks the second set of values was
presented with a random delay, Ss having to retain the values for a longer
period. The uncertainty resulting for Ss as to when the computer would
responded did not influence task-adequacy as can be seen from figure 6.

Interindividual differences in information processing for different coding
forms

In a number of investigations where the task could be solved on the basis
of both internal imagery and abstract semantic representations inter-
individual differences were found (Mac Leod, Hunt and Mathews 1978, Hoffmann
1982). They are apparent, in particular, in task solutions based on pictorial representation and are accounted for by the facility and speed with

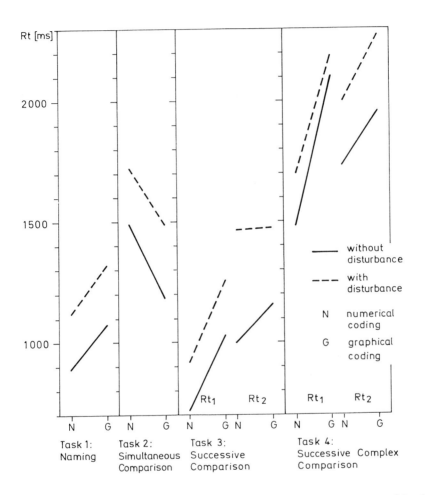

Fig. 5: Mean reaction times of all tasks for numerical and graphical coding on an additional task as a disturbance and in the undisturbed case.

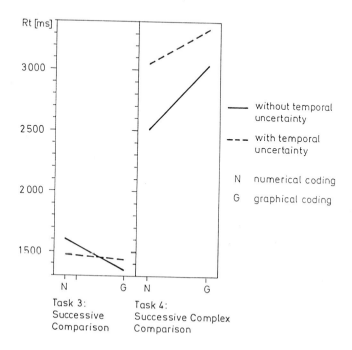

Fig. 6: Mean reaction times of the tasks 3 and 4 for numerical and
        graphical coding on temporal uncertainty for the second
        information presented and on immediately presented second
        information.

which the internal images can be produced and modified (Hoffmann 1982).
This could suggest that the performances achieved due to individual dispositions that are utilized processing imaginal coding forms and pictorial
representations might be superior to those, which we would obtain for
cognitive processing without those dispositions. In the hitherto examined
random samples of Ss such differences have, however, not been found.

This led us to perform an additional experiment with a sample of Ss with
very good performance in certain subtests of intelligence tests but no
overall high performance scores. These subtests (plane and cube tasks
from IST-Amtauer and subtests 9 and 10 from the LSP-Horn) are suitable for
the diagnosis of such differences (Putz-Osterloh and Lüer 1979).

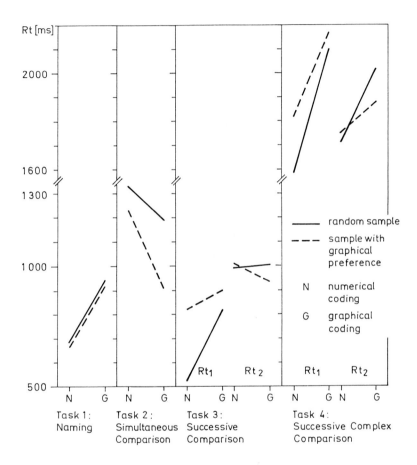

Fig. 7: Mean reaction times of all tasks for numerical and graphical coding for Ss with graphical preferences in information processing and for Ss of a random sample.

The results (figure 7) disprove the hypothesis. Task-adequacy is preserved as the major factor in spite of special individual ability to process graphic material. As would be expected, reaction times do decrease for graphic coding forms in the comparison tasks (task 2, 3, 4), but the shortest reaction times are in each case obtained with task-adequate coding (numerical in task 3 and 4).

CONCLUDING REMARKS

- A task-adequate coding on the screen was found to improve performances in human information processing. Its influence is neither exceeded by situational conditions in man-computer dialogue nor by individual abilities in processing graphic material and internal pictorial representation.

- To determine the task-adequate coding form we successfully used cognitive task analysis. Its theoretical part falls into a tentative description of the process, the description of essential properties of the internal representation and a comparison of the external coding form and the internal representation as to their compatibility. The aim of this part was to predict the task-adequate coding form. In the experimental part the predictions were examined and at the same time the process and representation properties essential for adequacy were determined.

- The approach suggests that the task-adequate coding form may well be predicted. Moreover, it seems to be an efficient method, because it helps in the design of an adequate coding form and the elucidation of the psychological basis of task-adequacy.

REFERENCES

(1) Geissler, H.-G. and Puffe, M., The inferential basis of classification: From perceptional to memory code system, in Geissler, H.-G. (ed.): Modern issues in perception (Deutscher Verlag der Wissenschaften, Berlin 1983).

(2) Hacker, W., Handlungsregulation: Zur aufgabenabhängigen Struktur handlungsregulierender mentaler Repräsentationen, Proceedings of the XXII ICP, Leipzig (1980) 80 - 89.

(3) Hoffmann, J., Das aktive Gedächtnis (Deutscher Verlag der Wissenschaften, Berlin, 1982).

(4) Klix, F., Information und Verhalten (Deutscher Verlag der Wissenschaften, Berlin, 1971).

(5) Klix, F., Über Grundstrukturen und Funktionsprinzipien kognitiver Prozesse, in Klix, F. (ed.), Psychologische Beiträge zur Analyse kognitiver Prozesse (Deutscher Verlag der Wissenschaften, Berlin, 1976).

(6) Klix, F., On structure and function of semantic memory, in Klix, F. and Hoffmann, J. (eds.), Cognition and memory (Deutscher Verlag der Wissenschaften, Berlin, 1980).

(7) Mac Leod, C. M., Hunt, E. B. and Mathews, N. N., Individual differences in the verification of sentence-picture relation-ship, J. verb. learn. verb. behav. 17 (1978) 493 - 507.

(8) McCormick, E.J., Human factors engineering (McGraw-Hill New York, 1970).

(9) Murrell, K.F.H., Ergonomics (Chapman and Hall, London, 1965).

(10) Neumann, J. und Timpe, K.-P., Psychologische Arbeitsgestaltung (Deutscher Verlag der Wissenschaften, Berlin, 1976).

(11) Paivio, A., Imagery and verbal Processes (New York, 1971).

(12) Paivio, A., Imagery, language and semantic memory, Research Builletin 385 (1976).

(13) Putz-Osterloh, W. und Lüer, G., Wann produzieren Probanden räumliche Vorstellungen beim Lösen von Raumvorstellungsaufgaben. Z. exp. u. angew. Psychol. XXVI (1979) 138-156.

(14) Sternberg, S., Memory-scanning: mental processes revealed by reaction-time experiments. Am. Scientist 57 (1969) 421-457.

(15) Wetzenstein-Ollenschläger, E., Scheidereiter, U. und Geissler, H.-G., Psychologische Beiträge zur anforderungsgerechten Informationsdarbietung bei Bildschirmarbeitsplätzen, Psychol. Praxis 4 (1984) 283 - 296.

Man-Computer Interaction Research
MACINTER-I
F. Klix and H. Wandke (Editors)
© Elsevier Science Publishers B.V. (North-Holland), 1986

VISUALIZATION OF PROCESS INFORMATION IN IMPROVING
WORK ORIENTATION

Leena Norros, Ari Kautto and Jukka Ranta
Technical Research Centre of Finland
Electrical Engineering Laboratory
Espoo
Finland

Recent advances in computer graphics provide the
possibility of utilizing visual information in
making the essential dynamics of the production
process more intelligible. This paper discusses
the methodology of deriving the criteria for visual
information in (the context of) nuclear power
plants. It shows how the results of the analysis
of the production process can be used in designing
both the process information system and operator
training.

INTRODUCTION

An automation system is a tool for supervising and controlling
the industrial production process. In this paper we will be
discussing the construction of an automation system in particular from the point of view of its function to mediate process
information. Thus we are studying automation system as an
information presentation system.

CRITICAL DEMANDS OF THE PROCESS CONTROLLING ACTIVITY

Independent of the developmental level of process control as
working activity the operators have to be able to aquire
mastery over the process, over their work in general. Mastery
could be defined as a readiness to take actions on the process
on the basis of conceiving it.

In order to be able to define the critical demands of process
control in todays complex systems an analysis of the history of
process control was carried out (Narros). In this context it
should be sufficient to make a comparison between the earliest
and latest developmental levels to demonstrate the differences
in their demands (on the derivation of the historical types
of work see Toikka et al., 1984).

In process control of the character of hand work the mastery is
based on individual experience and empirical generalizations.
Respectively process knowledge mainly comprises correlative
relations between process states and necessary control opera-

tions and it is typically acquired through immediate per-
ceptions. The critical demand in this work would be to control
i. e. to keep the process parameters within the prescribed
range and act accordingly if a deviation of the set values
occurs. "Process feel" and "autonomy" are abstractions of this
type of process control and describe the nature of mastery
in it.

Under the circumstances of the increasing social character of
the working process, i.e. growing organizational complexity
and developing production technology, the acquisition of the
mastery of the process through the prevailing empirical
working and training praxis becomes ineffective and partly
impossible. Many kinds of problems in process control that
are known from the field and described in the human engineering literature can be interpreted as a growing contradiction
between the inherently hand work type of mastery and the
potential, principally new level of mastery, the theoretical
comprehension of the process and the work as a whole. As tools
in mastering the totality of his work the operators need
scientific concepts.

This defines the critical demand of the process control activity at the developmental stage that could be called theoretical mastery. In its essence it is required of that the
operator is able to evaluate the particular process and
situation on the basis of socially formed and mediated
general concepts and to derive the necessary operative actions.
This is diagnosis in a broad sense, and as we have stated it
acquires its role as the critical demand mainly through the
process of the increasing social character of work. Learning
to fullfil this demand exceeds the limits of individual
working experience. At this stage scientific "concepts" sub-
stitute for "process feel" and "collectivity" for "autonomy"
as abstractions of the process control activity.

A widely examined method to enhance diagnostic activities is
to formulate and teach diagnostic rules. In the light of our
argumentation of the nature of the diagnostic activity this
solution would be principally an insufficient one. Yet, some
rules vaguely reflect the objective need of mastering concepts.
As an example we could mention rules of the type: "Don't loose
the overview".

This good advice helps only if one knows the referred totality.
And, to know that requires thinking activity that conceives
the object in its genesis, its internal relationships and
contradictions, as Davydov (1977) writes. This is the general
way of increasing the qualifications of the operators.

Our study is an attempt to test that approach. In this paper
we describe our efforts to analyze a particular industrial
process and to model it visually in the information presentation system. This analysis is the basis for the formation
of the adequate work orientation of the operators of the same
process.

THE STRUCTURE OF THE PROCESS INFORMATION SYSTEM

Our object was to examine the production of electricity using nuclear fuel and our task to develop the tools in mastering this production. From the methodological point of view our aim was to model the object on different explanatory levels and to organize knowledge adequately. A detailed description of the decomposition of information is given in Kautto et al. (1984). Table 1 should demonstrate the approach used in the design of the process information system.

Descending in a hierarchical information system is usually understood as a kind of zooming into the details of the system. Analogously operator activity is thought to descend into concrete details of the process which is experienced as a nuisance particularly in the case of a disturbance. That is why he is adviced to "keep the overview". The problem is that the totality is not the sum of the elements described in technical terms. Thinking in terms of concepts that represent deeper explanatory levels, and presentation of information in functional and systemic principles, is needed. The structure of the IPS described here should serve this basic idea. Furthermore, leaning on the notion that totality is identified through its history, we have paid extra attention on mediating historical data through the information system. This is concretized in two forms: The system includes particular support levels which give design basis for the realization of both the production process and the automation system. Along with the construction history also production of the process is given in the form of trends in the main parameters and productive goals (safety, availability, efficiency).

The information system is thought to be realized in a video based control room (VCR). This precondition puts extra demands on the design of the individual displays each of which should repeat the entity in one way or other. The different levels of modelling of the process should be represented in each of the displays to help the operator to orientate his thinking adequately. At least the following information should thus be available:

1. The state of functions with the help of the alarm system.

2. The most important interactions between the (sub)systems.

3. The design information of the (sub)systems.

4. The location of the present display in the total display system (see details in Kautto et al., 1984).

Essential contents of process mastery	Modelling of the process (explanatory depth of knowledge)	Organization of information (the level of organization of knowledge)	Hierarchial level of the IPS
Conceiving the process	Physical model – genetic = energy refinement and mE-balances – causal = physical phenomena and laws	Simplified functional representation with main variables – functionally organized presentation of processing stages and functions and subfunctions Support level (Design basis)	I s
		Operational overview with main systems (PI-displays) – systemic organization of main components and group control sequences	II
Readiness to operate	Technical model – descriptive: flow diagrams (pipe lines) and instrumentation systems	Operational control with components and variables – classified organization of operative procedures with corresponding components	III
		Support level (design basis) – plant protection – automatic control sequences – feedback controls – interlocks (etc.)	III s

TABLE 1. Description of the design of the information presentation system (IPS).

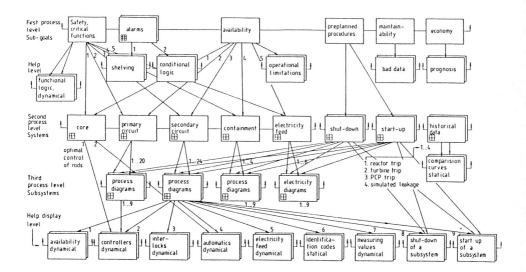

Figure 1: The structure of the information presentation system

The structure of the single Process and instrumentation (PI) display is seen in figure 2. The central space is reserved for the technical flow diagram.

A particular set of displays was created for the demonstration of a disturbance and to test the design idea with nuclear power plant operators (displays were not dynamical as they shall be in the realized process information system).

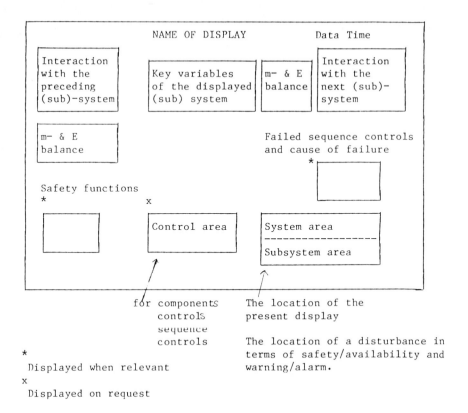

Figure 2: The structure of the single PI display

AN EXPERIMENT TO DEVELOP THE THEORETICAL WORK ORIENTATION
IN PROCESS CONTROL

Our starting point is a model of working activity that includes
a co-operative subject who by means of collectively established
tools produces useful values. This defines the entity called
"activity" that has a certain internal structure (Leontjew,
1973). Thus, working praxis that has a tendency to reduce
activity into immediate operations causes contradictions which
as such manifest the existence of the entity, i.e. the motives
and goals of activity are included in the operations which,
cannot be controlled without them (Toikka et al., 1984). Take
for an example our case, the control of the highly automated

power plant where every disturbance proves the operator's role as a mere "operator" to be false. These internal contradictions are easily seen in praxis, but their interpretation presupposes that they are reflected in the theory of human activity. If it is not, it turns out to be hard for us to act against the widespread mystifications that the machine becomes a subject and the robots carry out the production.

Man is human through this production of tools and the social mediation of their use. To realize this in automated production presupposes an assimilation of the theory of production and of tools by the production workers. They should know what their tools are in terms of the human actions they materialize, i.e. how do they work. In our training experiment, on the basis of the historical analysis of the process control activity and of the particular production process, attempts were made to mediate conceptual means for the operators and thus the operators for an analysis and development of their own work.

The trial was organized through training sessins that totalled 40 hours. One nuclear power plant operating shift (shift supervisor, reactor technician and turbine technician) from a Finnish power plant and two researchers (a nuclear physicist and a psychologist) formed the trainee-trainer research team. The experiment comprised a carefully planned sequence of sessions which included lectures, modelling tasks and practical work. These formed a combined learning research process in an experimental design of "the developmental work study" (Engeström et al., 1984, Toikka et al., 1984). The following scheme should demonstrate the phases in the work study (figure 3).

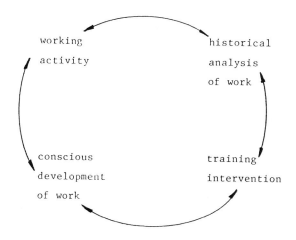

Figure 3: Scheme of the developmental work study design.

Learning on the knowledge gained in the process of producting the information presentation system it was in the learning intervention attempted to develope the operators ability to model their work, particularly the process and its control tools. Thus, talking about the substance of the work it was possible to investigate the level of the operators present mastery of the work.

The results of the training experiment are still under analysis. They shall be reported by concretely formulating the contradictions of the present working praxis. These can be abstracted for the analysis of the actual working activities and of the prevailing work orientation. Furthermore, attempts are made to show the main areas and particular objects in work which should and could be developed. As an anticipation of the final results we could mention the following broad questions upon which concrete development plans shall be formulated.

The first important area of work development is the realization of the information presentation system. The suggestion of its basic design principles was tested in the experiment and can be evaluated as principally approved.

Second, we shall propose a basic concept for an alarm system that could serve as a diagnostic support in identifying leaks in the process.

Third, we shall work out a program for further qualification of the operators. The leading thesis in this would be to make training more practical and work more theoretical. We hope to be able to formulate concrete methods for the use of the respective essential actions, modelling and planning, in order to start a developmental process among the operators in their work.

REFERENCES

(1) Davydow, V.V., Arten der Verallgemeinerung im Unterricht (Volk und Wissen, Berlin, 1977).

(2) Engeström, Y., Hakkarainen, P. and Hedegaard, M., On the Methodological Basis of Research in Teaching and Learning, in: Hedegaard, M., et al., (eds.), Learning and Teaching on a Scientific Basis (Aarhus Universitet, Psykologisk Institut, 1984).

(3) Kautto, A., Norros, L., Ranta, J. and Heimbürger, H., The role of visual information in improving the acquisition of adequate work orientation, in: Ergonomics Problems in Process Operations, Institution of Chemical Engineers, (Pergamon Press, London, 1984).

(4) Leontjew, A.N., Probleme der Entwicklung des Psychischen (Volk und Wissen, Berlin, 1973).

(5) Norros, L., Enhancing the mastery of work in process control (to be published).

(6) Toikka, K., Engeström, Y. and Norros, L., Entwickelnde Arbeitsforschung als arbeitsnehmerorientierte Strategie, Referat im III. Internationalen Kongress Kritische Psychologie, II-13 (Mai 1984).

Man-Computer Interaction Research
MACINTER-I
F. Klix and H. Wandke (Editors)
© Elsevier Science Publishers B.V. (North-Holland), 1986

EXPERIMENTAL AND THEORETICAL ANALYSIS
OF VISUAL SEARCH ACTIVITIES

Bohumir Chalupa
J. E. Purkyne University
Brno
Czechoslovakia

The visual search activities used in seeking and
identifying items of a list underlie a variety of
tasks. The difficulty of tasks can be defined in
terms of the elementary checking time. It varies,
on the average, between 200 and 800 ms for a single
item. The optimum identification is that of words
of a known language since, by contrast to numerical
materials, the length of item is of little relevance.

INTRODUCTION

The visual search activities, studied for the first time by
Jastrow in 1892, can be considered as a model of information
processing by a human operator identifying data of various
visual displays. They are the object of experiments designed
to investigate the effects of the different types of material
and their complexity, to make comparisons with reading and
to examine such factors as size of the list of items, adopted
search strategies, etc.

In our view, the general and experimental psychology, the
engineering psychology and other disciplines are far from
making the best use of all the known facts regarding the
psychical regulation of search activities, i.e. a specific
and dynamic activity quite different from other kinds of processes. The structure of search activities fundamentally differs from that of the selective motor reaction to optical and
acoustical signals, as is shown by comparisons of reaction
times (RT) and search times (ST). Whereas the signals are
usually one-dimensional, the search activities are based on
multi-dimensional stimuli (figures, letters, words, pictures
etc.) which are independent from each other as regards the
perceptive identification. The best approximation to the
visual search activity is the reading but a detailed analysis
reveals differences even in this respect. Being a highly
organized and systematic process, the reading leans upon
certain skills and knowledge whereas the search activities
appear in the man before he has learned to read. Besides,
there exist objects of perceptive identification that cannot
be taken in by means of reading (e.g. landscape, map, human
face, shop-window etc.). Of course, the search activities and

reading can be combined, e.g. the knowledge proper of a sought word is made possible by mechanisms developed for reading of lexical materials. The search through a display, however, may follow another way. Especially the search of a figurative material calls for very few reading routines and mechanisms. This fact finds its repercussion in differing times of reading and perceptive identification required by the search.

The objective of our study was to reveal some rules of the visual search activities considering the kind of material, number and lenght of items, global or partial search strategy, differences between perceptive identification, recognition and reproduction of identical materials, etc. Theoretically, the facts thus acquired can be applied in characterizing the methods of information processing and in describing the psychical structures and mechanisms of regulation relevant to this sphere of activities. Their practical application consists in optimization of the methods and technical means to be used in presenting visual data. They can also be instrumental in reducing the psychical stress inherent in the work with visual displays.

METHODS

Most experiments involved panels with 25,49 and 81 items arranged so as to form squares (5x5, 7x7, 9x9). The items were numbers of two up to six figures, groups of two letters, dials with two pointers, Czech and Portuguese words of three to six letters, patterns of two stripes in differing colours, etc.

The search time (ST) was the time taken by the person under test to find the target item. The item were distributed over the panel randomwise.

The experiments were made with pupils of secondary schools, aged 17 or 18 years.

The optical field used in applying the global or partial search strategy was left undivided or the subject had successively to go through several limited sections. When undergoing experiments with recognition and reproduction, the subjects started by searching for numbers and dials before engaging in recognition or reproduction of the test items.

RESULTS

Speaking generally, we can say that the search times were shortest for symbolic and semantic materials (figures, letters, words) whereas with such materials as dials and coloured stripes, it clearly increased with the same number of items.

2. Even strange, i.e. Portuguese, words of 3 and 4 letters were identified essentially within the same time as known Czech words. Yet the search time significantly increases with words of 5 and 6 letters. Though being meaningless for the experimental subjects, short Portuguese words can be perceptively identified with the same readiness as Czech known words. Longer words require successive checking of letters.

3. Extension of numerical items results in linear extension of search time (approximately 1 s per item element). This is consequent upon the successive checking of item elements.

The visual search activities are a complex process involving especially orientating search components as well as perceptive, memorial and logical operations, analysis and synthesis, planning, anticipation, etc., In general, they correlate poorly or medially with performance in intelligence tests but also with some personal features (emotional stability).

The elementary checking time required for perceptive identification of a single item is not identical to the time of silent reading as is evident from the comparison given in Table 4.

	ECT	SRT
Two-elements numbers	0.212 s	0.239 s
Couple of letters	0.270	0.249 s
Dials	0.724 s	1.269 s

Table 4: Elementary checking time (ECT) and silent reading time (SRT)

It is obvious than the searching and reading mechanisms do not differ a great deal for numbers and letters but as regards dials, the search activity is clearly more effective than successive reading of lines.

This is borne out by experiments using global and partial strategies to seek couples of numbers and dials. The division of panel into several sections to be successively processed had no practical effect on the search of numbers but brought about much longer searching times with dials.

The elementary checking time, i.e. time taken by perceptive identification of a single item, dependents on the following factors:

1. Method of material coding. Symbolic items are easier to identify than figural items.

2. Length of item. For non-integrated items such as numbers, the search time increases more or less linearly with the length of item and, consequently, so does the elementary reading time.

3. Simultaneous or successive processing of information. Words of mother tongue differing in length are identified in approximately the same time. The simultaneous processing of information is evidently conditioned by former learning.

4. Searching strategy. The global strategy proved useful with visual materials.

5. Age and other factors.

DISCUSSION

Effects of the categories of words (semantic and grammatical) were studied in experiments based on seeking words of 6 letters in a panel of 49 items. The average searching time for concrete words was 6.24s, for emotional words 6.63s and for abstract words 8.03s. Abstract material appears to involve also other cognitive operations. Identification of abstract words is a much more difficult operation, which is in agreement with the experiments carried out by Sasson, Fraisse (1972), Bower (1978) and others which were concerned with memorization of concrete and abstract words. The theoretical interpretation of this fact is not yet consistent (role of imagination, semantic networks, hierarchization of notional structures). The grammatical category easiest to identify was that of adjectives (7.33s) and concrete nouns whereas identification of verbs was rather difficult (9.12s). This seems to bear out the presupposition that the words are apt to be identified when containing some concrete attributes.

The cognitive processes participating in search activities are not identical to those of recognition and reproduction. While the search of dials was three times more difficult that that of two-elements numbers, a subsequent recognition did not register any differences between the two and the reproduction even went in favour of dials.

Our experiments allow to draw the following conclusions:

1. To transmit information with the help of figurative material is less advantageous in tasks involving visual search than to use symbolic and verbal material. It is probably due to the difficult perceptive differentiation of figurative material.

2. Numerical material is always processed successively, even within the framework of an item, which is inconvenient with increasing lengths of items.

3. Verbal material has a peculiar feature in that it can be processed either simultaneously like items (familiar words of native language) or successively (strange words).

4. Verbal material is subject to the effects inherent in the semantic and grammatical character of the words to be sought.

According to Anderson (1975) most information coming from the primary perception which forms an analogical model of the world is processed simultaneously whereas verbal and, in particular, numerical materials are processed successively. Though greatly influential in the visual search activity, these facts do not account for all the established aspects, especially as regards the role of the higher psychical processes in the handling of verbal materials.

REFERENCES

(1) Anderson, B.F., Cognitive Psychology. The Study of Knowing, Learning and Thinking (New York, 1975).

(2) Bower, G.H., Moderni koncepce lidské pameti (Modern Conception of Human Memory), Cs. psychologie 22 (1978) 232-242.

(3) Cizková, J., Effect of the quantity and complexity of visual stimuli on the operator activity, Studia psychologica 9 (1967) 241-247.

(4) Chalupa, B., Pozornost a jej úloha v psychichej regulácii cinnosti (Attention and its role in the psychic regulation of activity), (SPN, Bratislava, 1981).

(5) Chalupa, B., Cizková, J., Psychologické studium cinnosti operátora ve vyhledávacich pokusech (Psychological study of operator's activity in search tasks), Cs. psychologie 11 (1967) 598-601.

(6) Chalupa, B., Cizková, J., Psychologische Analyse der Tätigkeit des Operateurs bei den Suchaufgaben, Ergonomics in Machine Design (ILO Geneva, 1969, vol. 1, 69-78).

(7) Chalupa, B., Ulmanová, Y., Zkoumáni zrakové hledací cinnosti pri pouziti verbálnich podnetu (Examination of visual search activity with verbal stimuli), Sbornik praci filozofické fakulty brnenské univerzity I$_{17}$ (1982) 103-109.

(8) Jastrow, J., Studies from the Laboratory of experimental psychology of the University of Wisconsin, II., Amer. J. Psychol. 4 (1982) 381-428.

(9) Neisser, U., Beller, H. K., Searching through word list, Brit. J. Psychol. 56 (1965) 349-358.

(10) Raum, H., Stocklöw, Ch., Aufgabengerechte Optimierung des Informationsangebots auf Bildschirmen, in: Hacker, W., Raum, H., (Eds.), Optimierung von kognitiven Arbeitsanforderungen (Huber, Bern,1980).

(11) Sasson, R.Y., Fraisse, P., Images in memory for concrete and abstract sentences. Journal of Exper. Psychol. 94 (1972) 149-155.

Man-Computer Interaction Research
MACINTER-I
F. Klix and H. Wandke (Editors)
© Elsevier Science Publishers B.V. (North-Holland), 1986

ALTERNATIVE INFORMATION PRESENTATION IS A CONTRIBUTION TO USER CENTRED DIALOGUE DESIGN

Harald Raum
Technische Universität Dresden
Wissenschaftsbereich Psychologie
Dresden
GDR

The paper deals with (1) the efficiency of information presentation as it varies in accordance with
the task, person and situation in question; (2) the
capacity of information users for giving an intuitive
assessment of presentation forms; (3) the use being
made of an optional presentation offer; (4) the
conditions restricting application; and (5) general
conclusions from the experimental and field studies
discussed.

INTRODUCTION

The increased use made of visual display units (VDU use) is,
inter alia, an indication of the extension of automation to
the sphere of man's intellectual activity. Just as in the case
of the earlier automation of man's physical activity, the
automation of intellectual activity involves the risk of leaving man with an accumulation of residual functions that either
cannot be automated or have not as yet been automated. In
addition, man has to fulfil his tasks in interaction with the
computer, which imposes him the constraints of strictly
algorithmic activity (Friedrich, Schaff,1982). This leads to
a large number of complaints of the part of the operators
(see e. g. Johannsson/Aronsson, 1980), and challenges all
ergonomists to take remedial measures.

The aim that industrial psychologists pursue in designing intellectual activity is clear: even under the conditions of
automation one should set health and personality-promoting
tasks that man is capable of performing (Hacker, 1984).
Special attention must be paid to personality promotion, i. e
to. the "granting of cognitive and social competence" (Ulich,
1974; Volpert, 1974), the "formation of learning potentials"
(Frei, 1979), and the "guaranty of significance, autonomy,
variability, identity and feedback throughout the process"
(Hackman, Oldham, 1974).

The preservation of flexibility in VDU use is one way of
achieving the goal. The place of work should be adapted to
different individual needs and should allow tasks to be fulfilled
in an individualized manner. This requires and optionally

variable regime of information presentation and a special
kind of dialogue formation (Balzert, 1983).

If the use of VDU is linked with the above-mentioned comforts,
hardware and software expenditure goes up. This is why psychologists are often asked by technicians and economists what
advantages are provided by these comforts and what use should
be made of them. Answers are found in the investigations made
in recent years by our working group on information presentation
on screens.

ON THE EFFICIENCY OF DIFFERENT KINDS OF INFORMATION PRESENTATION

As we known from cognitive and differential psychology,human
information processing can be parallel or the different processing mechanisms can be used alternate, if required, in
accordance with the task, person or situation concerned.

The demand for compatible designs was first made by industrial
psychologists. The effects produced by compatible information
presentation result from the existence of specific "simple
perceptive structures" of considerable "vividness", "order" and
"gestalt quality". They are economical in terms of their
coding or transformation with regard to the corresponding processing mechanisms, thus minimizing the number of processing
steps, releasing innate and aquired individual interpretation
stereotypes and allowing cognitive operations to shift to
automatic perceptive preprocessing (Wandke, 1979; Raum, 1983).

If the diversity of human information processing modes that was
shown to be present is seen in the context of the demand for
compatibility, it will become clear that there cannot be one
single ideal version of information presentation, but that
similar kinds of presentation must produce different effects in
accordance with the task, person or situation concerned. This
was once again confirmed by laboratory investigations made
for the purpose of "reinsurance". Table 1 provides a survey of
the chosen variables and the use made of them in our experiments.

ON THE CAPACITY OF INFORMATION USERS FOR GIVING INTUITIVELY
CORRECT ASSESSMENTS OF ALTERNATIVE FORMS OF PRESENTATION

The reference to the usefulness of alternative information presentation based upon theoretical and scientific experience
gives rise to the question of how it can be carried out in
practice. From the point of view of a theory of work design, the
creation of a possibility of choice would doubtless be an
advantage since this would increase the freedom of dialogue
formation and allow operators to perform their tasks in a wider
variety of ways (Spinas, Troy, Ulich, 1982).

| Presentation variable | Task variable | | Criterion variable | | |
| | | | | | |
Content	Mode	Task	Reaction	Performance	Physiological	Assessments
Individual value	digital graphico-analogous -columns -scales -schemes	reading classifi-cation	writing	solution time fixation time coding time error	heart rate breathing	difficulty
Group of three values (like KLT-DÜKER)	digital graphico-analogous -columns mixed digital and ana-logous verbal	reading search for target value addition rating of (+/-) addition result comparison between two subsequent addition results	writing typing marking of column lengths announcement	time - fixation - coding - answering error - sign - amount - mixed decision contents	heart rate breathing	difficulty adequacy
Threefold classified group of 25 values (tables)	digital -table graphico-analogous -polygon -columns -polygons of diffe-rent arrange-ment	reading of individual values recognition and evaluation of functional dependencies recognition of general re-gression model	announcement or verbal answer	time error sequence of processing	xxx	difficulty adequacy degree of order

Table 1: Survey of variables of presentation, tasks and criteria investigated in laboratory experiments on alternative information presentation

Whether users can be allowed a choice will, however, depend on
his capacity for giving an intuitively correct assessment of the
modes of presentation offered in a specific case of utilization.
For this purpose we recorded assessments and inquiry data on
the "degree of difficulty", "adequacy" and "clearness" of presentation in our laboratory investigations.

The general result was that users who know the alternative presentation modes available are in a position to distinguish
in an intuitively correctly manner between appropriate and less
effective presentation in the sense of an order of precedence
at least after they have dealt with them for a short time, without making any comprehensive attributions to the reasons for
the differences (for further details, see Raum, 1984).

ON THE USE BEING MADE OF AN OPTIONAL OFFER OF ALTERNATIVE
INFORMATION PRESENTATION

The differential effect shown to be produced on performance by
information presentation (Item 1), and man's capacity for
giving an intuitively correct assessment of the presentation
forms offered (Item 2) will not, in the eyes of sceptics, be
convincing reasons for justifying technical efforts and
expenditure regarding the provision of an optional information
offer. The question is whether an offer of this kind would
actually be made use of.

We therefore proceeded to change the basic structure of the
experiments made until then (see Table 1), and began investigating the choice of the form of presentation on the basis of
a given content and knowledge of its presentation alternatives,
considering this as a functional criterion variable. We are
interested in the behaviour shown by subjects when the latter
were making a choice among the presentation alternatives related
to certain tasks that had to be repeatedly fulfilled in an
unpredictable sequence. Table 2 gives an example. The general
result showed that use was made of this even in cases of repetition (i.e not only as a novelty effect). Subjects may be
divided into three groups, each showing typical behaviour:
64 % of subjects were certain at once, about 33 % learnt rapidly, and about 3 % gambled.

Although in view of what has been said so far, the applications
of the optional offer of alternative information presentation
to real-life jobs appear obvious, a demonstration in field
surroundings is desirable if all doubt concerning the ecolo-
gical validity of the findings should be removed (Holzkamp,
1964). In co-operation with the Department of Physics of Dresden Technological University and the Centre of Scientific
Apparatus Construction of the Academy of Sciences of the GDR,
we were given an opportunity for testing and checking the
prototypes of Energy Dispersing X-ray Spectrometer EDR183. In
analogy to previous laboratory investigations, analyses were
made of the behaviour and performance of users (for further

	Classification of subjects/operators (in %)		
Tasks/Sub-tasks	Immediate deciders	Rapid learners	Gamblers

1. Processing of (KLT-DÜKER-like) data (experimental study, 37 subjects, four different presentations, for further details see Raum, 1982)

Reading the data	75	22	3
Search for target value	70	25	5
Adding all values	62	38	O
Rating of +/-addition result	51	46	3
Average	64	33	3

2. Processing of (EDR183) spectograms (field study, 20 operators, three different presentations, for further details see Raum, 1983)

Positioning peaks	65	25	10
Positioning half widths	65	25	10
Positioning background area	75	20	5
Average	69	23	8

Table 2: Decision behaviour of subjects/operators in relation to presentation versions with regard to different tasks/sub-tasks fulfilled by the subjects/operators

	Choice of presentation mode/task (in %)		
Task	Dots	columns	with black underneath
Positioning peaks	43	21	36
Positioning half widths	42	24	34
Positioning background area	32	32	36
Average	39	26	35

Table 3: Choice of three presentation versions for the fulfilment of tasks with the help of EDR183 (20 users assess 17 spectrograms each, for further details see Raum, 1983)

details, see Raum, 1983). We found that:

(a) the choice of presentation offered was indeed used. Utilization depended on the persons and tasks concerned (Table 3);

(b) the decision behaviour of the persons observed was similar to that detected under laboratory conditions in cases of repeated confrontation with the tasks (see Table 2); and

(c) the utilization of the kinds of presentation chosen led to a balance being established between inter-individual and task-specific qualitative and quantitative performance differences (Table 4).

CONDITIONS RESTRICTING THE APPLICATION OF OPTIONAL ALTERNATIVE INFORMATION PRESENTATION

The results described so far can be regarded as supporting the finding that optional information presentation is a suitable measure of user-centred dialogue design in VDU use. They do not however show, that an alternative presentation offer must used in every case.

Our investigations with two EDR183 versions have revealed that:

(a) Presentation selection must be as simple as possible. Simple selection (e.g. by means of operating keys) encourages even those "experienced users" to make intensive use of the presentation alternatives offered who usually "save" themselves the trouble of selection to make for fluent job processing (Table 5).

   This fits in with experimental laboratory findings made by the Department of Psychology of Berlin Humboldt University:

(b) The more complicated dialogue (selection of presentation) can result in added difficulties in the performance of tasks by casual users (Wetzenstein-Ollenschläger et al., 1983).

(c) Unsatisfactory ratios of the number of different tasks to be fulfilled and the number of presentation alternatives offered lead to this comfort being rejected and very limited use being made of it by operators (Wetzenstein-Ollenschläger, 1983).

   Further conditions that have a restricting effect can be as follows:

(d) Presentation should be in keeping with the needs of users. Presentation with vague or extremely scattered application advantages remains unused (no offer is made for the sake of making an offer).

| Task | Time for fulfilling the tasks (sec) | | | |
	Dot users	Column users	Users of black under- neath	Total
Positioning peaks	8.34	7.47	8.24	24.05
Positioning half widths	13.99	13.92	15.41	43.32
Positioning background area	11.88	13.54	12.22	37.74
Total	34.21	34.93	35.87	105.01

Table 4: Time needed for fulfilling the task by users of different presentation modes in accordance with the tasks fulfilled with the help of EDR183: no significant differences between users of different information presentations (for further details see Raum, 1983)

| Operation system | Sub-programme | Choice frequency/person per spectrogram | | |
		Laymen	Specialists	Total
EDR183/I	DASPE (presentation/ colour)	0.00	0.29	0.29
(sequence of indi- vidual commands)	MASST (change of scale/focusing)	1.29	1.14	2.43
Total		1.29	1,43	2.72
EDR183/II	DASPE	2.29	1.20	3.49
(operating keys)	MASST	2.57	5.20	7.77
Total		4.86	6.40	11.26

Table 5: Utilization of the optional offer of spectogram presen- tation (DASPE) and scaling/focusing (MASST) sub-program- mes by laymen and specialists in accordance with the simplicity of the dialogue with the help of EDR183 versions (see Herzberg, 1984)

(e) A certain critical number of presentation alternatives
    should not be exeeded. The limit might be set by the
    operative memory span (5 to 9 items), with the optimum
    probably being well below these figures (3 to 5 versions).

GENERAL CONCLUSIONS FOR DIALOGUE DESIGN

From the theoretical point of view, the re-creation of the
engineering-psychological construct of compatibility and its
connections with the general and differential psychological
fact of different modes ("strategies") of information processing as mentioned at the beginning seem to be well-suited
for our purpose. They may be used as additional explanation
of the efficiency of an optional work offer. An optional offer
of this kind does not only follow from the more ethical and
motivational aims of work design ("personality promotion",
"job satisfaction"), but also supports and simplifies human
task fulfilment activities through the opportunity for individualization.

The following conclusions result from the investigations discussed for the application of this basic idea to user-centred
VDU-based dialogue design:

(a) A well-designed dialogue program should involve optional
    opportunities for information presentation on the screen.
    This at least applies to information of the investigated
    type (indication of measurement data, compilation of data),
    but should also be suitable for mask formation in general
    (the grouping of information, the build-up of schemes, and
    the arrangement and structuring of texts).

(b) The offer of presentation versions should be restricted to
    a few (3 to 5) that can be assessed by the user, it should
    take account of existing individual modes of processing and
    types of task.

(c) Dialogue design must offer the user easy access to present-
    ation versions (e.g. by means of operating keys).

(d) The user should be enabled to make a preselection as to
    whether he wants to use the presentation versions offered
    or rather use a standard position for simplifying his
    operating actions (e.g. for casual users).

(e) The "added difficulty" of dialogue that is no doubt more or
    less recognized by VDU users is a no sufficient conter-
    argument against optional information presentation. The
    extention of work opportunities achieved by the "add diffi-
    culty" is the main argument in favour of this. It may even
    be possible that the "added difficulty" is a desirable
    sider-effect since it eliminates the uniformity of operation
    that may be conducive to the monotony of perceptiory.

The explanations give above are meant to give an impression of our approach to the problem of MAn-Computer-INTERaction design. This procedure is in keeping with modern trends in the development of software ergonomics (Balzert, 1983) and psychological, "differential" (Ulich, 1978), "personality-promoting" (Hacker, 1984) job design. This is why we propose that one of the subjects to be dealt with in our future cooperation in the MACINTER project should be: Opportunities and limits of individualization in man-computer interaction (VDU)-work.

REFERENCES

(1) Balzert, H., Software-Ergonomie. German Chapter of the ACM, Berichte 14 (Teubner, Stuttgart, 1983).

(2) Doss, B., Untersuchungen zur Abhängigkeit von Informations-gestaltung, Aufgabenstellung und Verarbeitungsökonomie, Diplomarbeit, Technische Universität Dresden, Wissen-schaftsbereich Psychologie (1980) (unpublished).

(3) Frei, F., Arbeit als Lernprozess und Qualifikationschance. ro-ro-ro, Psychosozial 1 (1979) 7-21.

(4) Friedrichs, G. and Schaff, A. (eds.), Auf Gedeih und Ver-derb (Europaverlag, Vienna/Munich/Zürich, 1982).

(5) Hacker, W. (ed.), Spezielle Arbeits- und Ingenieurpsycholo-gie, Band 2 (Springer, Berlin/Heidelberg/New York/Toronto, 1984).

(6) Hackman, J.R. and Oldham, G.R., The Job Diagnosis Survey. Techn. Rep. 4, Yale University (1974).

(7) Herzberg, H., Vergleich zweier Dialogvarianten am EDR 183 und Erarbeitung eines Lernprogramms, Diplomarbeit, Tech-nische Universität Dresden, Wissenschaftsbereich Psycho-logie (1984).

(8) Holzkamp, K., Theorie und Experiment in der Psychologie (Springer, Berlin (West), 1964).

(9) Johannsson, G. and Aronsson, G., Stress Reaction in Computerized Administrative Work. Reports Dept. Psychol. Univ. Stockholm, Suppl.Series 50 (November 1980).

(10) Raum, H., Zur Gestaltung von Anforderungen und Beanspru-chungen in automatisierten Informationsverarbeitungstechno-logien am Beispiel der Bildschirmarbeit (Materialien 7. Colloquium Dresdense, Technische Universität Dresden, 1982).

(11) Raum, H., Bildschirmarbeit und wählbares Informationsange-
     bot. Symposium "Wissenschaftlich-technischer Fortschritt
     und Entwicklungstendenzen der Arbeit", Symposiumsband,
     Technische Universität Dresden, 1983.

(12) Raum, H., Informationsgestaltung und Bildschirmarbeit,
     Psychol. Suppl. 5 (1983) 56-76.

(13) Raum, H., Bildschirmarbeit - eine Folge moderner Infor-
     mationsverarbeitungstechnologien. Psychol.f.d.Praxis, 4
     (1984).

(14) Raum, H., Zum Prinzip des alternativen Informationsan-
     gebots. Psychologie und Praxis, 1984 (forthcoming).

(15) Spinas, Ph.; Troy, N. and Ulich, E., Leitfaden zur Ein-
     führung und Gestaltung von Arbeit mit Bildschirmsystemen
     (Duttweiler-Institut, CH-8803, Rüschlikon, 1982).

(16) Ulich, E., Neue Formen der Arbeitsstrukturierung, Fort-
     schrittliche Betriebsführung 23, 3 (1974) 187-196.

(17) Ulich, E., Über das Prinzip der differentiellen Arbeits-
     gestaltung, Industrielle Organisation, 47 (1978) 281-286.

(18) Volpert, W., Handlungskompetenz und Sozialisation, in:
     Güldenpfennig, S.; Volpert, W. and Weinberg, W. (eds.),
     Sensomotorisches Lernen und Sport als Reproduktion der
     Arbeitskraft (Cologne, 1974).

(19) Wandke, H., Zur Prüfung der Transformationshypothese bei
     Zuordnungsleistungen unterschiedlicher Kompatibilität,
     in: Klix, F. and Timpe, K.-P. (eds.), Arbeits- und
     Ingenieurpsychologie und Intensivierung (DVW, Berlin,
     1979).

(20) Wetzenstein-Ollenschläger, E., Prinzipien der Informations-
     strukturierung auf dem Bildschirm, Vortrag Arbeitstagung
     "Psychologische Gestaltung rechnergestützter Bildschirm-
     arbeitsplätze", Humboldt-Universität Berlin, Sektion
     Psychologie (1983).

(21) Wetzenstein-Ollenschläger, E., Scheidereiter, U. and
     Geissler, H.-G., Informationsgestaltung in der automati-
     sierten Produktion..., 6. Kongress d.Ges.f.Psychol. d.DDR,
     Symposium 12, Kongressband, (Berlin, Ges.f.Psychol., 1983).

EVALUATION OF
MAN–COMPUTER INTERACTION

Man-Computer Interaction Research
MACINTER-I
F. Klix and H. Wandke (Editors)
© Elsevier Science Publishers B.V. (North-Holland), 1986

351

EFFECTS OF COMPUTERIZATION ON JOB DEMANDS AND STRESS:
THE CORRESPONDENCE OF SUBJECTIVE AND OBJECTIVE DATA

Anneli Leppänen, Raija Kalimo, Pekka Huuhtanen
Institute of Occupational Health
Helsinki
Finland

There are different opinions about the effects of computerization on job demands and stress (dequalification versus polarization hypothesis). In this article the impact of
computerization of text preparation, salary calculation, and
on the work of journalists is described. It can be shown
that computerization causes no general effects on job demands
and stress.

INTRODUCTION

It has been assumed that the effects of computerization on the work process
and well-being of man always follow certain general trends. Scientists
have different opinions about these trends.

The dequalification hypothesis assumes that computerization always decreases
occupational qualification demands and, as a consequence, causes stress
reactions in men. The polarization hypothesis contends that computerization
of the work process causes differentiation of occupational demands. Although
the qualification level of some occupations increases, most occupations
become more restricted. The requalification approach assumes that computerization increases qualification demands of all employees. According to this
view computerization makes the control of the work process more abstract.
As a result, employees need thorough knowledge about both the work process
and computer technology in order to be able to perform adequately.

From the viewpoint of psychology these views on the effects of computerization on work are too general and categorical. Prediction and control of
the consequencies of computerization requires a relatively detailed analysis of the mental processes active during a workprocess. The consequencies
of computerization also depend on the fit of demands with the volitional
and emotional characteristics of man.

CASE EXAMPLES

The effects of computerization on job demands and worker stress have been
studied in slightly varying conceptual frameworks and with varying methods.

Framework of a study on computerization of text preparation

The impact of computer technology on work contents, feedback, performance control, and mental stress was studied in text preparation branch in the printing shops in Finland. The conceptual framework of the study is presented in fig. 1.

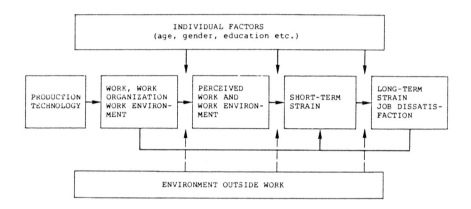

Figure 1: Framework of the study on computerization of text preparation

The characteristics of work and the reactions of perforator typesetters (N = 24), Visual display terminal (VDT) typesetters (N = 17), proof-readers (N = 10) and photocompositors (N = 30) were investigated in a quasi-experimental field setting (Kalimo and Leppänen, 1984). The concept of mental load refers to the use of an individual's psychic functions at work. Mental loads refer to those demands placed on an individual's mental functions such as perception, memory and thinking. If the characteristics of the individual do not coincide with the work characteristics work causes an unsuitable load which can lead to negative effects on the person. The methods of the study and the variables measured by each are described in fig. 2.

Measurements of vigilance were made with the critical flicker frequency technique (CFF) three times a day. The Bourdon-Wiersma perceptual-motor test was administered twice a day to assess psychomotor performance. The subjects assessed their state on a rating scale at the end of the work day.

A questionnaire was used to study long-term stress reactions. Work analysis and questionnaire techniques were used to assess the characteristics of work.

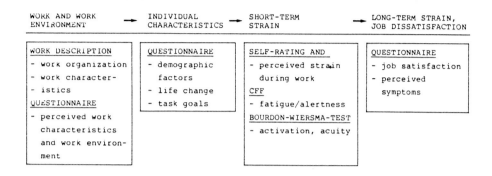

Figure 2: Methods in the study on computerization of text preparation

Framework in the study on computerization of salary calculation

The impacts of computerization of the demands of work, work organization and mental load in salary calculation were studied both from the organizational (Piispanen, 1983) and stress theoretical (Huuhtanen, 1983) framework. The conceptual framework of the study is presented in fig. 3.

THE FRAMEWORK OF THE STUDY

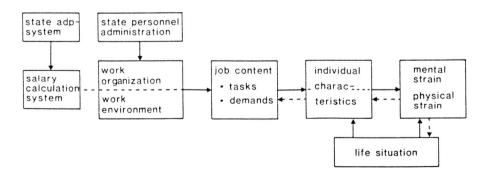

Figure 3: The framework of the study on computerization of salary calculation

Emphasis was placed on the investigation of the stressors in jobs and work organization, e. g., changes in job content, work flow, work organization, and the division of tasks. Interviews, self-appraisals and psychological tests were used as methods of the study. The interview covered topics on personal background, work history, position in organization, work flow, tasks, errors at work, work satisfaction, work environment, leisure activities, health, occupational interests and attitutes toward computerization.

Questionnaires were used to explore the dimensions of work content, daily mental strain and long-term stress reactions. Measurement of short-term memory, visual perception, verbal reasoning and self concept were made with psychological tests. A sample of 24 payroll clerks in nine institutions participated in this follow-up study through different stages of the implementation of an automatic data processing (ADP) system.

Framework of the study on the impact of computerization on the work of journalists

The development of production technology has changed the equipment used in editorial departments of publishing houses. A stress-theoretical approach and a questionnaire technique were adopted to study the consequences of computerization on work and journalists' reactions. Ninety-five journalists participated in the study. More than half of them used VDTs almost continuously and 29 % used VDTs half of their workhours.

RESEARCH FINDINGS

Computerization of a text input task

In the study of the effects of computerization of the text-preparation process in printing industry on the reactions of workers the group differed from each others in the way their state of vigilance changed during the work day. The critical flicker frequency threshold of perforator typesetters became lower during the work shift ($p < .05$) whereas no statistically significant change was found for the other groups. A tendency towards increased stability of performance on the Bourdon-Wiersma test was noted in all the groups, but it was less visible for perforator typesetters than for the others. The subjects' self-ratings of competence calmness, pleasantness, and alertness at the end of work day revealed two statistically significant differences between the groups. The perforator typesetters and the proofreaders rated themselves less competent and less active than VDT typesetters and photocompositors (Kalimo and Leppänen, 1984).

Computerization of calculation of salaries

The study on the computerization of the salary calculation revealed that payroll clerks considered the changes in job contents as primarily positive. Many laborious manual tasks (calculations, collecting and typing payroll lists for registers, etc.) had been computerized (Piispanen,1983), and the work now provided a possibility to learn new things (Huuhtanen, 1984). Although an increase of monotony and a simplification of job demands had been expected, such changes were not noted 8 - 10 month after the transition. Payroll clerks achieved a better understanding of the whole process of salary calculation, because through computerization the

vertical organization of tasks was eliminated. Despite these positive
effects, the study also revealed problems similar to those encountered
in some other studies. Time pressure and total dependence on the computer
system were considered problematic, and difficulties were experienced in
the correction of errors. The employees also had some difficulties in
adopting the new way of thinking necessary with the computerized system
(Huuhtanen, 1983).

Computerization of the work of journalists

Long response times and disruptions in the functioning of the computer
have been considered as two of the main problems in working with VDTs.
However, more than half of the journalists working with VDTs had rather
positive experiences. They reportes that long processing times or prosessing
disruptions of the computers seldom interrupted their work and seldom
forced them to wait. One in three respondents sometimes had and one in ten
more often had difficulties in working due to the long response times of
the computers.

The majority (91 %) of the journalists who used VDTs had no need to work
overtime because of the equipment. According to these results, VDTs do
not increase the quantitative workload of the journalists. The autonomy
of journalism was not affected by computers according to the respondents.

Insufficient and inadequate training is often a problem during and after
the introduction of computerized information systems. Two of ten journalists
considered the training for computerized editing systems as insufficient.
Forty-three percent of the respondents regarded the contents of the training
unsatisfactory regarding the demands of their work.

The journalists were either indifferent or had positive opinions about the
effects of computerization on job strain. Thirty-eight percent of the
respondents had not perceived any changes in strain due to computerization.
Thirty-six percent of the respondents felt that computerization reduced
strain.

DISCUSSION AND CONCLUSIONS

The correspondence of subjective and objective data on job demands and
worker stress can be assessed at least from two points of view. First the
compatibility of changes at work demands and the worker's appraisals of
them can be assessed. Secondly the experienced level of well-being can be
compared to numerous behavioral, psychophysiological and biochemical
measures.

In a study of the effects of computerization on the occupational demands
in salary calculation both the objective data about the changes in work
process: tasks, methods and division of work, and the subjective assessments
of the payroll clerks about the characteristics of work revealed comparable
trends. Several routine manual tasks e. g. calculations and typing lists
had disappeared after computerization. Simultaneously the payroll clerks
experienced that the possibility to learn new things, the challenge of
work, and the demands of knowledge and skills had increased.

Computerization did not affect the strain experienced by the journalists. Computerization had caused some minor difficulties in working e. g. long response times of computers. The main occupational demands of the journalists: creating ideas and decisions about the topics, contents, and realization of articles and interviewing for articles remain the same irrespective of the tool.

The results of the studies on the impact of computerization on the work and strain the payroll clerks and journalists revealed that when computerization changed the essential features of work contents and organization the subjective assessments about work changed accordingly (Huuhtanen,1983). When computerization did not have any effect on the contents of work no subjective changes were experienced either (Leppänen, 1984). The problems connected with the functioning of computers were, however, realized, but they did not affect the assessments of the other characteristics of work.

The study on computerization of the text-preparation branch of the printing industry revealed the comparability of the subjective and objective stress reactions. These results indicate that both subjective and objective data about the occupational demands and subjective and objective data about stress reactions of man reflect the consequences of computerization on the man-work interaction. To be able to predict, guide and control computerization of work processes knowledge about the consequences of computerization on different stages of interaction between man and work is needed.

REFERENCES

(1) Huuhtanen, P., Implementation of a computerized system and its effects on job content, work load, and work organization in office work (Institute of Occupational Health, Helsinki, 1983). (In Finnish).

(2) Huuhtanen, P., Implementation of an ADP-System to calculate salaries: evaluation of the implementation process and changes in job content and work load, in Grandjean, E. (ed.), Ergonimics and health in modern offices (Taylor and Francis, London, 1984).

(3) Kalimo, R. and Leppänen, A., Feedback from video display terminals, performance control and stress in text preparation in the printing industry. J. Occup. Psychol. 57 (1984) (in press).

(4) Leppänen, A, Stress at the work of the journalists (Institute of Occupational Health, Helsinki, 1984 (in Finnish).

(5) Piispanen, E., ADP-system and salary calculation (Valtion Painatuskeskus, Helsinki, 1983). (in Finnish).

Man-Computer Interaction Research
MACINTER-I
F. Klix and H. Wandke (Editors)
© Elsevier Science Publishers B.V. (North-Holland), 1986

ASSESSMENT OF MENTAL LOAD FOR DIFFERENT STRATEGIES
OF MAN-COMPUTER DIALOGUE BY MEANS OF THE HEART RATE
POWER SPECTRUM

Klaus W. Zimmer and Bojanka Guguljanova

Department of Psychology
Humboldt-University of Berlin
Berlin
GDR

Two strategies differing with respect to processing and
operational demands could be adopted by naive computer
users to complete the same type of tasks.
While the selection-ratio of the strategies obviously
was determined by the instruction (neutral vs. ego-involvement) task-difficulty and strategies could be discri-
minated by the power spectrum of the cardiac interval
signal with reduced power in the range of .o6-.12 cps
for tasks and those strategy which placed harder demands
on conscious processing.

INTRODUCTION

In their stimulating discussion of the various strategies people may use
to solve concept formation problems, Bruner, Goodnow, and Austin (1956)
point to the trade-off between memory and conscious processing which determines a good deal of the strategies used in solving one and the same problem. What has to be mentioned is that the problem of processing strategies,
along with the first and up to now not outdated ideas on this topic, arose
from a particularly scope of general psychology. Now, to find out efficient
strategies for different individuals in man-computer-interaction is a problem of considerable practical relevance (see also Klix, van der Veer, this
volume). Unfortunately the ideas of Bruner et al. have not been much improved upon since that time. This is because there remain at least two problems
to be solved: (1) the clearcut definition of all possible strategies which
could be adopted to any task, and, (2) the evaluation of the mental processing load which determines the efficiency of the solution. As to the first
problem we believe man-machine-interaction to be a good paradigm because
all contacts in the information exchange between man and computer may be
defined. On the other hand the cognitive processing load resulting from
this or that strategy could be reflected in time-locked analysed changes
of autonome controlled physiological indices like heart rate or respiratory
rate. There is now a lot of evidence available which turned out the demands
placed on controlled capacity-limited information processing (Shiffrin and
Schneider (1977, 1984)) related to changes in heart rate patterns (Posner
(1975),Richter et al. (1980)). Following an approach by Mulder and Mulder
(1980, 1981) we used the power spectrum of the cardiac interval signal as
a tool to evaluate the amount of controlled information processing necessary to complete the task. In a series of experiments (see Schönebeck and
Zimmer (1985)) it could be demonstrated that particularly the spectral component of about o.1 cps is more reduced if the demands placed on working
memory in the same type of task were increased. The type of task we investi-

gated was reading of short prose texts. The difficulty or readability of
the texts was estimated with reference to the model of text comprehension
proposed by Kintsch and van Dijk (1978). A typical result is illustrated
by the first Figure.

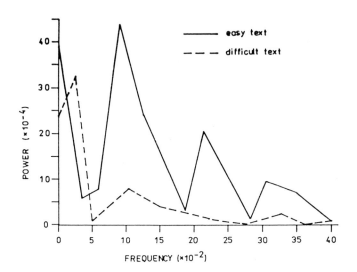

Fig. 1
Power spectra of the cardiac interval signal for an easy
compared with a difficult text (subject 13). The mean IBI
for the easy text is 757 ms and 8o8 ms for the difficult
text.

The component of o.1 cps revealed to be strongly reduced for the difficult
text. The estimated discriminant functions with typical frequencies as
variables, computed for all texts and all subjects provided this component
in almost all cases with the largest weight.
This results encouraged the use of the cardiac power spectrum to indicate
the cognitive processing load related to different strategies of man-computer dialogue for the same type of task. There were two points of further
interest: (a) There are well-known relations between heart rate and respiratory rate with lower degrees of coupling in harder physical work (Laurig
et al. (1971), Eckoldt et al. (198o)). Our question was if there could be
differentiated between degrees of coupling cardiac and respiratory activity
while comparing different strategies of man-computer dialogue.
(b) Which strategy is best depends along with other conditions (cf. Bruner
et al. (1956), Lindsay and Norman (1977)) on what purpose the task is needed
for. This points to the motivational state and motivational determined atten-
tional selectivity as conditions which control the free selection of strategies. While motivational states are discussed with respect to the general
availability of processing resources (see Kahneman (1973), Eysenck (1982),
for an elaborate discussion) or the availability of particular processing
resources (Hockey et al. (1981)), selectivity is discussed to result in typical stimulus and response sets (Broadbent (1971, 1977)) which may function
as instructions within the program that will be performed by the individual
to solve the problem. Therefore we investigated also the effect of a moti-

vational instruction on strategy selection for naive subjects.

METHOD

By strategy we mean simply different dialogue structures which could be
used as a mode of communication between our subjects and the computer to
perform simulated commercial orders in a sales division of a factory.
There was a specific constructed database stored in the computer (HP 9845 B).
The first dialogue structure consisted of a sequence of several single
commands for each dialogue step. We call this the chain-up strategy. To
follow this strategy successfully a good deal of learning the single commands was necessary and also more key strokes had to be performed. But there is not much of conscious processing to be done. The second dialogue
structure consisted of only one but complex command for each dialogue step.
To determine this complex command a good deal of mental arithmetics had
to be performed (please compare the paper by Wandke and Schulz, this volume, for further details). We call this the transformation strategy.
The adoption of the transformation strategy obviously placed harder demands
on controlled capacity-limited processing, but reduced operational demands.
Twelve subjects, psychology student volunteers, learned these two strategies before the experiment started. Some practice trials controlled for
the results of learning. During the experiment the subjects were left completely free to select one of the two strategies or to alternate within the
session to solve the above mentioned tasks. These taks differed in the degree of difficulty scaled by the number of characteristics (rangig from 2
up to 4) which had to be met by the retrieval orders. Each subject was re-
quiered to solve 14 tasks.
Six of the twelve subjects got an ego-involvement instruction. They were
told that the tasks are related to intelligence. Additionally they were
given a time-limit, estimated from practice trials. Exceeding the limit was
signalled by a warning tone. We call this the motivated group.
The ECG was recorded from surface electrodes placed on the left arm vs. the
left leg (extremities leak III by Einthoven). Interbeat intervals (R-R-dis-
tancies) were electronically measured. The respiratory rate was recorded by
means of a breathing-tape placed around the chest. All data were stored on-
line in digital manner on flexible magnetic discs.The power spectra of the
cardiac interval signal were estimated for each single task and each subject (168 spectra althogether) with Fast Fourier Transformation (FFT). Each
power spectrum was then normalized, and averaged with respect to conditions
of interest(task-difficulty, instruction, strategy).

RESULTS AND DISCUSSION

With respect to solution times there was an increase found from the lowest
level of task-difficulty up to the highest level within each strategy
(12o s up to 22o s in the mean). The level of task-difficulty was reflected
also in the pulse/respiration-quotient (mean heart rate divided by mean
respiratory rate). This index increased significantly with the level of
task-difficulty from 2.5 for the lowest level up to 3.o for the highest level of task-difficulty ($\hat{F}$ = 8.75> 4.3o, F o.o5; 1,22).
In general the chain-up strategy was preferred by our naiv Ss over the transformation strategy but this is due to the markedly preference of the motivated Ss which selected the chain-up strategy in 86 % of the cases, while
the neutral instructed Ss showed an ratio of 5o % which means in fact no
preference. We have to note, that the chain-up strategy secured a higher

chance to fall short of the required time-limit with fewer errors.
With respect to the power spectrum of the cardiac interval signal a stronger
reduction with increasing task difficulty had to be expected.
Figure 2 demonstrates that this expection was met by the data. The slower
frequency components in the range of .o6 - .12 cps differ with respect to
their relative energy between the levels of task difficulty.

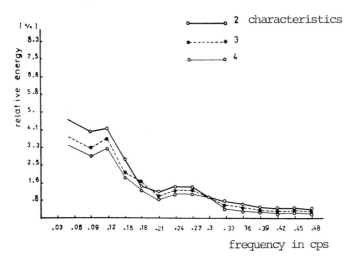

Fig. 2
Averaged power spectra of heart-beat intervals for
each level of task difficulty (12 Ss).

It should be noted that in this range of frequencies oscillations of blood
pressure are reflected (Sayers (1973)).
A similar result should hold also, if the averaged power spectrum of all
tasks solved with the chain-up strategy is compared with that belonging to
the transformation strategy.
Figure 3 presents the obtained result: the power spectrum belonging to the
transformation strategy is reduced not only in the slower but also in the
faster frequency components.

It is worth to notice that the demonstrated results with respect to the
cardiac interval power spectrum can not be reduced simply to an increase
in the tonic heart rate as a consequence of increased demands on overt behavior.
Table 1 demonstrates task-difficulty not to be related to tonic heart rate
in general but Table 2 demonstrates a markedly increase of tonic heart rate
for the transformation strategy which was connected with reduced motor demands.

A discriminant analysis with 16 frequencies of the power spectrum as variables resulted in a discriminant function which reclassified correctly 84 %
of the tasks solved with the chain-up strategy and 82 % of those solved
with the transformation strategy.
Only one word concerning the results obtained with respect to the coupling
between heart rate and respiratory rate. As a first step the computer
estimated the intervals between the R-peak of the ECG and inspiration onset.
In a further step histograms of these intervals were defined for each task.

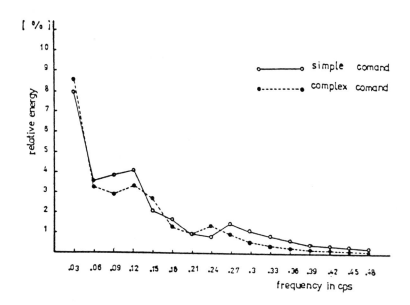

Fig. 3
Averaged power spectra (over 12 Ss) of heart rate intervals compared for the chain-up strategy (simple command)
and the transformation strategy (complex command).

Table 1
Mean heart rate in beats per minute, averaged over all
subjects and type of strategy used for the task completing
interval

taks difficulty	mean heart rate (bpm)
easy	76.7
medium	76.3
hard	75.o

Table 2
Mean heart rate in beats per minute, averaged over all subjects for the task completing intervals of the three task-difficulty groups and type of strategy used

taks difficulty	chain-up strategy	transformation strategy	difference
easy	73.9	8o.9	+ 7.o
medium	73.o	84.1	+ 11.1
hard	7o.o	83.o	+ 13.o

If the hypotheses of equal distributed events could not be rejected at the
5 % level of significance, decoupling was stated. To cut a long story
short: it was impossible by this method to differ between the levels of
task difficulty, simply because out of the overall 168 solved tasks only
for 21 there was a significant deviation of the histogram from a discrete
uniform distribution and these 21 cases over and above were uniform distributed over the levels of task difficulty. This could mean that the experimental situation in general placed strong demands on all subjects, because
the degree of coupling increases with more relaxed states of individuals.

CONCLUSIONS

If the presented results and those from preliminary experiments not mentioned in this context (see Zimmer et al. (1985)) are taken together, the
following conclusions may be drawn, of course with care:
(1) Man-computer interaction may well serve as an excellent paradigm to
investigate the underlying conditions of human strategies of information
processing. Such investigations may contribute to solve this old but also
contemporary problem of the psychology of cognition and memory. At the same
time some problems of practical relevance, as that of evaluation of different modes of communication between man and the computer may be dealt with.
(2) The power spectrum of the cardiac interval signal may be recommended
as a sensitive tool for evaluating the total amount of cognitive processing
load resulting from different strategies. It provides more information
than a simple index of heart rate variability. So the power spectrum seems
to reflect at least two different sources of mental processing load: (a)
in the range of o.o6 up to o.12 cps the amount of controlled information
processing in connection with a capacity-limited working memory, and (b)
the demands placed on motor operations and motivational effort which are
additionally reflected in the range of about o.2o up to o.5o cps.
(3) Some useful results in both scopes, computer-aided problem solving and
the evaluation of computer-aided jobs in the field, are expected by the
use of this method.

REFERENCES

(1) Broadbent, D.E., Decision and stress (Academic Press, London, 1971).
(2) Broadbent, D.E., Levels, hierarchies, and the locus of control,
    Quart. J. Exp. Psychol. 29 (1977) 181-2o1.
(3) Bruner, J.S., Goodnow, J.J. and Austin, G.A., A study of thinking
    (Wiley, New York, 1956).
(4) Eckoldt, K., Pfeifer, B. and Schubert, E., Sympathetic and parasympa-
    thetic innervation of the heart at rest and work in man as judged by
    heart rate and sinus-arrhythmia, in: Koepchen, H.D., Hilton, S.M. and
    Trzebski, A.T. (eds.), Central Interaction between Respiratory and
    Cardiovascular Control System (Springer, Berlin-Heidelberg-New York,
    198o).
(5) Eysenck, M.W., Attention and arousal: cognition and performance
    (Springer, Berlin-Heidelberg-New York, 1982).
(6) Hockey, R., MacLean, A. and Hamilton, P., State changes and the tempo-
    ral patterning of component resources, in: Long, J. and Baddeley, A.D.
    (eds.), Attention and Performance, IX (Erlbaum, Hillsdale-N.J., 1981).
(7) Kahneman, D., Attention and effort (Prentice Hall, Englewood Cliffs -
    N.J., 1973).

(8) Kintsch, W. and van Dijk, T.A., Toward a model of text comprehension and production, Psychol. Rev. 85 (1978) 363-394.
(9) Laurig, W., Luczak, H. and Philipp, U., Ermittlung der Pulsfrequenz-arrhythmie bei körperlicher Arbeit, Intern. Z. angew. Physiol. 3o (1971) 4o-51.
(1o) Lindsay, R.H. and Norman, D.A., Human information processing (Academic Press, London-New York, 1977).
(11) Mulder, G. and Mulder, L.J.M., Coping with mental work load, in: Levine, S. and Ursin, H. (eds.), Coping and health (Plenum Press, New York, 198o).
(12) Mulder, G. and Mulder, L.J.M., Information processing and cardiovascular control, Psychophysiology 18 (1981) 392-4o2.
(13) Posner, M.I., Psychobiology of attention, in: Gazzaniga, M. and Blakemore, C. (eds.), Handbook of Psychobiology (Academic Press, London-New York, 1975).
(14) Richter, P., Richter, P.G., Schmidt, Ch. and Straube, B., Psychophysiologische Aufwandsbestimmung als Grundlage der Effektivitätsbeurteilung von Arbeitstätigkeiten, Zeitschrift für Psychologie 188 (198o) 275-291.
(15) Sayers, B.McA., Analysis of heart rate variability, Ergonomics 16 (1973) 17-32.
(16) Schönebeck, B. and Zimmer, K., Cognitive strain in text comprehension and heart rate variability, in: Klix, F., Näätänen, R. and Zimmer, K. (eds.), Psychophysiological approaches to human information processing (North Holland, Amsterdam, 1985).
(17) Shiffrin, R.M. and Schneider, W., Controlled and automatic human information processing, Psychol. Rev. 84 (1977) 127-19o.
(18) Shiffrin, R.M. and Schneider, W., Automatic and controlled processing revisited, Psychol. Rev. 91 (1984) 269-276.
(19) Zimmer, K., Weimann, J. and Guguljanova, B., Phasic and tonic heart rate changes and different strategies of information processing, in: Klix, F., Näätänen, R. and Zimmer, K. (eds.), Psychophysiological approaches to human information processing (North Holland, Amsterdam, 1985).

Man-Computer Interaction Research
MACINTER-I
F. Klix and H. Wandke (Editors)
© Elsevier Science Publishers B.V. (North-Holland), 1986

PERFORMANCE IN COGNITIVE TASKS AND CARDIOVASCULAR PARAMETERS AS
INDICATORS OF MENTAL LOAD

Peter Quaas, Peter Richter, and Frank Schirmer
Sektion Arbeitswissenschaften
Technical University Dresden
Dresden
GDR

One approach is presented to measure load in mental work by
its effects on a subsequent cognitive task. Load effects may
change performance and activation on the task. Activation is
tried to be measured by cardiovascular parameters. Five tasks
are specified by their demands and patterns of parameter values.
Results of an experiment with inferencing an subsequent task
are shown.

INTRODUCTION

Work in modern information technology requires especially the analysis and
evaluation of mental load. In this paper one possible approach will be
presented for the measurement of load in mental work, which is followed
also by other authors (Sintschenko et al., 1977, Leonowa, 1984). We assume
that there is an after-effect from mental work affecting performance and
activation on subsequent cognitive tasks. This can be carried out in two
different ways:

1. In order to record actual effects specified cognitive tasks could be
   given within short breaks during work and could be repeated at definite
   intervals.

2. Long-time effects could be recorded with specified cognitive tasks in
   screenings outside worktime.

Thus we want to measure load from mental work by changes of performance and
activation on subsequent cognitive tasks. At the present time, five tasks
are being selected: visual search, memory search, calculating, inferencing,
and problem solving. They are described in the next section.

We suppose that load effects from mental work are reflected in the efficiency on subsequent cognitive tasks. This efficiency is regarded as a type of
ratio between performance and activation. Indicators of performance will
be reaction times, errors and changes in strategies of information processing. According to Mulder and Mulder (1980) changes in psychophysiological activation can be reflected by cardiovascular parameters. Therefore we
look for cardiovascular parameters suitable as indicators of activation.
In this paper tonic and phasic parameters of heart-rate are discussed. In
the third section specific activation patterns for the selected cognitive
tasks are demonstrated. In the last section we present some preliminary
results of recording actual effects of mental load.

DESCRIPTION OF COGNITIVE TASKS

In order to differentiate load effects by specific disturbed cognitive processes, the demands of the selected tasks have to be described. This will be based on our ideas about the microstructure of information processing in simple cognitive tasks. We start form a memory structure containing the following stages: sensory register, short-term store, long-term store, and response generator. Atkinson and Juola (vid. Klix, 1980) proposed control procedures regulating information processing within and between these stages. Generally it is assumed that controlled processes rather than automated processes can be disturbed by load. A demand analysis shows that different regulating procedures run under special control in visual search, memory search, calculating, inferencing, and problem solving. They are summarized as primary control processes in the following table:

Cognitive task	Primary control process	Authors
visual search	stimulus analysis	P.G. Richter (1982)
memory search	rehearsal and comparison	Sternberg (1975) Sintschenko et al. (1977)
calculating	arithmetical operations, rehearsal and comparison	KLT by Lienert and Düker (1959)
inferencing	logical operations, rehearsal and comparison	reduced Mastermind (Sielaff, 1983)
problem solving	heuristic operations rehearsal and comparison	Anagrams (Gordon et al., 1976) 5-puzzle (Heuser, 1978)

Deterioration of efficiency on anyone of these tasks will be interpreted as disturbance of the corresponding regulating procedure.

CHARACTERISTIC PSYCHOPHYSIOLOGICAL RESPONSES DURING COGNITIVE TASKS

There are close functional connections between cortical and automatic mechanisms of activation. Oriented on field studies, therefore we concentrate on cardiovascular parameters, which can be more easily recorded. Under load controlled cognitive processes rather than automated processes show functional deterioration caused by fatigue (Leonowa, 1984). According to Mulder and Mulder (1980) controlled processes run primarily under sympathetic activation, while in automated processes parasympathetic activation dominates. This parasympathetic dominance is especially typical for event-related arousal reactions in automated information processing (Obrist, 1981). Therefore we try to make use of methodic approaches allowing to record the interaction between both branches of the autonomic nervous system. In our project therefore we look for the following parameters:

average and dispersion of tonic heart-rate and the 0.10 component of the power spectrum, amplitude and latency of the phasic heart-rate, R-peak and T-wave of the ECG, blood pressure, skin conduct level and response. In this paper only results for tonic and phasic heart rate are presented

In order to record mental load by subsequent cognitive tasks, their stability under conditions without load has to be proved. For this we used the concordance analysis by Kendall. Furthermore it has to be proved that the hypothetically assumed demand differences between the cognitive tasks are reflected in different difficulty of the tasks measured by errors, different reported difficulty, and different psychophysiological responses. This was investigated in corresponding experiments. And these are the findings:

1. The number of errors, as an indicator of performance, increases monotonially with the reported difficulty of different tasks.

2. Besides the number of errors and reported difficulty phasic heart-rate patterns also differ between the tasks (fig. 1).

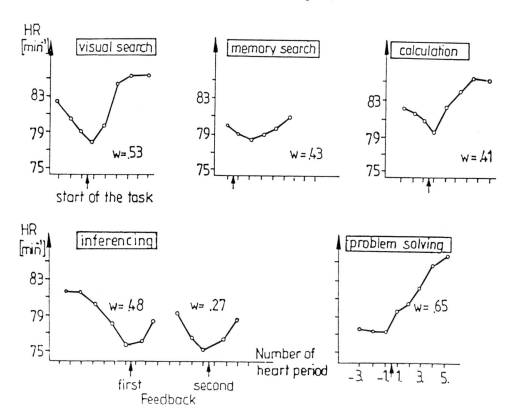

Figure 1: Phasic HR-reactions in several cognitive tasks

The phasic patterns were obtained by averaging 8 to 15 heart-rate
sequences triggered by the presentation of the task. The coefficients
of concordance W are significant, except with the second feedback in
the inference task.

3. Figure 1 shows a stronger anticipatory deceleration of the heart-rate
    before tasks of visual search and before the first feedback in the
    inference task. Figure 2 shows the amount of deceleration as a function
    of reported difficulty. In tasks with greater reported difficulty the
    deceleration of the heart-rate is reduced. In this case acceleration
    of heart-rate is dominant in the earlier phases of information pro-
    cessing. These patterns coincide with the frequently described pheno-
    menon of changes of heart-rate: deceleration with dominance of infor-
    mation intake and acceleration with dominance of information pro-
    cessing.

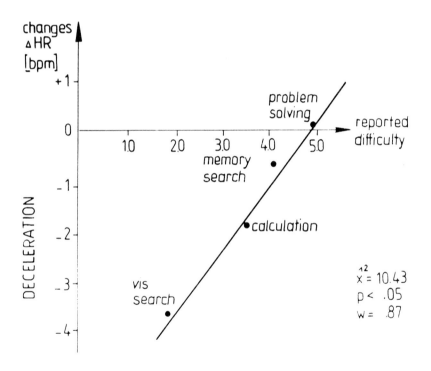

Figure 2: Deceleration of the phasic HR-reaction before the task and
          reported difficulty of the tasks

SOME PRELIMINARY RESULTS

In a labor experiment (Sielaff, 1983) it was asked whether or not actual effects of load from mental work, under different conditions, can be differentiated by an additional cognitive task. In this case an inference test was chosen and used in a pre-post comparison before and after one hour of mental work. The inference test used a task analogous to Mastermind. It demanded 40 times guessing a two-figure number using stepwise logical processing of feedback. The experimental design is presented in the following table (each group with 10 Ss):

	pretest	work (1 h)	posttest
Control group	inference	no work	inference
Group 1: load	inference	mental work with heat and noise	inference
Group 2: practice	inference	inference	inference
Group 3: practice + load	inference	inference with noise	inference

It contained four groups:

1. The control group relaxed between pretest and posttest.

2. In a condition of extreme load the experimental group 1 executed mental work under noise (90 dB) and heat (40 °C). The work required controlled visual search of definite numbers and subsequent calculation depending on the result of the search.

3. In the condition of practice reduction of load effects was predicted as the experimental group 2 solved inference tasks for one hour without noise and heat.

4. As with the experimental group 3, this group experienced a combination of load and practice, for Ss solved inference tasks under noise.

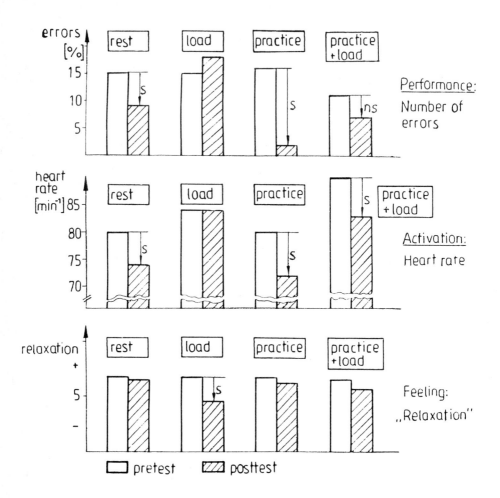

Figure 3: performance, activation and reported feeling in an inference
         task before and after different conditions of mental work

Only such parameters are discussed which differentiated between the
group:

1. Performance is reflected in the number of errors in pretest and
   posttest.

2. A first rough measure of activation is the averaged tonic heart-rate
   in pretest and posttest.

3. As a measure of subjective feeling the Eigenzustand-scale by Nitsch
   (1976) was applied before and after the experiment. Only the factor
   "relaxation" (Erholtheit) as one indicator of reported fatigue differentiated between the groups.

Examining fig. 3 allows us to discuss the effects of different conditions
of mental load on the performance and activation and reported feeling during the additional cognitive task:

1. Control group: Repeating the inference test after rest reduced the
   number of errors and the activation. This means an increase in efficiency. At the same time relaxation did not change.

2. Load: After load, the number of errors and activation were not reduced,
   i.e. efficiency did not improve. Thus there was no adaptation to the
   working conditions, while at the same time reported feeling deteriorated
   significantly.

3. Practice: Practice reduced the number of errors more than in the control
   group, while activation was reduced as in the control group. This
   means that efficiency after practice was greater than after rest. But
   this greater effeciency was not reflected by an improvement of reported
   relaxation.

4. Load and practice: Combining load and practice reduced activation as
   under conditions of rest or practice. But contrary to the control group,
   the reduction in the number of errors was not significant. This means
   that some Ss had a greater reduction of errors than others. In this
   case, the effect of practice dominated. With other Ss the number of
   errors remained constant or increased. Here the effect of load dominated. Both effects differed interindividually. Besides there was
   no significant reported deterioration.

Thus with performance and activation on a cognitive task following mental
work, positive and negative changes of effeciency can be shown. These
changes are caused by mental load or practice or their interaction. These
data reflected the different conditions better than subjective data only.

SUMMARY

It is possible to measure load from mental work by the efficiency on
subsequent cognitive tasks. Moreover different cognitive tasks can reflect load effects on different cognitive processes. The advantages of
this approach are its objectivity, differentiation and repeatable
application. Problems probably arise from the influence of covariables
like practice, personality and motivation. Further research must be
devoted to problems with such covariables, to test further cognitive tasks
and to search for more suitable physiological parameters of activation.

REFERENCES

(1) Gordon, V.M., Karacov, K.V. and Trus, V.D., Psichologiceskoje issledovanije dejatjelnosti v rezimje informazionogo poiska sritjelnoj i verbalnoj informazii (in Russian), Ergonimica 11 (1976) 137-169.

(2) Heuser, J., Zur differentiellen Wirkung von Streß auf das Problem-lösen. Zeitschrift für experimentelle und angewandte Psychologie 25 (1978) 379-406.

(3) Klix, F., Die kognitive Psychologie: Methodologie, methodische theoretische und praktische Konsequenzen für die Psychologie und angrenzende Wissenschaften, in: Kossakowski, A., (ed.), Psychologie im Sozialismus (Deutscher Verlag der Wissenschaften, Berlin, 1980).

(4) Leonova, A. B., Diagnostika funktionalnych sostojanij Isdatelstvo Moskovskogo Universiteta, Moscow (in Russian) 1984.

(5) Lienert, G.A. and Düker, H., KLT- Der Konzentrationsleistungstest (Hogrefe, Göttingen, 1959).

(6) Mulder, G. and Mulder, L.J.M., Coping with mental work load, in: Levine, S.S. and Ursin, H. (eds.), Coping and health (Pergamon Press, New York, 1980).

(7) Nitsch, J.R., Die Eigenzustandsskala (EZ-Skala) - Ein Verfahren zur hierarchisch-mehrdimensionalen Befindlichkeitsskalierung, in: Nitsch, J.R. and Udris, I. (eds.), Beanspruchung im Sport, Schriften-reihe Training und Beanspruchung 4 (Limpert, Bad Homburg, 1976).

(8) Obrist, P.A., Cardiovascular Psychophysiology - A perspective (Academic Press, New York, London, 1981).

(9) Richter, P.G., Möglichkeiten der Beanspruchungsindikation in Feld-situationen unter besonderer Berücksichtigung tätigkeitsspezifischer Leistungs- und Verhaltensparameter, Doctoral Dissertation, Step A, Fak. f. Nat.wiss. u. Math., Techn. Univ. Dresden (1981).

(10) Sielaff, H.-J., Vorbereitung eines Problemlöseparadigmas als Test für Beanspruchungsfolgen, Diploma Thesis, Techn. Univ. Dresden (1983).

(11) Sincenko, V.P., Leonova, A.B., Strelkov, Ju. K., Psichometrika utomlenija (in Russian), Isdatelstvo Moskovskogo Universiteta, Moscow, 1977).

(12) Sternberg, S., Memory scanning: New findings and current controversies, Quarterly Journal of Experimental Psychology 23 (1975) 1-32.

Man-Computer Interaction Research
MACINTER-I
F. Klix and H. Wandke (Editors)
© Elsevier Science Publishers B.V. (North-Holland), 1986

INFLUENCES OF MENTAL LOAD ON REACTION TIMES IN
MAN-COMPUTER-DIALOGUES

Frank M. Kühn, Klaus H. Schmidt[*], Klaus-Cl. Schoo, Uwe Kleinbeck[*]

Institut für Arbeitsphysiologie
Departments of Ergonomics and Work Psychology[*]
Universität Dortmund
Dortmund
FRG

Two skilled and two unskilled subjects were required
to read strings from VDT and to retype them on keyboard.
The strings varied in length (1 to 12) and in type
(random and meaningful material). On the basis of
measured response latencies and keystroke-intervals
two behavioural strategies in text transcription can
be identified: a sequential one and a parallel one for
matching reading and typing.

INTRODUCTION

One of the essential parts in the man-computer-interaction consists of the
transcription of visually displayed information (symbols like letters, digits and so on as well as strings) into motor outputs like typing commands
controlling the next computer operation. In the simplest case, this transcription involves the reading of text material and subsequent retyping on a
keyboard. This kind of task is similar for both computer keyboards and typewriters.
The analysis of typewriting has a long tradition. Throughout the research, a
main point of interest has been the fact that at least in skilled typing the
information processing is faster than would be expected under the assumption
that choice reaction times are the overall effective limiting factors for
human performance (Salthouse (1984)). From a theoretical point of view, the
question is, how skilled typists circumvent such reaction time limits. Retyping activities can be partitioned into at least three stages: 1. The perception and encoding of text material, 2. the storing of this material, including its organization and classification, 3. the preparation, execution,
and control of the motor output.

This description may lead to various explanations for the performance time
falling short of the expected reaction time limits. Up to now, three approaches have dominated the discussion about this phenomenon:
1. In the tradition of Book (1908), the skilled typists are not assumed to
analyse the information symbol by symbol and to respond to each character
separately, but they group the visual input into so-called perceptual chunks.
Evidence for this explanation is given by results showing the preview of the
text material to be a critical factor in the speed of typing.
2. In close connection with the idea of perceptual chunking, a process of
output grouping is assumed to work, too. In modern thinking, this output
grouping is managed by motor programs controlling a whole sequence of keystrokes in a more or less ballistic way (Sternberg et al. (1978)).

3. The third approach for explaining the circumvention of reaction time limits is the partial overlap in motor responses, i.e. parallel execution of
movements (Gentner et al. (1980)). As shown by high speed motion camera analyses, there is a strong overlap between doing the stroke with one finger
and parallel aiming for the next keyboard position with another one and so
on. Further support for this approach is given by analyses of typing errors.
As Shaffer (1978) reports, the majority of transposition errors occurs between cross hand movements indicating that the second movement reaches
stroke position faster than the intended first movement.

Concerning the way, in which the perceptual chunking and the motor chunking
may be interrelated, at least two modes of matching between them are possible.
1. The first mode of matching may be assumed to be a serial one. That means,
one group of symbols is chunked, stored and answered by a chunked sequence
of keystrokes, before the next group of symbols is read in, answered and so
on.
2. The second mode of matching may be assumed to be a parallel one. While
the first group of symbols is answered by a sequence of motor output, a subsequent group of symbols is read in simultaneously. There is an overlap in
the operation of the perceptual and the output stage. This must be distinguished from the overlap of motions within the output stage as pointed to
by the third traditional approach.
These two modes may reflect different user strategies in handling the task
demands. When accepting this, the question rises, what kind of mental load
and individual factors determine the selection of one or the other strategy.

In the following experiment two mental load factors were analysed in their
effect on performance. A precondition for examining a parallel or serial
matching of the perceptual and motor chunking operations is to vary the
string length of the exposed material. This is because only a string length
greater than a normal chunking span opens the possibility for a serial
matching. In addition, the types of string varied from strings consisting of
random characters (letters and digits) to meaningful words. It can be assumed that the random strings, as compared with meaningful words, need a
greater amount of capacity for perception, organization and classification
before preparing the subsequent motor programs than meaningful words. Therefore, the possibility for a simultaneous control of motor output and the
organization of the following characters might be reduced resulting in prolonged response latencies and keystroke-intervals, in comparison with the
processing of meaningful words. Skill level in typewriting may play an additional role in information processing (Salthouse (1984)). In the case of
meaningful material, it can be assumed that the differences between performance of skilled and unskilled subjects is mainly caused by differences
in the training of keyboard motor acts. Skilled and unskilled subjects
should have nearly the same level of experience in reading meaningful words.
In contrast, encoding random material requires a higher capacity for the
organization of the stored input material. This higher demand should more
heavily influence the resultant performance output at low skill levels in
typewriting. Unskilled typists must allocate a greater portion of capacity
into the motor output than skilled ones. This reduces the possibility for
parallel processes like encoding and storing. Consequently, the unskilled
subjects are expected to use a different information processing strategy
than the skilled ones, especially in the case of random material.

EXPERIMENT

Subjects: Three female and one male right-handed students participated in
the experiment. Two female subjects were skilled in typewriting, the others
were unskilled.
Apparatus: The test program was executed on a DEC VT-100 terminal with automatic time-keeping by the computer. Time was measured to the nearest 33 msec.
The numerical keypad was covered. Thus, subjects could only use the part of
the keyboard which is realised on nearly all terminals or typewriters.
Experimental procedure: All subjects were given 5 two-hours practice sessions. In these sessions all experimental conditions were **realized** as in the
experimental sessions. Only data of the latter are reported here. The experimental design was a 12x2x2 crossed classification, in which the independent variables were the string length (ranging from 1 to 12), the string
type (meaningful and random material) and finally the level of practice
(skilled and unskilled). String length and string type were varied independently. The order of presentation was randomly generated by the test-
program. Each subject performed 5 experimental sessions. Each session consisted of two working hours separated by an one hour rest period. The first
20 trials of each hour were used for absorbing short-term practice effects
and were not included in the final data analysis. Overall, each subject performed about 2500 trials depending on the individual performance speed.
Experimental task: Subjects were instructed to work as fast and as accu-
rately as possible. The strings to be copied as well as the strokes executed by the subjects were displayed side by side on the terminal screen (Figure 1). The last keystroke for one string (return key) was immediately
followed by the next string. When recognizing a typing error, subjects were
instructed to interrupt the input and to start over again. These trials
were excluded from the final time analysis.
Data analysis: Dependent variables were response latency (i.e. time interval between the presentation of the string and the first keystroke) and the
keystroke-intervals (i.e. time intervals between consecutive keystrokes).
These data were analysed by Repeated Measurement ANOVAs.

RESULTS

Response latencies: Figure 2 shows the influence of string length, string
type and skill level on response latencies.
As can clearly be seen, there is a strong effect of skill level on response
latency (F = 1106.26, DF 1/10825, P .01). This effect works across all
string lengths and string types.
Secondly, there is a strong effect of string type on response latencies
(F = 270.79, DF 1/10825, P .01) across all string lengths and skill levels.
The random strings cause longer response latencies than the meaningful
words.
Thirdly, irrespective of skill level and string type, the response latencies
differ depending on the string length (F = 25.39, DF 11/10825, P .01). The
latencies increase with increasing string lengths.
Additionally, the effect of skill level on response latencies is different
for the string types. The differences between meaningful strings are not as
great as the differences between the random strings. This effect results in
a highly significant interaction of string type and skill level on response
latencies (F = 73.12, DF 1/10825, P .01).
Skill level shows also an interaction effect with string length on response
latencies (F = 12.98, DF 11/10825, P .01). The increase of response latencies caused by an increase in string lengths is stronger for the un-

skilled subjects.

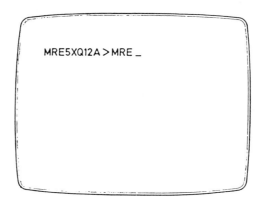

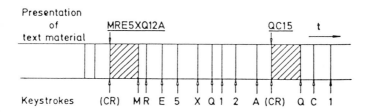

Figure 1
Experimental procedure

Response latencies are also dependent of the interaction of string length and string type (F = 12.37, DF 10/10825, P .01). The response latencies for meaningful strings are influenced less by the string length than the ones for the random strings. Finally, this interaction effect is more pronounced with unskilled subjects resulting in a 3 way-interaction of string length, string type and skill level (F = 4.09, DF 10/10825, P .01). From a theoretical point of view, the main effect of string length on response latencies as well as its interaction effects with string type and skill level are critical features in these results. Under the assumption that the response latencies at least reflect both the encoding of text material and the preparation of the subsequent motor acts, the main effect of string length is quite reasonable. The greater the amount of information to be processed, the greater the resultant response latencies should be. Interestingly, this effect is mainly caused by the increase of string lengths

of up to 6 characters. The further increase of string length above 6 characters produces no further significant increase of response latencies.
Statistically, an ANOVA including only the string lengths ranging from 6
to 12 characters shows no significant string length effect on response latency (F = 1.33, DF 6/6487, P .20). In this range of string lengths, the
interaction effects with skill level and string type prove also to be non-
significant.

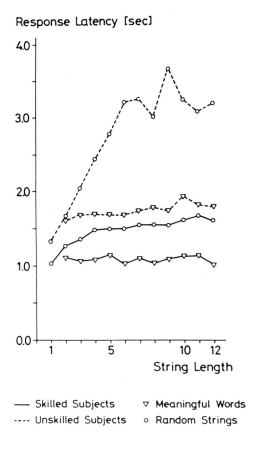

Response Latency [sec]

String Length

— Skilled Subjects   ▽ Meaningful Words
---- Unskilled Subjects   ○ Random Strings

Figure 2
The influence of string length, string type
and skill level on response latencies

Keystroke-Intervals: The inspection of the keystroke-intervals within all
string lengths and under the various string types and skill levels reveals
two typical patterns.
One consistent pattern of results can be identified for the keystroke-intervals with string lengths below 6 characters, the other critical pattern
concerns the keystroke-intervals for strings with more than about 7 cha-

racters. These typical patterns are exemplified by the keystroke-intervals within the strings of 5 and within the strings of 12 characters in Figure 3.

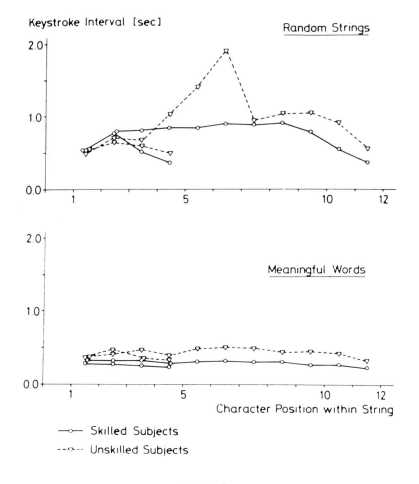

Figure 3
The keystroke-intervals in dependence of character position
for the random string type and for the meaningful words

The upper part of Figure 3 shows the keystroke-intervals for the 5- and 12-character-strings in dependence of character position within these strings and skill level for the random string type. The lower part of Figure 3 shows the results for the meaningful words.
As can clearly be seen, there is a strong effect of string type. The keystroke-intervals within random strings are longer than within meaningful words. This holds true for the 5-character-string as well as for the 12-character-string (5-character-string: $F = 275.66$, DF 1/3744, P .01; 12-character-string: $F = 939.58$, DF 1/10021, P .01).
The keystroke-intervals depend also on skill level (5-character-string:

F = 12.10, DF 1/3744, P .01; 12-character-string: F = 186.03, DF 1/10021, P .01). The skilled subjects produce shorter keystroke-intervals than the unskilled subjects. The only exception are the keystroke-intervals at the random string type up to the fourth keystroke. Here the unskilled subjects are little faster than the skilled subjects.

The effect of the position of characters within the string on keystroke-interval seems to be the most interesting one concerning the behavioural strategies mentioned above. For 5-character-strings, there is a strong position effect on keystroke-intervals (F = 59.16, DF 3/3744, P .01) independent of skill level and string type. From the beginning of the keystroke sequence, there is a slight increase of the intervals followed by a decrease towards the end of the sequence.

The keystroke-intervals within the 12-character-string not only show significant position effects (F = 66.27, DF 10/10021, P .01) but in addition highly significant interactive effects with string type (F = 16.43, DF 10/10021, P .01) and skill level (F = 26.64, DF 10/10021, P .01). The position effect is stronger for the random material and the position effect is also stronger for the unskilled subjects.

Moreover, there is a 3 way-interaction effect of skill level, character position and string type (F = 9.42, DF 10/10021, P .01). At random material, the unskilled subjects show stronger position effects than the skilled ones. At meaningful material, the difference between the skill levels concerning the position effect is not as great. This 3 way-interaction effect seems to be mainly caused by a strong increase of keystroke-intervals around the sixth and seventh character position within the 12-character-string at random material performed by the unskilled subjects.

Typing errors:

As mentioned above, all these data only refer to trials, where errors were not detected by the subjects themselves.

Concerning such errors, there is a main effect of string length on error frequency (F = 9.15, DF 11/45, P .01). One incorrect string constitutes one error. With increasing string lengths error frequency increases, too, from an average of around 1 % at 1- and 2-character-strings to about 7.5 % at 12-character-strings.

Furthermore, there is an interaction effect between string type and skill level on error frequency (F = 5.91, DF 1/45, P .05). The two skill levels differ more at meaningful material concerning error frequency than at random material.

DISCUSSION

What interpretations can be deduced from the present results for the question about the behavioural strategies involved in the transcription of visually displayed information into keystroke responses?

First of all, there are strong moderating effects of string type and skill level on the dependency of response latencies from string length. In the extreme case of unskilled subjects processing random material, a nearly linear dependency between response latency and string length is found for strings of up to 6 characters. Beyond this string length, the dependency disappears. At the other extreme, for the skilled subjects processing meaningful material, the dependency between string length and response latencies can never be found. Only in the case of processing random material, latencies of skilled subjects depend also on string length. This dependency seems to be restricted to shorter string lengths and is much weaker in comparison with that of the unskilled subjects.

Under the assumption, that the response latency includes the time for encoding text material as well as the time for preparating the first subsequent motor sequence (Sternberg et al. (1978)), the different curve characteristics for random strings may point to two different processing strategies. These strategies may be a sequential one used by the unskilled subjects and a parallel processing used by skilled subjects. The unskilled subjects seem to read in a certain amount of the text material, then switch
from input to output stage (eyes are turned from the exposed material to the
keyboard) and then perform the keystrokes. If the presented text material
overloads some kind of storage buffer, subjects return to the input stage
and repeat this sequence of operations. The critical loading limit seems to
be at about 6 random elements. In contrast, the skilled subjects seem to
use a simultaneous or overlapping strategy, which is characterized by parallel reading and typing. Text material is continuously perceived and keystrokes or chunks, resp., are also continuously executed. There is a span
of a few characters held in a storage buffer between reading and typing.
The perfection of handling parallel input and output and managing a storage
buffer containing an optimal amount of information expresses high experience
of subjects, i.e. high skill level. For shorter strings, this optimal amount
of stored information can not be reached. Consequently, additional capacity
becomes free to be used for motor programming, resulting in shorter latencies. As mentioned above, unskilled subjects are assumed to repeat the
sequence of input, storing and output execution for strings longer than 6
characters. This effect can also be proven by the results from the keystroke-intervals. The increase of keystroke-intervals in the range of the
fifth to the seventh character position seems to reflect the point, when
the unskilled subjects returned to input encoding before completing the
entire movement sequence (Figure 3).
Concerning the meaningful text material, skilled subjects show no effect of
string length on latencies. This is understandable under the assumption,that
the presented meaningful material leads to immediate storing. Input processing is very fast and does not have to be repeated for the same material.
Storing and handling of information for preparing the output is very easy
because of the characters' redundancy. For the unskilled subjects there is
a slight increase of response latencies with the string length (Figure 2).
It cannot be expected that unskilled typists differ from skilled with respect to encoding and storing meaningful strings. This slight increase of
response latencies with string length may therefore be mainly caused by
less effective motor programming.

In summary, the present results indicate that even at such simple tasks as
transcribing isolated strings, different behavioural strategies can be
identified, determined by operator variables as well as mental load factors.
The results concerning the influence of these factors in coping with tasks
in man-computer interaction may be a basis for analysing more complex task
demands. Such approaches may lead to more concrete user models accessible
to stronger experimental evaluation.

REFERENCES

(1) Book, W.F., The Psychology of Skill, with Special Reference to its Acquisition in Typewriting (University of Montana Press, 1908).

(2) Gentner, D.R., Grudin, J., Conway, E., Finger Movements in Transcription
Typing, Technical Report 8001, Center for Human Information Processing,
Univ. of California, San Diego (May 1980).

(3) Salthouse, T.A., Effects of Age and Skill in Typing, J. Exp. Psychol. 113 (1984) 3, 345 - 371.

(4) Shaffer, L.H., Timing in the Motor Programming of Typing, Quart. J. Exp. Psychol. 30 (1978) 333 - 345.

(5) Sternberg, S., Monsell, S., Knoll, R.L., Wright, C.E., The Latency and Duration of Rapid Movement Sequences: Comparisons of Speech and Type-writing, in: Stelmach, G.E. (ed.), Information Processing in Motor Control and Learning (Academic Press, New York, 1978).

(6) Summers, J.J., Motor programs, in: Holding, D.H. (ed.), Human Skills (John Wiley and Sons, Chichester, 1981).

Man-Computer Interaction Research
MACINTER-I
F. Klix and H. Wandke (Editors)
© Elsevier Science Publishers B.V. (North-Holland), 1986

SOME REMARKS ON A MEASURE OF COMPUTER OPERATOR
WORKLOAD: CHANGES IN PUPIL REFLEX

Tadeusz Marek, Czesław Noworol
Jagiellonian University, Institute of Psychology
Krakow
Poland

Mental workload is a highly important component of
computer operator workload. Presented research deals
with changes in acceleration of pupil reflex in
response to mental workload of VDT operators doing
two kinds of tasks: the monotonous one and the
various. It has been stated that changes in acceleration of pupil reflex may be treated as an indicator
of different mental workload of VDT operators.

INTRODUCTION

It has been stated for many years that mental workload is an
important problem area for man-computer interaction research.
In order to evaluate alternative solutions in man-computer
systems design, it is often deemed necessary to measure not only
system performance, but also human operator workload.

The research presented here deals with changes in acceleration
of pupil reflex in response to mental workload of VDT operators.
A field study on data entry VDT operators who were working for
a data service system is reported. The aim of our research was
to find out whether the changes in acceleration of pupil reflex
under the two kinds entry data tasks (monotonous and various)
are different.

PUPIL REFLEX AND MENTAL LOAD

Pupil reflex to changes in illumination is unconditional. The
increment of light intensity causes pupillary contraction.
Recently it has come to be known that the pupil diameter and
pupil reflex change under mental load (Beatty, 1976, Hamilton
et al., 1979, Marek et al., 1979, 1980, Marek, Noworol, 1982,
1984).

Two muscles are responsible for contraction and expansion of
the pupil. There are the sphincter and the retractor. Tension
in these muscles is directly responsible for the intensity of
the pupillary reflex to the light. The sphincter is innervated
by parasympathetic nerve fibres and the retractor by sympathetic
nerve fibres (Adler, 1965, Chusid, 1970, Delmas, 1974).

Activation of the special cells in the retina responsible solely
for the pupil reflex by a light stimulus releases an impuls
which is then transmitted by special pupillary fibres (Delmas,
1974). These fibres first reach the area praetectalis where they
are switched to the Westphal-Edinger nucleus and then from here
the impuls causing pupil contraction runs by pupillary fibres
to the sphincter. The state of the pupil and shape of the reflex
are determined by tension in the sphincter and retractor, but
the sphincter is clearly stronger. According to Adler (1965)
the pupil expansion is caused mainly by inhibition in the
sphincter. Many authors point out that reaction of the pupil to
light (under the same light condition) depends not only on
activity in the reflex arch but also on the functional state
of the whole nervous system. It can be particularly modified by
the functional state of the reticular formation.

As it follows from Magoun, Moruzzi, Bremer and many others investigations, the two subsystems can be distinguished within
this structure. There are activity and inhibitory subsystems.
The first determines the degree of readiness of organism to act
and maintain a high level of arousal. According to Hess (Grandjean, 1967) this subsystem causes functional dominance of the
sympathetic system over the parasympathetic. The inhibitory
system inhibits the cerebral cortex while at the same time
activates the parasympathetic system. It causes sleep in extreme
cases. The functioning of both these subsystems depends on
level of stimulation of the organism. The level of stimulation
depends on variability, complexity and intensity of stimuli.
When the level of stimulation is high the activity (arousal)
subsystem predominates. But when the stimulation prolongs the
inhibitory subsystems begins to predominate. This leads to
predominance of the sympathetic and then (in turn) parasympathetic system respectively. When the level of stimulation
is low the inhibitory subsystem predominates from the beginning.

According to the Cazamian's point of view the mental load may
be treated as a result of over or under-stimulation (Cazamian,
1979). As we point out above over and under-stimulation cause
two different kinds of the nervous system reaction. Because of
it we expected that the changes in acceleration of pupil reflex
under two kinds entry data tasks (monotonous and various) were
different.

METHOD

Subjects

A 2 h two kind of entry data tasks were carried out by two
groups of VDT operators. The first group of operators carried
out the monotonous, dull tasks and the second group the
various, complicted entry data. In the first group the tasks
of operators was to type entry data consisting of numbers
only. In the second group the entry data consisted of alpha-
numeric data - FORTRAN programs. The operators carried out
these programs in BASIC.

The sequential trials were analysed. It permitted to minimize
the number of examined operators in both groups. Because of it
only twenty female operators in both group were examined. The
operators were 24 - 29 years old. They had been employed for
four to five years. In all cases of below the ophtalmologycal,
neurological and neurotic disturbances were eliminated. Each
operator worked ICL video display terminal.

Pupil reflex registration

The operators were tested on the morning shift. In every thirty
minutes the pupil reflex was registered and analyzed by means
of a special pupillography (in both groups) (Marek and Noworol,
1984). Then, the operators were tested five times: I - before
work, II, III, IV, V - after 30, 60, 90, 120 minutes of work
respectively.

The basic registration element was a TV camera connected with
a videotape-recorder.

After darkness adaptation each subject was seated in front of
the TV camera lens. The faint phosphoric fixation point painted
on the lens was a test of darkness adaptation. Not until certain minimum of adaptation was reached did subjects notice the
point. When this happened the pupil reflex registration began.
In order to evoke the reflex a standard light stimulus (constant light - 100 Lx) was used. The reflex was registered on
the videotape. After registration the data were fed into the
computer and analyzed.

Mathematical and statistical base of analysis

For each operator five empirical curves of the pupil reflex
were obtained. An illustrative empirical curve for one operator
is presented in figure 1. Duration of the reflex and pupil
diameter are shown on the abscissa and on the ordinal respectively.

Obtained empirical curves of reflex were approximated using
functions from the class C^1. These functions are good for
approximating reflex dynamics (Marek et al., 1979). They have
the equation 1.

$$y = \exp(-\alpha t^2 - \beta t + \gamma) + C \qquad (1)$$

where:

    y - pupil diameter
    t - time
    α, β, γ - function parameters
    C - constant value

The α, a acceleration coefficient was analysed. The sequential
analysis of variance was used (Marek and Noworol, 1984a).

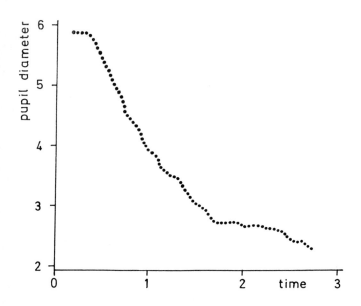

Figure 1
Empirical curve of the pupil reflex

RESULTS

The approximations of obtained empirical curves by the curves
in equation 1 were statistical satisfactory ($p < .05$).

The approximation error was insignificant in every cases.
The agregated means and standard deviations of the acceleration
coefficient α for the first group (monotonous task) and second
group (various task) are shown in table 1 and table 2 respectively.

As it can be seen from table 1, in the first group (monotonous
task) it was found that the acceleration of pupil reflex in
every thirty minutes increased.

Table 1. The means and the standard deviations of the
acceleration coefficient - monotonous task.

Number of registration	The acceleration coefficient	
	$\bar{\alpha}$	$\mathfrak{G}$
I	.152	.004
II	.160	.002
III	.171	.005
IV	.179	.002
V	.198	.003

Table 2. The means and the standard deviations of the
acceleration coefficient - various task.

Number of registration	The acceleration coefficient	
	$\bar{\alpha}$	$\mathfrak{G}$
I	.180	.002
II	.172	.006
III	.149	.005
IV	.177	.003
V	.190	.004

In the second group (various task) (table 2) the acceleration
of pupil reflex in the first sixty minutes decreased and then
increased. In both group all differences are statistically
significance ($p < .05$).

CONCLUSION

In conclusion, the different changes in acceleration of pupil
reflex in both examined groups may be treated as an indicator
of different mental workload of VDT operators (monotonous and
various). These two kinds VDT operators mental workload are
connected with understimulation and overstimulation.

The predominance of the inhibitory system followed understimulation or overstimulation when it is prolonged. The inhibitory
system activated the parasympathetic system. In this way the
sphincter becomes stronger then the retractor. Because of it
the acceleration of pupil reflex increased. It decreased when
the sphincter becomes weaker then the retractor, when arousal
system and connected with it the sympathetic system are pre-

dominant. It followed short term of overstimulation.

REFERENCES

Adler, F.H., Physiology of the eye (The C.V. Mosby Company, Saint Louis, 1965)

Beatty, J., Pupillometric measurement of cognitive workload in complex man-machine systems, in: Proceedings 12th Annual Conference on Manual Control (Urbana, Illinois, 1976)

Chusid, I.C., Correlative neuroanatomy and functional neurology (Lang Medical Publications, Los Altos, California, 1970)

Cazamian, P., Le syndrome general de fatigue - La fatigue mentale, Le Travail Human 2 (1979) 359

Delmas, A., Voies et centres nerveux (Masson et C-ie, Paris, 1974).

Grandjean, E., Physiologische Arbeitsgestaltung - Leitfaden der Ergonomie (Ott Verlag, Thun, München, 1967)

Hamilton, P., Mulder, G., Strasser, H. and Ursin, H., Final report of physiological psychology group, in: Moray, N. (ed.) Mental Workload (Plenum Press, New York, London, 1979)

Marek, T., Noworol, Cz. and Zarczyński, Z., Objective fatigue measurement by pupillography, Ergonomics 22 (1979) 721

Marek, T., Noworel, Cz. and Zarczyński, Z., Pupil reflex with light velocity changes in initial phase influenced by psychical load, in: XXIInd International Congress of Psychology - Abstract Guide (Leipzig, 1980)

Marek, T. and Noworol, Cz., Disturbances in curve smoothness of pupillary reflex under mental load, in: Noro, K. (ed.) Eighth Congress of the International Ergonomics Associasion (Tokyo, 1982)

Marek, T. and Noworol, Cz., Acceleration in initial phase of pupillary reflex in response to mental load. Polish Psychological Bulletin 2 (1984) 143 - 150

Marek, T. and Noworol, Cz., The sequential approach to analysis of variance, Polish Psychological Bulletin 3 (1984a)

Man-Computer Interaction Research
MACINTER-I
F. Klix and H. Wandke (Editors)
© Elsevier Science Publishers B.V. (North-Holland), 1986

389

SUBJECTIVE LOAD IN INTRODUCING VISUAL DISPLAY UNITS

Thomas Wolff, Heidemarie Hugler, Hans-Joachim Selle,
Jürgen Weimann and Eckard Schulz
Sektion Psychologie
Humboldt University
Berlin
GDR

The first part of the paper covers the objective, the
design, and preliminary results of the baseline-
investigation in a longitudinal study carried out in
a savings-bank which was introducing visual display
units. First implications for preventive and job-
organizing measures are briefly discussed. The second
part describes the modelling of the cognitive effort
by computer simulation for the purpose of analysing
the change in mental load resulting from the introduction of visual display units.

AIM OF THE STUDY

The introduction of visual display units (VDU) into office work results in
a great number of psychological problems neglected in past studies in favour
of ergonomic and hard-ware related investigations.
One of these problems consists in the question of what short- and long-term
consequences VDU have and how to design terminals in order to prevent
negative consequences for the users. To raise this question means the pursue
a longitudinal approach.

Our prospective study - consisting of a baseline-investigation, i.e. an
investigation before the introduction of VDU, and two follow-up studies:
one immediately and the other 6 month after the introduction of VDU - has
various objectives, two of which will be the subject of this paper:

1. We investigate the influence of information technology and organization
on the mental load in order to draw conclusions as to which task characteristics have positive and which have negative consequences.
The differential aspect of the study will help us to detect persons at risk,
i.e. persons who are in danger of developing a psychological or a psychoso-
matic disorder. In other words: we want to identify especially two groups
of persons: neurotics and psychosomatics. Two major personality characteristics that have time and again emerged from recent research as influential
in illness onset are alexithymia (i.e. impoverished fantasy life and
difficulty expressing feelings verbally, see Sifnoes 1973), and the coronaryprone behaviour pattern, which encompasses such psychological job-relevant
characteristics as ambition, a desire to dominate, high achievement motivation, resistance to relaxation, suppression of subjective states (e.g.
fatigue), and the continual struggle to assert and maintain control over
the environment when confronted with threatened loss of control and autonomy.
This hyperresponsiveness will turn into hyporesponsiveness when the efforts

at control have repeatedly failed (see Glass 1981). This behavioral style
will be monitored in our study.

2. Proceeding from the assumption that the introduction of VDU is connected
with a change in cognitive demands, the second aim of our analysis consists
in a differentiated description of the interaction process between perception
and memory. This is designed to provide information as to whether VDU have
effective consequences ensuring mental health and promoting personality
development, or whether they cause under- or overload. In order to achieve
sufficient precision and differentiation in the description of cognitive
operations, we used computer simulation to analyse the change in cognitive
effort resulting from the introduction of VDU.

Our study was carried out in two branch offices of a savings-bank. The results presented in this paper are those of the baseline-investigation, i.e.
before the introduction of VDU.

THE INTERACTION OF PERSONALITY TRAITS AND JOB CHARACTERISTICS WITHIN THE
MENTAL LOAD PROCESS

Concept of the Study and Methods Used

The starting point of our study is the well-known fact that the effect of
the task demands depends to a considerable extent on how a person experiences and evaluates the demands and executive conditions which are brought
in relation to the own capacities, skills, and available strategies. In
other words, the evaluation of task demands and consequently the subjective
load does not only depend on these demands themselves, but is influenced
(mediated) by the various personality and behavioral characteristics.

Proceeding from this we want to explain the concept of our study and the
diagnostic methods employed. The latter are depicted in Fig. 1.

We used:

- the TBS (Task Diagnosis Survey) to evaluate the objective job demands
  (this evaluation is made by experts),

- the JDS (Job Diagnosis Survey) to identify the subjective evaluation
  of different task demands,
  (While the subjectively evaluated task demands are to be brought in
  relation to the current load, the objective evaluation by experts
  produces concrete proposals for job design.)

- the EZ-scale to record the subjective load,

- the BVND (a multidimensional inventory of neurotic and personality
  disorders) to identify neurotic persons, who as such are persons at
  risk, and

- the modified SVF (a stress processing inventory) to identify what effective
  or ineffective coping strategies the person employs under stress
  conditions.

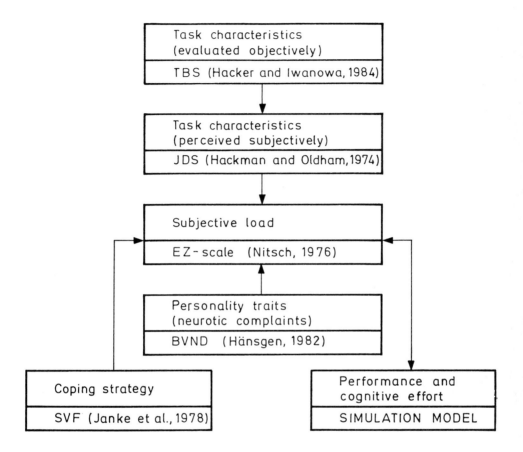

Fig. 1: Personality- and task-characteristics and their diagnostic
comprehension in the longitudinal study

Preliminary Results of the Baseline-Investigation

Let us now summarize some findings of our first cross-sectional analysis:

In evaluating objective job demands - derived from TBS - we found that the
task variety, the cooperation variety, and autonomy (control) are considered
to fall short of a desirable standard necessary for the conservation and
promotion of cognitive and social abilities.

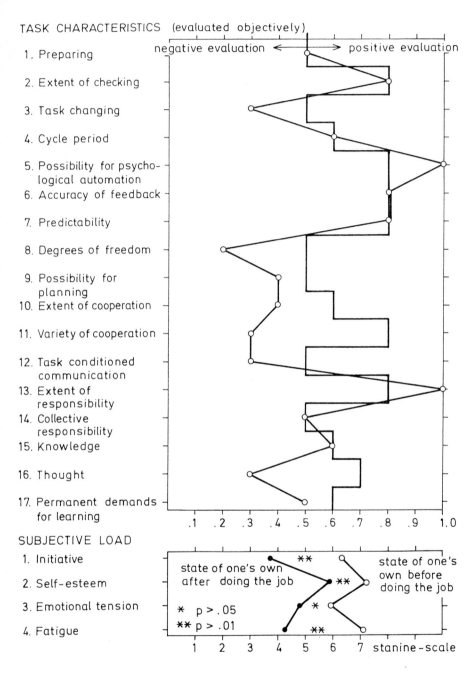

Fig. 2: Task characteristics and subjective load before and after doing
the job

By contrast, a favourable view can be taken - where the above-mentioned
standard of personality promotion is concerned - of the possibilities for
job-internal feedback, responsibility, and cooperation support (see fig.2).
These demands result in differences in mental load. A comparison of the
pre- and post-ratings of the EZ-scale reveals significant differences in the
factors "emotional tension", "fatigue", "initiative", and "self-esteem".

The persons at risk we identified used to a significantly higher degree ineffective coping strategies (i.e. resignation, self-accusation), while the
psychologically inconspicuous users preferred effective coping strategies
(i.e. relaxation under stressfull conditions, looking for social support).
As expected we found the following interactions between the subjective
mental load on the one hand and the job characteristics and personality
traits on the other.

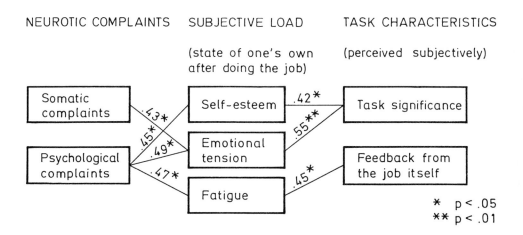

Fig. 3: Interaction between personality-, task-characteristics and
        subjective load

The schedule in figure 3 contains the significant correlations of the JDS-
scales and the BVND-scales with the EZ-scale. The results show that both
the psychopathologically relevant personality traits (neurotic tendency)
and the redef ed job demands significantly correlate with the subjective
load reflected in the EZ-scale.

Let us first regard the correlations between subjective load and internal
feedback: Persons who take a positive view of their job in terms of internal
job-related feedback indicate not experiencing emotional tension and
fatigue, i.e. they experience a low level of subjective load. They
describe themselves as being highly motivated, having initiative and self-
esteem. These findings correspond with results Schulz (1980) obtained in
his investigations.

The correlations between neurotic tendency and subjective load demonstrate
that neurotic persons experience a high subjective load, i.e. fatigue
and emotional tension, which is in accordance with the findings reported
in literature on the subject (see Kasielke 1982).

Implications for Preventive and Job-Organizing Measures

As far as implications for preventive and job-organizing measures are concerned we will have to wait for the first and second follow-up to be carried
out the next few months.
There can be no doubt, however, that the results of the baseline-investigation point to the importance of internal feedback for the motivation,
mental-health and general well-being of our users. Future job design must
ensure that the positive evaluation of job-internal feedback is preserved
and is not restricted by VDU. Additionally we have to find out which persons
misinterpret the real degree of job-internal feedback to make the extent
of such feedback transparent for them with the aim of diminishing the
subjective load and to improve well-being and motivation. Measures of job
design derived from the first results concern a more comprehensive organizational role of the individual in job design, i.e. a job rotation system,
and a flexible break system.

There is to be very careful follow-up on the identified persons at risk.
Since they use ineffective coping-strategies, we predict they will have
more problems in adapting to the new working conditions. The question
arising in this connection is whether special training related to the
requirements of the VDU will be sufficient to overcome their problems, or
whether a more comprehensive treatment of the personality is necessary.

DESCRIPTION OF EFFORT RELEVANT COGNITIVE PROCESS PARAMETERS OF THE WORKING MEMORY

Modelling of Cognitive Skills by Computer Simulation

The simulation model describing the cognitive effort consists of a set of
components connected with one another by a number of relations (see Fig. 4).

The following components are to be distinguished:

Interactions between the users and the objects (i.e. forms, information
displayed on the screen) with constitute recognition processes in the sense
of an operative compartment (see Klix 1984). Recognition processes activate
hierarchical-sequential goal structures which permit transformations of
status by different strategies. In order to control flexible strategies,
control compartments are necessary (see Klix 1984). As proposed by Card,
Moran and Newell (1983) we implemented control compartments by selection
rules. For the description of status transformations operators are to be
defined which have a time characteristic.

These components of the simulation model - interactions, recognition processes, flexible strategies, transformations of status - are connected by
a set of relations which have a task related function. The conceptual
recognition of the forms by their special characteristics leads to the
formation of a task goal (finality-relation). The task goal activates an

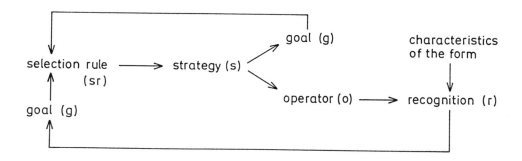

relation	task-oriented function	simulation
r ⟶ g	finality	list-processing
g ⟶ sr	control	production system
g ⟶ s	conditioning	list-processing
sr ⟶ s	option	— ,, —
s ⟶ g	opening a hierarchy	— ,, —
s ⟶ o	execution	— ,, —
o ⟶ r	processing	production system

Fig. 4: Components and relations within the simulation model

action scheme which admits to fulfil the task by different strategies. In order to decide which strategy is to be used actually a set of selection rules has to be controlled (control-relation). This control can consists in an autonomous decision (i.e. an option) concerning the succeeding action if different strategies of task performance are possible (option-relation). On condition that if the task does not admit any degree of freedom and enforces a dependent procedure a conditioning relation is activated. Proceeding on this assumption of an autonomous decision about strategy to be used (option-relation) either hierarchically interlocked subgoals or operators can be called. A hierarchically interlocked subgoal is called if its fulfilment is the prerequisite of the realization of a supergoal (opening a hierarchy-relation). Therefore hierarchically interlocked sub-goals always result in chunks to be preserved simultaneously in the working memory. These simultaneously stored chunks represent one crucial criterion of cognitive effort, since they restrict the available but limited capacity of the working memory.
If it is not necessary to interlock the goals an operator is directly executed for the goal attainment (execution-relation). In applying the operators information processing processes take place activated by a processing relation. Processing procedures latently are available as moduls.

They are called by the action part of the production rules (see Newell 1973) and admit performances of control, of identification etc.

In addition to the storage parameters we used selected process characteristics of processing procedures representing the second group of parameters of the cognitive effort. These process characteristics restricting the available capacity of the working memory and therefore having consequences for the cognitive effort consist of steps of comparison (i. e. condition controls), and of inputs from the task environment (identification, recognition) into the working memory and from the retrieval of information of the long-term memory into the working memory.

The defined components and relations represent a finite action grammar suitable for the process description of cognitive skills at VDU. For the computer simulation relations are of concern which are implemented as lists (see Graham 1982) or as production rules (see Newell and Simon 1972).

As far as the prediction of the cognitive effort is concerned, the production system is of importance for understanding the mechanism of information processing. It contains three elements: A long-term memory (representing the total amount of existing productions), a working memory (representing the storage and processing unit), and an interpreter controlling the storage and information processing. The validity of the simulation models depends on their data basis. To give you a general idea of our data basis we present an experimental investigation in the following section.

Laboratory-Experimental Results Serving as Parameter Estimations of the Simulation Model

The most important input for the counter business are the informations given by the forms. Varying slots which have to be complemented by arguments after being recognized are the different kinds of forms, the account number, and the monetary amount.
As the modelling of the working memory needs assumptions of the chunk formation, an experiment on the VDU-terminal was carried out with the aim to construct a suitable selection rule. The digit-range of the account-numbers as well as the users' pre-knowledge about the sequence of the numbers have been varied.

Using an indirect method we analysed whether the subjects divided the account in one or two chunks. Fig. 5 demonstrates in what manner the task characteristic influences the chunk formation (the proportion of tasks per experimental condition - solved by One-chunk- and Two-chunk-formations - amount to 100 %).

Let us immediately prevent a possible misunderstanding: The chunk formation as parameter of the load of the working memory has been found to be effective in different degree related to the subjects. The analysis of the experiment brought to light two different strategies of the users: Subjects using resources and subjects not using resources.

Concerning the information input the first group of the users flexibly organized the formation of the chunks, i.e. flexibly according to the demands of the memory (cf. Fig. 5). This strategy is to be considered optimal. The subjects not using resources used an effort minimizing strategy,

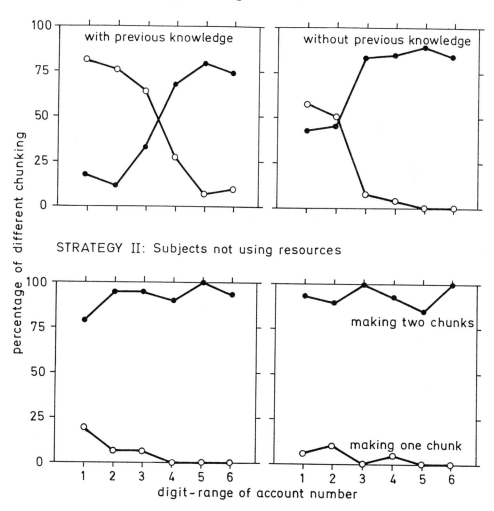

Fig. 5: Strategies of chunking while receiving information

generally forming two chunks regardless of the demands of the memory.
We conclude that the pre-knowledge of the users concerning the account-
numbers modifies the chunk formation and has to be taken into account
in our simulation model.

Results of Simulation Concerning Performance and Cognitive Effort

The estimation of the time characteristic of the operators is derived from
field studies in the savings-bank. The execution time was predicted by a
Monte-Carlo-simulation based on a Gamma-distribution.

PREDICTION OF PERFORMANCE

time	95% - confidence interval			N	standard deviation
	lower limit	mean (sec)	upper limit		
observed	33,56	37,27	40,97	41	11,74
simulated	36,63	38,93	41,22	41	7,27

PREDICTION OF COGNITIVE EFFORT

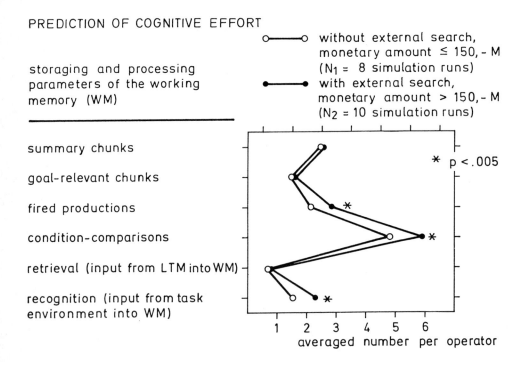

Fig. 6: Results of the simulation of performance and cognitive effort
related to payment in clearing account

After 41 simulation runs we got a good correspondence between observed and simulated times. The standard deviations of the empirical and the simulated performance data, however, are differing: The simulation neglects persons who are very fast in carrying out the task demands (see the lower limit of the 95 % level of confidence interval).

The simulated process description of the working memory permits to estimate the following parameters of the cognitive effort:

- the averaged number of the chunks which have to be present simultaneously in the working memory,

- the averaged number of fired productions,

- the averaged number of comparison steps in the condition part of the productions,

- the averaged number of retrieval (i.e. from the long-term memory) into the working memory,

- the averaged number of external inputs (i.e. from the task environment) into the working memory.

The hypothesis-making simulation demonstrates that even task demands with only slight differences in external action can be differentiated by their effort parameters of the working memory: Paying out in savings-banks without searching the account-number differs from paying out with searching the account-number concerning processing parameters only (cf. Fig. 6). Future job design has to reduce the interlocking of the subgoals in order to diminish the cognitive load of the users.

Our results show that the co-operation of Clinical, Working, and General Psychology can lead to complex intervention strategies when introducing VDU. Besides the design of organization conceptions also differential diagnostic studies of the user personality as well as optimization of cognitive effort by cognitive engineering become more important.

REFERENCES

(1) Card, S. K., Moran, T. and Newell, A., The Psychology of Human-Computer Interaction (Lawrence Erlbaum Associates, New Jersey, London, 1983)

(2) Glass, D. C., Typ-A Behavior: Mechanisms Linking Behavioral and Pathophysiologic Processes, in: Sigrist, J. and Halhuber, M. J. (eds.), Myocardial Infarction and Psychosocial Risks (Springer Verlag, Berlin, Heidelberg, New York, 1981)

(3) Graham, N., Künstliche Intelligenz (Luther Verlag, Sprendlingen, 1983)

(4) Hacker, W. and Iwanowa, A., Das Tätigkeitsbewertungssystem (TBS) - ein Hilfsmittel beim Erfassen potentiell gesundheits- und entwicklungsfördernder objektiver Tätigkeitsmerkmale, Psychologie für die Praxis 2 (1984) 104 - 114

(5) Hackman, J.R. and Oldham, G.R., The Job Diagnosis Survey: An Instru-
    ment for the Diagnosis of Jobs and the Evaluation of Job Redesign
    Projects, Techn. Report 4, Yale Univ. (May 1974)

(6) Hänsgen, K.-D., Zur Entwicklung eines Selbstbeurteilungsverfahrens
    für die Neurosendiagnostik, Diss. A, Fak. f. Nat.wiss. u. Math.,
    Humboldt-Univ. (1982)

(7) Janke, W., Erdmann, G. and Boucsein, W., Der Stressverarbeitungs-
    fragebogen, Ärztliche Praxis 38 (1978) 1208-1210

(8) Kasielke, E., Neurosendiagnostik (VEB Dt. Verlag der Wissenschaften,
    Berlin, 1982)

(9) Klix, F., Denken und Gedächtnis - Über Wechselwirkungen kognitiver
    Kompartments bei der Erzeugung geistiger Leistungen, Manuskript,
    Sektion Psychologie, Humboldt-Univ. (1984)

(10) Newell, A., Production Systems: Models of Control Structures, in:
     Chase, W. G. (ed.), Visual Information Processing (Academic Press,
     New York, 1973

(11) Newell, A. and Simon, H. A., Human Problem Solving (Prentice Hall,
     New Jersey, 1972)

(12) Nitsch, J. R., Die Eigenzustandsskala (EZ-Skala) - Ein Verfahren zur
     hierarchisch-mehrdimensionalen Befindlichkeitsskalierung, in: Nitsch,
     J. R. and Udris, I. (eds.), Beanspruchung im Sport, Schriftenreihe
     Training und Beanspruchung: 4 (Limpert-Verlag, Bad Homburg, 1976)

(13) Schulz, P., Regulation und Fehlregulation im Verhalten, V. Die wechsel-
     seitige Beeinflussung von mentaler und emotionaler Beanspruchung,
     Psychologische Beiträge 22 (1980) 633-656

(14) Sifneos, P.E., The Prevalence of Alexithymic Characteristics in Psycho-
     somatic Patients, Zeitschrift für Psychotherapie und Psychosomatik
     22 (1973)

JOB ORGANIZATION

JOB ORGANIZATION AND ALLOCATION OF FUNCTIONS BETWEEN MAN AND
COMPUTER: I. ANALYSIS AND ASSESSMENT

W. Hacker and E. Schönfelder
Department of Ergonomics
Institute of Psychology
Technical University
Dresden
GDR

Design of man-computer interaction means information-
centered task design. A supplement of the Task Diagnosis
Survey is used for the evaluation of a representative
sample of computerized white-collar jobs. There are no
cogent relationships between computerization of wide-
spread data- and text-processing tasks and the enhancement of the quality of working life because of the
potential efficiency of man-computer interaction depends on the health and personality promoting design
of the remaining task content. The most important task
characteristics are sequential and hierarchical completion including temporal and procedural freedom of
decision and goal-setting.

INTRODUCTION

Design of man-computer interaction means information-centered
task design. Before details of this interaction, e.g. the type
of dialogue, can be designed, two basic decisions often neglected must be thoroughly dealt with: the organizational
division of tasks between men, and the technological allocation
of functions between man and computer. Both key aspects of tasks
design first of all require a diagnosis and an evaluation of
the task demands.

We are engaged just in this diagnosis and evaluation on

- a macro-level by means of quasi-experimental task analyses
  and work studies in field settings, and on

- a micro-level by means of experimental studies of simulated
  real-life mental routine tasks in the laboratory (cf. Hacker,
  this symposium).

Unfortunately it turned out repeatedly that computerization will
not automatically generate human-centered job contents. On the
contrary: "It is surprising how badly technology matches human
capabilities... As a result we are slaves to technology", as
D.A. Norman emphatically summarized (1982; p. 113). The new
tasks may even be more monotonous and may provoke more mental
health risks than before (Friedrich et al. 1982). Thus, the

potential economic efficiency of man-computer system will not
completely be exhausted, too. This especially may happen with
the wide-spread mental routine tasks, e.g. book-keeping in
pay-offices. Computerization in addition to rationalization by
a Taylorist division of tasks here migh replace the relatively
demanding processing operations by narrow input operations.

PROBLEMS AND THEORETICAL BACKGROUND

Our main questions are:

- How to evaluate different versions of the division of tasks
  and the allocation of functions, esp. referring to the
  motivational and the learning potential of the resulting
  tasks?

- Is it possible to deal with human-related effects of
  computerization relatively independently of its organizational context?

- Which are the task dimensions mainly changing with computerization and its organizational context, that are relevant
  for the resulting human effects? Which cluster of changing
  task dimensions will result in which effects?

Our theoretical background is the approach of "complete versus
partialized or incomplete goal-directed actions" which was
repeatedly discussed in detail elsewhere (e.g. Hacker 1984):
Goal-directed actions are organized simultaneously in a
cyclic and in a hierarchic manner. Roughly, one can designate
those structures of activities as complete that include more
than routinized execution operations. Complete structure, thus,
leave opportunity for

- preparatory cognitive phases including autonomous goal setting requiring freedom to choose meaningful task-goals,
  predictibility of demands, and control;

- modification or even design of action programmes which weigh
  the consequences;

- a decision potential referring to alternative procedures,
  and, thus, for taking over responsibility; and

- checking of results based on sufficient feedback.

Consequently, from a hierarchic point of view, demands are
made on various levels of mental regulation of actions, including productive intellectual processes, at least sometimes.

This approach already enables to predict roughly the effects
of task characteristics on motivation and satisfaction, mental
health, and intellectual abilities.

METHODS

In the last few years we designed and validated the Task
Diagnosis Survey (TDS), an instrument designed to guide and
to compare task analyses and work studies of objective task
characteristics of blue collar jobs (Hacker, Iwanowa, Richter 1983).

The instrument makes possible to compare profiles of psychologically relevant task characteristics quantitatively and
in an objective, reliable, and valid manner (Hacker, Iwanowa,
Richter 1983). This paper reports first attempts made to
validate a TDS-Supplement for white coller jobs including man-
computer interaction.

For evaluation reasons a couple of subjective effects had to
be measured, too. We administered standardized and semistan-
dardized questionnaires and interviews aiming at psychophysiological complaints (BFB; Hoeck and Hess 1975), perceived fatigue, monotony, satiation, and stress (BMS II;
Plath and Richter 1984), reported satisfaction (AZA; Iwanowa
and Hacker 1984), and motivation (SAA; Aliot and Udris 1976).
The co-variation of age, sex, qualification, and some personality traits was tried to be considered.

RESULTS

The following data are preliminary results of a long-range
project. They relate on a systematically selected representative sample of 7 white-collar tasks with 67 employees.
Three of the selected tasks represent the lower third of the
total range of possible tasks diagnosed by the TDS, two the
medium, and two the upper third. Following a cluster analysis
of the 43 white-collar jobs analyzed so far, this sample represents mere data input jobs and problem-centered data processing tasks. The sample is not representative for the different kinds of routine clerk jobs.

The 22 task characteristics discussed here were selected from
the 56 characteristics of the instrument by means of a
cluster analysis (hierarchic agglomerative cluster analysis
following Ward 1963), and of their correlations with a couple
of task effects on the basis of 43 computerized white-collar
jobs with 220 employees.

Task demands of traditional versus VDU-work

We start with the comparision of traditional data input tasks
using punching card units with input tasks using VDU. The
division of labour is comparable. Thus, the differences of
demands are essentially determined by computerization. In the
special case there are two exeptions, the organizationally
determined higher variety of forms and lower time pressure

for the computerized version.

Demands: Both task versions are restricted to mere data
input in 98 % of the working time. Preparatory, organizational,
and checking subtasks do not appear (fig. 1). There are
neither temporal nor procedural degrees of freedom (i.e.
autonomy) to decide on task implementation or to set goals
autonomously. Planning demands do not exist. In both cases
automatic processing is prevailing; the lower degree of
possible routinization of the computerized version is due
to organizational reasons. Cooperation is demanded only ex-
ceptionally. Thus, the resulting cognitive demands are narrow:
Data are to be transfered without any intellectual processing.

A minimal learning potential, restricted to knowledge refresh-
ing is given.

Computerization altogether did not result in any kind of
enlarged or enriched demands. The task remains uncomplete
in the sequential and hierarchical dimension. Thus, un-
desired effects are to be expected.

Effects: Fig. 2 verifies this expectation. Autonomy is perceived being low, the variety of demands lacking. Qualification is utilized only partially and - within VDU-work - in
a one-sided manner. The employees perceive qualitative under-
load. Strong fatigue, monotony, and satiation are perceived
at the end of the shift at VDU-work.

This findings are typical for computerized data-input jobs,
according to our overview, hitherto. Thus, we are afraid
computerization of input tasks will not necessarily and automatically enhance the quality of task demands.

Demands of VDU-work with differently complete task structures

(a) Data input tasks

We compare two different versions of division of labour at
data input tasks with a comparable allocation of functions
between man and computer and identical VDU.

In version A the employee - additionally to input tasks -
accomplishs several subtasks including the finding and
correction of automatically marked faults. In version B
mere input prevails.

Demands: The percentage of input time is lower for version
A (80 %) than for B (98 %). The preparatory and checking
subtasks of A offer some temporal and procedural degrees
of freedom for decisions and goal-setting (fig. 3). Task A
is less repetitive and may be routinized to a smaller
extent. The resulting variety of cognitive demands is a
bit higher, however, it does not include intellectual demands. Thus, the task structure is partially incomplete

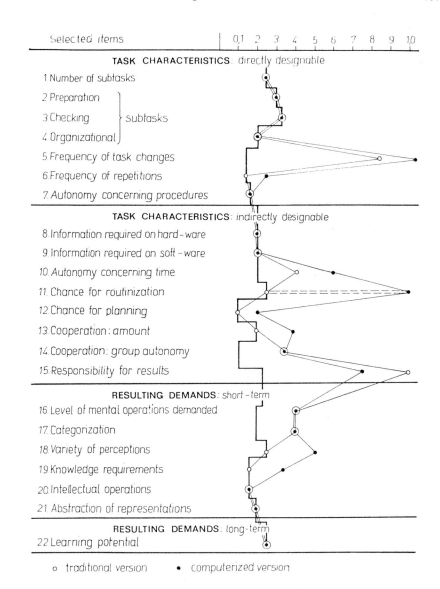

Fig. 1: Task demands of traditional versus computerized
VDU-work (transformed ordinal scales of selected
items of the Task Diagnosis Survey)
differences ≥ 2 scale points

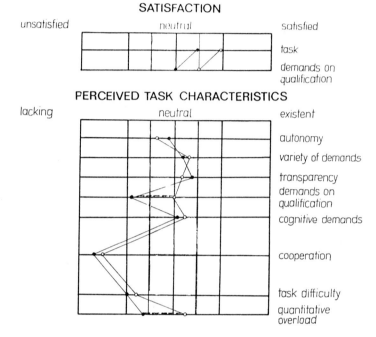

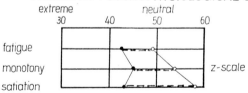

○ data processing, traditional version (n = 14)
● data processing, computerized version (n = 9)

Fig. 2: Effects of traditional versus computerized VDU-work
        p = 0.05.

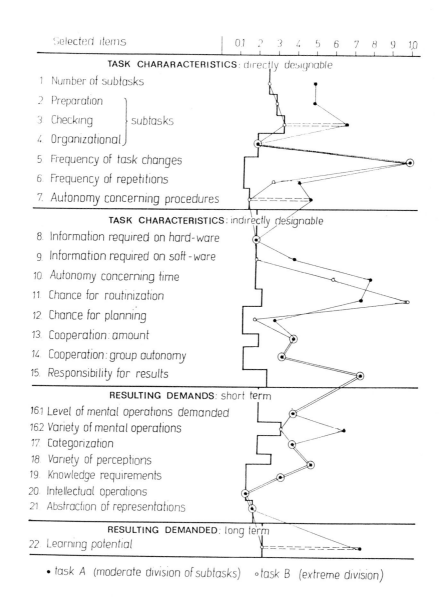

Fig. 3: Task demands of computerized VDU-work with different
division of labour (moderate vs extreme)
differences ≥ 2 scale points.

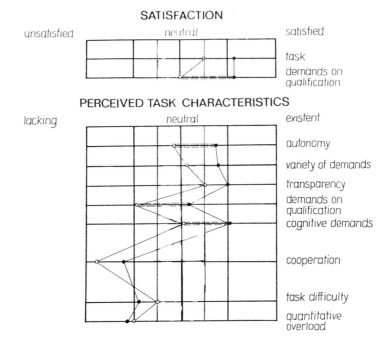

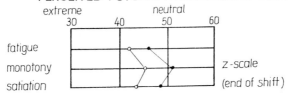

task A   •   computerized; moderate division of labour (n = 9)
task B   ∘   computerized; extreme division of labour (n = 4)

Fig. 4: Effects of computerized VDU-work with different
division of labour (moderate vs. wxtreme)
p = 0.05.

esp. referring to the hierarchic aspect. Consequently, we expect undesirable effects of task A, too, however with a much smaller extent.

Effects: Fig. 4 verifies this expectations. In task A satisfaction, the demands perceived and autonomy are significantly higher. Unlike task B, in task A neither monotony nor satiation or fatigue are perceived to a degree worth mentioning. The complaints are less numerous, probably depending on the extent of perceived social support in spite of a lacking necessity of cooperation, too. We conclude: A comparable allocation of functions given, the division of tasks strongly determines the mental task demands and the resulting perceived effects on man.

(b) Text processing: Computerized type setting

We compare two different types of division of tasks in computerized type setting with identical allocation of functions. A group of compositors (group A) composes German belletristic text only.

Another group (B) composes scientific and foreign language texts including tables and formulas and carries out all corrections, even for the first group.

Demands: The job of group B involves a higher variety of subtasks with differing demands, including preparation, checking, organization and correction. The percentage of mere input, i.e. typing, and repetition are significantly less than for A. There are broader possibilities of autonomous goal-setting, real decisions on procedures and their sequences, and of long-range planning (fig. 5). Both tasks are dominantly controlled processes.

Task B requires the reponsibility for a "whole", complete result. The demands on cooperation are higher. The resulting cognitive demands of task B show higher variety and include intellectual, even problem-solving demands - contrary to group A. The demanded internal representations are more abstract. The learning potential of B is much more extensive. Since both groups of compositors got the same qualification, we expect more undesirable effects for group A with the narrow and unchallenging division of tasks.

Effects: Fig. 6 verifies this expectation. The satisfaction with the task and the demands set on qualification are significantly lower for the narrow task content. Perceived autonomy, variety of demands, transparency of the working situation and demanded cooperation are significantly less. Perceived fatigue, satiation, and the amount of psychophysiological complaints)8.5 versus 3.0 per person; p = 0,05) are more marked.

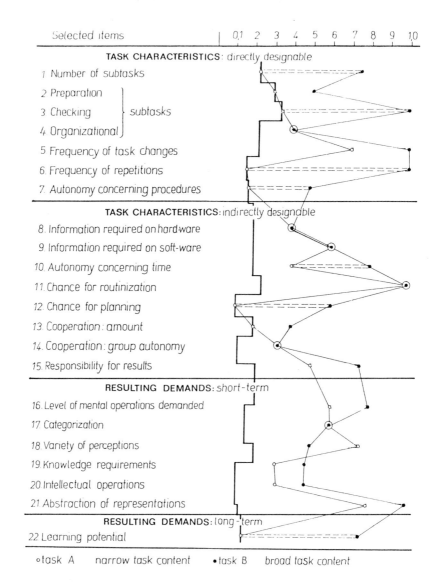

Fig. 5: Text-processing: Task demands of computerized type setting with narrow vs broad task content differences ≥ 2 scale point.

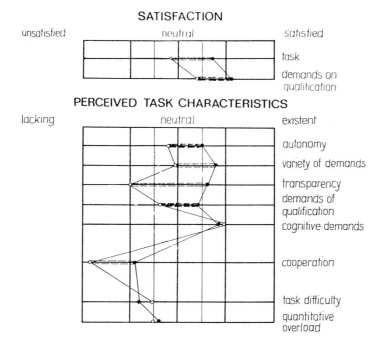

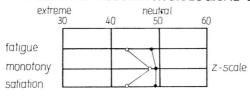

task A ∘ computerized type setting, narrow task content (n = 15)
task B • computerized type setting, broad task content (n = 7)

Fig. 6: Text-processing: Effects of computerized type
setting with narrow vs broad task content
p = 0.05.

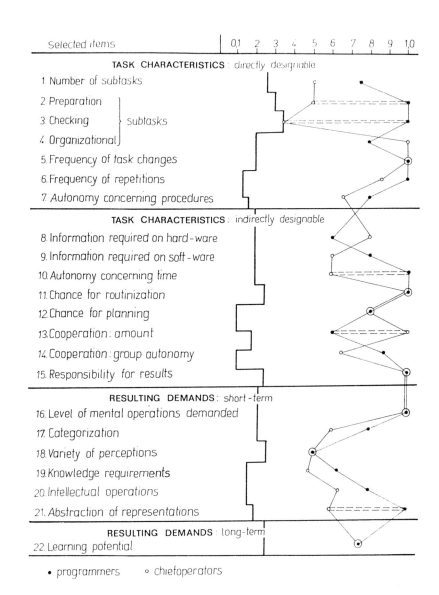

Fig. 7: Task demands in man-computer interaction: Differences
in terms of autonomy (Programmers vs chief-operators)
differences ≥ 2 scale points.

We conclude: The strong impact of the division and organization of tasks on the mental demands and their perceived effects on man may be verified in computerized text processing tasks.

Sequentially and hierarchically complete task structures in man-computer interaction:

Differences in terms of the decision potential ("control")

The comparisons discussed so far might provoke the impression, that tasks including some just noticeable preparatory, organizational, or checking operations, and, thus, some intellectual demands, would guarantee the desired positive effects on man.

For more profound examination we compare the tasks of programmers with those of chief-operators of computing centres. The programmers design complete programs, starting with the analysis of the problems and ending with the test of the program. The chief-operators are responsible for the management and organization of all activities of the computing center including the supervision of the operators monitoring the computers and peripheral units.

Demands: Both jobs involve a variety of tasks with differing demands including organization, preparation, and checking. The repetition rate is low. The variety is higher and the percentage of mere task implementation lower for the programmers. There are high planning demands (fig. 7). Both jobs demand problem solving: for the programmers even creative identification of problems is necessary. The temporal autonomy of the chief-operators is strikingly low - both absolutely and in comparison with the programmers. Prompt reactions on unexpectable events are required. The share of reactive responding is higher than for programmers. Temporarily time pressure occurs. The extent of collective responsibility is lower.

Referring to the Karasek-Paradigm (Karasek 1979, or to Savage and Perlmutter 1979) we expect negative effects for the chief-operators inspite of their sequentially and hierarchically nearly complete task structure. Namely, there is an exception concerning an essential detail: Contrasting with the high disposition demands of organization and preparation, the chief-operators' temporal and procedural autonomy or "control" is low.

Effects: Fig. 8 verifies this expectation: The chief-operators are highly unsatisfied with their task and the demands set on their qualification. Perceived autonomy is relatively low. There is a tendency towards perceived quantitative and qualitative overload. Whereas fatigue and monotony are uncritical, strong satiation is perceived. Just the contrary applies for the programmers. They leave the office just as fit, activated, and challenged as they entered it in the morning. We conclude: The decisive role of autonomous goal setting and actual freedom

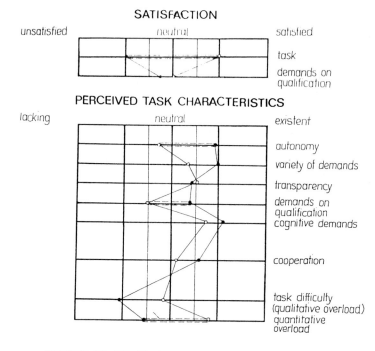

PERCEIVED PSYCHOPHYSIOLOGICAL STATE

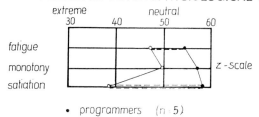

Fig. 8: Man-computer interaction: Effects of different
        autonomy (programmers vs chief-operators)
        p = 0.05.

of decisions, i.e. "control" referring to task content and timing is stressed for a human-centered division of labour and allocation of function for computerized white-collar tasks, too.

CONCLUSIONS

1. There are no cogent relationships between computerization of white-collar tasks and enhancement of quality of working life because of the co-varying work structure.

2. In wide-spread computerized data- and text-processing tasks the demands set on man are not determined exclusively or predominantly by technology, esp. the allocation of functions between man and computer, but to a high extent by organization and work structuring, esp. the division of labour between men. Since analogues results were obtained for robots (Edwards 1984, Noack 1984), a general regularity might be identified.

3. The exhaustion of the potential efficiency of man-computer interaction heavily depends on the health and personality promoting design of the remaining task content.

4. The approach of complete versus partialized action should be further elaborated as a guideline of the human-centered allocation of function and division of labour, the basics of task design.

5. The following marco-characteristics of tasks are important for the effects of computerized white-collar tasks on man:

   - Sequential completion, i.e. the combination of task implementation with organization, preparation, checking, and correcting;

   - hierarchic completion, i.e. the share of real information processing including non-algorithmic intellectual demands - in contrast to pure information transmission -, which coincides with

   - temporal and procedural freedom of (individual or collective) decision and goal-setting, i.e. control.

Consequently, work design in computerized technologics should enhance predominantly these characteristics.

Footnote

[1] The field studies were carefully carried out by B.Hoepfner in partial fulfilment of her diploma-thesis.

REFERENCES

(1) Alioth, A. and Udris, I., Fragebogen zur subjektiven
    Arbeitsanalyse (SAA), Arbeitsmaterial am Lehrstuhl für
    Arbeits- und Betriebspsychologie, ETH Zürich (Zürich 1977).

(2) Edwards, M., Robots in industry: An overview, Applied
    Ergonomics 15 (1984) 45-53.

(3) Friedrich, J., Wicke, F. and Wicke, E., Computereinsatz:
    Auswirkungen auf die Arbeit, Humane Arbeit 3 (Reinbeck,
    1982).

(4) Hacker, W., Activity - a fruitful concept in Psychology
    of Work, in: Frese, M. and Sabini, J. (eds.), Goal-
    directed Behavior (Hillsdale, Erlbaum, 1984).

(5) Hacker, W. and Iwanowa, A., Kurzverfahren zur Analyse der
    Zufriedenheit bei der Arbeit (AZA), Preprint, Sektion
    Arbeitswissenschaft, Technische Universität (Dresden 1984).

(6) Hacker, W., Iwanowa, A. and Richter, P., Verfahren zur
    objektiven Tätigkeitsanalyse (TBS), (Berlin, 1983).

(7) Haider, E. and Rohmert, W., Anforderungsermittlung DTV
    für Tätigkeiten der Daten- und Textverarbeitung mit dem
    AET, in: Landau, K. and Rohmert, W. (eds.), Fallbeispiele
    zur Arbeitsanalyse. Ergebnisse zum AET-Einsatz (Bern,
    Stuttgart, Wien, 1981).

(8) Hoeck, K. and Hess, H., Der Beschwerdefragebogen (BFB)
    (Berlin, 1975).

(9) Hoepfner, B., Validierung des TBS bei geistigen Routine-
    tätigkeiten. Diplomarbeit, Sektion Arbeitswiss., Techn.
    Univ. Dresden (Dresden, 1984).

(10) Karasek, R.A., Job demands, job decision latitude, and
     mental strain, Administrative Science Quarterly 24 (1979)
     285-311.

(11) Noack, B., Abhängigkeit der Arbeitsanforderungen und -aus-
     wirkungen vom Automatisierungsgrad in der Teilefertigung,
     Diplomarbeit, Sektion Arbeitswiss., Techn. Univ. Dresden
     (Dresden, 1984).

(12) Normann, D.A., Learning and Memory, (Freeman, San Francis-
     co, 1982).

(13) Plath, H.-E. and Richter, P., Der BMS-I-Erfassungsbogen -
     ein Verfahren zur skalierten Erfassung erlebter Bean-
     spruchungsfolgen, Probleme und Urgebnisse der Psychologie
     65 (1978) 45-85.

(14) Savage, R.E. and Perlmutter, L.C., The freedom to choose is not always so choice, Journal of Experimental Psychology: Human Learning and Memory 5 (1979) 170-178.

(15) Ward, J.H., Hierarchical grouping to optimize an objective function, Journal of the American Statistical Association 58 (1963) 236-244.

Man-Computer Interaction Research
MACINTER-I
F. Klix and H. Wandke (Editors)
© Elsevier Science Publishers B.V. (North-Holland), 1986

421

JOB ORGANIZATION AND ALLOCATION OF FUNCTIONS
BETWEEN MAN AND COMPUTER:
II. JOB ORGANIZATION

Eberhard Ulich and Norbert Troy

Department of Industrial Psychology
Swiss Federal Institute of Technology
Zurich
Switzerland

By presenting some results of experimental studies,
advantages of flexible types of man-computer dialogues
are proved. The described case studies on different
applications of VDU work underline the relations between primary task and man-machine interaction.
Finally, the modification of boundaries between organizational units is demanded in cases, where departments' tasks are restricted by data processing
systems.

INTRODUCTION

The use of information technology in the office has often resulted in the
continued or even extended division of labour. In spite of technological
possibilities, it seems that those forms of interaction between man and
machine still predominate, which impose on the user practically every single
step on his way to the attainment of a specific goal. Here, we are no longer
presented with the user of a machine, as it is the case with conventional
tools, but we are rather left with the servant or (passive) operator of the
machine, which, in addition, has been programmed by others.

This mostly concerns jobs which through their limited requirements already
lead to a one-sided use of skills, for example, work in centralized word
processing pools or data entry tasks. It should be mentioned though, that
this is not as much a matter of software design as one of work organization.

ASPECTS OF INTERACTION

In respect to the individual's experience of man-machine interaction it
seems to be of essential importance whether the operator can use the computer as a tool at one's own disposition. This, however, requires the existence of different alternatives to choose, that is flexible software for
the dialogue control. Ackermann (1984) was able to show this in a study at
our institute. In this experiment, the possibilities of choosing different
command sequences in a computer game were not only made use of, but this
also turned out to be more efficient than precisely determined commands.

Various advantages of flexible interaction were proved in another experimental study carried out at our institute (Aschwanden and Zimmermann
(1984)). The 30 subjects in this experiment, all of them experienced in
daily VDU work had to fulfill commercial tasks such as the ordering and

settlement of merchandise on the video display.

	type of dialogue 1	type of dialogue 2
screen masc 1	non adaptable layout	adaptable layout
screen masc 2	<u>procedure</u>: fixed, field-to-field, horizontal start execution automatically	<u>procedure</u>: free choice execute-key
all screen mascs and lists	no line for user notes <u>corrections</u>: – backspace – 1 cursor control key field-to-field – go-key for screen masc 2	line for user notes <u>corrections</u>: – 4 cursor control keys field-to-field – 4 c.c.keys sign-to-sign – insert – delete
operating keys total	9 keys, each 1 function	17 keys, each 1 function + 2 keys, each 2 functions + 1 key with 3 functions

Table 1
Main differences between the two types of dialogue,
used in the experiment (source: Aschwanden and Zimmermann (1984))

There were no significant differences between the two types of dialogue regarding time needed to perform the tasks, although variance was much larger for the flexible type of dialogue. With the rigid type of dialogue, more severe mistakes and more corrections on the video display were made. Evaluation of subjective strain by Nitsch's (1976) method of self-rating psychic state showed no significant differences between the two types of dialogue. The subjects in the flexible interaction setting estimated their possibilities of self-determination far higher than their colleagues who had to work with the simpler but rigid type of dialogue.

Further remarkable results relate to the proposals made by the participants regarding task improvements. Under the condition of the rigid interaction, many propositions were made concerning directly the operating of the system. In contrast, subjects in the group using a flexible interaction came up with twice as many proposals regarding the general use of the system or the work-flow as the first group.

Another observation contained in an additional field study by Aschwanden and Zimmermann (1984) refers to a connection between the instruction on the computer functions and the description of the technical system by the user: Persons who were instructed only superficially, often used terms which identified them as servants of the technical system. By using expressions such as "he wants to" or "he cannot", they proved their mental model of the computer to be strongly determined by black-box conceptions. More thoroughly instructed persons more often seemed to use expressions, which identified them as users of a technical system with tool characteristics. This observation reminds of Duncker's (1935) principle of the 'functional attachment of thinking'.

RELATIONS BETWEEN PRIMARY AND SECONDARY TASK

There seem to be close relations between (a) the type of interaction, (b) the specifity of the instructions needed for a reliable use of the system and (c) the primary task. This is one result of case studies based on interviews and shift observations of 25 different applications of VDU work. It became clear that the secondary task which concerns the use of the computer, has great objective significance for the design of the primary task.

type of department and branch	primary task	secondary task
newspaper setting	simple	simple *) **)
newspaper distribution	simple	intermediate
printing office	intermediate	intermediate
airline company: space control	complex	complex *)
airline company: seat reservation	intermediate	complex *)
trust office	complex	intermediate
insurance company	intermediate	intermediate
small banking house	intermediate	intermediate
large banking house I	simple	simple *) **)
large banking house II	simple	simple
personnel department	intermediate	simple
library (project)	(complex)	(intermediate)
public administration	simple	simple
telephone information	simple	intermediate

Table 2
Requirements of primary and secondary tasks for 14 VDU applications
(source: Aschwanden and Zimmermann (1984))

---

*) exclusive VDU work

**) exclusive data entry task

It should be mentioned here that primary tasks, meaning the employee's original tasks, with only low skill requirements entirely correspond with
rather easy secondary tasks. That means that these tasks are often connected
with simple, highly formalized handling of the means of work. This concerned
6 out of 14 applications observed, including 2 cases of exclusive data entry
tasks. The opposite was found in 4 other cases of clerical work, that is
complex requirements of the primary task correlating with a rather demanding
secondary task. The relating task could be done with help of flexible systems, the operating of which required a more specific knowledge of the system in order to make full use of all the possibilities.

ORGANIZATIONAL ASPECTS

These results make clear that one-sided skill requirements are mainly the
result of organizational concepts which determine the type of interaction
between man and machine, also by the effects of certain forms of software.
Apart from this, organizational aspects seem to be responsible for the determination of the primary tasks, as human functions are allocated in an
organizational unit.

Centralized hierarchic applications of electronic data processing and the
corresponding division of labour caused by organizational structures, were,
in most cases known to us, responsible for repetitive VDU work.

The results of a number of recent case studies carried out by Spinas and
Mussmann (in prep.) at our institute confirm the importance of organizational aspects: Here the different applications of video terminals in ad-
ministrative work ranged from simple data entry tasks, done by temporary
employees, up to the demanding responsibility of handling entire meaningful
tasks. In this last case, the terminal seemed to be an important and valuable support for the acquisition, modification and retrieval of data.

Obviously, these different applications of data processing systems are related to different notions of rationalization. Traditional strategies of
rationalization follow the Tayloristic principle of the separation of mental
and manual work. They also tend to eliminate all mental tasks from work
processes. Consequence of such rationalization concepts is the classical separation in the three task units: planning, performing and controlling.
Example #4 of this case studies gives a demonstration of such working structures.

Example #4: Large Banking House

The Clearance Department for Swiss currency handles all in- and
out-payments. The incoming payment documents are first dealt with
by a group responsible for the preparatory work. Subsequently,
the documents are entered into the computer by (female) data
typists and, finally, controlled by a third group of employees,
belonging to a special department. The data typists each have an
average entry of about 15'000 documents per day, work cycles ranging between one and two seconds.

Strategies of rationalization of the integrating type attempt to re-establish the unit of planning, performing and controlling. This does not hold
true for the rationalization approaches of the fragmenting type.

Example #5 shows a form of organization where a systematical re-integration of mental requirements into task performance is attempted.

Example #5: Airline Company

It is the responsibility of the Space Control Department to attain seat occupancy which is for all flights as close as possible to full capacity. For this purpose the space controller determines the varying 'over-booking' rate depending on the day of the year, the destination and the time until take-off. It lies within his authority to fix a rate that is higher than the statistical record would suggest. The competence of the space controller even extends to order an additional aircraft if demand increases unexpectedly. In this case, all task elements, from preparatory planning to self-control, have been allocated to one job.

Thus it becomes evident that microelectronics allow alternative ways of using technology. They can be a means of continuing or even strengthening centralized organizational structures, with the consequence of fragmented tasks, or, technology can be used to preserve or re-establish decentralized organizational structures with the (possible) consequence of complete tasks. The latter strategy implies that even the so-called 'intelligent instruments' can have the functions of a tool, supporting meaningful tasks. Martin (1984) characterized such applications in the field of production as a new combination of "advanced technology and skilled production work".

TASK CRITERIA AND ORGANIZATIONAL BOUNDARIES

In connection with the concepts of Hackman and Oldham (1976) as well as Emery and Thorsrud (1982) the following criteria for analysis and design of tasks can be formulated: completeness, variety of demands, cooperation requirements, learning possibilities and autonomy.

It must be admitted that even relatively complex and meaningful tasks may undergo a reduction of variety and an increase of strain when interactive VDU work is introduced. This is on the one hand due to the lower amount of routine work connected with these tasks. On the other hand, tasks are becoming more uniform when adjusting them to technological requirements. At our institute, Spinas (1984) interviewed 179 females in a service enterprise who, when working with the VDU, were mainly occupied with recalling information. The following is a representative statement by one of these women: "Work has become easier, but somehow more exerting".

In a research project that took place in an insurance company we observed very similar tendencies: Even if the tasks of employees do not get more fragmented by the introduction of interactive VDU work, intensity of work and homogenity of strain obviously increase - as long as the actual range of tasks remains unchanged.

As a consequence of these results, we strongly advocate Job Enrichment, especially in those areas where individual employees are responsible for merely partialized tasks. In the insurance company mentioned this could be achieved through combining the handling of insurance policies and damage claims. In this way, the employee's duties would not only include completion and up-dating of insurance contracts, but also dealing with damage cases and the clients concerned.

A more general way to formulate this point is: If tasks do not meet the criteria mentioned above and where an organization does not offer opportunities for improvements, it will be necessary to change the boundaries between the units of the organization.

In this case it is needed to get to a higher level viewing point. Only in such a way it becomes possible not just simply to preserve existing <u>social</u> units, but to create useful <u>socio-technical units</u> with meaningful tasks. Without changing the boundaries, it is only possible to redistribute the tasks within the existing organizational units.

Especially in departments, where data-processing tasks consist of simple preparation of computer data, it is necessary to enlarge the task variety, by means of a change of boundaries between the departments. This can be applied to the mentioned policy departments in the insurance company. Without boundary changes, tasks in such departments would just be the "handling of data", which represents only one of several different stages of working on a single 'product'.

Within a national research program in Switzerland, we have been able to make some similar observations in the personnel department of an industrial company. If interactive video terminals were introduced and existing boundaries as well as the range of tasks remained unchanged, the employees' tasks would be reduced to a smaller scope.

In this project, an attempt at stimulating employees to reflect upon their actual situation and to develop possible future states was made by the method of Subjective Work Analysis. Following this method, the employees listed positive and negative aspects of their work situation and possible ways of improvement.

It was quite impressing how quickly the employees came to the conclusion that only the enlargement of task variety for the whole department would permit to achieve or re-establish meaningful tasks for all individuals. Especially the older employees had very concrete ideas about an optimal work situation. They all remembered the type of work organization before the introduction of centralized data processing, which was the manual handling of 'entire' tasks by each employee.

One of the consequences is: Interactive video terminals can be used as tools in order to preserve or re-establish meaningful and complex tasks. This, however, often requires organizational structures to be modified, even if a considerable redistribution of tasks between different organizational units should be necessary. This especially applies to structures that have been created by introducing centralized data processing.

This is the only way to guarantee the desired reorganization by making technical innovations. It is also the only way to avoid that organizational structures - as it has been formulated by Clark (1972) - result as the "unplanned consequence of the design of technical systems".

REFERENCES

(1) Ackermann, D., Untersuchungen zum individualisierten Computerdialog, in:
      Dirlich, G. et al. (eds.), Mensch-Computer-Interaktion. Ergebnisse eines
      interdisziplinären Workshops (Urban & Schwarzenberg, München, in press).

(2) Aschwanden, C. and Zimmermann, M., Flexibilität in der Arbeit am Bild-
      schirm, Lizentiatsarbeit, Lehrstuhl für Arbeits- und Betriebspsycholo-
      gie, ETH Zürich (February 1984).

(3) Clark, P.A., Organizational Design (Tavistock Publications, London,
      1972).

(4) Duncker, K., Zur Psychologie des produktiven Denkens (Springer, Berlin,
      1935).

(5) Emery, F.E. and Thorsrud, E., Industrielle Demokratie (Huber, Bern,
      1982).

(6) Hackman, J.R. and Oldham, G.R., Development of the Job Diagnostic Sur-
      vey, Journal Appl. Psychol. (1975) 159 - 170.

(7) Martin, T., Manless Factory: The Wrong Alternative, International Fe-
      deration Automatic Control, Newsletter 2 (1984).

(8) Nitsch, J.R., Die Eigenzustandsskala - Ein Verfahren zur hierarchisch-
      mehrdimensionalen Befindlichkeitsskalierung, in: Nitsch, J.R. and
      Udris, I., Beanspruchung im Sport (Limpert, Bad Homburg, 1976).

(9) Spinas, P., Bildschirmeinsatz und psycho-soziale Folgen für die Be-
      schäftigten, Referat am Kongress des Berufsverbands Deutscher Psycho-
      logen, Lübeck (May 1984).

(10) Spinas, P. and Mussmann, C. (in preparation).

Man-Computer Interaction Research
MACINTER-I
F. Klix and H. Wandke (Editors)
© Elsevier Science Publishers B.V. (North-Holland), 1986

PSYCHOLOGICAL PRINCIPLES FOR ALLOCATION OF
FUNCTIONS IN MAN–ROBOT–SYSTEM

Klaus Peter Timpe
Sektion Psychologie
Humboldt University
Berlin
GDR

Depending on the performance class of a given industrial
robot, a number of design principles with a view to robot-
assisted techniques have been formulated.
The application of these psychological principles to
manufacturing sections provided with robotic equipment
yielded, apart from an improvement in design quality, also
an effective economic benefit, as compared with the variant
envisaged.

STATEMENT OF THE PROBLEM

Psychological problems evolving from robot applications in production
engineering can be assigned to two classes:

- Development of industrial robots
- Preparation for operation of industrial robots.

Of relevant interest in the following is only the case of preparation for
operation on condition that robot application does not result in man's
total removal from the production process. It is the objective of contributions made by industrial and engineering psychology to this subject-matter
to ensure, by the advance of technology for the workers, even more and more
ambitious job requirements. This, on the one hand, means, as far as
production preparation is concerned, to meet to the greatest extent possible
the psychological criteria as to the allocation of tasks. On the other hand,
the design concept must be of such a flexibility that it is possible to
remove, by job–design measures, socalled residual functions which, it is
true, it is necessary to exclude from the automation concept but which it
is impossible to predict in systems design in the particular case. In
contrast to the analysis apparatuses available, the psychological synthesis
techniques necessary to this end are still in an inadequate stage of
development. Therefore, an essential partial objective of psychological
research is to derive useful principles for an optimum layout of tasks from
which the allocation of functions will evolve (Edwards, 1984).

STUDIES CONCERNING THE ALLOCATION OF FUNCTIONS

The starting point for the approach chosen is a systematic set of engineering and technological activities in the production process. From this
systematic representation evolves what object areas are to be covered
and will be covered, respectively, by technical means of work, and what
tasks men are to take charge of and will take charge of respectively. For
the design phase a planning heuristic has been developed, serving as a
starting point for a global description of function allocation. Figure 1
is an illustration of this.

The following analytic steps will derive:

1. Recording all partial activities necessary at the workplace and in the
   manufacturing section respectively (task analysis, possible both for
   activity design and correcting job layout);

2. Assessment of all the activity components not covered by automation
   (activity assessment);

3. Deriving - depending on the result of the activity assessment - new
   forms of task combinations and task assignments according to the
   results following from the activity assessment.

For our studies we selected 10 different manufacturing sections provided
with robotic equipment. The robots were of the class of fixed and
variable sequence control robots.

Following the outline concept described, an activity analysis was made
with the objective of identifying in detail cognitive requirements as
well as forms of cooperation not used. This analysis was prepared both for
the individual sub-systems of the production process according to figure 1
and for the overall systems. In addition the load data on the individual
workers were registered.

Figure 2 shows the procedures applied and gives a survey of the objectives
set.

SELECTED RESULTS CONCERNING TASK ALLOCATION

The following results refer to studies made in connection with correcting
job layout. The hitherto studies made as to designing job layout sub-
stantiate, however, the hypothesis that basically similiar approaches and
results are to be expected even as far as activity design is concerned.

Figure 3 shows what characteristic features for differing applications
have been obtained in the assessment of job activities.

The broken line stand for shortcomings found in job layout. Summarizing
the data obtained from these empirical studies, the following major
trends results with a view to the psychological activity assessment:

	Sub-systems/Activities (acc. to Rockstroh 1980)								Psychological procedural steps in the inter-disciplinary workteam
	Operational system	Object flow system	Storage system	Information and control system	Handling system	Supply and waste disposal system	Appliance, tool and testing means syst.	Auxiliary system	
Designed (as well as realized) allocation of functions	M	M	M	R-ƏL	R	ƏL1	ƏL1	ƏL1	1. Task analysis
Systems analysis				?		?	?	?	2. Job evaluation
Corrected allocation of funktions	M	M	M	R	R	M	ƏLK	ƏLK	3. Deriving measures as to job layout

M : Technical means of work (except industrial robots)
R : Industrial robot
ƏL1 : Individual worker
ƏLK: Collective group in major manufacturing sections and preparation of production respectively

Fig. 1: System of activities necessary in the production process (acc. to ROCKSTROH, 1980)

Data acquisition means	Objectives
1. Analysis of documents - technical and technological documents - Workplace Master Index Card - job classification, Part A	Registration of requirements applying to the worker and evolving from the job task and execution conditions
2. Standardized psychological procedures - job evaluation system (TBS-K) - Load and Exertion - Monotony - Saturation - Acquisition Sheet (BMS) - methods concerning the industrial-psychological assessment and design of job contents and job conditions with a view to juvenile workers (STB)	- Analysis, assessment and design of personality - conducive conditions of job activities - scaled identification of experienced exertion sequences - registering the subjective assessment of the job activity in the worker's judgment
3. Semi-standardized procedures - interview with members of the Preparatory Group concerning problems involved in preparation for operation of industrial robots - interview with workers concerning problems in connection with robot technology	Acquisition of data on general conditions and priority tasks in connection with robot applications (attitudes towards training issues, cooperation, availability etc.)

Fig. 2: Summary of the study methods employed

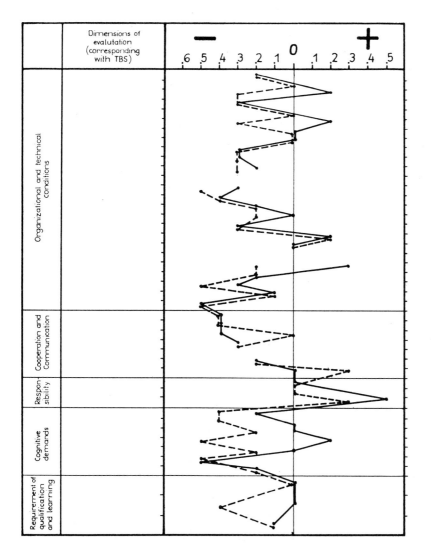

Fig. 3: Example of an IR application of an inadequate (———) design level and of an improved (——) design level

1. It is potentially possible to increase task variety.

2. Scope of action has rarely been used to full capacity.

3. The engineering and technological determination of the working process needs to be reduced.

4. More attention should be paid to communication and cooperation.

In general, the studies made with reference to the changes made in function assignment have once again proved that disjoining production preparation, production realization and production assurance from each other has a negative effect with a view to the improvement of job contents. It is obvious to further requirements by developing new forms of allocation of tasks and task combination. This can be facilitated by assessing the job tasks in the sub-sections according to the heuristic planning approach and, depending on that, by re-allocating and combining respectively the assissgnments within the work-team (M in figure 1). To this, however, no reference will be made now, instead, two generalizations will be derived from the hitherto studies.

GENERALIZATION: PRINCIPLES CONCERNING FUNCTION ALLOCATION AND AUTOMATION STRATEGIES

In contrast to the concepts suggested by other authors (e. g. Simbios, by Parsous and Kearsley or Noro and Okada's Step Model), it is our understanding that a maximum of efficiency of psychological measures taken in job layout will be achieved when it is possible to take them into account right in the design stage. Depending on the performance class of the given industrial robot, two design principles have been formulated as a result of the studies made for robot-assisted techniques which have to be observed in job preparation, in connection with additional principles of labour sciences and industrial economy.

Principle 1:

Proceeding from a personality-conducive tasking approach, only a complete acquisition of all the partial activities can lead to a psychologically efficient system design. If, in robot application design, only rarely occuring but necessary information processing jobs done by workers (for example, in connection with trouble-shooting, or maintenance tasks) are neglected, production disturbances are apt to come to pass. Therefore, the designing engineer must know about the action-relevant piece of information, allowing of an assessment of the partial activities executed and, hence, of making effective corrections in job layout as early as in the designing stage of the man-robot system. The principle is illustrated in figure 4, with its differentiation being to be illustrated by the following example of a concrete particular case: In order to skim the slag off a steel bath, a worker made seemingly superfluous movements. So a robot was programmed in a way that it effected the skimming operation with economy of movement. Since the steel was of minor quality as a result of the robot operation, the worker's manipulations were analysed afterwards, and it was found that the seemingly superfluous movements were intended to obtain information on the thickness of the slag layer, on its toughness and so on. It is on the basis of such proprioceptive information that the worker would coordinate his movements, an information that was lacking in the robot programme, because the design engineer was ignorant of those facts. These shortcomings would have been prevented as early as in the design stage, if an analysis of the information processing processes necessary for the motor controls had been made according to the decision pattern.

Principle 2:

As the degree of automation of the whole system increases, in particular, the increased 'intelligence' of the industrial robot, extended activities concerning preparation, planning and maintenance have to be envisaged for the workers included in a man-robot system. This necessity results from the principal possibility of extending the scope of action as the degree of automation will increase, that is to say, to envisage, in contrast to the conventional splitting between production-preparatory and production-executive tasks, in further developments such techniques and solutions that will comprise parts of the two areas of responsibility. Then, the most convenient form of organization in case of a high degree of automation will be the employment of a work-team in such a way that each member of the team, depending on the working conditions, will derive his concrete tasks in a flexible way, and solve them.

Such a form of organization will be of particular effectiveness in connection with the application of the 1st principle. Moreover, based on the technical and organizational prerequisites, changes in the qualifications of the workers as to the hitherto forms of assignment are necessary. Results achieved in the translation of the principles expounded confirm the approach as has been outlined (Giesel et al.). Figure 3 gives an example (complete line).

The improvement of the design level concerning this concrete case has been achieved to the effect that it has been possible to assign quality control and error correction to those workers who continue to be involved in the production process. The economic benefit - established in terms of saving of living labour - has been proved.

CONCLUSION

The findings show that for determining the assignment of functions according to the criteria of psychological job layout near-optimum solutions become possible. In the course of shop-floor studies different classes of psychological catchment possibilities have been elaborated, permitting to derive principles which make it possible to also take into account the basic object of personality development, besides the economic and scientific-technological target criteria, of relevance above all to the design of new techniques and engineering methods.

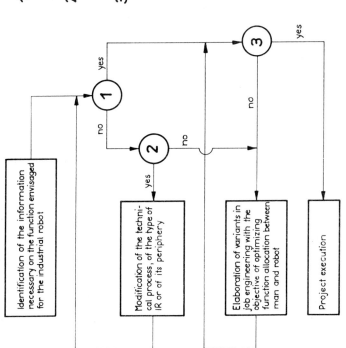

1. Is the industrial robot able to register/process completely the information necessary

2. Can the information processing operations not registered be realized technically

3. Is there any efficient (technical, economic, social) use in assigning the activity to a robot

Identification of the information necessary on the function envisaged for the industrial robot

Modification of the technical process, of the type of IR or of its periphery

Elaboration of variants in job engineering with the objective of optimizing function allocation between man and robot

Project execution

Fig. 4: Decision complexes with a view to the examination of robot application prerequisites from the aspect of utilization of activity-relevant process information

REFERENCES

(1) Edwards, M., Robots in industry: An overview, Applied ernonomics 1 (1984) 56-63

(2) Giesel, B., J. Neumann und K.P. Timpe, Funktionsverteilung beim Einsatz der Industrierobotertechnik, Soz. Arbeitsw. 6 (1984) 429-438

(3) Noro, K. and Okada, Y., Robotization and Human factors, Ergonomics, 10 (1983) 985-1000

(4) Parsons, H. and Kearsley, P.; Robotics and Human factors, Human factors, 5 (1982) 535-552

Man-Computer Interaction Research
MACINTER-I
F. Klix and H. Wandke (Editors)
Elsevier Science Publishers B.V. (North-Holland), 1986

SOCIAL PSYCHOLOGICAL PREREQUISITES AND CONSEQUENCES OF NEW INFORMATION TECHNOLOGIES

Bernhard Wilpert
S. Antonio Ruiz Quintanilla

Technical University Berlin
Berlin (West)
FRG

The paper starts out by evoking the danger that psychology, in connection with new technologies, might end up with an individualistic myopia due to neglecting social and organizational aspects of the introduction and use of such techniques. It presents a four-level analytic approach to the study of social prerequisites and consequences of using new information technologies by discussing individual, group, organizational and societal level issues derived from received theory and research paradigms. The paper presents illustrative materials on those four levels from relevant research projects with special emphasis on projects conducted at the Technical University Berlin.

INTRODUCTION

It has been claimed that the history of psychology is marked by an astounding neglect of the world of things, a neglect that is due to the discipline's "organismic preoccupation" (Graumann, 1974). The author goes on to argue that almost all things/objects of our daily life have an important social significance. While it may be true that psychology as a whole has paid little attention to the world of things, the same cannot be claimed for engineering psychology and ergonomics which exclusively address the problems of man and his/her work environment, the interaction between man and machine, man and computers, man and technology. However, it appears that in these disciplinary context we face another danger - a preoccupation with the individual and his/her work environment at the expense of neglecting its social determinants and implications: the danger of an individualistic myopia.

The rest of the paper will address some of the social factors relating to new technologies by considering four analytic levels: the individual, the work group, the organizational system as a whole, and the societal level. This tour de force implies that we argue on the basis rather of examples of own and others' research findings than on the basis of a comprehensive discourse.

INDIVIDUAL LEVEL PERSPECTIVE

The lion's share of publications in recent years which treat man-machine interaction problems are guided by theoretical approaches that might be considered as deriving from a general psychological (software psychology/ ergonomy, cognitive ergonomy, cognitive engineering etc.) or physiological framework. The very nature of such frameworks suggest an individualistic bias of focus and attention. This is even true of more advanced models which suggest the explicit consideration of the respective knowledge bases of user and computer (Fischer, 1984). Saying this is not to be little their important contributions to the analysis and understanding of man-machine interactions. It is only to say that already on the individual level analysis it may be necessary to introduce a social-psychological theoretical framework which considers man-machine communication as a special case of general human communication (Maaß, 1984, Oberquelle et al., 1983).

Any technological device - whether a simple instrument or a complex computing system - is part of the world of things and as such is an "agendum" (Graumann, 1974) which due to its specific technical features presents itself with a specific demand structure that has been incorporated into it by its designer. As such it might be considered as "frozen action structure". Man-computer dialogues, by virtue of this imputed action structure, become a virtual social interaction process between the user and the machine's designer. The latter bases his design on a set of assumptions about the user's characteristics and produces a virtual machine in terms of semantic, syntactic and action sequencing norms which constitute the user conventions. They are largely determined by the designer with hitherto little or no feedback and bargaining opportunities from the side of the user. Dialogue conditions are thus characterized by a power differential which is often aggravated by a lack of harmony among conventions of different program units. Dialogue can only succeed if the user acts in line with the internal user image of the designer. It follows that all such interaction can be conceptualized as a communication process, liable to the same differential degrees of understanding, comprehension or misunderstanding as all communication. The implications of this for task and performance requirements are similarly underresearched as for adequate methods of user participation in systems design.

With respect to different program feedback modalities experiments at our institute have shown that feedback which excessively uses normal 'conversational' modes may be counterproductive for performance levels because users tend to develop unrealistic images of the program structure and capabilities (Porsch, 1984). Similarly, some beginning is made for the progressive inclusion of users in the design of computer systems (Floyd and Keil, 1983).

GROUP LEVEL PERSPECTIVE

The heuristic usefulness of considering man-computer dialogue as a special case of human communication may further be illustrated on the level of work groups.

The growth of computerization in office settings seems increasingly to affect formal and informal information flows and communication patterns within work groups (Brandt et al., 1978). Standardization and restrictivity in the use of codes characterize formal communication modes while the advance of accoustic input-output media and the trend towards multifunc-

tional work places appear to progressively reduce opportunities and needs
for immediate human face-to-face communication (Friedrich et al., 1982;
Faerber et al., 1983). This is particularly true, as one of our field
studies underscores (Ruiz Quintanilla, 1983) for employees with major data
input tasks. From work socialization research we can draw ample evidence
of the negative effects of restrictive work settings on personality development (cf. Kohn and Schooler, 1983), however, little to nothing is known
about the long range impact of lacking social contact opportunities and
the growing predominance of formalized interaction requirements on the
development of social competence. The need for intensified research efforts
in this domain becomes so much the more plain as similar media begin to
pervade schools and the private sphere (Teletex, video games and home
computer).

ORGANIZATIONAL LEVEL PERSPECTIVE

The discussion of new technologies as imposing new and rigid technological
and organizational imperatives (Volpert, 1984) versus their inherent
flexibility as opening up new organizational and structural degrees of
freedom for the division of labor and job designs has by no means come to
an end (Troy, 1983, Spinas, 1984). Irrespective of how this problem will
ultimately be resolved, computer assisted information techniques confront
the organizational system as a whole with two inevitable decision tasks,
one relating to the modalities of the introductory process, the other to
the intended overall division of labor.

The introduction of new information techniques poses problems analogous
to the ones discussed in part 1 of this paper except that here they
require a whole systems perspective: they relate to the question of how
appropriate structures can be designed to allow for an adequate articulation of employee interests on issues that are traditionally seen to belong
to managerial prerogatives (choice of production system). Case studies on
the cooperation and conflicts between management, employee representatives
and affected employees during different phases of introducing new information techniques demonstrated that two factors tend to obfuscate these
processes even under bona fide conditions among all parties involved:
lack of competence among employees and their representatives to deal with
highly technical, complex issues in the introductory phase and inability
of management to provide sufficiently accurate information on likely
long-range effects of the use of these techniques (Dirrheimer and Wilpert,
1983). One solution to mitigate both factors seems to be to introduce
process bargaining (i. e. iteratively during all phases of the introduction) instead of outcome bargaining (e. g. one-time agreement to maintain
pay levels) (Kubicek et al., 1981).

Treu (1984) pointed out that different organizational choice options are
possible with regard to the ultimate use of new technologies. In our context they must take into account at least the following systemic aspects:

- distribution of competences within the organization and their developmental potential through training

- legal framework (e. g. privacy rules for data use)

- leadership styles and control structures

- labor market consequences.

Thus the problem is not only whether to implement a centralized versus a decentralized system but beyond this a question of how to take account of a. m. factors in their inextricable interrelatedness. This, however, presupposes the availability of new organizational models which are capable of incorporating the prerequisites and dynamics of directed organizational change, i. e. models we are badly amiss.

SOCIETAL LEVEL PERSPECTIVE

Various authors have noted and lamentad a recent decline of traditional (protestant) work ethics among the work force of Western industrialized countries (Noelle-Neumann, 1978, Yankelovich, 1978, Yankelovich et al., 1983). Their worries are based on changing response frequencies to identical survey research items repeatedly used over a period of some 20 years. Indeed, their concern may be warranted if one can assume that work demands in the 80-ies are still the same as in the 60-ies. However, somewhat different evaluations seem more appropriate if more differentiated concepts and models of work related value patterns guide the research. Findings form an eight-country comparison of target group and representative samples (total N $\simeq$ 14,000, Mow, 1985) show that people continue to identify strongly with their work and profession and consider working as a significant part of their life, provided their work setting meets certain criteria (Ruiz Quintanilla, 1984). Such criteria may be described as discretionary freedom or the potential for self-regulatory work activities in organizations. As Triebe (1981) has shown, identical tasks can be solved by different individuals with comparable efficiency via different action strategies. In other words, what we are noting then are continued high levels of work as a central life role but changing expectations as to specific content aspects of work.

Changing societal values regarding work, rather than perceived as a threat, may in connection with new information technologies be considered as an opportunity to provide more individually tailored work settings by exploiting technological flexibilities. If individualization of work settings means basically to leave the choice of task solving strategies to the working person then such an approach also means that qualifications such as the readiness to take on responsibility and planning competence are in demand to a growing extent. They are usually seen as crucial aspects of individual growth. Work related values and expectations of the work force and technological potential seem to offer the opportunity for a selcome convergence. Maybe this view is too optimistic in the eyes of many observers, but research evidence reported here and our evaluation of technical possibilities make it appear to be a definite possibility.

However that may be, in concluding this paper we summarize its main thrust to be a plea for a widening of scope when dealing psychologically with man-computer-interaction. We deem it necessary to draw on more than only psychological knowledge and models derived from general and cognitive psychology but to draw as well on the body of knowledge, the theoretical and methdological competence developed in social psychology, organizational and even cultural psychology, as it seems inevitable when it comes to the study of technology related values.

REFERENCES

(1) Brandt, G., Kündig, B., Paradimitriou, Z., Thomae, I., Computer und Arbeitsprozeß. Eine arbeitssoziologische Untersuchung in ausgewählten Betriebsabteilungen der Stahlindustrie und des Bankgewerbes (Campus Verlag, Frankfurt (M), 1978)

(2) Dirrheimer, A., Wilpert, B., Einführung neuer Informationstechnik: Fallstudien zur Kooperation von Management, Betriebsräten und Mitarbeitern, Institut für Psychologie, Technische Universität Berlin (1983)

(3) Faerber, B., Reichle, S., Schrade, K.-F., Ergonomische, physiologische und organisationspsychologische Parameter der Bildschirmarbeit, Psychologisches Institut der Universität Tübingen, Bericht Nr. 10, Tübingen (1983)

(4) Fischer, G., Wie intelligent können und sollen Computersysteme sein? Bedeutung für die Gestaltung wissensbasierter Systeme in der Büroautomatisierung, Vortrag, Online 1984, Berlin

(5) Floyd, C., Keil, R., Softwaretechnik und Betroffenenbeteiligung, in: Mambrey, P., Opermann, R. (Hrsg.), Beteiligung von Betroffenen bei der Entwicklung von Informationssystemen (Campus Verlag, Frankfurt, New York, 1983)

(6) Friedrich, J., Wicke, F., Wicke, W., Computereinsatz: Auswirkungen auf auf die Arbeit (rowohlt Reinbek, 1982)

(7) Graumann, C. F., "Psychology and the World of Things", Journal of Phenomenological Psychology (1974) 389-404

(8) Kohn, M. L., Schooler, C., Work and Personality. An Inquiry into the Impact of Social Stratification (Ablex Publ. Corp., Norwood, N. J. 1983)

(9) Kubicek, H., Berger, P., Döbele, C., Seitz, D., Handlungsmöglichkeiten des Betriebsrates bei Rationalisierung durch Bildschirmgeräte und computergestützte Informationssysteme (Arbeitskammer des Saarlandes Saarbrücken, 1981)

(10) Maaß, S., Mensch - Rechner - Kommunikation. - Herkunft und Chancen eines neuen Paradigmas -, Diss., Fachbereich Informatik, Universität Hamburg, 1984 (Bericht Nr. 104, Juli 1984)

(11) Mow the Meaning of Work International Research Team, The Meaning of Work: An International View (Academic Press London, 1985)

(12) Noelle-Neumann, E., Werden wir alle Proletarier? (Interfrom, Zürich, 1978)

(13) Oberquelle, H., Kupka, I. Mass, S., A View of Human-Machine Communication and Cooperation, International Journal on Man-Machine Studies 19 (1983) 309-333

(14) Porsch, U., Experimentelle Untersuchungen zu Feedbackmodalitäten und Kontrollbewußtsein im Leistungsverhalten von Computer-Nutzern, unpublished Diploma thesis, Technische Universität Berlin (1984)

(15) Ruiz Quintanilla, S.A. et al., Die Auswirkungen der Bildschirmarbeit auf das Sozialverhalten - Ein Untersuchungsbericht für die Beteiligten - Berlin (August 1983)

(16) Ruiz Quintanilla, S. A., Bedeutung des Arbeitens. Entwicklung und empirische Erprobung eines sozialwissenschaftlichen Modells zur Erfassung arbeitsrelevanter Werthaltungen und Kognitionen (Eigenverlag, Berlin, 1984)

(17) Treu, T., The technology debate (II). The impact of new technologies on employment, working conditions and industrial relations, Labour and Society (1984)

(18) Triebe, J. K., Aspekte beruflichen Handelns und Lernens, Phil. Diss. (Selbstverlag, Bern, Berlin, 1981)

(19) Troy, N., Psychologische Probleme der Büroautomation, Psychosozial 18 (1983 51-69

(20) Spinas, P., Bildschirmeinsatz und Psycho-Soziale Folgen für die Beschäftigten, Paper, ETH Zürich (1984)

(21) Volpert, W., Das Ende der Kopfarbeit oder: Daniel Düsentrieb enteignet sich selbst, Psychologie heute (10, 1984) 29-39

(22) Yankelovich, D., Wer hat noch Lust zu arbeiten?, Psychologie heute (11, 1978) 14-21

(23) Yankelovich, D., Zetterberg, H., Strümpel, B. Skonks, M., Work and Human Values: An international report on jobs in the 1980s and 1990s, Aspen Institute for Humanistic Studies, New York (1983)

Man-Computer Interaction Research
MACINTER-I
F. Klix and H. Wandke (Editors)
© Elsevier Science Publishers B.V. (North-Holland), 1986

WHAT SHOULD BE COMPUTERIZED?
Cognitive demands of mental routine tasks and mental load

Winfried Hacker
Department of Ergonomics
Institute of Psychology
Technological University
Dresden
GDR

With the computerization of mental routine tasks the
question raises whether some components of these tasks
should be automated primarily and some others might be
useful for man. In a 2 x 2 x 4 experimental design with
simulated pay offices man-computer tasks we varied
tasks complexity, working memory demands, and some
categories of cognitive operations. Subjects prefer
tasks of medium complexity. In case of man-computer
interaction these preferences are nearly equalized.
The advantages of medium task complexity depend on the
variety of different operations, esp. the share of non-
arithmetic cognitive ones. Mnemonic aids do not produce
significant performance shifts; however, they diminish
uncertainty.

INTRODUCTION

"The 'man' in man-machine interaction is not primarily interacting with a machine but is interacting with information,
programme logic, knowledge, another intelligence" (Stores,
Rivers and Canter 1984, p. 62).

With the automation of mental routine tasks arise improvements
and risks (Norman 1982, Hess 1982). Thus, the question gains
interest, whether some components of these tasks should be
automated primarily to make work more comfortable, and whether
some others should further be performed by man, since they
might be useful for him, e.g. since they might contribute to
well-being or task-related intrinsic motivation.

We are dealing with this problem of allocation of functions in
a joint project of field and laboratory research (cf. Hacker
and Schönfelder, this volume). A laboratory simulation allows
to isolate effects of allocation of functions between man and
computer from the organizational context-effects, esp. division
of labour and, moreover, to ask more detailed questions on
cognitive task components.

PROBLEM

We ask: Which components of mental routine tasks are mainly
loading and which are predominantly challenging, and to which
extent? In particular we are interested in the effects of
(table 1):

- varying task complexity, operationalized by the number of
  operations per task,
- varying demands set on working memory, and
- varying demands set by different categories of cognitive
  operations (esp. arithmetic versus non-arithmetic ones).

| COGNITIVE AID (Computer) | MNEMONICS (Working rules) | C O M P L E X I T Y | | | | MO |
		low	medium	medium	high	
	without	7 18 9	16 41 18	17 50 20	139 200 38	IBT P LT
with- out	with	7 18 (9)	16 42 (18)	17 50 (20)	139 200 (38)	IBT P LT
	without	9 8 9	17 27 18	20 27 20	35 10 36	IBT P LT
with	with	9 8 (9)	17 27 (18)	20 27 (20)	35 10 (36)	IBT P LT

Table 1: Experimental design. (MO = mental operations,
         IBT = input-buffer-transmission, P = processing
         operations, LT = long-term memory items)
         (Cells: mental demands; the values given only may
         illustrate orders of magnitude because of arbitrary
         counting units!).

We suppose that an answer will not depend on the type of cognitive processes per se, but on their functions within action
control. Thus, the concept of complete versus partialized
action becomes a theoretical background (cf. Hacker and Schönfelder, this volume).

METHOD

We simulate cognitive demands of the tasks of a pay-office.
The representativeness of the simulation was checked by work
studies (Hacker, Iwanowa, Richter 1983; Muendelein and Schoen-
pflug 1984). For the description and comparison of the cognitive demands we use a modification of the YALC-system (Anonymus 1974).

We apply an analysis - by - synthesis approach: By means of
microcomputers the arithmetic processing operations could be
eliminated. Additionally, by means of mnemonic aids for the
task rules the demands on working memory were eliminated. In
both cases, however, the overall structure of the tasks remains
unchanged.

Four matched groups with 40 paid subjects of different occupational background performed the simulated pay-office tasks
in a balanced design for three hours after a training period.
Performance data including faults were recorded. Perceived
fatigue, motivation, emotional tension etc. were rated with
the self-rating system by Nitsch and Udris (1976).

RESULTS

How did the subjects assess the task of different complexity?

Task assessment

All assessments were made at the end of the final session.

1. Two thirds of the subjects prefer tasks of medium complexity.
   Even 90 % reject extreme, i.e. high and low complexity
   (table 2 and fig. 1).

2. Perceived difficulty, attention demands, and risks of faults
   are monotonically increasing with complexity, whereas
   fatigue is perceived earlier with low and high complexity,
   than with medium (figure 2).

   Thus, the demands are perceived corresponding to the objective task complexity, whereas the preferences and rejections
   seem to depend on the perceived effects on the subjects.

3. The use of a microcomputer dimishes task complexity: Many
   arithmetic processing operations of man will drop out,
   only a smaller number of input operations is added. Corres-
   pondingly, through the allocation of functions between man
   and computer the preferences nearly become equalized. Tasks
   of low and high complexity are perceived as more acceptable;
   the rejections of high complexity are reduced to the debit
   of medium (figure 1).

operations per task	task		complexity		
	low		medium		high
	30		70 70		200
preferences	15		30 37		18 %
			67		
rejections	45		2 8		45 %
			10		

Table 2: Preferences and rejections of tasks with
         varying complexity

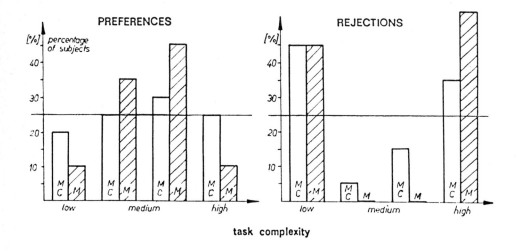

task complexity

Figure 1: Preferences and rejections of tasks with varying
          complexity
          MC ... Tasks with use of computer (man-computer)
          M ... Tasks without use of computer (man only)

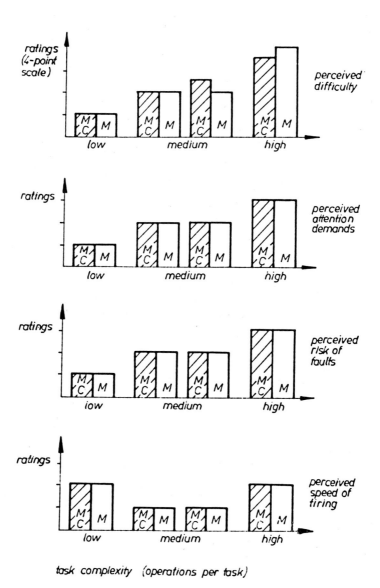

Figure 2: Perceived demand characteristics (difficulty;
attention; risk of faults) and perceived effects
(fatigue) of tasks with varying complexity.

4. On the contrary, mnemonic aids do not alter the preferences
   essentially.

A detailed analysis of the performance and activation data
recorded during the working periods might be more important
than these assessments. We will try to decompose the tasks
stepwise according to the scheme (figure 3).

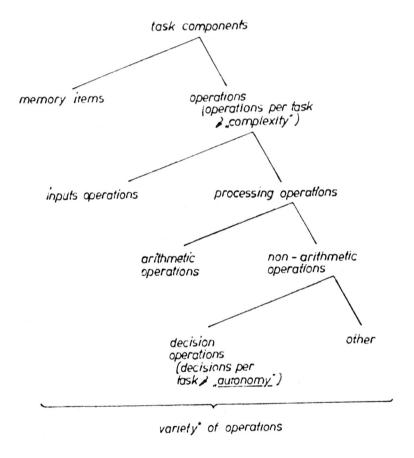

Figure 3: Task components

Effects of memory demands

Referring to Leonowa and Medwejdew (1981), Scheidereiter, Geißler and Reimer (1983), and own results (Hacker 1982) we expect diminished fatigue and increased performance with reduced working memory load.

We compare groups working with and without mnemonics for the task rules:

1. The use of these aids is increasing with the number of requisite working memory items per task. After a strong reduction within the first working hour having occured the use of mnemonics is increasing at the end of the tiring work period (figure 4). Although the rules could be reproduced, the subjects feel prompted by an increasing uncertainty to ascertain. Thus, offering mnemonics might contribute to diminish mental strain even in a well-trained state.

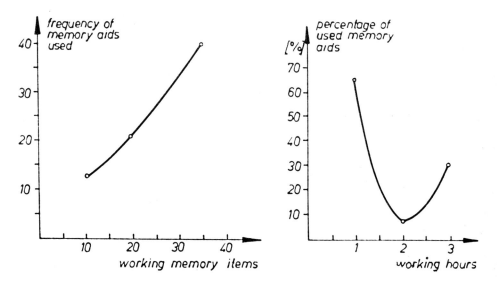

Figure 4: Use of memory aids:

   - Frequency of memory aids used as a function of the working memory load (written task rules) (memory items/task)

   - Percentage of memory aids used per working hour (100 % ... total within the 3 hours).

2. The effects of memory aids on performance, failure rate, reported motivation, and perceived fatigue are not significant. However, there is a tendency towards higher performance, lower failure rate, and later deterioration of reported motivation if mnemonics are available.

These findings contradict the strong effects of mnemonics we found in earlier research with more artificial calculating tasks (Hacker 1982). Preliminarly, we try to explain these differences by the "natural" memory aids available within the real-life tasks simulated here by their semantic context and the headings etc. of the forms and tables used.

Effects of task complexity

Referring to the literature (e.g. Hackman and Oldham 1974, Locke et al. 1981) and own results (Hacker 1982) we expect improved outcomes with enhaced task complexity.

The relationship we found shows two different sections (figure 5): In a broad range of increasing complexity performance is enhancing without any growth of failure rate, perceived fatigue, and deterioration of reported motivation. Fatigue is even perceived later in the working period. But this increase of efficiency is limited. With very high complexity the efficiency becomes worse.

Former findings of a monotonically increasing efficiency with task complexity are restricted to a section of complexity, only. Instead of speculating on possible reasons we will continue the decomposition:

Effects of the ratio of processing operations to operations total

Our hypothesis is (referring e.g. to Schneider and Shiffrin 1977): Processing operations are more challenging than input operations. Thus, with an increasing share of processing, motivation and performance should improve, but failures and fatigue reduce.

This hypothesis could not be verified. There is no relationship between the ratio mentioned and effects, as is illustrated in figure 6.

What about different kinds of processing operations?

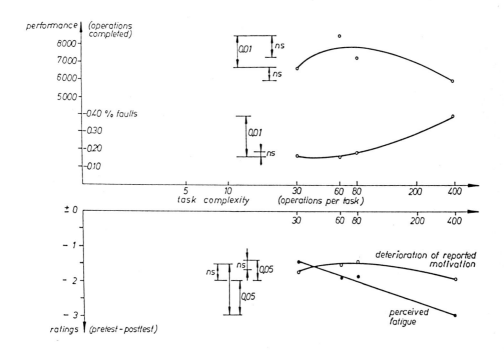

Figure 5: Effects of task complexity (operations per task) on
  - performance (operations completed)
  - quality (percentage of faults)
  - deterioration of reported) pretest - posttest
    motivation   ) differences of ratings
  - perceived fatigue   )

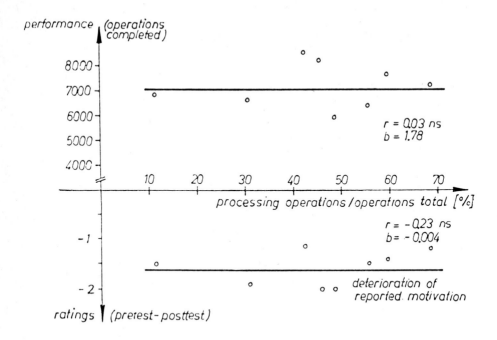

Figure 6: Effects of the ratio of processing operations/
          operations total on performance and reported
          motivation

Effects of the ratio of arithmetic / non-arithmetic
processing operations

At first we compare tasks with a varying share of artihmetic
operations performed without computers.

For a moderate dominance of arithmetic operations (5 : 1) we
did not find significant effects. Only in case of an extreme
dominance (30 : 1) performance, quality, fatigue, and motivation deteriorate significantly.

Thus, a further hypothesis is suggested: The interaction with
computers may shift the ratio of arithmetic to non-arithmetic
operations to sections more beneficial for performance and
strain.

For verification we compare identic tasks, performed with and
without computer: The use of computers strongly reduces
arithmetic processing operations in favour of non-arithmetic
ones and of input operations, with the latter being even
absolutely increasing. The results are:

1. Working with computers is preferred nearly without any
   exception (95 %).

2. The performance is higher and the failure rate lower, even
   if comparing only the remaining operations done by man.
   This is due to the higher share of simple input operations
   performed by man.

3. There are no significant differences concerning the increasing fatigue and the deteriorating motivation. However,
   subjects using computers, later in the working period felt
   tired and later became less motivated.

Both strings of results suggest that the ratio of non-arithmetic processing operations / operations total might be a task
characteristic determining performance and task perception.

Effects of the ratio of non-arithmetic processing operations/
operations total

With a decreasing share of non-arithmetic operations motivation,
performance and quality deteriorate and fatigue increase
(figure 7). Consequently, a significant correlation exists
between the ratio discussed and the ranks averaged on the four
effects parameters. This is the only significant correlation
of all the possible ones (table 3).

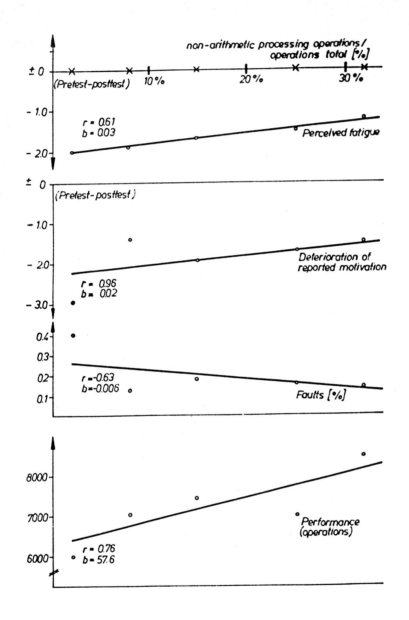

Figure 7: Effects of the ratio of non-arithmetic processing
operations/operations total on
    - perceived fatigue   } pretest-posttest
    - deterioration of reported   } differences of
      motivation   } ratings
    - quality (percentage of faults)
    - performance (operations completed)

	r_s	p
1. processing operations/ operations total	0.08	ns
2. non-arithmetic processing operations/operations total	0.71	0.025
3. do / processing operations total	0.57	(0.10)
4. decisions/operations total	0.56	(0.10)
5. do / processing operations total	0.26	ns

Table 3: Correlations between outcome variables (ranks averaged on performance, quality, perceived fatigue, reported motivation) and task characteristics.

The consequences for the allocation of functions are illustrated by Figure 8: Tasks with a sufficient share of non-arithmetic processing operations performed by man - briefly the "processing tasks" - will deteriorate motivation significantly less and will produce higher performance of the man-computer system than narrow tasks of man with extremly predominant input operations ("input tasks").

Effects of the share of decisions

Finally, according to the well-known decisive effects of task discretion or autonomy we expect the share of decisions being the most essential task characteristic (Kotik 1978; Iwanowa 1981).

The correlation coefficient between the decision share and the task effects just fails the level of significance. However, the reported task preferences coincide with one task characteristic only, namely the number of decision operations.

An explanation of the moderate correlation might be the lacking importance of these decisions for the subjects' task control (Savage and Perlmutter 1979).

Further research is indispensible; preliminarily, the following conclusions may be drawn:

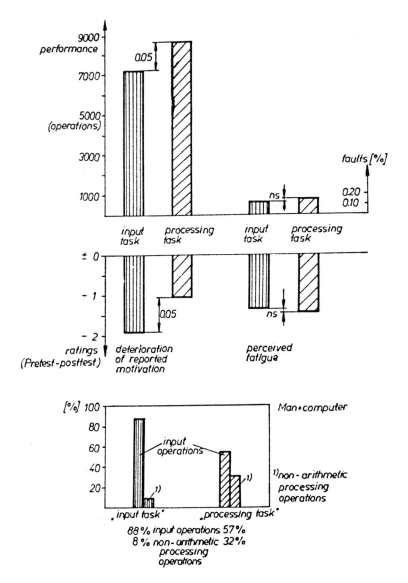

Figure 8: Consequences resulting from the ratio of non-arith-
           metic processing operations/operations total for the
           allocation of functions between man and computer:
           Task with a sufficient share of non-arithmetic pro-
           cessing operations ("processing task") produce higher
           performance and deteriorate reported motivations less
           than narrow tasks of man with predominant input
           operations ("input task"). The boxed lower part of
           the figure illustrates the shares of input and pro-
           cessing operations compared.

CONCLUSIONS

The subjects prefer tasks of medium complexity. Simultaneously their efficacy proofs optimal: Performance is highest without increased perceived fatigue.

Through the use of computers tasks of low and of high complexity become more acceptable.

Former findings of a monotonically increasing efficacy with task complexity are restricted to a section of the complexity dimension: With enhancing complexity performance is increasing without any growth of failure rate, perceived fatigue, and deteriorations of reported motivation. However, with extreme high complexity efficacy becomes worse.

The adventages of medium complexity heavily depend on the variety of different operations. With a decreasing share of non-arithmetic operations motivation, performance, and quality deteriorate but fatigue raises. It seems, the allocation of functions between man and computer should produce an optimal variety of demands which remains to be defined, however.

The improving effects of the decision potential depend on a minimum of importance of the decisions for task control. For the simulated type of real-life tasks mnemonic aids do not cause significant effects on performance. However, they dimish uncertainty even in case the rules being completely memorized.

All in all, computerization of mental routine tasks offers opportunities to shift the shares of different mental processes of man to beneficial proportions. The identification of these proportions remains to be performed.

Footnote

[1] The experiments were carefully carried out in partial fulfilment of her diploma-thesis by Bettina Halibrand.

REFERENCES

(1) Anonymus, A classification and terminology of mental work, Work Study, June 1974, 23-29.

(2) Hacker, W., Beanspruchungskomponenten von geistigen Routinetätigkeiten, Z. Psychol. 190 (1982) 3, 234-258.

(3) Hacker, W., Iwanowa, A. und P. Richter, Das Tätigkeitsbewertungssystem, Psychodiagnostisches Zentrum der Humboldt-Universität: Berlin 1983.

(4) Hackman, J.R. and G.R. Oldham, The Job Diagnosis Survey: An instrument for the diagnosis of jobs and the evaluation of job redesign projects, Technical Report 4. Yale University 1974.

(5) Halibrand, B., Beanspruchung durch operative Gedächtnisanforderungen und kognitive Operationen bei geistigen Routinetätigkeiten, Diplomarbeit: Technische Universität Dresden, Sektion Arbeitswissenschaften, Bereich Psychologie 1983.

(6) Hess, K.-D., Automatisierung geistiger Prozesse - Was bedeutet: Menschliche Fähigkeiten verschwinden im Computer? (124 - 145), in: Millert, N. (eds): Schöne elektronische Welt. ro ro ro - aktuell: Technologie und Politik 19,1982.

(7) Iwanowa, A., Validierung eines Tätigkeitsbewertungsverfahrens, Dissertation: Naturwissenschaftlich-mathematische Fakultät der Technischen Universität Dresden. 1981.

(8) Kotik, A.M., Human Engineering (russian), Tallin 1978.

(9) Leonowa, A.B. and A.N. Medwejdew, Functional states of man at work (russian), Medgis Moscow: 1981.

(10) Locke, E.A., L.M. Saari, K.N. Shaw, and G.P. Latham, Goal setting and task performance: 1969-1980, Psychol.Bull. 90 (1981) 1, 125-152.

(11) Mündelein, H. und W. Schönpflug, Ökologische Validierung eines im Labor nachgebildeten Büroarbeitsplatzes mittels FAA, Psychologie und Praxis 28 (1984) 1, 2-10.

(12) Nitsch, J. and I. Udris, Beanspruchung im Sport, Training und Beanspruchung Vol. 4. Bad Homburg v.d.H.: Limpert 1976.

(13) Norman, D.A., Learning and Memory, Freeman: San Francisco 1982.

(14) Savage, R.E. and L.C. Perlmuter, The freedom to choose is not always so choice, J. of Exp. Psychol. (Human Learning and Memory) 5 (1979) 2, 170-198.

(15) Scheidereiter, U., H.-G. Geißler und K. Reimer, Kognitive Faktoren bei der Verarbeitung von bildschirm-gebundener Information, Z. Psychol. Suppl. 5 (1983) 124-137.

(16) Schneider, W. and R.M. Shiffrin, Controlled and automatic human information processing (I, II), Psychol. Rev. 84 (1977) No. 1, 1-66; No. 2, 127-190.

(17) Stons, G., R. Rivers, and D. Canter, The future of man-machine interface research: A discussion and a frame work for research Applied Ergonomics 15 (1984) 1, 61-63.

NAME INDEX

Abernathy, W. J. 131, 138

Ackermann, D. 421, 427

Adler, F. H. 383, 384

Aliot, A. 405, 418

Anderson, B. F. 337

Anderson, J. R. 24, 80, 86, 90, 91, 95, 118, 123, 152, 179, 181

Apostolakis, G. 301

Arblaster, A. 249

Aronson, G. 339

Aschwanden, C. 421, 422, 427

Askwall, S. 190

Austin, G. A. 357

Backhaus, K. O. 281

Balad, I. P. 188, 191

Balzert, H. 340, 347

Barnard, G. 85

Barnard, P. J. 189, 235

Barr, A. 214

Battmann, W. 131

Beatty, J. 383

Becker, J. D. 93, 95

Beishuizen, J. J. 15, 198, 199

Belawine, I. G. 86

Berger, P. 443

Besseret, A. 236

Bobrow, D. G. 93, 95

Boettger, H. 90, 96

Bonar, J. 253, 258

Book, W. F. 373

Boucsein, W. 302

Bower, G. H. 94, 95, 118, 123, 336, 337

Brandt, G. 440, 443

Barsch, Chr. 161

Brauer, J. S. 7

Broadbent, D. E. 358

Bruner, J. S. 357, 358

Canter, D. 445, 461

Carbonell, J. G. 9

Card, S. K. 141, 144, 150, 152, 394

Carroll, J. M. 235

Cazamian, P. 384

Chalupa, B. 337

Chapanis, A. 236

Chusid, J. C. 383

Cizková, J. 337

Clancey, W. J. 79, 85

Clark, I. 85

Clark, P. A. 189, 426, 427

Colquhoun, P. 302

Craig, A. 302

Cronbach, L. J. 214, 216

Curtis, B. 257 258

Darlington, J. 47

Davies, D. R. 301 - 303, 305

Davydov, V. V. 161, 165, 166, 322, 328

Delmas, A. 383, 384

Dijk van, T. A. 358

Dirrheimer, A. 443

Döbele, C. 443

Dörner, D. 12, 24, 39, 80, 85, 163

Doss, B. 347

Doyle, J. 96

Draper, S. W. 139, 150

Dumais, S. T. 212, 214

Duncker, K. 423, 427

Durnin, J. H. 174

Dzida, W. 22, 23, 47, 79, 85, 139, 142, 144, 150, 161

Egan, D. E. 210, 211

Edwards, M. 417 418, 429, 437,

Eckoldt, K. 358

Ehrenpreis, W. 174, 178

Ehrlich, K. 253, 258

Emery, F. E. 425, 427

Engeström, Y. 327, 328

Enwistle, N. J. 196

Eysenck, M. W.134, 138, 358

Faerber, B. 441, 443

Fabeck, J. 120, 121, 123

Falzon, P. 236

Feigenbaum, E. A. 12, 214

Fillmore, C. J. 99, 115

Fischer, F. 151

Fischer, G. 79, 85, 440, 443

Fitter, J. J. 254, 258

Fitter, M. 189

Flammer, A. 27, 81, 85

Floyd, C. 440, 443

Fraisse, P. 336

Frei, F. 339, 347

Friedrichs, G. 339, 347

Friedrich, J. 403, 418, 441, 443

Furmas, G. W. 212, 214

Gagne, R. M. 174

Geißler, H. G. 308, 318, 451, 461

Genov, P. 51

Gentner, D. R. 29, 43, 374

Gillmore, D. 255, 257, 258

Giesel, B. 435, 437

Glaser, R. 182

Glass, D. C. 390

Goede, K. 11

Gomez, L. M. 210, 211, 212, 214

Goodnow, J. J. 357

Goranzon, B. 187

Grandjean, E. 384

Graham, N. 396

Graumann, C. F. 439, 443

Green, T. R. G. 46, 189, 249, 251, 253, 257, 258

Gross, B. 269

Guest, D. J. 253, 258

Gunzenhäuser, R. 36

Hacker, W. 308, 318, 339, 347, 403, 404, 405, 418, 445, 446, 447, 451, 452, 460

Hackman, J. R. 161, 339, 347, 425, 427 452, 460

Hagen ten, P. J. W. 273

Halibrand, B. 459, 460

Hamilton, P. 383

Hammond, N. 79, 85, 189, 235

Hansen, W. J. 136, 138

Hartley, J. 254, 258

Hayes, P. 247

Hayes, Roth, F. 257, 258

Helbig, H. 89, 90, 94, 96

Hess, H. 405, 418

Hess, K. D. 445, 460

Hesse, F. W. 81, 85

Herzberg, J. 345, 347

Hoare, C. A. R. 251, 258

Hoc, J. M. 253, 258

Hockey, R. 358

Hoeck, K. 405, 418

Hoepfner, B. 417, 418

Hoffmann, C. 144, 150

Hoffmann, J. 117, 119, 123, 308, 309, 314, 316, 318

Hollnagel, E. 79, 80, 85, 86

Holzkamp, K. 342, 347

Holzman, T. G. 174

Hunt, E. B. 314

Hunter, I. M. L. 125, 130

Huuhtanen, P. 353 - 356

Ichbiah, J. 251, 258

Iwanowa, A. 405, 418, 447, 457, 460

Jagodzinski, A. P. 45, 46

Jarke, M. 285

Jastrow, J. 331

Johannsson, G. 339, 347

Johnson-Laird, Ph. N. 92, 96

Kahneman, D. 358

Kalimo, R. 352, 354, 356

Karasek, R. A. 415, 418

Kasielke, E. 394

Kautto, A. 323, 328

Kearsley, P. 434, 437

Kelly, M. J. 236

Keil, R. 440, 443

Kieras, D. 151

Kiesewetter, H. 279

Kinnucan, J. 178

Kintsch, W. 118, 123, 358

Klahr, D. 175

Klix, F. 3, 7, 9, 24, 80, 86, 91, 93, 96, 104, 115, 152, 308, 309, 318, 394, 366

Koch, D. 287

Kohn, M. L. 441, 443

Kohonen, T. 91, 92, 96

Kopsteim, F. F. J. 195

Kornilova, T. V. 82, 86

Kotik, A. M. 457, 460

Krause, B. 80, 86

Krause, J. 285, 292

Krause, W. 11, 80, 81, 86

Kruesi, E. 257, 258

Kubicek, H. 441, 443

Kulka, F. 11

Kündig, B. 443

Kupka, I. 23, 38

Laird, I. E. 80, 86

Landauer, T. K. 212, 214, 235

Langer, J. 158

Latham, G. P. 460

Laurig, W. 358

Lederberg, J. 12

Lenat, D. B. 12, 107, 115, 257, 258,

Lehwald, G. 85, 86

Leonowa, A. B. 365, 366, 451, 460

Leontjew, A. N. 125, 130, 163, 326, 329

Leppänen, A. 352, 354, 356

Levine, M. 174

Lindsay, R. H. 358

Locke, E. A. 452, 460

Lohmann, H. 86

Long, J. 85, 189

Lord, F. M. 217

Luchmann, D. 104, 105, 115

Lüer, G. 12, 80, 86, 316

Maaß, S. 23, 440, 443

Mackie, R. E. 301

Maguire, M. 246

Marek, T. 383

Martin, T. 425, 427

Matern, B. 161, 168

Mathews, N. N. 314

Maver, R. E. 191

Mc Cormick, E. J. 307, 319

Mc Dermott, D. 95, 96

Mc Keachie, W. 179

Mc Leod, C. M. 314, 318

Medwejdew, A. N. 451, 460

Meer van der, E. 108, 115

Michaelis, P. R. 236, 285

Michalski, R. S. 114, 115, 9

Miller, G. A. 92, 96

Moran, T. P. 35, 37, 38, 39, 152, 221 394

Morrison, D. L. 251, 258

Morton, J. 85, 189

Mulder, G. 357, 365, 366

Mulder, L. J. M. 357, 365, 366

Müller, G. 161

Mündelein, H. 447, 460

Murrell, K. F. M. 307, 319

Mussmann, C. 424, 427

Muthig, K. P. 125, 130

Muylwijk van, B. 15, 48, 192

Nachreiner, F. 301

Napoleon, I. 93

Neisser, U. 338

Neumann, J. 307, 319, 437,

Neumann v., J. 93

Newell, A. 80, 86

Newell, A. 152, 176, 394, 396

Nilsson, N. J. 152

Nitsch, J. R. 167, 371, 422, 427,
    447, 460

Noack, B. 417, 418

Noelle-Neumann, E. 442, 443

Norman, D. A. 29, 35, 43, 95, 165
    191, 358, 403, 418, 445, 460

Noro, K. 434, 437

Norros, L. 329

Noworol, Cz. 383

Nullmeier, E. 161

Oberquelle, H. 23, 142, 150, 440,
    443

Obrist, P. A. 366

Oerter,   81

Oldham, G. R. 425, 427, 452, 460

Okada, Y. 434, 437

Pellegrino, J. W. 182

Perlmutter, L. C. 415, 419, 43,
    460

Paivio, A. 309, 319

Paradimitrion, Z. 443

Parasuraman, R. 301 - 303, 305

Parsons, H. 434, 437

Pask, G. 15, 195, 197, 198, 199,
    200, 203, 204

Payne, S. J. 46, 189, 254, 258

Piispanen, E. 353, 354, 356

Plath, H. E. 405, 418

Polson, P. 151

Porsch, U. 440, 444

Posner, M. I. 357

Pountain, D. 249, 258

Preuß, M. 103, 104, 115

Puffe, M. 308

Putz-Osterloh, W. 316, 319

Rasmussen, J. 36, 44, 79, 80, 86

Raum, H. 70, 338, 340, 347, 348

Reichle, S. 443

Reimer, K. 451, 461

Reisner, P. 131, 138

Rich, J. 36

Richter, P. 357, 405, 418, 447, 460

Rivers, R. 445, 461

Rockstroh, P. 431

Rödiger, K. J. 161

Rohr, G. 35, 37, 46

Rosenbloom, R. S. 131, 138

Rothkopf, E. Z. 217, 218, 219

Ruiz Quintanilla, S. A. 439, 441, 442,
    444

Rühle, R. 168

Rumelhart, D. E. 121, 123

Saari, L. M. 460

Sackmann, H. 79, 86

Salthouse, T. A. 373, 374

Sasson, R. Y. 336, 338

Savage, R. E. 415, 419, 457, 460

Scandura, J. M. 173, 174, 176, 178,
    179, 180, 181

Scapin, D. O. 235, 236, 245

Schaff, A. 339

Schank, R. C. 99, 115

Scheidereiter, U. 308, 451, 461

Scheller, B. 269

Schindler, R. 79, 86, 151

Schmitt, R. 255

Schmuck, P. 119, 123

Schneider, W. 33 .

Schönebeck, B. 357

Schönfelder, E. 403, 446, 460

Schönpflug, W. 80, 86, 125, 130, 134, 256, 447, 460

Schooler, C. 441, 443

Schrade, K. F. 443

Schuhmacher, A. 81, 83, 86

Schulz, J. 251

Schulz, P. 393

Scott, B. C. E. 198, 199

Seifert, R. 117

Seigler, R. S. 174, 175

Seitz, D. 443

Seligman, M. 228

Shackel, B. 22

Shaffer, L. H. 374

Shaw, A. C. 251, 258

Shaw, K. N. 460

Sheppard, S. B. 257, 258

Shneider, W. 452, 461

Shneiderman, B. 131, 138, 189

Shiffrin, R. M. 357, 452, 461

Siddigi, J. I. A. 253, 258

Sielaff, H. J. 369

Sifneos, P. E. 389

Sime, M. E. 253, 258

Simon, H. A. 7, 80, 86, 176, 396

Sintschenko, V. P. 365

Skell, W. 168

Skonks, M. 444

Sloboda, J. 254, 258

Snow, R. E. 214, 216

Soloway, E. 253, 258

Spinas, Ph. 161, 228, 340, 348, 424, 427, 441, 444

Sternberg, R. J. 210

Sternberg, S. 309, 319, 373, 380

Stevens, A. 29, 43

Stores, G. 445, 461

Streitz, N. 21, 27, 28, 79, 81, 87, 249

Strümpel, B. 444

Sydow, H. 80, 87

Tauber, M. J. 9, 15, 35, 37, 46, 47, 48, 161

Thomae, I. 443

Thorndyke, P. W. 121, 123

Thorsrud, E. 425, 427

Tikhomirov, O. K. 79, 81, 87

Timpe, K. P. 307, 429, 437

Toikka, K. 321, 326, 327, 328

Traunmüller, R. 36

Treu, T. 441, 444

Triebe, J. K. 442, 444

Troy, N. 161, 340, 421, 441, 444

Udris, I. 405, 418, 447, 460

Ulich, E. 161, 339, 347, 348, 421

Unger, S. 11

Urry, V. W. 217

Veer van der, G. C. 15, 48, 192, 202, 203, 253

Volpert, W. 144, 150, 339, 348, 441, 444

Waern, Y. 15, 48, 185, 188, 189, 190, 191, 192

Wahlster, W. 230

Wandke, H. 251, 340, 348

Ward, J. H. 405, 419

Wasserman, T. 136, 138

Watermann, D. A. 176, 257, 258

Weinberg, G. M. 262

Wetzenstein, Ollenschläger, E. 308, 319, 344, 348

Name Index

Wicke, F. 418, 443

Wicke, W. 418, 443

Wilpert, B. 439, 443

Wingert, B. 23

Winogard, T. 12

Wolde van de, G. J. E. 202, 203

Woods, D. D. 79, 86

Wysotzki, F. 11

Yankelovich   442, 444

Zadeh, L. 95, 96

Zetterberg, H. 444

Ziessler, M. 117

Zimmer, K. 225, 228, 357, 362

Zimmermann, M. 421, 422, 427

Zoeppritz, M. 293

Zoltan, E. 285, 292

SUBJECT INDEX

acceleration of heart rate 368

activity
  process control 321 - 322, 327

Ada 251 - 252, 270

alexithymia 389

Algol 264 - 270

allocation of functions
  between robots and men 429 - 437

american ergonomics 59 - 63

aptitude 210, 216, 219

artificial intelligence 90 - 95

automated production
  and personality traits 53
  functions of the workers 52

automation strategies 434 - 435

Basic 250 - 253, 264, 266, 269 - 270

cardiovasular parameters 365

C 253

chain-up strategy 359, 360

chunk formation 396

classification procedures 11

color
  preference 295, 296, 298

coding
  graphical 309, 311 - 317
  numerical 209, 311 - 317
  task-adequate 308, 311, 313 - 314, 317 - 318

Cobol 264 - 266

cognitive compatibility 27

cognitive effort 390, 394, 396, 399

cognitive ergonomics 22, 62

command entry 221 - 229

command language 235, 246

Command Language Grammar 39

command parameters 244 - 245

command verbs 244 - 245

communication
  face-to-face 440 - 442

comparison procedure 101

compatibility 340

competence 197, 200, 203

complexity of commands 221, 228 - 229, 231 - 233

computers
  social impacts 3
  in the classroom 13

computer-commands
  design of 210

computerization of
  calculation of salaries 354 - 355

computerization of
  the work journalists 355

concept representation 91 - 93

content of mental representations 163

content problem 24

content related load 134, 136, 157,
  reduction of 131, 132

context 237

coping strategy 393, 394

coronaryprone behaviour pattern 389

critical flicker frequency 352 - 355

data input task 406 - 407

data processing task classes 66 - 67, 69

deceleration of heart rate 368

decision
  behaviour 343 - 344

design of userfriendly software 79

detection
  signal 295 - 299, 301 - 305
  feature 295 - 300

dialogue
  design 344, 346

dialogue interpreter 139, 142, 144

dialogue related load 132, 134, 135,
  136, 137
  reduction of 131

dialogue steps 140, 143, 145
  automated interpretation of 139
  work content of 141

types of 142, 144
model of 142, 144
sequence of 144
relationships between 148
protocol analysis of 149

dialogue
structure of 221 - 223
style of 221

dialogue
types of 422 - 423

dialogue work 65 - 68

differences among learners 215 - 219

dimensions of man-computer
interactions 72

discrimination
simultaneous 302 - 303, 305
successive 302 - 303, 305

encoding 310, 313 - 314

european ergonomics 59 - 63

event-related concepts 98, 107, 113

external storage of information
125, 130

eye movements 262 - 263, 265

fatigue 405

flowcharts 252

focal knowledge 125, 126, 127
functionalyty of 127
memory load for 129
acquisition of 129

Fortan 264, 266, 269 - 270

heart rate 361, 367, 368

holism 197 - 199

human-computer interaction
research fields of psychology 5
models 23, 35, 42
and personality traits 55

hyper-micro computer 73 - 74

hyperresponsiveness 389

identification
perceptive 332 - 336

inferential reasoning 94

information complexity 131

information
coding 307 - 318
presentation 321 - 325, 339 - 347

information
retrieval systems 131

instruction
adaptive 214 - 215, 218

interaction problem 24

interactive problem solving 79 - 80

interaction 273
structure 275 - 282

interface 7, 35, 45

interface
natural-language 285 - 293

internal job-related feed back 393

intuitive functions 240 - 241

job evaluation 431

keystroke - intervals 377, 379, 380

knowledge-based systems 26

knowledge components 151

knowledge engineering 97

knowledge generation 105

knowledge of the operators 59, 61 -
62

knowledge on strategies 80

knowledge representation 97, 105

knowledge representation in
computers 90 - 95

language comprehension 94

language
programming 261 - 270

learning problems in computer
aided task 185

learning processes 161
design of
content of 163

learning processes in automated
industry 163

learning strategies 197 - 200

Lisp 264 - 266, 268 - 269

long-term memory 91 - 92

man-computer system
job organization 403 - 419

memory demands 451

memory types 91 - 92

mental load 228 - 230, 352 - 355
   processing vs input operation
   452 - 453

mental model 29, 43

mental routine 446 - 460

metacommunication 44, 47, 190

mnemonics 446

micro computer 73 - 74

misconceptions 30

modul for analogical reasoning 109

modules of relation detection 106

monotony 405

motor chunking 374

motor programms 373, 380

natural language 235, 246

natural language understanding
   system 90 - 95

network of statements
   construction of a 119
   reduction of the 120, 121

neurotics 389

operative compartment 394

operator workload 383

operator's competence 59, 61 - 62

organizational aspects
   in computerization 441

Pascal 249 - 254, 264 - 270

pattern recognition 264

perceptual chunking 373, 374

PL/1 264, 266

power spectrum 357, 358, 359, 361,
   362

primary control processes 366

problem
   algorithmic 274, 278
   creative 274, 278
   solving
   interactive 273 - 275

problem solving 24, 39
   behaviour 80
   competence 132, 134, 135, 138
   research 173

procedure 237, 245

production rule systems 90 - 92
   production systems 175

program
   closeness 262
   compactness 262, 269
   keywords 262, 264
   linearity 262
   locality 262
   structured 265 - 266

programming language
   discriminibality 250

programming language
   size of 250 - 254

programming language
   structure 250 - 254

Prolog 269 - 270

property-related concepts 98

propositional representation
   of the contents of the text 118

protocol analysis 144, 149
   computer assisted 139
     approach 141
     of dialogue steps 149

prototypic knowledge 174

psychosomatics 389

pulse / respiration-quotient 359

pupil reflex
   acceleration of 383, 385, 387

qualification in data
   processing 66

question - answering systems 89 - 91

question asking 80 - 83

reliability
   human 301 , 305

representation of concepts 98, 106

respiratory rate 358, 359

response latencies 375, 380

retractor 383, 384, 387

retyping activities 373

routine cognitive skill 152

search
   visual 331 - 337
   time 332 - 334

semantic networks 90, 94

semantic relations 93

serialism 197 - 199

short-term memory 91 - 92

sizes of computers 71

social psychology in
    computerization 439 - 443

societal aspects in
    computerization 442

sphincter 383, 384, 387

stress 351 - 356, 405

structural learning theories 173,
    174

structure of an analogy 110

subjective load 392

Subjective Work Analysis (SWA)
    426

super ordinated concept 106

source difficulty 127

source knowledge 125, 127
    categories of 126
    memory load for 129
    acquisition of 129

task analysis 431

task characteristics 392

task complexity 446 - 458

task complexity
    preference of 448

task demands of VDU-work 423

task demands
    traditional vs VDU-work 405

task-design 210

Task Diagnostic Survey(TDS) 405

task
    dimensions 404 - 413

task, division of 404 - 410

task model 187

task of chief-operators 415 - 416

tasks of programmers 415 - 416

task space 36

task-solving knowledge 151

TBS 432 - 433

teaching strategies 161, 198 - 200

text assembling procedure
    special rules for the 117
    organization of the 121

text assembling systems
    cognitive demands in the use of 117
    faultless use of 117
    methods for the building up of 117

text difficulty 127

text-editing system 151

text input tasks 354

text processing 415 - 416

text units
    the manner of calling up the 117
    setting up the list of 117
    appropriate derivation of 118
    the structure of 121

training 327 - 328

training programme 156

transformation strategy 359, 360

types of operative units 152 - 159

type of representation 175

type setting, computerized 415 - 416

ultra-short-term memory 91 -92

Unix 250, 255

user
    types 285 - 286, 290 - 292
    requirements 290 - 292

user frequency 68 - 69

user-system communication 188

utilisation duration 68 - 69

utilisation intensity 68 - 69

VDU-work in airline companies 425

VDU-work in banking houses 424

video screen
    colors 295 - 300

vigilance 352 - 355

white coller jobs 405

Word Star 249

work flow 144, 149
    model of 139, 144

analysis 146, 149
    rules 149

work structure 144, 149
    models of 139, 144
    subjective and objective 145
    analysis of 144
    rules 149

working memory 446